THE
Scholarship
BOOK

FIFTH EDITION

The Complete Guide to Private-Sector Scholarships, Grants, and Loans for Undergraduates

PRENTICE HALL
Englewood Cliffs, New Jersey 07632

Daniel J. Cassidy

Library of Congress Cataloging-in-Publication Data

Cassidy, Daniel J.
    The scholarship book : the complete guide to private-sector
scholarships, grants, and loans for undergraduates / Daniel J.
Cassidy.—5th ed.
        p.   cm.
    Includes indexes.
    ISBN 0-13-476078-6 (case).—ISBN 0-13-476060-3 (pbk.)
    1. Scholarships—United States—Directories. 2. Student aid—
United States—Directories. 3. Associations, instituitions, etc.—
Charitable contributions—United States—Directories. I. Title.
LB2337.2.C37 1996
378.3'4'0973—dc20   96-8138
                                                      CIP

Warning!
Copy at your peril!

Printed in the United States of America

10 9 8 7 6 5 4 3

ISBN 0-13-476078-6 (case)   ISBN 0-13-476060-3 (pbk.)

> **ATTENTION: CORPORATIONS AND SCHOOLS**
> Prentice Hall books are available at quantity discounts with bulk purchase for educational,
> business, or sales promotional use. For information, please write to: Prentice Hall Career &
> Personal Development Special Sales, 113 Sylvan Avenue, Englewood Cliffs, NJ 07632. Please
> supply: title of book, ISBN number, quantity, how the book will be used, date needed.

PRENTICE HALL
Career & Personal Development
Englewood Cliffs, NJ 07632
A Simon & Schuster Company

On the World Wide Web at http://www.phdirect.com

Prentice Hall International (UK) Limited, *London*
Prentice Hall of Australia Pty. Limited, *Sydney*
Prentice Hall Canada, Inc., *Toronto*
Prentice Hall Hispanoamericana, S.A., *Mexico*
Prentice Hall of India Private Limited, *New Delhi*
Prentice Hall of Japan, Inc., *Tokyo*
Simon & Schuster Asia Pte. Ltd., *Singapore*
Editora Prentice Hall do Brasil, Ltda., *Rio de Janeiro*

I want to thank all of those who have made this fifth edition of THE SCHOLARSHIP BOOK a reality. My sincere thanks and gratitude to:

The staff at NSRS

especially:

My wife, Deirdre Carlin Cassidy, Vice President/Controller

Research & Computer Engineering
Keri L. Grafe, Director of Research
Richard Merwin, Computer Systems
Ray Baker, Programming
William L. Sheppard, Director Emeritus

Administration & Public Relations
Joe Gargiulo, Public Relations Director
Julanne C. Lorimor, Administrative Coordinator
Janie G. Ramirez, Executive Secretary
Kathleen Sherman, Assistant to Mr. Cassidy

A very special thank you to
Jim Eason
KGO Radio, San Francisco
The man who made NSRS possible

And, at Prentice Hall

Neal Goff, President
Prentice Hall Direct
Eugene Brissie, Vice President/Editorial Director
Sally Hertz, Vice President, Sales
Tom Power, Senior Editor
Zsuzsa Neff, Production Editor
Audrey Kopciak, Electronic Production Editor
Joan Ellen Messina, Publicity Director
Grace Li, Director of Marketing
Carmine Lepore, National Accounts Manager
Mark Walter, Marketing

And as always . . .
Barbara Palumbo, Manager, Electronic Production

Preface

INTRODUCTION

The information in THE SCHOLARSHIP BOOK was compiled from the database of the largest private sector financial aid research service in the world. Located in Santa Rosa, California, NATIONAL SCHOLARSHIP RESEARCH SERVICE (NSRS) began tracking private sector scholarships in the late 1970s, using a specialized computer system. As awards increased and research uncovered new sources for today's student, the addition of the INTERNATIONAL SCHOLARSHIP RESEARCH SERVICE (ISRS) doubled the size of this independently-developed database. Prospective college students and present undergraduates will find the information in this book valuable in directing their application and broadening their prospects for scholarship selection.

THE FACTS

According to the Association of Fund Raising Counsel, more than 80% of the grant applications that went to the 37,500 foundations in the United States, were either misdirected or filled out improperly.[1] In 1983, the National Commission on Student Financial Assistance and the House Subcommittee on Post-secondary Education "concluded that financial aid from the private sector was an 'overwhelmingly neglected' resource. In particular, the commission found that education benefits for their employees are widely available, but that a large portion of that aid had gone unused each year."[2] A 1996 NSRS survey of private sector sources responses indicated that undistributed scholarships equaled three and one half percent (3.5%).[3] There is a great need to organize this "paper-chase" of information into a workable source for today's student. Utilizing the data collected in this book, students will have a broad base of information to convert to their advantage. The monies are there. Apply for them!

PRIVATE SECTOR FUNDS

Philanthropy in the United States is alive and well. More than 53.64% of the available scholarships, fellowships, grants, and loans are from the private sector. Philanthropy in the United States totaled $58.67 billion in 1982, increased to a whopping $184.21 billion in 1993.[4] Of that amount, 15% (or $28.38 billion) goes into the United States educational system.[5] An additional $20 to $30 plus billion is dispersed worldwide.

And that amount increases daily. The interest alone on a properly invested $2 million is easily $200,000 annually. Private sector resources for higher education are as varied as the awards themselves.

Many scholarships are renewable. You simply apply for them year after year. Others allow you to "piggyback" several individual scholarships. The average undergraduate scholarship is $4,000 per year, ranging from a low of $100 to a high of $20,000. Graduate-level fellowships range from $10,000 to $60,000. Some research projects can yield a quarter of a million dollars or more. As inflation spirals, so does the cost of education and the need for financial assistance.

INVESTIGATE THE POSSIBILITIES

Don't think you can't apply because you earn too much money; 80% of the private sector does not require a financial statement or proof of need. Don't think that application deadlines occur only in the fall; private sector deadlines are passing daily because often they are set to coincide with the tax year or organizational meeting dates. Don't believe that grades are the only consideration for an award; many

---

[1] *Annual Register of Grant Support* (1997 30th Edition)
[2] *The Chronicle of Higher Education* (November 1983)
[3] 1996 National Scholarship Research Service (NSRS) private sector survey
[4] *Foundation Giving: Yearbook of Facts and Figures on Private, Corporate and Community Foundations* (1995)
[5] *The Chronicle of Philanthropy* (April 1990)

application questions deal with personal, occupational, and educational background, organizational affiliation, talent or ethnic origins; 90% are not concerned with grades. Don't be concerned with age; many organizations are interested in the re-entry student and the mid-career development student. The Business and Professional Women's Foundation awards hundreds of scholarships to applicants who must be older than 25 or even 35. There is a scholarship at the California state colleges for students over the age of 60.

PLAN TO COMPETE AND QUALIFY

The plan is simple—use this book and every other resource you can find. Inquire at your institution's financial aid office about government assistance and private endowments. If you are a high school sophomore, write to ten or more schools. Select a range of institutions that interest you, both large and small, public and private. Request the application materials and catalogs—many private endowments are available in the forms of scholarships and fellowships bequeathed by alumni. A significant number of these go unclaimed because qualified students do not know they exist! The information is available, but the commitment and determination to find it belongs to the individual.

The private sector is easily accessed with this book. The student can use the tables provided to cross-reference the scholarships applicable to his or her personal background and educational goals. Choose twenty or more sources and request application forms and any pertinent materials. Some have specific requirements for applicants such as a personal interview, the submission of an essay or related work, or a promise to work for the company on completion of study and/or the earning of a degree. Others may have paid internships or work advancement programs. Still others may simply require that you fill out an application form.

The money is there. Billions go unclaimed. Students who do not take the time to inquire lose every advantage. The opportunity to advance to a graduate degree will widen many avenues for your future and the rewards are incalculable. Information is merely a passage waiting to be used. The resources to achieve your goals are available to you; you need only pursue them.

'A human mind, once stretched to a new idea,
never returns to its former dimension.'

— Oliver Wendell Holmes, Sr.

Just for Fun: A Potpourri of Scholarships

1. The **Countess of Munster Musical Trust** has scholarships in varying amounts to British and Commonwealth citizens studying music. (K74/R19)

2. Don't be bugged by a lack of funds. Money really does grow on trees. The **International Society of Arboriculture** invites horticulturists, plant pathologists, and entomologists to pluck a grant for the study of shade trees. (K24/R12)

3. Your tuition troubles could be gone with the wind! If you are a lineal descendant of a worthy Confederate soldier, contact the **United Daughters of the Confederacy** about their $400 to $1,500 scholarships. (K22/R7)

4. If you or your parents are actively involved in harness racing, you just might hitch yourself to one of the **Harness Tracks of America** scholarships worth $2,500 to $3,000. (K18/R147)

5. You could lace up a scholarship of up to $2,000 for undergraduate study if you are a dependent child of a worker in the footwear industry. It's a patent idea from **Two/Ten International Footwear Foundation**. (K17/R157)

6. Don't let financial woes cast a pall over your dreams. Bury those worries with a **Hilgenfeld Foundation for Mortuary Education** scholarship! It's available to qualified individuals interested in the funeral service or funeral education fields. (K99/R5)

7. *Jen unu mil pundo—nun EK!* (Here's a thousand pounds - now go!) If you understood that, you might be eligible for a **Norwich Jubilee Esperanto Foundation** scholarship paying $500 to study Esperanto in the United Kingdom. (K19/R10)

8. For a left-handed freshman enrolled at Juniata College and who needs the money, **Beckley Scholarship Foundation** offers $700. (K17/R127)

9. For students whose ancestors put their John Hancocks on the Declaration of Independence, have scholarships worth $1,200 to $2,000. **Descendants of the Signers of the Declaration of Independence**. (K19/R152)

10. Investigating scholarship possibilities? The **Association of Former Agents of the US Secret Service** offers scholarships of $500 to $1,500 to undergraduate law enforcement and police administration students. You do have to give your real name, but fingerprints won't be necessary. (K95/R32)

THE TOP TEN CELEBRITY SCHOLARSHIPS

1. The proof is in the pudding! **Bill Cosby** and his wife Camille have been acclaimed 'The First Family of Philanthropy' for their generous donations to various colleges in excess of $28 million.

2. The **Eddie Murphy/Paramount Pictures $25,000 Writing Fellowship**. Silver Screen? Let your talent shine with a postgraduate film & television writing internship at Paramount Pictures presented to eligible bachelor degree grads of Hampton and Howard Universities who are tuned into television and screen writing.

3. The cost of college doesn't go for the price of peanuts these days, so **The Scripps Howard Foundation** is offering the **Charles M. Schultz Award**. $2,000 for an outstanding college cartoonist, working at a college newspaper or magazine. Don't be a Blockhead! Apply! (K71/R17)

4. "Average yet creative" is the punch line for junior telecommunications majors at Ball State University. **The David Letterman Telecommunications Scholarship Program** could pay your way to graduation if you are an average student with a very creative mind. (K93/R23)

5. Don't make a big production out of the high cost of filmmaking! All it takes is "Forty Acres and a Mule"! **Spike Lee & Columbia Pictures** offer production fellowships to students in their second or third year of graduate study at the New York University Tisch School of Film. Two $5,000 fellowships are awarded per year to graduates rolling in action in production, filmmaking, and acting. (K71/R25)

6. This is certainly one house with high equity! Morehouse College received $1 million dollars from celebrity Oprah Winfrey to establish the **Oprah Winfrey Endowed Scholarship Fund**. (K24/R128)

7. Is the cost of college a dramatization? The right stage for you could be **Debbie Allen** and **Phylicia Rashad's** applause for their father in the **Dr. Andrew Allen Creative Arts Scholarship** of $10,000. A command performance is requested from undergraduate juniors and seniors at Howard University who portray excellence in drama, song, and dance. (K74/R37)

8. Are you between the ages of 17 and 22, living in the Golden State? If you are a Mexican-American resident of California in an undergraduate program, you may just strike gold with the **Vikki Carr Scholarship** of up to $1,500! (K19/R85)

9. College costs driving you up the wall? Go ahead and dance on the ceiling! **Lionel Richie** has made students of Tuskegee University lighter than air with his $500,000 donation for an endowment in the business school at Tuskegee. (K26/R111)

10. Well Hee-Haw, Y'all! Miniere's Network offers the **Minnie Pearl Scholarships** to financially-needy high school seniors who have a significant bilateral hearing loss, good grades, and who have been accepted for enrollment by an accredited university, college or technical school. (K17/R156)

TOP SCHOLARSHIPS FOR WOMEN

1. The **California Junior Miss Program** scholarship competition is open to girls in their junior year of high school who are US citizens and California residents. Winner receives $10,000 for books, fees, and tuition at any college in the world. (K21/R103)

2. The **Women's Western Golf Foundation** has $2,000/year awaiting female high school seniors who are US citizens and who have high academic standing, financial need, and an involvement with golf . . . skill is NOT a criterion! (K18/R57)

3. The **National Federation of the Blind** (Anne Pekar Memorial Scholarship) offers $4,000 to legally blind women between the ages of 17 and 25, pursuing or planning to pursue full-time study in any field. (K16/R99)

4. For women re-entry students, the **Jeanette Rankin Foundation** awards $1,000 to the winning woman aged 35 or older who is a US citizen enrolled in a program of vo-tech training or in an undergraduate program. (K16/R18)

5. The **National Federation of Press Women, Inc**. (Helen M. Malloch Scholarship), offers $500-$1,000 to undergraduate women who are juniors or seniors or to grad students majoring in journalism at any college or university. (K93/R6)

6. The **Landscape Architecture Foundation** (Harriett Barnhart Wimmer Scholarship) offers $1,000 to women who have demonstrated excellent design ability in landscape

architecture, have sensitivity to the environment, and who are going into their final year of undergraduate study at a university in the USA or Canada. (K63/R2)

7. **National Physical Science Consortium Graduate Fellowships for Minorities & Women in the Physical Sciences** offers $12,500 (years 1–4) and $15,000 (years 5 & 6) to US citizens studying astronomy, chemistry, computer science, geology, materials science, mathematical science, physics, and sub-disciplines. (K20/R89)

8. **Alpha Delta Kappa's International Teacher Education Scholarship** enables as many as 7 women from foreign countries to study in the USA. Unmarried women (with no dependents) who are under 30 years of age are eligible for this $10,000 scholarship if they reside outside of the USA and are non-US citizens. (K60/R49)

9. The **Astrae National Lesbian Action Foundation** (Margot Karle Scholarship) gives $500 to women students whose career path or extracurricular activities demonstrate political or social commitment to fighting for the civil rights of gays and lesbians. (K24/R5)

10. The **International Society of Women Airline Pilots** (ISA International Career Scholarship/Fiorenze de Bernardi Merit Award) offers $500-$1,500 to women throughout the world who are pursuing careers as airline pilots and have at least 350 hours of flight experience. (K62/R5)

TOP SCHOLARSHIPS FOR MEN

1. The **Fred A. Bryan Collegiate Students Fund** (Trust Fund Scholarships) offers scholarships for male graduates of South Bend Indiana High School with preference to those who have been Boy Scouts. Recipients receive between $1,400 and $1,600 for undergraduate study at an accredited college or university. (K16/R47)

2. The **Phi Kappa Theta National Foundation** (Scholarship Program) offers undergraduate scholarships to members of the Phi Kappa Theta Fraternity. Five scholarships are awarded based on financial need. (K19/R46)

3. The **ConRail-Consolidated Rail Corporation** (Frank Thomson Scholarships for Males) offers a $2,000 scholarship to high school seniors who are sons of ConRail or Predecessor Railroad company employees. Applicants must be studying in the engineering field. Twelve scholarships are awarded based on financial need and competitive exams. (K20/R95)

4. The **Iowa American Legion** (Boy Scout of the Year Contest Scholarship) offers a $1,000 scholarship for undergraduate study to Iowa Boy Scouts who have received the Eagle Scout award. Qualification is based on the scout's outstanding service to his religious institution, school, and community. (K21/R124)

5. The **Iowa American Legion** (Outstanding Citizen of Boys State Scholarship) offers $1,500 scholarships to males who attend Boys State. This scholarship is open to all fields of study. (K21/R125)

6. **The Boys & Girls Clubs of San Diego** (Spence Reese Scholarship Fund) offer scholarships to male high school students planning a career in: medicine, law, engineering, or political science. Preference to students who live within a 250-mile radius of San Diego. Boys Club affiliation in not required. (K25/R156)

7. The **Elmer O. & Ida Preston Educational Trust** (Grants and Loans) offers an award that is half grant and half loan to male residents of Iowa who are pursuing a collegiate or professional study at an Iowa college or university. Applicants must be planning on a career in Christian Ministry and must provide a recommendation from a minister commenting on the student's potential. (K75/R25)

RECOMMENDATIONS

By using this book to track down all your potential sources of funding, you may need additional help. Following are some excellent sources that NSRS recommends:

THE INSTITUTE OF INTERNATIONAL EDUCATION (IIE)

ACADEMIC YEAR ABROAD, $42.95 and $4.95 handling. The most complete guide to planning study abroad describes over 1900 post-secondary study programs outside the USA. Concise descriptions provide the information you need on costs, academic programs and credits, dates and application, and more. (K11/R60)

VACATION STUDY ABROAD, $36.95. Describes over 1450 summer or short-term study abroad sponsored by United States colleges and universities and foreign institutions. (K11/R58)

All orders must be prepaid. IIE pays domestic postage. If you have questions, write or phone:

Institute of International Education (IIE)
Publications Service, IIE
809 United Nations Plaza, New York, NY 10017
(212) 984-5330

MAKING IT THROUGH COLLEGE, $1.00. Handy booklet describing how to make it through college. Includes information on how to cope with competition, getting organized, study techniques, solving work overloads, and much more. (K11/R16)

Write to:

Professional Staff Congress
25 West 43rd Street, 5th Floor
New York, NY 10036

10 STEPS IN WRITING THE RESEARCH PAPER, $7.95. Arranged to lead the student step-by-step through the writing of a research paper from finding a suitable subject to checking the final copy. Easy enough for the beginner, complete enough for the graduate student. 160 pages. (K11/R5)

Write to:

Barron's Educational Series Inc.
250 Wireless Blvd.
Hauppauge, NY 11788

NEED A LIFT? $3. Outstanding guide to education & employment opportunities. Contains complete information on the financial aid process (how, when, and where to start), scholarships, loans, and career information addresses. (K11/R24)

Write to:

American Legion Education Program
P.O. Box 1050
Indianapolis, IN 46206

COLLEGE FINANCIAL AID EMERGENCY KIT, $5.95 (prepaid). 40-page booklet filled with tips on how to meet the costs of tuition, room and board, and fees. Tells what is available, whom to ask, and how to ask! (K11/R66)

Recommendations

Write to:

Sun Features Inc.
Box 368-K
Cardiff, CA 92007

FISKE GUIDE TO COLLEGES, $18. Describes the 265 top-rated four-year colleges in the USA and rates for academics, social life, and quality of life. (K11/R28)

Write to:

Times Books
400 Hahn Road
Westminster, MD 21157

INDEX OF MAJORS, $17.00. Describes over 500 major programs of study at 3000 undergraduate and graduate schools. Also lists schools with religious affiliations, special academic programs, and special admissions procedures. (K11/R95)

Add $3.95 postage. Write to:

College Board Publications
P.O. Box 886
New York, NY 10101

PETERSON'S GUIDE TO FOUR-YEAR COLLEGES, $19.95. Detailed profiles of over 1900 accredited four-year colleges in the USA and Canada. Also includes entrance difficulty directory, majors directory, and college cost directory. (K11/R98)

INTERNSHIPS, $29.95. Are you a college student? Looking for your first job? Re-entering the work force? Thinking about making a career change? Or just taking a break before higher education and would like to try a particular career field? This books lists numerous job training opportunities, arranged by career field and indexed geographically. (K11/R92)

> *"If you are somewhat undecided on the question of a career, simply browsing through the myriad possibilities may spark an unexpected interest."*
>
> — Business Week

Add $6.75 for shipping and handling. Write to:

Peterson's Inc.
Dept. 7707, P.O. Box 2123
Princeton, NJ 08543

COLLEGE DEGREES BY MAIL, $12.95 plus $2.50 shipping and handling. John Bear, Ph.D, describes every approach known to earning a degree without ever taking a single traditional course! It lists 100 reputable colleges that offer bachelors, masters, doctorates, and law degrees through home study. The book also lists colleges reputed to be diploma mills and cautions against them. (K11/R102)

HAPPIER BY DEGREES, $8.95. The complete guide for women returning to college or just starting out. It is the kind of resource that you can depend on for everything from financial aid to using campus programs. A step-by-step guide for selecting the right college and incorporating a student role into an already busy life, and concludes with advice on making your career choice. (K11/R61)

"I have never seen a more useful guide to the puzzling world of academia."

— Carolyn See, Professor, Loyola Marymount University

This is my most recommended book for women attending college today; it is full of good advice. Pam has done a great job! Include $3.50 for shipping and handling.

Write to:

Ten Speed Press
P.O. Box 7123
Berkeley, CA 94707

HOW TO WIN A SPORTS SCHOLARSHIP, $14.95 plus $3.00 shipping and handling. This is an easy-to-use workbook that teaches high school students and their families a step-by-step process for winning sports scholarships. You don't have to be a superstar! $100,000 scholarships offered in 35 sports each year! Over $500 million awarded annually! There is a special section for female athletes. 250 pages (K11/R8)

Write to:

Hastings Communications
P.O. Box 14927
Santa Rosa, CA 95402

SAMPLE FORM LETTER
REQUESTING APPLICATION INFORMATION

Use this sample letter as a guide to create a general letter requesting information. Photocopy your letter and address the envelopes for mailing. Include the name of the scholarship you are applying for with the address on the envelope. Remember to apply well in advance of the deadlines. You should keep a calendar to keep track of them.

Date

Scholarship Program Office

Dear Scholarship Director:

Please send me application forms for the scholarships or fellowships you might offer. I am enclosing a self-addressed, stamped envelope for your convenience in replying.

Sincerely,

Thomas Allen Cassidy
2280 Airport Boulevard
Santa Rosa, California 95403

THE PLAN

Once you have written to scholarship sources for complete information, you might consider starting three financial aid boxes to maintain your information. You might call them "Government Funding," "School Endowments," and "Private Sector."

The Government Funding Box

Put all information from state and federal programs in this box.
Remember:
Dept. of Educ. 1-800-433-3243
The Coordinating Board for your state is in your phone book under "Government."

The School Endowments Box

The college catalogs will usually list the endowments from alumni and local businesses. Put the catalogs in this box.

The Private Sector Box

This box should contain material you have gleaned from this book and/or from your NSRS computer printout.

Call 1-800-432-3782.

THE SEARCH

Believe it or not, just about everything about you will come into play in your search for scholarships—your ancestry, religion, place of birth and residence, parent's union or corporate affiliation, or simply your interest in a particular field can all be eligibility factors.

Using the tables in this book, select 20 to 30 different private sector scholarship sources. Next, write to them and ask for their scholarship application and requirements. The letter can be a general request for information "form" letter that can be photocopied, but you should be specific about the name of the scholarship you are inquiring about on the envelope.

Write to each source as far in advance of their scholarship deadline as possible and don't forget to send a self-addressed, stamped envelope—it not only expedites their reply, but some organizations won't respond without one.

Remember, on the outside of the envelope, list the name of the specific scholarship you are inquiring about. That way the person opening the mail will know where to direct your inquiry. Replies to these letters should be sorted into the appropriate boxes.

THE GOVERNMENT BOX

On a quiet Saturday or when you have time, sit down and review the information. In the "Government" box, you will find that the state and federal forms are very similar, asking a multitude of questions regarding income, assets, and expenses. Don't automatically exclude yourself from state and federal funding thinking that you or your family make too much money. These programs vary tremendously from state to state and the federal programs have changed quite a bit. For example, there is no longer a $32,500 limit on the amount parents can earn in order to qualify for a student loan; but since that limit has been raised to $45,000, there will be less federal money to go around, so be sure to get in line quick.

A bit of good news in the student loan arena is that the federal government no longer will consider the value of your house or farm in determining the amount of aid you qualify for.

THE SCHOOL ENDOWMENTS BOX

You will usually find a list of endowments from alumni listed in the financial aid section of the college catalog. Often endowments to schools are not advertised and may go unclaimed. For example, at a small school like USF, the total endowments average $20 million to $30 million per year. At Ivy League schools, endowments range from $100 million to $200+ million each year. Of those endowments, 10% to 15% goes to the financial aid office in the form of scholarships, fellowships, grants, and loans.

You will discover that sources in the "School Endowments" box are really just other forms of private sector scholarships. The difference is that endowment money is given directly to the school and is administered exclusively by the school's financial aid office, so you must deal directly with the college. You'll find that the myths I talked about earlier also apply to these private endowments—again, don't exclude yourself because of those old clichés regarding your grades, financial status, deadlines, or age.

THE PRIVATE SECTOR BOX

With your "Private Sector" box, you will find that once you have seen one or two forms, you have pretty much seen them all. Usually they are two pages asking where you are going to school, what you are going to major in, and why you think you deserve the scholarship. Some scholarship sources require that you join their organization. If the organization relates to your field of study, you should strongly consider joining because it will keep you informed (via newsletters, etc.) about developments in that field.

Other scholarship organizations may want you to promise that you will work for them for a period of time. The Dow Jones Newspaper Fund offers up to $80,000 in scholarships annually for journalism and mass communications students. In addition, a two-week intensive course (equivalent to advanced editing courses at most journalism departments) is followed by summer employment at a newspaper—interns receive a minimum weekly salary of $225. This could even yield a permanent job for the student.

THE ESSAY

Most organizations awarding scholarships require an essay as part of the application process. The essay is the most important part of the private sector scholarship search.

The following excerpt from the University of California at Los Angeles (UCLA) application material emphasizes the importance of the essay and contains good advice no matter where you are going to college:

> The essay is an important part of your application for admission and for scholarships.
>
> For these purposes, the University seeks information that will distinguish you from other applicants. You may wish, therefore, to write about your experiences, achievements, and goals. You might, for example, discuss an important life experience and what you learned from it. You might also describe unusual circumstances, challenges, or hardships you have faced. School activities and experiences are also topics to discuss in your essay but they do not need to be the focus.
>
> Rather than listing activities, describe your level of achievement in areas you have pursued—including employment or volunteer activities—and the personal qualities revealed by the time and effort you have devoted to them.
>
> Also, discuss your interest in your intended field of study. If you have a disability, you may also include a description of its impact on your experiences, goals, and aspirations.
>
> The University seeks information about any exceptional achievements such as activities, honors, awards, employment or volunteer work that demonstrates your motivation, achievement, leadership, and commitment.

Make sure your essay is neatly typed, well written, and does not contain grammatical errors or misspelled words.

THE APPLICATION

When filling out scholarship application forms, be complete, concise, and creative. People who read these applications want to know the real you, not just your name. Scholarship applications should clearly emphasize your ambitions, motivations, and what makes you different from everyone else. Be original!

Your application should be typewritten and neat. I had a complaint from one foundation about a student who had an excellent background and qualifications but used a crayon to fill out the application.

Once your essay is finished, make a master file of it and other supporting items. Photocopy your essay and attach it to each application. If requested, also include: a resume or curriculum vitae, extra-curricular activities sheet (usually one page), transcripts, SAT or ACT scores, letters of recommendation (usually one each from a teacher, employer, and friend) outlining your moral character and, if there are any newspaper articles, etc., about you, it is a good idea to include them as well.

Application Checklist

The following supporting documents may be requested with your application. I suggest you make a master file for these documents and photocopy them. You can then just pull a copy from your file and attach it to the application upon request.

- ❑ 1. Include your essay.
- ❑ 2. Include resume or curriculum vitae.
- ❑ 3. Include extra-curricular activities sheet.
- ❑ 4. Include transcripts.
- ❑ 5. Include SAT or ACT scores.
- ❑ 6. Include letters of recommendation.
- ❑ 7. Include any newspaper articles, etc., about yourself (if you have any).

You might also include your photograph, whether it's a high school picture or a snapshot of you working at your favorite hobby. This helps the selection committee feel a little closer to you. Instead of just seeing a name, they will have a face to match it.

Mail your applications in early—at least a month before the deadline.

THE CALENDAR

I also find it helpful to keep a calendar with deadlines circled so you can stay organized. You can hang it above your three scholarship boxes so it is easily visible. Each application should have its own file. On the outside of the file, you might rate your chances of getting the scholarship on a scale of 1 to 10.

If a scholarship application deadline has passed, save it for the next year. If you are turned down for a scholarship, don't worry. Some organizations want to see if you will apply a second time. The important point is to stay motivated and be persistent.

Calendar						
Sun	M	T	W	Th	F	Sat
1	2	3	4	5	6	7
8	9	10	11	12	13	14
15	16	17	18	19	20	21
22	23	24	25	26	27	28
29	30	31				

Government Box	**Endowment Box**	**Private Sector Box**

Box With Master Files 1–7.

WHERE THE INFORMATION IN THIS BOOK CAME FROM

The information in this book was compiled from the database of the largest private sector college financial aid research service in the world: National Scholarship Research Service (NSRS) located in Santa Rosa, California.

Since the late 1970's, NSRS had been using computers to research and update information on potential sources of financial assistance for college students. Many thousands of students have used NSRS's services to locate sources offering financial aid.

NATIONAL SCHOLARSHIP RESEARCH SERVICE (NSRS)

NSRS computers store information on thousands of private sector aid programs for all levels of college study: from high school seniors just entering college to postdoctoral researchers.

Applicants for NSRS services first complete a biographical questionnaire, indicating their particular area(s) of interest. This information is entered into the computer which searches NSRS files for the scholarships the applicant may qualify for. Since each applicant has a different background and each of the thousands of aid programs has different requirements, this computer search can save valuable time and often provides students with potential sources of aid that they might never have considered applying for.

If you consider that all the financial aid programs listed in this book are constantly changing, with new application dates, qualifying requirements, etc., you may want to utilize these services.

Since NSRS is a privately-owned company, there is a modest fee for the services provided. For a product list, write or call:

NATIONAL SCHOLARSHIP RESEARCH SERVICES
Box 6609
Santa Rosa, California 95406-0609
24-Hour Phone: (707) 546-6777
24-Hour Fax: (707) 546-6785

THE WORLDWIDE WEB

This year, National Scholarship Research Service (NSRS) started traveling on the new worldwide WEB's super highway.

For the first time in 1995, computer operators throughout the world can communicate with "Mr. Scholarship," Daniel Cassidy, president of NSRS, by using the worldwide highway at the following NSRS addresses:

Internet
Information can be found at:
800headstart.com or
Scholarshipbook.com or
edworks.com
Example: http://www.800headstart.com

America Online
NSRS.COM
Example: NSRS@AOL.COM

CompuServe
Dan Cassidy (Address 75534.1425)
and Dan Cassidy (AKA) Mr. Scholarship on:
U.S. News and World Report's "College Forum"
Example: GO USNCOL

MicroSoft Network
NSRS.COM
Example: NSRS.@MSN.COM

IMPORTANT NOTE

This book is an abridged version of the NSRS database. For a more comprehensive search for sources of educational financing, write to NSRS.

Every effort has been made to supply you with the most accurate and up-to-date information possible, but—even as this book goes to print—awards are being added and application requirements are being changed by sponsoring organizations. Such circumstances are beyond our control.

Since the information we have supplied may not reflect the current status of any particular award program you are interested in, you should use this book only as a guide. Contact the source of the award for current application information.

If questions arise during your search for educational funding, you are welcome to call a NSRS counselor at 707/546-6781.

SCHOLARSHIP SEARCH SCAMS

A disturbing number of scholarship sponsoring organizations have reported in recent months that they are receiving a high volume of inquiries from students who are unqualified for the awards about which they are asking.

Because of the number of these types of reports, we are investigating the origins of the misguided inquiries. Most often we find that someone has taken *only* names and addresses from our scholarship books and is selling the information—a general listing of scholarships available in a particular field of study—to students without regard to the student's qualifications. Most of these "rip-off operations" make no effort to match the student's educational goals and personal background with the requirements of the scholarships.

The books that we publish contain 40 tables along with the source description, providing accurate cross-matching of the student's characteristics to the requirements at scholarship sources. National Scholarship Research Service (NSRS) and the publishers of our books are doing all we can to stop any abuse of our copyright which might result in an inconvenience to our scholarship sponsoring organizations. We've assisted the Federal Trade Commission (FTC) in closing down one "rip-off operation" and we are currently pursuing six others. In September of 1996, the FTC announced Project $cholar$cam. For a period of one year, Project $cholar$cam will force scams in this industry to "cease and desist."

Lastly, if any scholarship service guarantees a scholarship, savings bond, or a fountain pen, "buyer beware!" If it sounds too good to be true, then it probably is. Since it is solely at the discretion of the scholarship sponsoring organizations to choose their scholarship recipients each year, these scholarship search scans cannot guarantee that users of their service will get a scholarship. Use this book to accurately cross-match scholarship sources you are eligible for and avoid those scholarship search scams that merely copy information from our books.

How to Use This Book

Each award, book, and resource listed has a record number preceding it. All of our indexes are based on these record numbers.

Here is a short guide to finding the information you need:

"QUICK FIND" INDEX

Most private-sector awards have certain eligibility qualifications. We have selected several of the most common requirements for this "Quick Find" index.

Here you can find awards targeted for people of a particular race, religion, or family ancestry, for people who will be studying in a particular state or community, for the physically handicapped, and much more. Simply go through each of the tables and write down the reference numbers that apply to you. Then proceed to those sources and read each one carefully to see if you qualify.

FIELD OF STUDY INDEX

Since the awards listed in this book are also based on your intended field of study, we have structured this index along the lines of a college catalog.

First, look under your particular field of study (e.g., "School of Business"). Then, look under your area of interest (e.g., "Accounting") and, finally, under your specific subject (e.g., "Banking"). In this section, you will find record numbers that reference both financial aid awards and other resources that can help you in your career. Again, since there might be several eligibility requirements you must meet in order to be able to qualify for any listed award, be sure you read each listing *carefully* and that you *meet the requirements of the award* before requesting an application.

SCHOLARSHIP AND AWARD LISTINGS

Each listing contains a very condensed description of the award, its eligibility requirements, deadline dates, and where to get more information or an application.

You will notice a large "General" section. These are awards that do not usually specify a particular field of study in their eligibility requirements. You need to use the indexes provided and read each listing carefully to see if you might qualify for one of these awards.

Use the information we have provided only as a guide. Write to the source for a complete description of qualifications.

HELPFUL PUBLICATIONS

This section contains a selection of books and pamphlets that we consider helpful to the student. These publications are excellent sources of information on a wide variety of college and financial aid subjects.

If you discover a publication you find particularly helpful, let us know so we can share the information with others.

CAREER INFORMATION

This is a list of organizations that can help you decide where to study, give you information on job opportunities available in your field of study, and much more. We encourage you to write to these organizations for information.

ALPHABETICAL INDEX

A to Z, this index lists the reference number of every award, book, and career organization that is included in this book.

Quick Find Index

DEGREES RECEIVED

ETHNIC BACKGROUND

EXTRACURRICULAR ACTIVITIES

FAMILY ANCESTRIES

FOREIGN LANGUAGES SPOKEN

HONORS/AWARDS/CONTESTS

LEGAL CITY OF RESIDENCE

LEGAL STATE/PROVENCE OF RESIDENCE

MARITAL STATUS

OCCUPATIONAL GOALS

OCCUPATIONS

ORGANIZATIONS

PHYSICAL HANDICAPS

PRE/CUR/FUT SCHOOLS

RELIGIOUS AFFILIATION

SEX

SORORITY/FRATERNAL

STATE/PROVINCE INTENDED STUDY

UNIONS

UNUSUAL CHARACTERISTICS

Field of Study Index

SCHOOL OF BUSINESS

General, 1, 1106, 1212

BUSINESS ADMINISTRATION

General, 3, 4, 9, 11, 22, 24, 28, 31, 34, 38, 39, 46, 48, 72, 85, 87, 102, 104, 117, 169, 174, 180, 183, 184, 186, 197, 213, 229, 252, 256, 316, 337, 399, 407, 413, 419, 433, 461, 478, 480, 489, 490, 499, 500, 503, 504, 507, 526, 536, 556, 592, 623, 627, 648, 656, 672, 720, 752, 873, B1276, C1378

Accounting, 2, 14, 15, 18, 20, 27, 30, 38, 39, 178, 183, 184, 195, 207, 503, 504, 581, 756, C1348, C1349, C1350

Actuarial Science, 13, 25, 37, 38, 39, 183, 184, 503, 504, C1351, C1436

Advertising, 8, 257, 658, 663, C1352

Aviation/Airport Management, 19, 123, 754

Banking, 21, C1372

Economics, 5, 16, 21, 22, 34, 38, 39, 47, 104, 174, 180, 183, 184, 197, 500, 503, 504, 672, 699, 704, 719, 720, 729

Finance, 21, 38, 39, 183, 184, 503, 504

Hotel Administration, 23, 40, 643, 644, 652, C1434

Industrial & Labor Relations, 26

Insurance, 13, 25, 38, 39, 183, 184, 503, 504, C1436, C1437

Management, 9, 12, 17, 21, 39, 184, 504, C1347, C1446

Marketing, 8, 17, 34, 38, 39, 104, 174, 180, 183, 184, 197, 257, 413, 500, 503, 504, 658

Public Administration, 32, 33, 150, 151, 725, 726, 743, 744

Public Relations, 6, 657, 663, C1486

Real Estate, 10, 35, C1364, C1489

Traffic Management, 41, 42, 43, 44, 45

Transportation, 29, 41, 42, 43, 44, 45, 147, C1360

Travel & Tourism, 7, 20, 84, 581, 756

SCHOOL OF EDUCATION

General, 49, 543, 1106, 1212

EDUCATION

General, 31, 50, 55, 56, 57, 59, 60, 61, 62, 63, 64, 66, 67, 68, 69, 72, 73, 74, 75, 77, 79, 82, 83, 91, 93, 102, 177, 221, 239, 252, 316, 337, 399, 407, 463, 474, 480, 485, 490, 495, 499, 512, 526, 541, 556, 592, 623, 648, 656, 708, 750, 873, B1277, C1402, C1495

Administration, B1292, C1494

Blind/Visually Impaired Education, 51, 52, 53, 65, 570, 571, 730, 731, 732, 812, B1306, C1400

Deaf/Hearing Impaired Education, 65, B1306, C1400

Elementary Education, 76, 78, 81

Learning Disabled Education, B1306, C1400

Physical Education, 70, 71, 84, 555, 591

Secondary Education, 76, 78, 81

Special Education, 58, 63, 65, 80, 579, 734, 741, 812, B1265, B1306, C1400, C1500

Youth Leadership, 48, 54, 85, C1512, C1513

SCHOOL OF ENGINEERING

General, 4, 31, 34, 46, 55, 57, 72, 86, 87, 88, 89, 90, 91, 92, 93, 94, 95, 96, 97, 98, 99, 100, 101, 102, 103, 104, 105, 106, 107, 108, 109, 110, 111, 112, 113, 114, 115, 116, 117, 118, 127, 152, 174, 177, 180, 181, 186, 197, 237, 239, 243, 252, 316, 337, 399, 401, 405, 407, 420, 433, 440, 453, 460, 461, 462, 463, 464, 465, 467, 468, 470, 473, 474, 475, 480, 483, 485, 486, 487, 490, 491, 495, 496, 497, 499, 500, 507, 510, 511, 512, 519, 526, 528, 536, 539, 541, 549, 556, 557, 592, 623, 627, 648, 655, 656, 697, 707, 708, 711, 717, 718, 733, 736, 750, 858, 873, 1106, 1212, B1278, C1355, C1404, C1405, C1493

AERONAUTICS

General, 19, 119, 120, 123, 125, 127, 129, 130, 175, 179, 196, 200, 208, 223, 232, 233, 443, 476, 498, 506, 628, 754, 767, B1338, C1353, C1359, C1360

NURSING

NUTRITION

SCHOOL OF SOCIAL SCIENCE

COMMUNICATIONS

HISTORY

Historical Writing, 328, 459, 703
Military Science, 328, 459, 703

LAW

General, 55, 89, 91, 98, 177, 241, 406, 466, 474, 485, 487, 495, 511, 512, 519, 523, 541, 549, 554, 614, 707, 708, 709, 710, 711, 713, 715, 717, 750, B1247, B1276, C1440
Law Enforcement, 705, 706, 712, 714, 759, C1409

POLITICAL SCIENCE

General, 16, 22, 47, 89, 94, 243, 420, 453, 475, 497, 511, 672, 697, 699, 704, 707, 716, 717, 718, 719, 720, 724, 729, 733, 873, 1106, B1269, C1483
Foreign Policy, 702, 727
Government, 16, 32, 33, 47, 150, 151, 699, 704, 719, 721, 724, 725, 726, 728, 729, 743, 744
International Relations, 723
Public Service, 32, 33, 150, 151, 721, 722, 724, 725, 726, 728, 743, 744

PSYCHOLOGY

General, 94, 103, 243, 253, 420, 453, 467, 475, 497, 501, 562, 606, 689, 697, 718, 733, 735, 736, 738, 745, 873, 1106, B1326, C1485
Developmental Disabilities-G, B1306, C1400
Human Sexuality, 739
Parapsychology, 737, B1291
Rehabilitation Counseling, 51, 52, 53, 58, 562, 570, 571, 579, 606, 730, 731, 732, 734, 735, 741, 812, B1265, C1490

SOCIOLOGY

General, 253, 501, 689, 738, 745, 873, 1106, B1326, C1498
Social Work, 58, 522, 553, 579, 586, 613, 734, 740, 741, 742, C1497
Urban Affairs, 32, 33, 150, 151, 725, 726, 743, 744

SCHOOL OF VOCATIONAL ED

General, 11, 419, 751, 752, 761, 762, 765, 766, 873, 960, 967, 1098, 1181, 1188, 1212, C1365
Aerospace studies, 753, B1338
Aviation Maintenance Technology, 19, 122, 123, 124, 748, 749, 754, 755, 763, 764, B1338, C1408
Baking Science, 747
Cosmetology/Barber, C1389
Court Reporting, 20, 581, 756
Fire Service, 588, 712, 759, 760, C1411
Funeral Service, 746, 758, C1421
Gemology, 757
Musical Instruments, 768
Paralegal, 20, 55, 91, 177, 474, 485, 495, 512, 541, 581, 708, 750, 756
Secretarial School, 20, 581, 756, C1496
Vertical Flight, 122, 124, 130, 200, 233, 748, 755, 767, 769

Scholarships and Award Listings

SCHOOL OF BUSINESS

1

PRESIDENT'S COMMITTEE ON EMPLOYMENT OF PEOPLE WITH DISABILITIES
(Scholarship Program)
1331 F St. NW
Washington DC 20004
202/376-6200; TDD 202/376-6205

AMOUNT: $2000
DEADLINE(S): Announced annually
FIELD(S): Business
Open to high school seniors & 4-year college or university undergrads having a disability (a physical or mental impairment that substantially limits 1 or more major life activities). US citizenship required.
Write for complete information.

BUSINESS ADMINISTRATION

2

AMERICAN ACCOUNTING ASSOCIATION
(Arthur H. Carter Scholarships)
5717 Bessie Dr.
Sarasota FL 34233
941/921-7747; FAX 941/923-4093

AMOUNT: $2500
DEADLINE(S): April 1
FIELD(S): Accounting
Applicants must be US citizens who have completed at least two years of study at an accredited college and have at least one year left. During scholarship period student must have at least 12 hours of classroom work.

Students must also be enrolled in at least two accounting classes each semester. Awards are based on merit; financial need is not considered. Write for complete information.

3

AMERICAN COLLEGE FOR THE APPLIED ARTS
(Emilio Pucci Scholarships)
3330 Peachtree Rd. NE; Admissions Office
Atlanta GA 30326
404/231-9000

AMOUNT: $1800 (distributed over 6 quarters)
DEADLINE(S): May 1
FIELD(S): Fashion Design; Fashion Marketing; Interior Design; Commercial Art; Business Administration; Video Production
Scholarships are for high school seniors who are interested in either a 2-year or 4-year program at one of the American Colleges for the Applied Arts in Atlanta, Los Angeles, or London. Scholarship is applied toward tuition.
Write for applications and complete information.

4

AMERICAN INDIAN SCIENCE & ENGINEERING SOCIETY
(Santa Fe Pacific Foundation Scholarships)
1630 30th St.; Suite 301
Boulder CO 80301
303/939-0023

AMOUNT: Up to $2500 per year for 4 years
DEADLINE(S): March 31
FIELD(S): Business; Engineering; Science; Health Administration
Open to graduating high school seniors with 1/4 or more Indian blood. Must reside in

1

KS, OK, CO, AZ, NM, or San Bernardino County, CA (AT&SF Railway service area). Two of the five scholarships are designated for Navajo tribe members.

Must plan to attend a 4-year post-secondary accredited educational institution. Write for complete information.

5

AMERICAN INSTITUTE FOR ECONOMIC RESEARCH
(Summer Fellowships; In Absentia Awards)
Division St.; P.O. Box 1000
Great Barrington MA 01230
413/528-1216

AMOUNT: Tuition; room & board; $125 per week stipend

DEADLINE(S): March 31

FIELD(S): Economics

Summer fellowships in economic science at the institute. Open to college seniors applying to graduate programs leading to a Ph.D. in economics and to students already enrolled in such programs. Preference to grad students & US citizens.

Successful summer fellows are eligible for in absentia awards which will pay total or partial tuition or monthly stipend for all or part of the following academic year or both. Write for complete information.

6

AMERICAN INSTITUTE OF POLISH CULTURE INC.
(Scholarships)
1440 79th Street Causeway; Suite 117
Miami FL 33141
305/864-2349

AMOUNT: $2500

DEADLINE(S): January 15

FIELD(S): Journalism/Public Relations

Scholarships to encourage young Americans of Polish descent to pursue the above professions. Award can be used at any accredited American college. The ruling criteria for selection are achievement/talent & involvement in public life.

For full-time study only. Renewable. Contact Prof. Zdzislaw Wesolowski at address above for complete information.

7

AMERICAN SOCIETY OF TRAVEL AGENTS
(ASTA Scholarship Foundation Scholarship Funds)
1101 King St.
Alexandria VA 22314
703/739-2782

AMOUNT: $250–$3000

DEADLINE(S): June/July

FIELD(S): Travel & Tourism

Foundation administers various scholarship funds which are open to students enrolled in accredited proprietary schools, 2-year or 4-year undergraduate schools, or graduate schools. Minimum 2.5 GPA required.

Each fund has specific eligibility requirements & some awards are renewable. US or Canadian citizenship or legal residency required. Write for complete information.

8

AMERICAN WOMEN IN RADIO & TELEVISION
(Houston Internship Program)
Aprille Meek; AWRT—Houston; P.O. Box 980908
Houston TX 77098
Written inquiry

AMOUNT: $500 per year

DEADLINE(S): March 1

FIELD(S): Radio; Television; Film & Video; Advertising; Marketing

Internships open to students who are juniors, seniors, or graduate students at greater Houston area colleges & universities.

Write for complete information.

9

APICS EDUCATIONAL & RESEARCH FOUNDATION INC.
(International Student Paper Competition)
500 West Annandale Rd.
Falls Church VA 22046
703/237-8344

AMOUNT: Up to $1700
DEADLINE(S): May 15 (submit papers to local APICS chapter)
FIELD(S): Integrated Resource Management
Awards for winning papers open to full-time or part-time undergraduate or graduate students.
Write for complete information.

10

APPRAISAL INSTITUTE EDUCATION TRUST
(Scholarships)
875 N. Michigan Ave.; Suite 2400
Chicago IL 60611-1980
312/335-4136; FAX 312/335-4200

AMOUNT: $3000 graduate; $2000 undergrad
DEADLINE(S): March 15
FIELD(S): Real Estate Appraisal; Land Economics; Real Estate or allied fields

Open to USA citizens for graduate or undergraduate study in the above fields. Awards are made on the basis of academic excellence. Applications will be distributed starting September 1.
Approximately 50 scholarships per year. Write for complete information.

11

CDS INTERNATIONAL INC.
(Congress-Bundestag Youth Exchange Program)
330 Seventh Ave.; 19th Floor
New York NY 10001
212/760-1400; FAX 212/268-1288

AMOUNT: Airfare; partial domestic travel & host family payment
DEADLINE(S): December 15
FIELD(S): Business; Vo-tech Fields; Agricultural Fields.

Year-long work/study programs in Germany for USA citizens aged 18–24 & in the USA for German citizens aged 18–21. Program for Americans includes 2-month language study, 4-month tech or professional school study, & 6-month internship.
Professional target and applicable work experience is required. Participants must provide their own spending money of $300–$350/month. Write or call for complete information.

12

CLUB FOUNDATION
(Scholarship Awards)
1733 King Street
Alexandria VA 22314
703/739-9500; FAX 703/739-0124

AMOUNT: Varies
DEADLINE(S): May 1
FIELD(S): Management

Open to students who have completed their freshman year at an accredited US college or university and are interested in a career in private club management. Applicants should have 2.5 or better GPA. Awards are not based solely on need.
Write for complete information.

13

COLLEGE OF INSURANCE
(Scholarships)
101 Murray Street; Admissions Office
New York NY 10007
212/962-4111

AMOUNT: $2200 to $9144 per semester
DEADLINE(S): May for following September

FIELD(S): Insurance Management; Actuarial Science

Awards tenable at the College of Insurance only. Open to applicants who are USA citizens; high school graduates.

50 scholarships per semister. Renewable. Write for complete information.

14

COLORADO SOCIETY OF CPAs
(Educational Foundation Scholarships for H.S. Seniors)
7979 E. Tuft Ave.; #500
Denver CO 80237
303/773-2877

AMOUNT: $750

DEADLINE(S): March 1

FIELD(S): Accounting

Colorado residents. Open to high school seniors with at least 3.75 GPA who intend to major in accounting at Colorado colleges & universities which offer an accredited accounting major.

Financial need is a consideration. Write for complete information.

15

COLORADO SOCIETY OF CPAs
(Educational Foundation Scholarships for Undergraduates)
7979 E. Tuft Ave.; #500
Denver CO 80237
303/773-2877

AMOUNT: $500/semester

DEADLINE(S): June 1; November 30

FIELD(S): Accounting

Open to undergraduates who have completed at least their 1st year and have 3.0 or better GPA & are majoring in accounting at one of the 13 Colorado colleges & universities which offer accredited accounting majors.

Scholarships are awarded each semester & are renewable with reapplication. Financial need is a consideration. Write for complete information.

16

DAUGHTERS OF THE AMERICAN REVOLUTION
(Enid Hall Griswold Memorial Scholarship Program)
Office of the Committee/Scholarships;
National Society DAR; 1776 'D' St. NW
Washington DC 20006-5392
202/879-3292

AMOUNT: $1000 (one-time award)

DEADLINE(S): February 15

FIELD(S): History; Political Science; Government; Economics

Open to undergraduate juniors & seniors attending an accredited college or university in the USA. Awards are judged on the basis of academic excellence and financial need & commitment to field of study. Must be US citizen.

DAR affiliation is not required but applicants must be sponsored by a local DAR chapter. Not renewable. Write for complete information (include SASE).

17

DECA
(Harry A. Applegate Scholarships)
1908 Association Drive
Reston VA 22091
703/860-5000

AMOUNT: Varies

DEADLINE(S): March 1

FIELD(S): Marketing; Management; Merchandising

Open to high school seniors or graduates who are members of DECA. Scholarships are for undergraduate study at accredited colleges or universities. USA citizens.

Scholarships are renewable. Write for complete information.

18

DEVRY INC.
(Scholarship Program)
One Tower Lane
Oakbrook Terrace IL 60181
708/571-7700; 800/323-4256

AMOUNT: Full tuition (40); 1/2 tuition (80)
DEADLINE(S): March 22
FIELD(S): Electronics Engineering
Technology; Computer Information
Systems; Business Operations;
Telecommunications Management;
Accounting

40 full-tuition & 80 1/2-tuition undergraduate
scholarships. Open to US high school graduates who wish to enroll in a fully-accredited bachelor of science degree program at
one of the DeVry Institutes located
throughout North America.

Awards renewable provided 2.5 GPA is maintained. Contact your guidance counselor,
nearest Devry Institute, or address above
for complete information.

19

EAA AVIATION FOUNDATION
(Scholarship Program)
P.O. Box 3065
Oshkosh WI 54903-3065
414/426-4888

AMOUNT: $200 to $1500
DEADLINE(S): April 1
FIELD(S): Aviation

Ten different scholarship programs open to
well-rounded individuals involved in school
and community activities as well as aviation.
Applicants' academic records should verify
their ability to complete their educational
program.

Financial need is a consideration; a financial
need statement may be required.

20

EMPIRE COLLEGE
(Dean's Scholarship)
3033 Cleveland Ave.
Santa Rosa CA 95403
707/546-4000

AMOUNT: $250–$1500
DEADLINE(S): April 15
FIELD(S): Court Reporting; Accounting;
Secretarial; Legal; Medical (Clinical &
Administrative); Travel & Tourism; General
Business

Open to high school seniors who meet admis-
sion requirements and want to attend
Empire College in Santa Rosa California.
US citizenship required.

Ten scholarships per year. Contact Ms. Carole
A. Bratton at the above address for complete information.

21

**FIRST INTERSTATE BANK OF
WASHINGTON**
(Scholarship Program)
P.O. Box 160; MS 803
Seattle WA 98111
206/292-3482

AMOUNT: $1000–$1500
DEADLINE(S): Established by institutions
making awards
FIELD(S): Business; Finance; Economics

Open to Washington state residents who are
entering specified colleges in Washington
state as freshman. Must exhibit need for
financial aid and demonstrate academic or
extracurricular achievement in business,
finance, or economics.

Apply directly to financial aid office of college
or university.

22

FUND FOR AMERICAN STUDIES
(Institutes on Political Journalism, Business &
Government Affairs, & Comparative Political
& Economic Systems)
1526 18th St. NW
Washington DC 20036
202/986-0384

AMOUNT: Up to $3500
DEADLINE(S): January 31 (early decision);
March 15 (general application deadline)
FIELD(S): Political Science; Economics;
Journalism; Business Administration

Scholarships cover cost to attend annual 6-
week summer institute at Georgetown Univ.
Courses are worth 6 credits & include foreign policy lectures, media dialogue series,
and site briefings. Open to college sophomores, juniors, and seniors.
Approx. 100 awards per year. For Fund's programs only. Write for complete information.

23

GOLDEN GATE RESTAURANT ASSN.
(David Rubenstein Memorial Scholarship
Foundation Awards)
720 Market St.; Suite 200
San Francisco CA 94102
415/781-5348

AMOUNT: $1000–$1500
DEADLINE(S): March 31
FIELD(S): Hotel & Restaurant
Management/Food Science

Open to students who have completed the
first semester of college as a food service
major and have a 2.75 or better GPA (4.0
scale) in hotel and restaurant courses.
Seven awards per year. Write for complete
information.

24

GOLDEN STATE MINORITY
FOUNDATION
(College Scholarships)
1055 Wilshire Blvd.; Suite 1115
Los Angeles CA 90017
213/482-6300

AMOUNT: Up to $2000
DEADLINE(S): August 1 (northern CA);
February 1 (southern CA)
FIELD(S): Business Administration

Open to minority students attending school in
California or California residents attending
school elsewhere. Awards support study at
the undergrad college junior/senior levels.
Must maintain a 3.0 GPA or better.
May not work more than 25 hours a week.
Income must be insufficient to cover
expenses. Approx. 75 awards per year.
Write for complete information.

25

GRIFFITH FOUNDATION FOR
INSURANCE EDUCATION
(Gamma Iota Sigma Scholarships)
941 Chatham Lane; Suite 210
Columbus OH 43221
614/442-8357

AMOUNT: varies
DEADLINE(S): None
FIELD(S): Insurance; Risk Management;
Actuarial Science

Open to students studying in the above fields
and who have completed at least two years
of college. Must be a student at Ohio State
University.
Write for complete information.

26

HOTEL EMPLOYEES & RESTAURANT
EMPLOYEES INTERNATIONAL UNION
(Ed S. Miller Scholarship)
1219 28th Street NW
Washington DC 20007
202/393-4373

AMOUNT: $3500

DEADLINE(S): February 28

FIELD(S): Industrial & Labor Relations

Open to HERE union members, their wards, children, & grandchildren. Must have been union member at least 1 year prior to November. 1 of the application year. Application requests are in October, November, & December editions of "Catering Industry Employee."

Candidates living east of the Mississippi apply in odd-numbered years & attend Cornell. Those west of the Mississippi apply in even-numbered years & attend UCLA. Renewable. Write for complete information.

27

INDEPENDENT ACCOUNTANTS INTERNATIONAL EDUCATIONAL FOUNDATION INC.
(Robert Kaufman Memorial Scholarship Award)
9200 S. Dadeland Blvd.; Suite 510
Miami FL 33156
305/670-0580

AMOUNT: $250–$1500

DEADLINE(S): February 28

FIELD(S): Accounting

Open to students who are pursuing or planning to pursue an education in accounting at recognized academic institutions throughout the world. Must demonstrate financial need for larger sums; not required for $250 honorary textbook award.

Up to 20 scholarships per year. Write for complete information.

28

NATIONAL ASSOCIATION OF WATER COMPANIES—NEW JERSEY CHAPTER
(Scholarship)
c/o NJ-American Water Co.
66 Shrewsbury Ave.
Shrewsbury NJ 07702
908/842-6900; FAX 908/842-7541

AMOUNT: $2500

DEADLINE(S): April 1 (postmark)

FIELD(S): Business Administration; Biology; Chemistry; Engineering

Open to USA citizens who have lived in NJ at least 5 years and plan a career in the investor-owned water utility industry in disciplines such as those above. Must be undergrad or graduate student in a 2 or 4 year NJ college or university.

GPA of 3.0 or better required. Write for complete information.

29

NATIONAL DEFENSE TRANSPORTATION ASSOCIATION— SAN FRANCISCO BAY AREA CHAPTER
(NDTA Scholarship)
P.O. Box 24676
Oakland CA 94623
Written inquiry

AMOUNT: $2000

DEADLINE(S): March 31

FIELD(S): Transportation-related Business; Engineering; Planning & Environmental fields

Open to USA citizens enrolled in a California accredited undergraduate degree or vocational program in the above fields who plan to pursue a career related to transportation. Financial need is considered.

Write for complete information.

30

NATIONAL SOCIETY OF PUBLIC ACCOUNTANTS SCHOLARSHIP FOUNDATION
(Scholarships)
1010 North Fairfax St
Alexandria VA 22314
703/549-6400; FAX 703/549-2984

AMOUNT: $500 - $1000

DEADLINE(S): March 10

FIELD(S): Accounting

Open to full-time accounting students in an accredited 2-year or 4-year college in the USA. Must maintain an overall grade point average of 3.0 (4.0 scale).

Approx. 22 awards per year. Selection based on academic attainment, leadership ability, and financial need. Write for complete information.

31

NELLIE MARTIN CARMAN SCHOLARSHIP TRUST
(Scholarships)
18223 73rd Ave. NE; #B101
Bothell WA 98011
206/486-6575

AMOUNT: Up to $1000
DEADLINE(S): March 15
FIELD(S): All fields of study except those noted below

Open to high school seniors in King, Pierce, & Snohomish Counties (WA). For undergraduate study in the state of Washington in all fields EXCEPT music, sculpting, drawing, interior design, & home economics. US citizenship required.

Applications available only through high schools & nomination by counselor is required. Awards are renewable. Write for complete information.

32

NEW YORK CITY DEPT. OF PERSONNEL
(Government Scholars Internship Program)
2 Washington St.; 15th Floor
New York NY 10004
212/487-5698

AMOUNT: $3000 stipend
DEADLINE(S): January 13
FIELD(S): Public Administration; Urban Planning; Government; Public Service; Urban Affairs

10-week summer intern program open to undergraduate sophomores, juniors, &

seniors. Program provides students with unique opportunity to learn about NY City government. Internships available in virtually every city agency & mayoral office. Write for complete information.

33

NEW YORK CITY DEPT. OF PERSONNEL
(Urban Fellows Program)
2 Washington St.; 15th Floor
New York NY 10004
212/487-5698

AMOUNT: $18,000 stipend
DEADLINE(S): January 20
FIELD(S): Public Administration; Urban Planning; Government; Public Service; Urban Affairs

Fellowship program provides one academic year (9 months) of full-time work experience in urban government. Open to graduating college seniors and recent college graduates. US citizenship required. Write for complete information.

34

PACIFIC GAS & ELECTRIC CO.
(Scholarships for High School Seniors)
77 Beale St.; Room 2837
San Francisco CA 94106
415/973-1338

AMOUNT: $1000–$4000
DEADLINE(S): November 15
FIELD(S): Engineering; Computer Science; Mathematics; Marketing; Business; Economics

High school seniors in good academic standing who reside in or attend high school in areas served by PG&E are eligible to compete for scholarships awarded on a regional basis. Not open to children of PG&E employees.

36 awards per year. Applications & brochures are available in all high schools within PG&E's service area and at PG&E offices.

35

**REAL ESTATE EDUCATORS ASSN.
(REEA—Harwood Scholarship Program)**
11 S. LaSalle St.; #1400
Chicago IL 60603
312/201-0101

AMOUNT: $250
DEADLINE(S): December 31
FIELD(S): Real Estate

Open to undergrads (who have completed at least 2 semesters) & graduate students who are studying full-time at an accredited US school, have a 3.1 minimum GPA, & intend to pursue a career in real estate.

10 scholarships per year. Write for complete information.

36

**SISTERS OF SALISAW FOUNDATION
(Scholarship)**
911 Bartlett Pl.
Windsor CA 95492
Written inquiry

AMOUNT: $500
DEADLINE(S): August 1
FIELD(S): Business

Open to children of migrant farm laborers residing in Windsor CA whose family migrated to California from Salisaw OK during the Dust Bowl era of the 1930s. Family must have worked at least six months in the Hernesto Onexioca Vineyards.

For undergraduate or graduate study leading to a degree in business. Write for complete information.

37

**SOCIETY OF ACTUARIES
(Actuarial Scholarships for Minority Students)**
475 N. Martingale Rd.; Suite 800
Schaumburg IL 60173-2226
708/706-3500

AMOUNT: Varies
DEADLINE(S): May 1
FIELD(S): Actuarial science

Open to students who are members of ethnic minorities and are enrolled or accepted in an actuarial science program at an accredited college or university. Must demonstrate financial need and be a USA citizen or legal resident.

Amount varies according to student's need and credentials. Approximately 40 awards per year. Write for complete information.

38

**STATE FARM COMPANIES
FOUNDATION
(Exceptional Student Fellowship)**
1 State Farm Plaza
Bloomington IL 61710
309/766-2039

AMOUNT: $3000
DEADLINE(S): Febuary 15 (apps. available November 1)
FIELD(S): Accounting; Business Administration; Actuarial Science; Computer Science; Economics; Finance; Insurance; Investments; Marketing; Mathematics; Statistics; & Related Fields

Open to current full-time college juniors and seniors majoring in any of the fields above. Only students nominated by the college dean or a department head qualify as candidates. Applications without nominations will NOT be considered.

USA citizen. 3.4 or better GPA (4.0 scale) required. 50 fellowships per year. Write for complete information.

39

**STATE FARM COMPANIES
FOUNDATION
(Exceptional Student Fellowship Awards)**
One State Farm Plaza; SC-3
Bloomington IL 61710
309/766-2039

AMOUNT: $3000

DEADLINE(S): February 15

FIELD(S): Business-related Fields; Computer Science; Mathematics; Accounting; Actuarial Science; Business Admininstration; Economics; Finance; Insurance; Investments; Marketing; Management & Statistics

Must be junior or senior undergrad at time of application & have at least a 3.4 GPA (on 4.0 scale). Nominations by Dean or department head only. USA citizenship required.

50 fellowships per academic year. Applications and nominations available November 1. Write for complete information and state your current year in college.

40

STATLER FOUNDATION
(Scholarships)
107 Delaware Ave.; Suite 508
Buffalo NY 14202
716/852-1104

AMOUNT: $500 per year

DEADLINE(S): April 15

FIELD(S): Food Management; Culinary Arts; Hotel-Motel Management

Open to undergraduate or graduate students who are accepted to or enrolled full-time at a US institution in an accredited program of study in any of the above areas.

Approximately 900 awards per year. Renewable. Write for complete information.

41

TRANSPORTATION CLUBS INTERNATIONAL
(Charlotte Woods Memorial Scholarship)
1275 Kamus Dr.; Suite 101
Fox Island WA 98333
206/549-2251

AMOUNT: $1000

DEADLINE(S): April 15

FIELD(S): Transportation; Traffic Management

Open to TCI members & dependents who are in their sophomore year at an accredited college or university. Must be enrolled in a program in transportation, traffic management, or related area & considering a career in transportation.

Awards are based on scholastic ability & potential, professional interest, & character. Financial need is also considered. Send SASE (business size) for complete information and application.

42

TRANSPORTATION CLUBS INTERNATIONAL
(Hooper Memorial Scholarships)
1275 Kamus Dr.; Suite 101
Fox Island WA 98333
206/549-2251

AMOUNT: $1000

DEADLINE(S): April 15

FIELD(S): Transportation; Traffic Management

Open to sophomore students enrolled in an accredited college or university in a degree or vocational program in transportation; traffic management or related fields (marketing, economics, etc.) & preparing for a career in transportation.

Awards are based on scholastic ability & potential, professional interest, & character. Financial need is also considered. Send SASE (business size) for complete information.

43

TRANSPORTATION CLUBS INTERNATIONAL
(Mexico Traffic & Transportation Scholarships)
1275 Kamus Dr.; Suite 101
Fox Island WA 98333
206/549-2251

AMOUNT: $500
DEADLINE(S): April 15
FIELD(S): Transportation; Traffic Management

Open to students of Mexican nationality who are enrolled in a Mexican institution of higher learning in a degree or vocational program in the above or related areas.
Write for complete information.

44

TRANSPORTATION CLUBS INTERNATIONAL
(Michigan Transportation Scholarships)
1275 Kamus Dr.; Suite 101
Fox Island WA 98332
206/549-2251

AMOUNT: $1000
DEADLINE(S): April 15
FIELD(S): Transportation; Traffic Management

Open to college sophomores who have attended school in Michigan at any level (even elementary) & are now enrolled in an accredited institution of higher learning in a degree or vocational program in the above or related areas.
Send self-addressed stamped envelope (business size) for complete information.

45

TRANSPORTATION CLUBS INTERNATIONAL
(Texas Transportation Scholarship)
1275 Kamus Dr.; Suite 101
Fox Island WA 98333
206/549-2251

AMOUNT: $1000
DEADLINE(S): April 15
FIELD(S): Transportation; Traffic Management

Open to students who have been enrolled in a school in Texas during elementary, secondary, or high school & are now in their

sophomore year at an accredited college or university in a degree or vocational program relating to transportation.
Awards are based on scholastic ability & potential, professional interest, & character. Financial need is also considered. Send SASE (business size) for complete information.

46

TYSON FOUNDATION INC.
(Scholarship Program)
2210 W. Oaklawn
Springdale AR 72762-6999
501/290-4955

AMOUNT: Up to $1200/semester
DEADLINE(S): June 21
FIELD(S): Business; Agriculture; Engineering; Computer Science; Nursing

Open to a US citizen who was raised in and still lives in the vicinity of a Tyson Food's facility. Must maintain a 2.5 while working and going to school full time. For undergrad study at schools in USA.
Recipients sign a pledge either to repay the scholarship money or help another deserving student not related by blood or marriage to attend college. Write for complete information.

47

WILLIAM RANDOLPH HEARST FOUNDATION
(U.S. Senate Youth Program)
90 New Montgomery St; Suite 1212
San Francisco CA 94105
415/543-4057, FAX 415/243-0760

AMOUNT: $2000 plus all expenses paid week in Washington
DEADLINE(S): None specified
FIELD(S): U.S. Government; History; Political Science; Economics

Open to any high school junior or senior who is serving as an elected student body officer at a USA high school. Student receives a week's stay in Washington as guest of the Senate and a $2000 scholarship.

Student must become a candidate for a degree at an accredited USA college or university within two years of high school graduation. USA permanent resident. Contact high school principal for complete information.

48

Y'S MEN INTERNATIONAL; US AREA
(Alexander Scholarship Loan Fund)
 7242 Natural Bridge Road
 Normandy MO 63121
 Written inquiry only

AMOUNT: $1000 to $1500 per year

DEADLINE(S): May 1; October 1

FIELD(S): Business Administration; Youth Leadership

Open to US citizens or permanent residents with a strong desire to pursue professional YMCA service. For undergrads or grad students (YMCA staff only). Financial need must be demonstrated.

Repayment of loan is waived if recipient enters YMCA employment after graduation. Write for complete information.

SCHOOL OF EDUCATION

49

CHARLES E. SAAK TRUST
(Educational Grants)
 Wells Fargo Bank Trust Dept. 5262 N. Blackstone
 Fresno CA 93710
 Written inquiry only

AMOUNT: Varies

DEADLINE(S): March 31

FIELD(S): Education; Dental

Undergraduate grants for residents of the Porterville-poplar area of Tulare County CA. Must carry a minimum of 12 units, have at least a 2.0 GPA, be under age 21, and demonstrate financial need.

Approximately 100 awards per year; renewable with reapplication. Write for complete information.

EDUCATION

50

ALASKA COMMISSION ON POST-SECONDARY EDUCATION
(Paul Douglas Scholarship Loan Program)
 3030 Vintage Blvd.
 Juneau AK 99801-7109
 907/465-6741

AMOUNT: $5000 per year for up to 4 years

DEADLINE(S): May 30

FIELD(S): Education

Alaska residents. Federally funded program to encourage outstanding high school seniors & undergraduate students to pursue teaching careers at the elementary or secondary levels.

Recipients are required to teach 2 years for each year of funding or 1/2 that for teaching in a critical teacher shortage area. Write for complete information.

51

AMERICAN FOUNDATION FOR THE BLIND
(Delta Gamma Foundation Florence Harvey Memorial Scholarship)
 15 W. 16th St.
 New York NY 10011
 212/620-2000; TDD 212/620-2158

AMOUNT: $1000

DEADLINE(S): None specified

FIELD(S): Rehabilitation and/or Education of the Visually Impaired and Blind

Open to legally blind undergraduate and graduate college students of good character who have exhibited academic excellence and are studying in the field of education and/or rehabilitation of the visually impaired and blind.

Must be USA citizen. Write for complete information.

52

AMERICAN FOUNDATION FOR THE BLIND
(Rudolph Dillman Memorial Scholarship)
15 West 16th St.
New York NY 10011
212/620-2000; TDD 212/620-2158

AMOUNT: $2500
DEADLINE(S): April 1
FIELD(S): Rehabilitation; Education of Blind & Visually Impaired

Open to legally blind undergrad or graduate students accepted to or enrolled in an accredited program within the broad areas of rehabilitation and/or education of the blind and visually impaired. USA citizen.

Three awards per year. Write for complete information.

53

AMERICAN FOUNDATION FOR THE BLIND
(TeleSensory Scholarship)
15 West 16th St.
New York NY 10011
212/620-2000; TDD 212/620-2158

AMOUNT: $1000
DEADLINE(S): April 1
FIELD(S): None specified

Open to full-time undergrad students who are legally blind and do not meet the criteria for other AFB scholarships. Must be USA citizen; provide proof of acceptance to a college or university and three letters of recommendation.

Write for complete information.

54

BOY SCOUTS OF AMERICA—DR. HARRY BRITENSTOOL SCHOLARSHIP COMMITTEE
(Greater New York City Councils' Scholarships)
345 Hudson Street
New York NY 10014
212/242-1100

AMOUNT: Varies
DEADLINE(S): June 1
FIELD(S): Youth Leadership

Undergraduate scholarships open to students who have been NYC Boy Scouts or Explorer Scouts for at least 2 years, show academic excellence, financial need, service to greater NYC councils, and strong scouting history. US citizens only.

Write for complete information.

55

BUSINESS & PROFESSIONAL WOMEN'S FOUNDATION
(Career Advancement Scholarships)
2012 Massachusetts Ave. NW
Washington DC 20036
202/293-1200

AMOUNT: $500–$1000
DEADLINE(S): April 15 (postmark)
FIELD(S): Computer Science; Education; Paralegal; Engineering; Science; Law; Dentistry; Medicine

Open to women (30 or older) within 12–24 months of completing undergrad or grad study in US (including Puerto Rico & Virgin Islands). Studies should lead to entry/reentry in work force or improve career advancement chances.

Not for doctoral study. Must demonstrate financial need. Send self-addressed stamped ($.64) #10 envelope for complete info. Applications available October 1–April 1.

56

CALIFORNIA STUDENT AID COMMISSION
(Paul Douglas Teacher Scholarship Program)
P.O. Box 510624
Sacramento CA 94245-0624
916/322-2294

AMOUNT: $5000 maximum per year for up to 4 years
DEADLINE(S): July 1
FIELD(S): Education

Open to top (10%) high school seniors & college students who demonstrate commitment to pursuing teaching careers; for undergrad & grad teacher preparation study at eligible California schools. Must be resident of California.

Must be US citizen or eligible noncitizen & agree to teach 2 years full-time (anywhere in USA) for each year the scholarship is received. Renewable. Contact college counselor, financial aid office, or address above for more information.

57

CIVIL AIR PATROL
(CAP Undergraduate Scholarships)
National Headquarters
Maxwell AFB AL 36112
205/293-5315

AMOUNT: $750
DEADLINE(S): October 1
FIELD(S): Humanities; Science; Engineering; Education

Open to CAP members who have received the Billy Mitchell Award or the senior rating in level II of the senior training program. For undergraduate study in the above areas.

Write for complete information.

58

EASTER SEAL SOCIETY OF IOWA
(Scholarships & Awards)
P.O. Box 4002
Des Moines IA 50333
515/289-1933

AMOUNT: $400–$600
DEADLINE(S): April 15
FIELD(S): Physical Rehabilitation; Mental Rehabilitation; Related Areas

Open to Iowa residents who are full-time undergraduate sophomores, juniors, seniors, or graduate students at accredited institutions, planning a career in the broad field of rehabilitation, financially needy, & in top 40% of their class.

6 scholarships per year. Must reapply each year.

59

FLORIDA DEPT. OF EDUCATION
(Critical Teacher Shortage Tuition Reimbursement Program)
Office of Student Financial Assistance; 1344 Florida Education Center
Tallahassee FL 32399-0400
904/487-0049

AMOUNT: Tuition reimbursement payments
DEADLINE(S): Specified on application
FIELD(S): Education

Open to full-time Florida public school employees certified to teach in Florida and who are teaching or preparing to teach in critical teacher shortage subject areas approved by the State Board of Education. Minimum 3.0 GPA required.

Will reimburse up to $78 per credit hour for up to 9 hours per academic year for up to a total of 36 credit hours. Write for complete eligibility requirements & information.

60

FLORIDA DEPT. OF EDUCATION
(Critical Teacher Shortage Student Loan
Forgiveness Program)
Office of Student Financial Assistance; 1344
Florida Education Center
Tallahassee FL 32399-0400
904/487-0049

AMOUNT: $2500 - $5000 per year
DEADLINE(S): July 15
FIELD(S): Teaching

Open to certified Florida public school teachers. Program provides repayment of education loans in return for teaching in Department of Education designated critical teacher shortage subject areas in Florida public schools.

Write for additional requirements and complete information.

61

FLORIDA DEPT. OF EDUCATION
(Florida Teacher Scholarship & Forgivable
Loan Program)
Office of Student Financial Assistance; 1344
Florida Education Center
Tallahassee FL 32399-0400
904/487-0049

AMOUNT: $1500/year (scholarship);
$4000/year (undergrad loan); $8000/year
(graduate loan)
DEADLINE(S): March 1
FIELD(S): Teaching

Two-year scholarship program provides assistance to lower division undergrads; two-year loan program provides assistance to upper division undergrads & grads and may be repaid through teaching service in critical shortage area in Florida.

Eligibility requirements vary with academic level. Write for complete information.

62

ILLINOIS CONGRESS OF PARENTS AND
TEACHERS
(Lillian E. Glover Illinois PTA Scholarship
Program)
901 S. Spring St.
Springfield IL 62704
217/528-9617

AMOUNT: $500 - $1000
DEADLINE(S): March 1
FIELD(S): Education

Illinois residents. Open to graduating public high school seniors who plan to major in education at an accredited college or university in the US and are in the upper 20% of their class.

52 awards per year. Applications are available after January 1. Write for complete information.

63

INDIANA STATE STUDENT
ASSISTANCE COMMISSION
(Minority Teacher & Special Education
Teacher Scholarship Program)
150 W. Market St.; 5th Floor
Indianapolis IN 46204
317/232-2350

AMOUNT: $1000 - $4000
DEADLINE(S): Varies with college
FIELD(S): Education

Open to Black or Hispanic residents of Indiana or Indiana residents working toward a certificate in special education. For full-time undergraduate or graduate study at an Indiana college. GPA of 2.0 or better (4.0 scale) is required.

Must demonstrate financial need (FAF). Write for complete information.

64

INDIANA STATE STUDENT ASSISTANCE COMMISSION
(Paul Douglas Teacher Scholarship Program)
150 W. Market St.; 5th Floor
Indianapolis IN 46204
317/232-2350

AMOUNT: $5000
DEADLINE(S): March 1
FIELD(S): Education

Open to Indiana residents for undergraduate or graduate study leading to a teaching credential. Must be in top 10% of high school graduating class or (if in college) have GPA of 3.0 or better (4.0 scale).

Must be USA citizen. Write for complete information.

65

INTERNATIONAL ORDER OF THE ALHAMBRA
(Scholarship Fund and Endowment Fund)
4200 Leeds Ave.
Baltimore MD 21229
410/242-0660

AMOUNT: Varies
DEADLINE(S): January; April; July; October
FIELD(S): Special Education

Open to undergraduate students who will be entering their junior or senior year in an accredited program for teaching the mentally challenged & the handicapped. Available to graduate students in Canada & the states of California & Virginia

USA citizenship required. Write for complete information.

66

IOWA COLLEGE STUDENT AID COMMISSION
(Paul Douglas Teacher Scholarships)
914 Grand Ave.; Suite 201
Des Moines IA 50309
515/281-3501

AMOUNT: $5000 per year (4 year maximum)
DEADLINE(S): May 1
FIELD(S): Education

Open to Iowa high school seniors who have applied to Iowa state scholarship program, are in top 10% of their class & want to teach in specific areas of need at elementary or secondary level. Must show financial need.

Must be USA citizen or legal resident and agree to teach for 2 years for each year of funding. Contact your counselor or write to address above for complete information.

67

MARYLAND HIGHER EDUCATION COMMISSION
(Sharon Christa McAuliffe Critical Shortage Teacher Program)
State Scholarship Administration
16 Francis St.
Annapolis MD 21401-1781
410/974-5370

AMOUNT: Up to $8000 for tuition; fees & room & board
DEADLINE(S): December 31
FIELD(S): Education (critical shortages determined annually)

For Maryland residents who agree to teach in critical shortage area in Maryland for up to 1 year for each year of funding. Open to full or part-time undergraduates or graduates studying at a Maryland degree-granting institution.

Minimum of 60 credits of undergraduate course work & GPA of 3.0 or better required. Renewable if 3.0 GPA is maintained. Write for complete information.

68

MINNESOTA FEDERATION OF TEACHERS
(Flora Rogge College Scholarship)
168 Aurora Ave.
St. Paul MN 55103
612/227-8583

AMOUNT: $1000

DEADLINE(S): First Friday in March

FIELD(S): Education

Candidate for this scholarship must currently be a high school senior. He/she must be recommended by two senior high school teachers on the basis of financial need, academic achievement, leadership ability, and good character.

Write for complete information.

69

MISSISSIPPI BOARD OF TRUSTEES OF STATE INSTITUTIONS OF HIGHER LEARNING

(William Winter Teacher Education Program)
3825 Ridgewood Rd.
Jackson MS 39211
601/982-6570

AMOUNT: Up to $3000 per year

DEADLINE(S): March 31

FIELD(S): Teacher (critical shortage subject areas)

Open to full-time undergraduate students in a Mississippi college or university who are in a teacher education program which will lead to "Class A" certification.

Recipients must agree to teach in a critical shortage area in Mississippi upon completion of the program.

70

NATIONAL COLLEGIATE ATHLETIC ASSOCIATION

(NCAA Ethnic Minority Internship Program)
6201 College Blvd.
Overland Park KS 66211
913/339-1906

AMOUNT: $1300 per month (includes $200 housing allowance)

DEADLINE(S): February 15

FIELD(S): Sports Administration; Coaching; Officiating

Internships of approximately one year at the NCAA national office open to members of ethnic minorities who have completed the requirements for an undergraduate degree and demonstrated an interest in a career of athletics administration.

Write for complete information.

71

NATIONAL STRENGTH & CONDITIONING ASSN.

(Challenge Scholarships)
P.O. Box 38909
Colorado Springs CO 80937
719/632-6772

AMOUNT: $1000

DEADLINE(S): March 1

FIELD(S): Fields related to Strength & Conditioning

Open to National Strength & Conditioning Association members. Awards are for undergraduate or graduate study.

Write for complete information.

72

NELLIE MARTIN CARMAN SCHOLARSHIP TRUST

(Scholarships)
18223 73rd Ave. NE; #B101
Bothell WA 98011
206/486-6575

AMOUNT: Up to $1000

DEADLINE(S): March 15

FIELD(S): All fields of study except those noted below

Open to high school seniors in King, Pierce, & Snohomish Counties (WA). For undergraduate study in the state of Washington in all fields EXCEPT music, sculpting, drawing, interior design, & home economics. US citizenship required.

Applications available only through high schools & nomination by counselor is required. Awards are renewable. Write for complete information.

73

NORTH CAROLINA ASSOCIATION OF EDUCATORS
(Mary Morrow Scholarship)
P.O. Box 27347; 700 S. Salisbury St.
Raleigh NC 27611
919/832-3000

AMOUNT: $1000
DEADLINE(S): January 13
FIELD(S): Education—Teaching

Awards given in junior year to students in an accredited North Carolina undergraduate institution for use in their junior year. Recipients must live in North Carolina & agree to teach in the state for at least 2 years after graduation.

Financial need is a consideration. 4–7 scholarships per year. Apply in junior year of college. Write for complete information.

74

NORTH CAROLINA DEPARTMENT OF PUBLIC INSTRUCTION
(Scholarship Loan Program for Prospective Teachers)
301 N. Wilminston St.
Office of Teacher Education
Raleigh NC 27601-2825
919/715-1120

AMOUNT: Up to $2000 per year
DEADLINE(S): February 15
FIELD(S): Education; Teaching

Open to NC residents interested in teaching in NC public schools. Awards are based on academic performance, scores on standardized tests, class rank, congressional district, and recommendations. USA citizenship required.

200 awards per year. Write for complete information.

75

OREGON PTA
(Teacher Education Scholarships)
531 S.E. 14th
Portland OR 97214
503/234-3928

AMOUNT: $250
DEADLINE(S): March 1
FIELD(S): Education

Open to outstanding students who are Oregon residents and are preparing to teach in Oregon at the elementary or secondary school level. The scholarships may be used to attend any Oregon public college.

Scholarships based on scholastic record, leadership, citizenship, and need. Send a self-addressed stamped envelope for application.

76

PENNSYLVANIA HIGHER EDUCATION ASSISTANCE AGENCY
(Paul Douglas Teacher Scholarship Program)
P.O. Box 8114
Harrisburg PA 17105-8114
717/257-5220

AMOUNT: $5000 per year for up to 4 years
DEADLINE(S): May 1
FIELD(S): Education—Teaching

H.S. seniors who have lived in PA at least 1 year & are in the top 10% of their class. For undergrad study in an accredited program leading to credential to teach at pre-school, elementary, or secondary level.

US citizen or legal resident. Recipients are required to teach in any state for 2 years for each year of funding or 1/2 that time if they teach in a critical teacher shortage area. Write for complete information.

77

PHI DELTA KAPPA INC.
(Scholarship Grants for Prospective Teachers)
P.O. Box 789; 8th & Union Ave.
Bloomington IN 47402-0789
812/339-1156

AMOUNT: $1000 (48-each); $2000 (1-each)
DEADLINE(S): January 31
FIELD(S): Teaching

Open to high school seniors in upper 1/3 of their class who plan to pursue career as teacher or educator. Based on scholastic achievement, school/community activities, recommendations, & an essay. USA or Canadian citizen or legal resident.

49 scholarships per year. Write to the attention of Scholarship Grants for complete information.

78

RHODE ISLAND HIGHER EDUCATION ASSISTANCE AUTHORITY
(Paul Douglas Teacher Scholarship Program)
560 Jefferson Blvd.
Warwick RI 02886
401/763-1100

AMOUNT: $5000 per year for up to 4 years
DEADLINE(S): April 1
FIELD(S): Education—Teaching

Federally funded program to encourage outstanding undergraduate students to pursue teaching careers at pre-school, elementary, & secondary levels. For study at eligible institutions. US citizen or legal resident.

Recipients are required to teach in any state for 2 years for each year of funding or 1/2 that for teaching in a critical teacher shortage area. Write for complete information.

79

TECHNOLOGY STUDENT ASSOCIATION
(Scholarships)
1914 Association Dr.
Reston VA 22091
703/860-9000

AMOUNT: $250 to $500
DEADLINE(S): May 1
FIELD(S): Technology Education

Open to student members of the Technology Student Association who can demonstrate financial need. Grade point average is NOT a consideration but applicants must be accepted to a 4-year college or university.

Funds are sent to and administered by the recipient's college or university. Write for complete information.

80

UNITED COMMERCIAL TRAVELERS OF AMERICA
(Retarded Citizens Teacher Scholarships)
632 North Park Street; P.O. Box 159019
Columbus OH 43215-8619
614/228-3276

AMOUNT: $750/year
DEADLINE(S): None
FIELD(S): Special Education

Open to undergraduate juniors & seniors, graduate students, teachers, & persons who plan to teach the mentally challenged in the US or Canada. Awards tenable at accredited institutions. US or Canadian citizenship required.

Approximately 500 awards per year. Preference (but not limited) to UCT members. Write for complete information.

81

UTAH STATE OFFICE OF EDUCATION
(CAREER TEACHING SCHOLARSHIPS)
250 E. 500 SO.
Salt Lake City UT 84111
801/538-7741

AMOUNT: Full tuition and fees
DEADLINE(S): March 30
FIELD(S): Education—teacher

Awards to outstanding Utah High School graduates or college freshmen. At undergrad soph/junior/or senior level awards open to any student (resident) studying in a

Utah State college or university to be a
teacher.
Approx 150 scholarships per year. Must
demonstrate financial need. Write for complete information.

82

**VIRGINIA STATE COUNCIL OF HIGHER
EDUCATION**
(Paul Douglas Teacher Scholarship Program)
101 N. 14th St.; James Monroe Bldg.
Richmond VA 23219
804/225-2141

AMOUNT: Up to $5000 per year
DEADLINE(S): Varies
FIELD(S): Education

Federal program open to Virginia residents in
top 10% of high school class & accepted to
or enrolled in full-time undergraduate
teacher education program. Scholarships
are renewable for up to 4 years. USA citizen or legal resident.
Recipients agree to teach in a designated
teacher shortage area for each year of funding received. Otherwise the scholarship
becomes a loan & must be repaid. Write for
complete information.

83

**WISCONSIN CONGRESS OF PARENTS
AND TEACHERS INC.**
(Brookmire-Hastings Scholarships)
4797 Hayes Rd.; Suite 2
Madison WI 53704-3256
608/244-1455

AMOUNT: $1000
DEADLINE(S): February 15
FIELD(S): Education; Teaching

Open to Wisconsin residents who are seniors
in public high schools. Awarded to outstanding high school graduates who intend
to pursue a career in the field of child
care/education.
Write for complete information.

84

**WORLD LEISURE & RECREATION
ASSN. (Tom & Ruth Rivers Scholarship
Program)**
P.O. Box 309
Sharbot Lake Ontario K0H 2P0 Canada
613/279-3173

AMOUNT: Varies
DEADLINE(S): January 1
FIELD(S): Recreation; Leisure Studies;
Resources Education

Scholarships intended to allow college seniors
or graduate students in recreation or leisure
services programs to attend international
meetings/conferences or conventions, there-
by gaining a broader perspective of world
leisure & recreation.
Write for complete information.

85

**Y'S MEN INTERNATIONAL; US AREA
(Alexander Scholarship Loan Fund)**
7242 Natural Bridge Road
Normandy MO 63121
Written inquiry only

AMOUNT: $1000 to $1500 per year
DEADLINE(S): May 1; October 1
FIELD(S): Business Administration; Youth
Leadership

Open to US citizens or permanent residents
with a strong desire to pursue professional
YMCA service. For undergrads or grad students (YMCA staff only). Financial need
must be demonstrated.
Repayment of loan is waived if recipient
enters YMCA employment after graduation. Write for complete information.

SCHOOL OF ENGINEERING

86

ALEXANDER GRAHAM BELL ASSOCIATION FOR THE DEAF
(Robert H. Weitbrecht Scholarship Award)
3417 Volta Place
Washington DC 20007
202/337-5220

AMOUNT: $750

DEADLINE(S): April 1

FIELD(S): Engineering/Science

Open to oral deaf students who were born with a profound hearing impairment or who suffered such a loss before acquiring language. Must be accepted into a full-time academic program for hearing students. Preference to N. American citizens.

Write for complete information.

87

AMERICAN INDIAN SCIENCE & ENGINEERING SOCIETY
(Santa Fe Pacific Foundation Scholarships)
1630 30th St.; Suite 301
Boulder CO 80301
303/939-0023

AMOUNT: Up to $2500 per year for 4 years

DEADLINE(S): March 31

FIELD(S): Business; Engineering; Science; Health Administration

Open to graduating high school seniors with 1/4 or more Indian blood. Must reside in KS, OK, CO, AZ, NM, or San Bernardino County CA (AT&SF Railway service area). Two of the five scholarships are designated for Navajo tribe members.

Must plan to attend a 4-year post-secondary accredited educational institution. Write for complete information.

88

ARTHUR & DOREEN PARRETT SCHOLARSHIP TRUST FUND
(Scholarships)
c/o US Bank of Washington; P.O. Box 720;
Trust Dept.; 8th Floor
Seattle WA 98111-0720
206/344-4653

AMOUNT: Up to $3500

DEADLINE(S): July 31

FIELD(S): Engineering; Science; Medicine; Dentistry

Washington state resident who has completed her/his first year of college by July 31. Open to students enrolled in above schools. Awards tenable at any accredited undergrad college or university.

Approximately 15 awards per year. Write for complete information.

89

BOYS & GIRLS CLUBS OF SAN DIEGO
(Spence Reese Scholarship Fund)
3760 Fourth Ave.; Suite 1
San Diego CA 92103
619/298-3520

AMOUNT: $2000 per year for 4 years

DEADLINE(S): May 15

FIELD(S): Medicine; Law; Engineering; Political Science

Open to male high school seniors planning a career in above fields. Preference to students within a 250-mile radius of San Diego. Boys Club affiliation is not required.

Applications are available in January. Must enclose a self-addressed stamped envelope to receive application. A $10 processing fee is required with completed application. Write for complete information.

90

BUSINESS & PROFESSIONAL WOMEN'S FOUNDATION
(BPW Loans for Women in Engineering Studies)
2012 Massachusetts Ave. NW
Washington DC 20036
202/293-1200

AMOUNT: Up to $5000 per year
DEADLINE(S): April 15 (postmark)
FIELD(S): Engineering

Open to women accepted for undergraduate or graduate study in a program accredited by the Accrediting Board for Engineering and Technology. For last 2 years of study. US citizenship required.

Must demonstrate financial need. Applications available between October 1 & April 1 ONLY. Send double-stamped self-addressed envelope for complete information.

91

BUSINESS & PROFESSIONAL WOMEN'S FOUNDATION
(Career Advancement Scholarships)
2012 Massachusetts Ave. NW
Washington DC 20036
202/293-1200

AMOUNT: $500–$1000
DEADLINE(S): April 15 (postmark)
FIELD(S): Computer Science; Education; Paralegal; Engineering; Science; Law; Dentistry; Medicine

Open to women (30 or older) within 12–24 months of completing undergrad or grad study in US (including Puerto Rico & Virgin Islands). Studies should lead to entry/reentry in work force or improve career advancement chances.

Not for doctoral study. Must demonstrate financial need. Send self-addressed stamped ($.64) #10 envelope for complete info. Applications available October 1–April 1.

92

CAPE CANAVERAL CHAPTER RETIRED OFFICERS ASSOC.
(Scholarships)
P.O. Box 4186
Patrick AFB FL 32925
Written inquiry

AMOUNT: Approximately $1500 per year
DEADLINE(S): May 31
FIELD(S): Science; Mathematics; Engineering; Liberal Arts; Chemistry

Open ONLY to Brevard County Florida residents who are undergraduate juniors or seniors at any 4-year college in the USA and the son or daughter of active duty or retired military personnel. Must be US citizen.

Awards renewable for one year. Write to the scholarship program committee (address above) for complete information.

93

CIVIL AIR PATROL
(CAP Undergraduate Scholarships)
National Headquarters
Maxwell AFB AL 36112
205/293-5315

AMOUNT: $750
DEADLINE(S): October 1
FIELD(S): Humanities; Science; Engineering; Education

Open to CAP members who have received the Billy Mitchell Award or the senior rating in level II of the senior training program. For undergraduate study in the above areas.
Write for complete information.

94

COMMITTEE ON INSTITUTIONAL COOPERATION
(CIC Pre-doctoral Fellowships)
Indiana University; 803 East 8th St.
Bloomington IN 47408
812/855-0823

AMOUNT: $11,000 + tuition (4 years)

DEADLINE(S): December 1

FIELD(S): Humanities; Social Sciences; Natural Sciences; Mathematics; Engineering

Pre-doctoral fellowships for US citizens of African American, American Indian, Mexican American, or Puerto Rican heritage. Must hold or expect to receive bachelor's degree by late summer from a regionally accredited college or unviersity.

Awards for specified universities in IL, IN, IA, MI, MN, OH, WI, PA. Write for details.

95

CONSULTING ENGINEERS COUNCIL OF NEW JERSEY
(Louis Goldberg Scholarship Fund)
66 Morris Ave.
Springfield NJ 07081
201/379-1100

AMOUNT: $1000

DEADLINE(S): January 27

FIELD(S): Engineering

Open to undergraduate students who have completed at least 2 years of study at an ABET accredited college or university in New Jersey; are in top 1/2 of their class & are considering a career as a consulting engineer. Must be US citizen.

Recipients will be eligible for American Consulting Engineers Council national scholarships of $2000 to $5000. Write for complete information.

96

ENGINEERING FOUNDATION
(Grants for Exploratory Research)
345 E. 47th St.; Suite 303
New York NY 10017
212/705-7835

AMOUNT: $25,000 maximum

DEADLINE(S): October 1

FIELD(S): Engineering

Seed funding for unique approaches in significant areas of engineering research. Project

should be outside the scope of conventional funding sources. These grants are NOT intended for students—undergraduate or graduate.

Write for complete information.

97

GENERAL LEARNING CORPORATION
(Dupont & GLC Science Essay Awards Program)
60 Revere Dr.
Northbrook IL 60062-1562
708/205-3000

AMOUNT: Up to $1500

DEADLINE(S): January 27

FIELD(S): Sciences

Annual essay competition open to students in grades 7–12 in USA & Canada. Cash awards for 1st, 2nd, 3rd, & honorable mention. 1st-place essayists, their science teacher, & 1 parent receive trip to space center Houston; April 27–29

Contact your science teacher or address above for complete information official entry blank must accompany essay entry.

98

H. FLETCHER BROWN FUND
(Scholarships)
c/o PNC Bank; Trust Dept.; P.O. Box 791
Wilmington DE 19899
302/429-2827

AMOUNT: Varies

DEADLINE(S): April 15

FIELD(S): Medicine; Dentistry; Law; Engineering; Chemistry

Open to US citizens born and still residing in Delaware. For 4 years of study (undergrad or grad) leading to a degree that enables applicant to practice in chosen field.

Scholarships are based on need, scholastic achievement, and good moral character. Applications available in February. Write for complete information.

99

JOSEPH BLAZEK FOUNDATION
(Scholarships)
  8 South Michigan Ave.
  Chicago IL 60603
  312/372-3880

AMOUNT: $750 per year for 4 years
DEADLINE(S): February 1
FIELD(S): Science; Chemistry; Engineering;
  Mathematics; Physics

Open to residents of Cook County (Illinois)
  who are high school seniors planning to
  study in the above fields at a four-year college or university.
20 scholarships per year. Renewable. Write for
  complete information.

100

NATIONAL ACTION COUNCIL FOR
MINORITIES IN ENGINEERING—
NACME INC.
(Incentive Grants Program)
  3 West 35th St.; 3rd floor
  New York NY 10001
  212/279-2626; fax 212/629-5178

AMOUNT: $500–$3000
DEADLINE(S): Set by colleges
FIELD(S): Engineering

Open to students of American Indian, African
  American, Mexican American, or Puerto
  Rican heritage. Demonstrate need or be
  designated to receive a merit award. For
  full-time enrollment in one of the participating colleges. US citizen or permanent
  resident.
Must be an entering freshman or transfer student for the initial award. Write for complete information & list of participating colleges.

101

NATIONAL SOCIETY OF
PROFESSIONAL ENGINEERS
EDUCATIONAL FOUNDATION
(Scholarships and Grants)
  1420 King Street
  Alexandria VA 22314
  703/684-2830

AMOUNT: $1000 to $4000 + some full
  scholarships
DEADLINE(S): November 15
FIELD(S): Engineering

Scholarships open to high school seniors who
  are in the top 25% of their class. Awards
  tenable at accredited colleges & universities
  in the US. US citizenship required.
Approximately 150 awards per year.
  Applications available in August,
  September, & October of year preceding
  college entry. Special scholarships for
  minorities & females also. Write for complete information.

102

NELLIE MARTIN CARMAN
SCHOLARSHIP TRUST
(Scholarships)
  18223 73rd Ave. NE; #B101
  Bothell WA 98011
  206/486-6575

AMOUNT: Up to $1000
DEADLINE(S): March 15
FIELD(S): All fields of study except those
  noted below

Open to high school seniors in King, Pierce, &
  Snohomish Counties (WA). For undergraduate study in the state of Washington in all
  fields EXCEPT music, sculpting, drawing,
  interior design, & home economics. US citizenship required.
Applications available only through high
  schools & nomination by counselor is
  required. Awards are renewable. Write for
  complete information.

103

NORTH CAROLINA STUDENT LOAN PROGRAM FOR HEALTH, SCIENCE, & MATHEMATICS
(Loans)

3824 Barrett Dr.; Suite 304
Raleigh NC 27619
919/733-2164

AMOUNT: $2500 to $7500 per year
DEADLINE(S): January 8 to May 5
FIELD(S): Health Professions; Sciences; Engineering

Low-interest scholarship loans open to North Carolina residents of at least 1 year who are pursuing an associates, undergraduate, or graduate degree in the above fields at an accredited institution in the US.

Loans may be retired after graduation by working (1 year for each year funded) at designated institutions. Write for complete details.

104

PACIFIC GAS & ELECTRIC CO.
(Scholarships for High School Seniors)

77 Beale St.; Room 2837
San Francisco CA 94106
415/973-1338

AMOUNT: $1000–$4000
DEADLINE(S): November 15
FIELD(S): Engineering; Computer Science; Mathematics; Marketing; Business; Economics

High school seniors in good academic standing who reside in or attend high school in areas served by PG&E are eligible to compete for scholarships awarded on a regional basis. Not open to children of PG&E employees.

36 awards per year. Applications & brochures are available in all high schools within PG&E's service area and at PG&E offices.

105

ROBERT SCHRECK MEMORIAL FUND
(Grants)

c/o Texas Commerce Bank—Trust Dept;
P.O. Drawer 140
El Paso TX 79980
915/546-6515

AMOUNT: $500–$1500
DEADLINE(S): July 15; November 15
FIELD(S): Medicine; Veterinary Medicine; Physics; Chemistry; Architecture; Engineering; Episcopal Clergy

Grants to undergraduate juniors or seniors or graduate students who have been residents of El Paso county for at least two years. Must be USA citizen or legal resident and have a high grade point average. Financial need is a consideration.

Write for complete information.

106

SOCIETY OF AUTOMOTIVE ENGINEERS
(SAE Scholarships)

400 Commonwealth Drive
Warrendale PA 15096-0001
412/776-4841

AMOUNT: $500 to $1500
DEADLINE(S): December 1
FIELD(S): Engineering

Open to US citizens who are high school seniors pursuing an engineering program accredited by ABET. Must have 3.25 GPA or better & rank in a high percentile in both verbal & math on ACT and/or SAT scores.

A variety of scholarships are available with varying scholastic requirements; one scholarship is offered for Philadelphia area residents only. Write for complete information.

107

SOCIETY OF HISPANIC PROFESSIONAL ENGINEERS FOUNDATION
(SHPE Scholarships)
5400 E. Olympic Blvd.; Suite 210
Los Angeles CA 90022
213/888-2080

AMOUNT: $500 to $3000
DEADLINE(S): April 15
FIELD(S): Engineering & Science

Open to deserving students of Hispanic descent who are seeking careers in engineering and science. For full-time undergraduate or graduate study at a college or university. Academic achievement and financial need are considerations.
Write for complete information.

108

SOCIETY OF WOMEN ENGINEERS
(Admiral Grade Murray Hopper Scholarship)
120 Wall St.; 11th Floor
New York NY 10005
800/666-ISWE; FAX 212/509-0224

AMOUNT: $1000
DEADLINE(S): May 15 (postmark)
FIELD(S): Engineering; Computer Science

Open to women who are USA citizens and are entering a four-year program for the study of engineering or computer science as freshmen. Applications available March–May.
Send self-addressed stamped envelope for complete information.

109

SOCIETY OF WOMEN ENGINEERS
(Dorothy Lemke Howarth Scholarships)
120 Wall St.; 11th Floor
New York NY 10005
800/666-ISWE; FAX 212/509-0224

AMOUNT: $2000
DEADLINE(S): February 1
FIELD(S): Engineering

Open to entering female sophomore students who are majoring in engineering and are USA citizens.
Applications available October–January only. Send self-addressed stamped envelope for complete information.

110

SOCIETY OF WOMEN ENGINEERS
(General Electric Foundation Scholarships; Westinghouse Bertha Lamme Scholarships; TRW Scholarships)
120 Wall St.; 11th Floor
New York NY 10005
212/705-7855

AMOUNT: $1000–$2500
DEADLINE(S): May 15
FIELD(S): Engineering

Open to women who are US citizens and are entering an ABET accredited school as freshmen with an engineering major. Applications available March through April ONLY and are due by May 15 (postmark).
GE scholarships are renewable up to three years. Send self-addressed STAMPED envelope for complete information.

111

SOCIETY OF WOMEN ENGINEERS
(Ivy Parker Memorial Scholarship)
120 Wall St.; 11th Floor
New York NY 10005
800/666-ISWE; FAX 212/509-0224

AMOUNT: $2000
DEADLINE(S): February 1
FIELD(S): Engineering

Open to a female engineering student who is entering her sophomore, junior, or senior year. Applicants must demonstrate financial need.
Applications available October–January only. Send self-addressed stamped envelope for complete information.

112

SOCIETY OF WOMEN ENGINEERS
(Lillian Moller Gilbreth Scholarship)
120 Wall St.; 11th Floor
New York NY 10005
800/666-ISWE; FAX 212/509-0224

AMOUNT: $5000
DEADLINE(S): February 1
FIELD(S): Engineering

For women of outstanding potential and
achievement who are entering their sophomore, junior, or senior year of college as an
engineering student.

Applications available October–January only.
Send self-addressed stamped envelope for
complete information.

113

SOCIETY OF WOMEN ENGINEERS
(MASWE Memorial Scholarships)
120 Wall St.; 11th Floor
New York NY 10005
800/666-ISWE; FAX 212/509-0224

AMOUNT: $2000
DEADLINE(S): February 1
FIELD(S): Engineering

For women of outstanding potential and
achievement who are entering their sophomore, junior, or senior year of college as an
engineering student.

Applications available October–January only.
Send self-addressed stamped envelope for
complete information.

114

SOCIETY OF WOMEN ENGINEERS
(Olive Lynn Salembier Reentry Scholarships)
120 Wall St.; 11th Floor
New York NY 10005
800/666-ISWE; FAX 212/509-0224

AMOUNT: $2000
DEADLINE(S): May 15 (postmark)
FIELD(S): Engineering

Open to women who have been out of the
engineering job market for a minimum of
two years. Award is to enable recipient to
obtain the credentials necessary to reenter
the job market as an engineer. For any year
of undergrad or grad study.

Applications available March–May only with
completed application to be postmarked by
May 15. Send self-addressed stamped envelope for complete information.

115

SOCIETY OF WOMEN ENGINEERS
(United Technologies Corporation
Scholarship/Northrop Corp./Digital
Equipment Corp. Scholarship)
120 Wall St.; 11th Floor
New York NY 10005
212/705-7855

AMOUNT: $1000
DEADLINE(S): February 1
FIELD(S): Engineering

For sophomore women who are majoring in
engineering at accredited colleges & pursuing an engineering degree. Northrop &
Digital scholarships require recipients to be
student SWE members.

Digital requires attendance at a NY or New
England college. United Technologies
award is renewable for two years.
Applications available October through
January ONLY. Send self-addressed
stamped envelope for complete information.

116

THOMAS ALVA EDISON FOUNDATION
(Edison/McGraw Scholarship Program)
3000 Book Building
Detroit MI 48226
313/965-1149

AMOUNT: $3000; $5000; $1500; $1000
DEADLINE(S): December 1
FIELD(S): Science; Engineering &
Technology

Outstanding high school students. No formal application. Submit a proposal not to exceed 1000 words on a completed experiment or a project idea that would have "practical application" in fields of science and or engineering.

Include letter of recommendation from a teacher or sponsor which describes how you exemplify creativity & ingenuity demonstrated by life & work of Thomas Edison & Max McGraw. Mail entry to Dr. K.R. Roy; P.O. Box 380057; E. Hartford CT 06138.

117

TYSON FOUNDATION INC.
(Scholarship Program)
2210 W. Oaklawn
Springdale AR 72762-6999
501/290-4955

AMOUNT: Up to $1200/semester
DEADLINE(S): June 21
FIELD(S): Business; Agriculture; Engineering; Computer Science; Nursing

Open to a US citizen who was raised in and still lives in the vicinity of a Tyson Food's facility. Must maintain a 2.5 GPA while working and going to school full time. For undergrad study at schools in USA.

Recipients sign a pledge either to repay the scholarship money or help another deserving student not related by blood or marriage to attend college. Write for complete information.

118

WASHINGTON INTERNSHIPS FOR STUDENTS OF ENGINEERING
1899 L St. NW #500
Washington DC 20036
202/466-8744

AMOUNT: $2700 stipend + travel allowance
DEADLINE(S): December 10
FIELD(S): Engineering—Public Policy

For top 3rd-year engineering students. ten-week summer internship in Washington DC to learn how engineers contribute to public policy decisions on complex technological matters. Students receive 5 quarter credits from Univ. of Washington.

15 internships per summer. Write for complete information.

AERONAUTICS

119

AIR TRAFFIC CONTROL ASSOCIATION INC.
(Scholarship Awards Program)
2300 Clarendon Blvd. #711
Arlington VA 22201
703/522-5717

AMOUNT: $1500 to $2500
DEADLINE(S): August 1
FIELD(S): Aeronautics; Aviation; Related Areas

Scholarships open to promising men & women who are full-time undergraduate or graduate students in the above fields. Scholarships of up to $600 also available for part-time students. USA citizen.

Financial need is a consideration but not determinative. Write for complete information.

120

AMERICAN INSTITUTE OF AERONAUTICS AND ASTRONAUTICS
(Scholarships)
Student Programs Dept.; 370 L'Enfant Promenade SW
Washington DC 20024
202/646-7458

AMOUNT: $1000
DEADLINE(S): January 31
FIELD(S): Aeronautics; Aeronautical Engineering

Scholarships open to undergraduate students enrolled at accredited colleges or universities who have completed at least one semester & have at least a 3.0 GPA. US citizenship or legal residency required.

20–30 awards per year. Applicant should be planning entry into an aerospace engineering technology field. Write for complete information.

121

AOPA AIR SAFETY FOUNDATION
(Mcallister & Burnside Scholarships)
421 Aviation Way
Frederick MD 21701
301/695-2170

AMOUNT: $1000 (Mcallister); $1200 (Burnside)
DEADLINE(S): March 31
FIELD(S): Aviation

Scholarships open to undergraduate juniors & seniors who are enrolled in an accredited aviation degree program with an academic proficiency of 3.0 or better; USA citizen.
Write for complete information.

122

AVIATION DISTRIBUTORS AND MANUFACTURERS ASSOCIATION INTERNATIONAL
(ADMA International Scholarship Fund)
1900 Arch Street
Philadelphia PA 19103
215/564-3484

AMOUNT: Varies
DEADLINE(S): May 1
FIELD(S): Aviation Management; Professional Pilot

Open to students seeking a career in aviation management or as a professional pilot. Emphasis may be in general aviation, airway science management, aviation maintenance, flight engineering, or airway a/c systems management.

Applicants must be studying in the aviation field in a four-year school having an aviation program and must have completed at least two years of the program. Write for complete information.

123

EAA AVIATION FOUNDATION
(Scholarship Program)
P.O. Box 3065
Oshkosh WI 54903-3065
414/426-4888

AMOUNT: $200 to $1500
DEADLINE(S): April 1
FIELD(S): Aviation

Ten different scholarship programs open to well-rounded individuals involved in school and community activities as well as aviation. Applicant's academic records should verify their ability to complete their educational program.

Financial need is a consideration; a financial need statement may be required.

124

EASTERN NEW ENGLAND NINETY-NINES INC.
(Marjorie VanVliet Aviation Memorial Scholarship)
P.O. Box 19
Waterford VT 05848
802/259-0222

AMOUNT: $2000
DEADLINE(S): January 31
FIELD(S): Aeronautics; Aviation Maintenance; Flight Training

Open to high school seniors or beyond who live in one of the New England states, plan a career in aviation, and have applied to an aviation-related education or training program. Must demonstrate financial need.

Can use for tuition and/or flight training. Write for complete information.

125

ELECTRONIC INDUSTRIES FOUNDATION
(Scholarship Fund)
919 18th St.; Suite 900
Washington DC 20006
202/955-5814

AMOUNT: $2000

DEADLINE(S): February 1

FIELD(S): Aeronautics; Computer Science; Electrical Engineering; Engineering Technology; Applied Mathematics; Microbiology

Open to disabled students who are pursuing careers in high-tech areas through academic or technical training. Awards tenable at recognized undergraduate & graduate colleges & universities. Must be US citizen. Financial need is considered.

6 awards per year. Renewable. Write for complete information.

126

INTERNATIONAL SOCIETY OF WOMEN AIRLINE PILOTS
(ISA International Career Scholarship/ Fiorenze De Bernardi Merit Award)
P.O. Box 66268
Chicago IL 60666
Written inquiry

AMOUNT: $500–$1500

DEADLINE(S): April 1

FIELD(S): Airline pilot career (pursuit of)

Open to women throughout the world who are pursuing careers as airline pilots & have at least 350 hours of flight experience. Selection based on need, demonstrated dedication to career goal, work experience, & history and recommendations.

Personal interview is required. Write for complete information.

127

NATIONAL SPACE CLUB
(Dr. Robert H. Goddard Space Science and Engineering Scholarship)
655 15th St. NW #300
Washington DC 20005
202/639-4210

AMOUNT: $10,000

DEADLINE(S): January 9

FIELD(S): Science and Engineering

Open to undergraduate juniors & seniors who have scholastic plans leading to future participation in the Aerospace sciences and technology. USA citizen.

Send a self-addressed stamped envelope for more information.

128

SOCIETY OF WOMEN ENGINEERS
(Judith Resnik Memorial Scholarship)
120 Wall St.; 11th Floor
New York NY 10005
800/666-ISWE; FAX 212/509-0224

AMOUNT: $2000

DEADLINE(S): February 1

FIELD(S): Space Science

Open to a rising senior female studying an engineering field with a space-related major who will pursue a career in the space industry. Must be a member of the Society of Women Engineers.

Applications available OctoberJanuary only. Send self-addressed stamped envelope for complete information.

129

US AIR FORCE ROTC
(4-Year Scholarship Program)
AFROTC/RROO; Recruiting Operations Branch
Maxwell AFB AL 36112
205/953-2091

AMOUNT: Tuition; fees & books + $100 per month stipend

DEADLINE(S): December 1

FIELD(S): Aeronautical Engineering; Civil Engineering; Mechanical Engineering; Mathematics; Physics; Nursing & some Liberal Arts

Open to USA citizens who are at least 17 and will graduate from college before age 25. Must complete application, furnish SAT/ACT scores, high school transcripts, and record of extracurricular activities.

Must qualify on Air Force medical examination. About 1600 scholarships awarded each year at campuses which offer Air Force ROTC.

ARCHITECTURE

130

VERTICAL FLIGHT FOUNDATION
(Undergraduate/Graduate Scholarships)
217 N. Washington St.
Alexandria VA 22314
703/684-6777

AMOUNT: Up to $2000
DEADLINE(S): February 1
FIELD(S): Mechanical Engineering; Electrical Engineering; Aerospace Engineering

Annual scholarships open to undergraduate & graduate students in the above areas who are interested in pursuing careers in some aspect of helicopter or vertical flight. For full-time study at accredited school of engineering.
Write for complete information.

131

VIRGINIA AIRPORT OPERATORS COUNCIL
(VAOC Aviation Scholarship Award)
c/o John Lillard; Box A-3
Richmond VA 23231
804/236-2110

AMOUNT: $2000
DEADLINE(S): Changes yearly/early spring
FIELD(S): Aviation

Open to Virginia high school seniors who have been accepted into an accredited post-secondary aviation education program. Applicants need a 3.0 or better GPA and should be planning a career in aviation.
College students and non-Virginia residents are NOT eligible. Write for complete information.

132

AMERICAN ARCHITECTURAL FOUNDATION
(Minority/Disadvantaged Scholarship Program)
1735 New York Avenue NW
Washington DC 20006
202/626-7511

AMOUNT: Varies
DEADLINE(S): December 4 (nomination); January 15 (application)
FIELD(S): Architecture

Open to minority &/or disadvantaged students who are entering an NAAB school of Architecture or college freshmen entering a program leading to a professional degree (bachelor or master of Architecture).
Nomination by an individual familiar with student's interest and potential to be an architect is required. 20 scholarships per year. Write for complete information.

133

AMERICAN INSTITUTE OF ARCHITECTS
(AIA/AIAF Scholarship Program)
1735 New York Avenue NW
Washington DC 20006
202/626-7511

AMOUNT: $500–$2500
DEADLINE(S): February 3
FIELD(S): Architecture

Open to undergraduate students in their final 2 years & graduate students pursuing their master's degree. Awards tenable at accredited institutions in the USA & Canada.
Applications available ONLY through the office of the dean or department head at an NAAB or RAIC school of architecture.

134

ARTS INTERNATIONAL; INSTITUTE OF INTERNATIONAL EDUCATION
(Cintas Fellowship Program)
809 United Nations Plaza
New York NY 10017
212/984-5370

AMOUNT: $10,000
DEADLINE(S): March 1
FIELD(S): Architecture; Painting;
Photography; Sculpture; Printmaking;
Music Composition; Creative Writing

Fellowships open to artists who are of Cuban ancestry or Cuban citizens living outside of Cuba. They are intended to foster & encourage the professional development & recognition of talented creative artists in the above areas.

Fellowships are not awarded for furtherance of academic study. 5–10 awards per year. Write for complete information.

135

LANDSCAPE ARCHITECTURE FOUNDATION
(CLASS Fund Scholarships)
4401 Connecticut Ave. NW; Suite 500
Washington DC 20008
202/686-0068

AMOUNT: $500–$2000
DEADLINE(S): April 3
FIELD(S): Landscape Architecture

Open to Southern California students enrolled at California Polytechnic Institute (Pomona or San Luis Obispo), USC, UCLA, & UC-Irvine who show promise & a commitment to landscape architecture as a profession.
Write for complete information.

136

LANDSCAPE ARCHITECTURE FOUNDATION
(Edward D. Stone Jr. & Associates Minority Scholarship)
4401 Connecticut Ave. NW; Suite 500
Washington DC 20008
202/686-0068; FAX 202/686-1001

AMOUNT: $1000
DEADLINE(S): May 4
FIELD(S): Landscape Architecture

Open to African American, Hispanic, & minority students of other cultural & ethnic backgrounds entering their final 2 years of undergrad study in landscape architecture.
Two scholarships per year. Write for complete information.

137

LANDSCAPE ARCHITECTURE FOUNDATION
(Edith H. Henderson Scholarship)
4401 Connecticut Ave. NW; Suite 500
Washington DC 20008
202/686-0068

AMOUNT: $1000
DEADLINE(S): May 4
FIELD(S): Landscape Architecture

Scholarship available to any landscape architecture student who is in the beginning or final year of undergraduate work or in any year of graduate study.
Write for complete information.

138

LANDSCAPE ARCHITECTURE FOUNDATION
(Harriett Barnhart Wimmer Scholarship)
4401 Connecticut Ave. NW; Suite 500
Washington DC 20008
202/686-0068

AMOUNT: $1000
DEADLINE(S): May 4
FIELD(S): Landscape Architecture

Open to women going into their final year of undergraduate study at a USA or Canadian university who have demonstrated excellence in their design ability & sensitivity to the environment.
Write for complete information.

139

LANDSCAPE ARCHITECTURE FOUNDATION
(LANDCADD Inc. Scholarship)
4401 Connecticut Ave. NW; Suite 500
Washington DC 20008
202/686-0068

AMOUNT: $500
DEADLINE(S): May 4
FIELD(S): Landscape Architecture

Scholarships open to undergraduate & graduate students who wish to utilize technological advancements such as computer-aided design, video imaging, and/or telecommunications in their career.
Write for complete information.

140

LANDSCAPE ARCHITECTURE FOUNDATION
(Lester Walls III Scholarship)
4401 Connecticut Ave. NW; Suite 500
Washington DC 20008
202/686-0068

AMOUNT: $500
DEADLINE(S): May 4
FIELD(S): Landscape Architecture

Scholarship open to handicapped students pursuing a degree in landscape architecture or for research on barrier-free design for the disabled.
Write for complete information.

141

LANDSCAPE ARCHITECTURE FOUNDATION
(Raymond E. Page Scholarship)
4401 Connecticut Ave. NW; Suite 500
Washington DC 20008
202/686-0068

AMOUNT: $500
DEADLINE(S): May 4
FIELD(S): Landscape Architecture

Scholarships open to any undergraduate or graduate student who is in need of financial assistance.
Write for complete information.

142

LANDSCAPE ARCHITECTURE FOUNDATION
(Student Research Grants)
4401 Connecticut Ave. NW; Suite 500
Washington DC 20008
202/686-0068

AMOUNT: $1000
DEADLINE(S): May 4
FIELD(S): Landscape Architecture

Research grants to encourage student efforts in practical research & expand the knowledge base of the profession. Open to undergraduate & graduate students.
Write for complete information.

143

LANDSCAPE ARCHITECTURE FOUNDATION (The Rain Bird Company Scholarship)
4401 Connecticut Ave. NW; Suite 500
Washington DC 20008
202/686-0068

AMOUNT: $1000
DEADLINE(S): May 4
FIELD(S): Landscape Architecture

Open to landscape architecture students in their final 2 years of undergraduate study who have demonstrated commitment to the profession through participation in extracurricular activities & exemplary scholastic achievements.

Write for complete information.

144

LANDSCAPE ARCHITECTURE FOUNDATION
(William J. Locklin Scholarship)
  4401 Connecticut Ave. NW; Suite 500
  Washington DC 20008
  202/686-0068

AMOUNT: $500

DEADLINE(S): May 4

FIELD(S): Landscape Architecture

Scholarships open to undergraduate & graduate students who are pursuing a program in lighting design. Purpose is to stress the importance of 24-hour lighting in landscape design.

Write for complete information.

145

NATIONAL ASSOCIATION OF WOMEN IN CONSTRUCTION
(El Camino Real Chapter #158 Scholarship)
  Marie Revere; 1737 1st St.; Suite. 300
  San Jose CA 95112
  408/452-4644

AMOUNT: $1000

DEADLINE(S): May 1

FIELD(S): Civil Engineering; Construction; Architecture; Architectural Engineering

Open to men or women undergraduates who are going into their junior year at an accredited 4-year California college. USA citizen.

Write for complete information.

146

NATIONAL ASSOCIATION OF WOMEN IN CONSTRUCTION
(Founders' Scholarship Foundation Awards)
  327 S. Adams
  Fort Worth TX 76104
  817/877-5551

AMOUNT: Not specified

DEADLINE(S): February 1

FIELD(S): Fields Related to a Career in Construction

Open to full-time students (men or women) enrolled in a construction-related program leading to an associate's or bachelor's degree. Applicants should be in at least their 1st year of college and have at least one year remaining.

Awards committee considers grades, interest in construction, extracurricular activities, employment experience, financial need, & evaluation by academic advisor. Write for complete information.

147

NATIONAL DEFENSE TRANSPORTATION ASSOCIATION— SAN FRANCISCO BAY AREA CHAPTER
(NDTA Scholarship)
  P.O. Box 24676
  Oakland CA 94623
  Written inquiry

AMOUNT: $2000

DEADLINE(S): March 31

FIELD(S): Transportation-related Business; Engineering; Planning & Environmental fields

Open to USA citizens enrolled in a California accredited undergraduate degree or vocational program in the above fields who plan to pursue a career related to transportation. Financial need is considered.

Write for complete information.

148

NATIONAL ROOFING FOUNDATION
(NRF Scholarship Awards Program)
  O'Hare International Center; 10255 W. Higgins Rd.; Suite 600
  Rosemont IL 60018
  708/299-9070

AMOUNT: $2000

DEADLINE(S): January 15

FIELD(S): Architecture; Construction

Open to high school seniors; undergraduate and graduate architectural students or students of another curriculum related to the roofing industry. Applicants must be US citizens.

For full-time study at an accredited 4-year college or university. Send a self-addressed stamped envelope (#10) to receive an application.

149

NEW JERSEY SOCIETY OF ARCHITECTS
(AIA/NJ Scholarship Program)
900 Route Nine; 2nd Floor
Woodbridge NJ 07095
908/636-5680

AMOUNT: $250–$1500
DEADLINE(S): April 16
FIELD(S): Architecture

Open to New Jersey residents who are enrolled in or accepted to an accredited school of architecture and have completed one year of study toward the first professional architectural degree. Must demonstrate talent and financial need.

Must be USA citizen and intend to pursue an architectural career in New Jersey. 20 awards per year. Write for complete information.

150

NEW YORK CITY DEPT. OF PERSONNEL
(Government Scholars Internship Program)
2 Washington St.; 15th Floor
New York NY 10004
212/487-5698

AMOUNT: $3000 stipend
DEADLINE(S): January 13
FIELD(S): Public Administration; Urban Planning; Government; Public Service; Urban Affairs

10-week summer intern program open to undergraduate sophomores, juniors, &

seniors. Program provides students with unique opportunity to learn about NY City government. Internships available in virtually every city agency & mayoral office.
Write for complete information.

151

NEW YORK CITY DEPT. OF PERSONNEL
(Urban Fellows Program)
2 Washington St.; 15th Floor
New York NY 10004
212/487-5698

AMOUNT: $18,000 stipend
DEADLINE(S): January 20
FIELD(S): Public Administration; Urban Planning; Government; Public Service; Urban Affairs

Fellowship program provides one academic year (9 months) of full-time work experience in urban government. Open to graduating college seniors and recent college graduates. US citizenship required.
Write for complete information.

152

ROBERT SCHRECK MEMORIAL FUND
(Grants)
c/o Texas Commerce Bank—Trust Dept;
P.O. Drawer 140
El Paso TX 79980
915/546-6515

AMOUNT: $500–$1500
DEADLINE(S): July 15; November 15
FIELD(S): Medicine; Veterinary Medicine; Physics; Chemistry; Architecture; Engineering; Episcopal Clergy

Grants to undergraduate juniors or seniors or graduate students who have been residents of El Paso county for at least two years. Must be USA citizen or legal resident and have a high grade point average. Financial need is a consideration.
Write for complete information.

153

SKIDMORE OWINGS & MERRILL FOUNDATION
(Travelling Fellowship Program)
  224 S. Michigan Ave.; Suite 1000
  Chicago IL 60604
  312/554-9090; FAX 312/360-4545

AMOUNT: $10,000
DEADLINE(S): None specified
FIELD(S): Architecture

Open to undergraduate and graduate architecture students. Candidates must be USA citizens attending or recently graduated from an accredited architecture school.
Write for complete information.

154

SMITHSONIAN INSTITUTION
(Cooper-Hewitt Museum of Design Summer Internships)
  Cooper-Hewitt Museum; 2 East 91st St.
  New York NY 10128
  212/860-6868; FAX 212/860-6909

AMOUNT: Varies
DEADLINE(S): March 31
FIELD(S): Art; Design; Architecture;
  Museum Studies

10-week summer internships at the Cooper-Hewitt Museum open to undergraduate and graduate students.
Write for complete information.

155

SMITHSONIAN INSTITUTION
(Minority Undergraduate & Graduate Internship)
  Office of Fellowships & Grants
  955 L'enfant Plaza; Suite 7000
  Washington DC 20560
  202/287-3271

AMOUNT: $250 to $300/week stipend +
  travel
DEADLINE(S): February 15; June 15;
  October 15

FIELD(S): Design; Architecture; Art;
  Museum Studies

Internships open to minority students for research & study at the Smithsonian or Cooper-Hewitt Museum of Design in New York City. The museum's collection spans 3000 years of design from ancient pottery to modern fashion & advertising.
Undergraduates receive $250 per week stipend & graduate students receive $300 per week stipend. Write for complete information.

156

UNIVERSITY OF ILLINOIS AT URBANA-CHAMPAIGN
(Lydia E. Parker Bates Scholarship)
  Student Services Bldg.
  610 East John Street
  Champaign IL 61820
  217/333-0100

AMOUNT: Varies
DEADLINE(S): March 15
FIELD(S): Art; Architecture; Landscape
  Architecture; Urban Planning; Dance;
  Theater

Open to undergraduate students in the college of fine & applied arts who are attending the University of Illinois at Urbana-Champaign. Must demonstrate financial need and have 3.85 GPA.
175 awards per year. Recipients must carry at least 14 credit hours per semester. Contact office of student financial aid.

157

VAN ALEN INSTITUTE
(Fellowship in Public Architecture—Lloyd Warren Fellowship/Paris Prize)
  30 West 22nd St.
  New York NY 10010
  212/924-7000

AMOUNT: Up to $7000
DEADLINE(S): TBA
FIELD(S): Architecture

Architectural design competition open to students who have received or anticipate receiving their first professional degree in architecture between June of competition year & June three years hence.

Awards are to support travel/study. Write for complete information.

158

VAN ALEN INSTITUTE
(Projects in Public Architecture—Dinkeloo Travelling Fellowship in Architectural Design & Technology)
30 West 22nd St.
New York NY 10010
Written inquiry only

AMOUNT: $7000

DEADLINE(S): March of every other year (1997; 1999; etc.)

FIELD(S): Architectural Design & Technology

Open to US citizens who have or anticipate receiving 1st professional degree in architecture between June of competition year & June four years hence. Travelling fellowship includes 2 months tenable at the American Academy in Rome, Italy.

Applicants submit a portfolio and project proposal. Write for complete information.

159

VAN ALEN INSTITUTE
(Projects in Public Architecture—Van Alen Fellowship)
30 West 22nd Street
New York NY 10010
Written inquiry only

AMOUNT: Up to $8000

DEADLINE(S): Fall (date TBA)

FIELD(S): Architecture

Design competition open to students, faculty, and practitioners. Winners will receive awards for travel & study abroad.

Write to address above for complete information.

160

WAVERLY COMMUNITY HOUSE INC.
(F. Lammont Belin Arts Scholarships)
Scholarships Selection Committee
P.O. Box 142
Waverly PA 18471
717/586-8191

AMOUNT: $9000

DEADLINE(S): December 15

FIELD(S): Painting; Sculpture; Music; Drama; Dance; Literature; Architecture; Photography

Applicants must reside in the Abington or Pocono regions of Northeastern Pennsylvania. They must furnish proof of exceptional ability in their chosen field but need no formal training in any academic or professional program.

USA citizenship required. Finalists must appear in person before the selection committee. Write for complete information.

161

WEBB INSTITUTE
(Naval Architecture Scholarships)
Crescent Beach Rd.
Glen Cove NY 11542
516/671-2213

AMOUNT: Full tuition for 4 years

DEADLINE(S): February 15

FIELD(S): Naval Architecture; Marine Engineering

Open to high school students aged 16–24 who are in the top 10% of their class & have at least a 3.2 GPA (4.0 scale). Selection based on college boards, SAT scores, demonstrated interest in above areas, & interview. US citizenship required.

20 to 25 four-year full tuition undergrad scholarships per year to Webb Institute. Write for complete information.

162

WEST VIRGINIA SOCIETY OF ARCHITECTS/AIA
(Scholarship)
  P.O. Box 813; 405 Capitol St. Suite I
  Charleston WV 25323
  304/344-9872

AMOUNT: $2000
DEADLINE(S): May 30
FIELD(S): Architecture

Open to West Virginia residents enrolled in at least their second year of an accredited architectural program. Candidates must submit letter stating need, qualifications, and desire.
Write for complete information.

CIVIL ENGINEERING

163

AMERICAN SOCIETY OF CIVIL ENGINEERS
(ASCE Construction Engineering Scholarship & Student Prizes)
  345 East 47th Street
  New York NY 10017-2398
  800/548-ASCE (outside NY); 800/628-0041 (within NY)

AMOUNT: $1000
DEADLINE(S): February 15
FIELD(S): Construction Engineering

Open to undergrad freshmen, sophomores, or juniors of ASCE Student Chapter/Club. Must submit paper relating to specified construction-related topics. Papers may not have been previously published or appeared in connection with course work.
A team of up to 4 students may submit a joint entry & share equally in the single stipend. Write for complete information.

164

AMERICAN SOCIETY OF CIVIL ENGINEERS
(B. Charles Tiney Memorial ASCE Student Chapter Scholarship)
  345 East 47th Street
  New York NY 10017-2398
  800/548-ASCE (outside NY); 800/628-0041 (within NY)

AMOUNT: $2000
DEADLINE(S): February 15
FIELD(S): Civil Engineering

Open to undergrad freshmen, sophomores, or juniors of an ASCE Student Chapter & also a National Student Member in good standing (NSM application may be submitted along with scholarship application). Financial need must be demonstrated.
Award must be used to continue formal education at an accredited educational institution. Write for complete information.

165

AMERICAN SOCIETY OF CIVIL ENGINEERS
(Freeman Fellowship)
  345 East 47th Street
  New York NY 10017-2398
  800/548-ASCE (outside NY); 800/628-0041 (within NY)

AMOUNT: Varies
DEADLINE(S): February 15
FIELD(S): Civil Engineering

Fellowship to encourage research in civil engineering. Open to young engineers (under 45) who are National ASCE members. Grants are made toward expenses for experiments, observations, & compilations to discover new & accurate data.
Write for complete information.

166

AMERICAN SOCIETY OF CIVIL ENGINEERS
(Samuel Fletcher Tapman ASCE Student Chapter Scholarships)
345 East 47th Street
New York NY 10017-2398
800/548-ASCE (outside NY); 800/628-0041 (within NY)

AMOUNT: $1500
DEADLINE(S): February 15
FIELD(S): Civil engineering

Open to undergrad freshmen, sophomores, & juniors of an ASCE Student Chapter & also a National Student Member in good standing (NSM applications may be submitted along with scholarship applications). Only 1 application per Student Chapter.

Award must be used to continue formal education at an accredited educational institution. Write for complete information.

167

ASSOCIATED GENERAL CONTRACTORS EDUCATION AND RESEARCH FOUNDATION
(Undergraduate Scholarships)
1957 E Street NW
Washington DC 20006
202/393-2040; FAX 202/347-4004

AMOUNT: $1500 per year for up to 4 years
DEADLINE(S): November 1 (applications available September 1)
FIELD(S): Construction; Civil Engineering

Open to college freshmen, sophomores, & juniors enrolled in or planning to enroll in a 4- or 5-year degree program in construction and/or civil engineering.

Must be US citizen or legal resident and desire a career in the construction industry. Write for complete information.

168

CONSTRUCTION EDUCATION FOUNDATION
(Associated Builders & Contractors Scholarship Program)
1300 N. 17th St.
Rosslyn VA 22209
703/812-2000

AMOUNT: $500 to $2000
DEADLINE(S): December 15
FIELD(S): Construction

Open to undergrads enrolled in an accredited 4-year degree program who have completed at least 1 year of study in construction (other than a design discipline). Must have at least 1 full year remaining subsequent to application deadline.

Approximately 20 scholarships per year. Applications available October 1 each year. Write for complete information.

169

NATIONAL ASSOCIATION OF WATER COMPANIES—NEW JERSEY CHAPTER
(Scholarship)
c/o NJ-American Water Co.
66 Shrewsbury Ave.
Shrewsbury NJ 07702
908/842-6900; FAX 908/842-7541

AMOUNT: $2500
DEADLINE(S): April 1 (postmark)
FIELD(S): Business Administration; Biology; Chemistry; Engineering

Open to USA citizens who have lived in NJ at least 5 years and plan a career in the investor-owned water utility industry in disciplines such as those above. Must be undergrad or graduate student in a 2- or 4-year NJ college or university.

GPA of 3.0 or better required. Write for complete information.

170

NATIONAL ASSOCIATION OF WOMEN IN CONSTRUCTION
(El Camino Real Chapter #158 Scholarship)
Marie Revere; 1737 1st St.; Suite. 300
San Jose CA 95112
408/452-4644

AMOUNT: $1000
DEADLINE(S): May 1
FIELD(S): Civil Engineering; Construction; Architecture; Architectural Engineering

Open to men or women undergraduates who are going into their junior year at an accredited 4-year California college. USA citizen.
Write for complete information.

171

NATIONAL ASSOCIATION OF WOMEN IN CONSTRUCTION
(Founders' Scholarship Foundation Awards)
327 S. Adams
Ft. Worth TX 76104
817/877-5551

AMOUNT: Not specified
DEADLINE(S): February 1
FIELD(S): Fields Related to a Career in Construction

Open to full-time students (men or women) enrolled in a construction-related program leading to an associate's or bachelor's degree. Applicants should be in at least their 1st year of college and have at least one year remaining.
Awards committee considers grades, interest in construction, extracurricular activities, employment experience, financial need, & evaluation by academic advisor. Write for complete information.

172

NATIONAL ROOFING FOUNDATION
(NRF Scholarship Awards Program)
O'Hare International Center; 10255 W. Higgins Rd.; Suite 600
Rosemont IL 60018
708/299-9070

AMOUNT: $2000
DEADLINE(S): January 15
FIELD(S): Architecture; Construction

Open to high school seniors, undergraduate and graduate architectural students, or students of another curriculum related to the roofing industry. Applicants must be US citizens.
For full-time study at an accredited 4-year college or university. Send a self-addressed stamped envelope (#10) to receive an application.

173

NORTH DAKOTA DEPARTMENT OF TRANSPORTATION
(Grants)
Human Resources Division
608 East Blvd. Ave.
Bismarck ND 58505
701/328-2574

AMOUNT: $1000 per year
DEADLINE(S): February 15
FIELD(S): Civil Engineering; Civil Engineering & Survey Technology; Construction Engineering

Financial aid grants open to undergraduate students at recognized colleges & universities in North Dakota who have completed at least one year of study in the above fields.
2–4 grants per year. Renewable. Write for complete information.

174

PACIFIC GAS & ELECTRIC CO.
(Scholarships for High School Seniors)
77 Beale St.; Room 2837
San Francisco CA 94106
415/973-1338

AMOUNT: $1000–$4000
DEADLINE(S): November 15

FIELD(S): Engineering; Computer Science; Mathematics; Marketing; Business; Economics

High school seniors in good academic standing who reside in or attend high school in areas served by PG&E are eligible to compete for scholarships awarded on a regional basis. Not open to children of PG&E employees.

36 awards per year. Applications & brochures are available in all high schools within PG&E's service area and at PG&E offices.

175

US AIR FORCE ROTC
(4-Year Scholarship Program)
AFROTC/RROO; Recruiting Operations Branch
Maxwell AFB AL 36112
205/953-2091

AMOUNT: Tuition; fees & books + $100 per month stipend
DEADLINE(S): December 1
FIELD(S): Aeronautical Engineering; Civil Engineering; Mechanical Engineering; Mathematics; Physics; Nursing & some Liberal Arts

Open to USA citizens who are at least 17 and will graduate from college before age 25. Must complete application, furnish SAT/ACT scores, high school transcripts, and record of extracurricular activities.

Must qualify on Air Force medical examination. About 1600 scholarships awarded each year at campuses which offer Air Force ROTC.

COMPUTER SCIENCE

176

AT&T BELL LABORATORIES
(Summer Research Program for Minorities & Women)
101 Crawfords Corner RD; RM 1B-222
Holmdel NJ 07733
Written Inquiry

AMOUNT: Salary + travel & living expences for summer
DEADLINE(S): December 1
FIELD(S): Engineering; Math; Sciences; Computer Science

Program offers minority students & women students technical employment experience at Bell Laboratories. Students should have completed their third year of study at an accredited college or university. USA citizen or permanent resident.

Selection is based partially on academic achievement and personal motivation. Write special programs manager—SRP for complete information.

177

BUSINESS & PROFESSIONAL WOMEN'S FOUNDATION
(Career Advancement Scholarships)
2012 Massachusetts Ave. NW
Washington DC 20036
202/293-1200

AMOUNT: $500–$1000
DEADLINE(S): April 15 (postmark)
FIELD(S): Computer Science; Education; Paralegal; Engineering; Science; Law; Dentistry; Medicine

Open to women (30 or older) within 12–24 months of completing undergrad or grad study in US (including Puerto Rico & Virgin Islands). Studies should lead to entry/reentry in work force or improve career advancement chances.

Not for doctoral study. Must demonstrate financial need. Send self-addressed stamped ($.64) #10 envelope for complete info. Applications available October 1–April 1.

178

DEVRY INC.
(Scholarship Program)
One Tower Lane
Oakbrook Terrace IL 60181
708/571-7700; 800/323-4256

AMOUNT: Full tuition (40); 1/2 tuition (80)

DEADLINE(S): March 22

FIELD(S): Electronics Engineering Technology; Computer Information Systems; Business Operations; Telecommunications Management; Accounting

40 full-tuition & 80 1/2-tuition undergraduate scholarships. Open to US high school graduates who wish to enroll in a fully-accredited bachelor of science degree program at one of the DeVry Institutes located throughout North America.

Awards renewable provided 2.5 GPA is maintained. Contact your guidance counselor, nearest DeVry Institute, or address above for complete information.

179

ELECTRONIC INDUSTRIES FOUNDATION (Scholarship Fund)
919 18th St.; Suite 900
Washington DC 20006
202/955-5814

AMOUNT: $2000

DEADLINE(S): February 1

FIELD(S): Aeronautics; Computer Science; Electrical Engineering; Engineering Technology; Applied Mathematics; Microbiology

Open to disabled students who are pursuing careers in high-tech areas through academic or technical training. Awards tenable at recognized undergraduate & graduate colleges & universities. Must be US citizen. Financial need is considered.

6 awards per year. Renewable. Write for complete information.

180

PACIFIC GAS & ELECTRIC CO.
(Scholarships for High School Seniors)
77 Beale St.; Room 2837
San Francisco CA 94106
415/973-1338

AMOUNT: $1000–$4000

DEADLINE(S): November 15

FIELD(S): Engineering; Computer Science; Mathematics; Marketing; Business; Economics

High school seniors in good academic standing who reside in or attend high school in areas served by PG&E are eligible to compete for scholarships awarded on a regional basis. Not open to children of PG&E employees.

36 awards per year. Applications & brochures are available in all high schools within PG&E's service area and at PG&E offices.

181

SOCIETY OF WOMEN ENGINEERS
(Admiral Grade Murray Hopper Scholarship)
120 Wall St.; 11th Floor
New York NY 10005
800/666-ISWE; FAX 212/509-0224

AMOUNT: $1000

DEADLINE(S): May 15 (postmark)

FIELD(S): Engineering; Computer Science

Open to women who are USA citizens and are entering a four-year program for the study of engineering or computer science as freshmen. Applications available March–May.

Send self-addressed stamped envelope for complete information.

182

SOCIETY OF WOMEN ENGINEERS
(Hewlett-Packard Scholarships)
120 Wall St.; 11th Floor
New York NY 10005
800/666-ISWE; FAX 212/509-0224

AMOUNT: $1000

DEADLINE(S): February 1

FIELD(S): Electrical Engineering; Computer Science

Open to women who are juniors or seniors majoring in electrical engineering or computer science at an accredited school. Applicants must be active supporters and contributors to SWE.

Applications available October–January only. Send self-addressed stamped envelope for complete information.

183

STATE FARM COMPANIES FOUNDATION
(Exceptional Student Fellowship)
1 State Farm Plaza
Bloomington IL 61710
309/766-2039

AMOUNT: $3000

DEADLINE(S): February 15 (apps. available November 1)

FIELD(S): Accounting; Business Administration; Actuarial Science; Computer Science; Economics; Finance; Insurance; Investments; Marketing; Mathematics; Statistics; & Related Fields

Open to current full-time college juniors and seniors majoring in any of the fields above. Only students nominated by the college dean or a department head qualify as candidates. Applications without nominations will NOT be considered.

USA citizen. 3.4 or better GPA (4.0 scale) required. 50 fellowships per year. Write for complete information.

184

STATE FARM COMPANIES FOUNDATION
(Exceptional Student Fellowship Awards)
One State Farm Plaza; SC-3
Bloomington IL 61710
309/766-2039

AMOUNT: $3000

DEADLINE(S): February 15

FIELD(S): Business-related fields; Computer Science; Mathematics; Accounting; Actuarial Science; Business Administration; Economics; Finance; Insurance; Investments; Marketing; Management; & Statistics

Must be junior or senior undergrad at time of application & have at least a 3.4 GPA (on 4.0 scale). Nominations by Dean or department head only. USA citizenship required.

50 fellowships per academic year. Applications and nominations available November 1. Write for complete information and state your current year in college.

185

TANDY TECHNOLOGY SCHOLARS
(Student Awards; Teacher Awards)
TCU Station; Box 32897
Fort Worth TX 76129
817/924-4087

AMOUNT: $1000 students; $2500 teachers

DEADLINE(S): October 14

FIELD(S): Mathematics; Science; Computer Science

Program recognizes academic performance and outstanding achievements by Mathematics, Science, and Computer Science students and teachers. Students and teachers receive cash awards.

Must be a senior in an enrolled high school located in one of the 50 states. 100 of each awarded each year. Nomination packets sent to high schools.

186

TYSON FOUNDATION INC.
(Scholarship Program)
2210 W. Oaklawn
Springdale AR 72762-6999
501/290-4955

AMOUNT: Up to $1200/semester

DEADLINE(S): June 21

FIELD(S): Business; Agriculture; Engineering; Computer Science; Nursing

Open to a US citizen who was raised in and still lives in the vicinity of a Tyson Food's facility. Must maintain a 2.5 GPA while working and going to school full time. For undergrad study at schools in USA.

Recipients sign a pledge either to repay the scholarship money or help another deserving student not related by blood or marriage to attend college. Write for complete information.

ELECTRICAL ENGINEERING

187

AMERICAN RADIO RELAY LEAGUE FOUNDATION
(Dr. James L. Lawson Memorial Scholarship)
225 Main St.
Newington CT 06111
806/594-0230

AMOUNT: $500
DEADLINE(S): February 15
FIELD(S): Electronics; Communications

Open to radio amateurs holding at least a general license and residing in CT, MA, ME, NH, RI, VT, or NY and attending a school in one of those states.
Write for complete information.

188

AMERICAN RADIO RELAY LEAGUE FOUNDATION
(Edmund A. Metzger Scholarship Fund)
225 Main St.
Newington CT 06111
203/666-1541

AMOUNT: $500
DEADLINE(S): February 15
FIELD(S): Electrical Engineering

Open to ARRL members who are residents of ARRL Central Div. (Illinois, Indiana, Wisconsin), attend a 4-year university in the ARRL Central Division, & are currently licensed radio amateurs.
Write for complete information.

189

AMERICAN RADIO RELAY LEAGUE FOUNDATION
(Irving W. Cook Waocgs Scholarship)
225 Main St.
Newington CT 06111
203/666-1541

AMOUNT: $1000

DEADLINE(S): February 15
FIELD(S): Electronics; Communications

Open to residents of Kansas who hold any class of radio amateur license and are seeking a baccalaureate or higher degree. For study in any USA college or university.
Write for complete information.

190

AMERICAN RADIO RELAY LEAGUE FOUNDATION
(L. Philip & Alice J. Wicker Scholarship Fund)
225 Main St.
Newington CT 06111
203/666-1541

AMOUNT: $1000
DEADLINE(S): February 15
FIELD(S): Electrical Engineering; Communications

Open to students who are residence of ARRL Roanoke Div. (N. Carolina, S. Carolina, Virginia, W. Virginia), attend a school in the Roanoke Div. as an undergraduate or graduate student, & are at least general class licensed radio amateurs.
Write for complete information.

191

AMERICAN RADIO RELAY LEAGUE FOUNDATION
(Paul & Helen L. Grauer Scholarship Fund)
225 Main St.
Newington CT 06111
203/666-1541

AMOUNT: $1000
DEADLINE(S): February 15
FIELD(S): Electrical Engineering; Communications

Open to ARRL Midwest Div. residents (Iowa, Kansas, Missouri, Nebraska) who are licensed radio amateurs & enrolled full-time as undergrad or grad students at an accredited institution in the ARRL Midwest Division.
Write for complete information.

192

AMERICAN RADIO RELAY LEAGUE FOUNDATION (Perry F. Hadlock Memorial Scholarship Fund)
225 Main St.
Newington CT 06111
806/594-0230

AMOUNT: $1000
DEADLINE(S): February 15
FIELD(S): Electrical Engineering

Open to students who are general class licensed radio amateurs, have demonstrated enthusiasm in promoting amateur radio, & are enrolled full time as an undergraduate or graduate student at an accredited institution.

Preference given to Clarkson University, Rotsdam, NY; Mr. Hadlock's alma mater students.

193

AMERICAN RADIO RELAY LEAGUE FOUNDATION
(Senator Barry Goldwater [#K7UGA] Scholarship Fund)
225 Main St.
Newington CT 06111
203/666-1541

AMOUNT: $5000
DEADLINE(S): February 15
FIELD(S): Communications

Open to students who are licensed radio amateurs & enrolled full time as an undergraduate or graduate student at an accredited institution in a field related to communications.

Write for complete information.

194

AT&T BELL LABORATORIES
(Summer Research Program for Minorities & Women)
101 Crawfords Corner RD; RM 1B-222
Holmdel NJ 07733
Written Inquiry

AMOUNT: Salary + travel & living expenses for summer
DEADLINE(S): December 1
FIELD(S): Engineering; Math; Sciences; Computer Science

Program offers minority students & women students technical employment experience at Bell Laboratories. Students should have completed their third year of study at an accredited college or university. USA citizen or permanent resident.

Selection is based partially on academic achievement and personal motivation. Write special programs manager—SRP for complete information.

195

DEVRY INC.
(Scholarship Program)
One Tower Lane
Oakbrook Terrace IL 60181
708/571-7700; 800/323-4256

AMOUNT: Full tuition (40); 1/2 tuition (80)
DEADLINE(S): March 22
FIELD(S): Electronics Engineering Technology; Computer Information Systems; Business Operations; Telecommunications Management; Accounting

40 full-tuition & 80 1/2-tuition undergraduate scholarships. Open to US high school graduates who wish to enroll in a fully-accredited bachelor of science degree program at one of the DeVry Institutes located throughout North America.

Awards renewable provided 2.5 GPA is maintained. Contact your guidance counselor, nearest DeVry Institute, or address above for complete information.

196

ELECTRONIC INDUSTRIES FOUNDATION
(Scholarship Fund)
919 18th St.; Suite 900
Washington DC 20006
202/955-5814

AMOUNT: $2000

DEADLINE(S): February 1

FIELD(S): Aeronautics; Computer Science; Electrical Engineering; Engineering Technology; Applied Mathematics; Microbiology

Open to disabled students who are pursuing careers in high-tech areas through academic or technical training. Awards tenable at recognized undergraduate & graduate colleges & universities. Must be US citizen. Financial need is considered.

6 awards per year. Renewable. Write for complete information.

197

PACIFIC GAS & ELECTRIC CO.
(Scholarships for High School Seniors)
77 Beale St.; Room 2837
San Francisco CA 94106
415/973-1338

AMOUNT: $1000–$4000

DEADLINE(S): November 15

FIELD(S): Engineering; Computer Science; Mathematics; Marketing; Business; Economics

High school seniors in good academic standing who reside in or attend high school in areas served by PG&E are eligible to compete for scholarships awarded on a regional basis. Not open to children of PG&E employees.

36 awards per year. Applications & brochures are available in all high schools within PG&E's service area and at PG&E offices.

198

RADIO FREE EUROPE/RADIO LIBERTY
(Engineering Intern Program)
Personnel Division; 1201 Connecticut Ave. NW
Washington DC 20036
202/457-6936

AMOUNT: Daily stipend of 55 German marks + accommodations

DEADLINE(S): February 22

FIELD(S): Electrical Engineering

Internship in Germany open to graduate or exceptionally qualified undergrad electrical engineering students. Preference to those who have completed courses in subjects related to the technical aspects of international broadcasting.

At least basic ability to speak German is highly desirable. Write for complete information.

199

SOCIETY OF WOMEN ENGINEERS
(General Motors Foundation Scholarships)
120 Wall St.; 11th Floor
New York NY 10005
800/666-ISWE; FAX 212/509-0224

AMOUNT: $1000

DEADLINE(S): February 1

FIELD(S): Mechanical; Electrical; Chemical; Industrial; Materials; Automotive or Manufacturing Engineering or Engineering Technology

Open to women entering their junior year at selected universities having a declared major in one of the fields listed above. Recipients must demonstrate leadership characteristics.

Renewable for senior year. Applications available October–January only. Send self-addressed stamped envelope for complete information.

200

VERTICAL FLIGHT FOUNDATION
(Undergraduate/Graduate Scholarships)
217 N. Washington St.
Alexandria VA 22314
703/684-6777

AMOUNT: Up to $2000

DEADLINE(S): February 1

FIELD(S): Mechanical Engineering; Electrical Engineering; Aerospace Engineering

Annual scholarships open to undergraduate & graduate students in the above areas who are interested in pursuing careers in some aspect of helicopter or vertical flight. For full-time study at accredited school of engineering.

Write for complete information.

ENGINEERING TECHNOLOGY

201

AMERICAN NUCLEAR SOCIETY
(John & Muriel Landis Scholarships)
555 North Kensington Ave.
La Grange Park IL 60526
312/352-6611

AMOUNT: $3500
DEADLINE(S): March 1
FIELD(S): Nuclear Engineering

Open to any undergraduate or graduate student who has greater-than-average financial need & is planning a career in nuclear engineering or a nuclear-related field. Awards tenable at accredited institutions in the US.

Must be US citizen or have a permanent resident visa. 8 awards per year. Write for complete information & include a SASE.

202

AMERICAN NUCLEAR SOCIETY
(Undergraduate Scholarships)
555 North Kensington Ave.
La Grange Park IL 60526
312/352-6611

AMOUNT: Varies
DEADLINE(S): March 1
FIELD(S): Nuclear Engineering

Scholarships open to undergraduate students who have completed at least 1 year of study in an accredited nuclear engineering (or nuclear-related area) program at a college or university in the US. Must be US citizen or legal resident.

Write & include a SASE for complete information.

203

AMERICAN SOCIETY OF HEATING, REFRIGERATION, & AIR-CONDITIONING ENGINEERS
(ASHRAE Scholarship Fund)
1791 Tullie Circle NE
Atlanta GA 30329
404/636-8400

AMOUNT: $2000–$5000
DEADLINE(S): December 1
FIELD(S): Heating; Refrigeration & Air-conditioning; Ventilation

Open to undergraduate students who plan a career in the above fields. Must have at least 1 full year of undergraduate study remaining. Minimum 3.0 GPA (4.0 scale). Awards tenable at accredited institutions in the USA & Canada.

Awards renewable. Financial need is considered. Write for complete information.

204

AMERICAN SOCIETY OF MECHANICAL ENGINEERS
(Auxiliary Student Loans)
345 E. 47th St.
New York NY 10017
212/705-7375

AMOUNT: Up to $2500
DEADLINE(S): April 1; November 1
FIELD(S): Mechanical Engineering; Engineering Technology

Loans to student members of ASME who are undergrad or grad students enrolled in schools with accredited mechanical engineering or engineering technology curricula. Minimum 2.2 GPA for undergrads; 3.2 GPA for grads. US citizenship required.

First preference given to undergraduate juniors and seniors. Write for complete information.

205

AMERICAN WELDING SOCIETY
(Scholarship Program)
550 NW Lejeune Rd.; P.O. Box 351040
Miami FL 33135
305/443-9353

AMOUNT: Varies
DEADLINE(S): June 1
FIELD(S): Welding Technology

Open to students who reside in the US & are
enrolled in an accredited welding and joint
material joining or similar program. Awards
are tenable at junior colleges, colleges, universities, & institutions in the US.
Write for more information.

206

AT&T BELL LABORATORIES
(Summer Research Program for Minorities &
Women)
101 Crawfords Corner RD; RM 1B-222
Holmdel NJ 07733
Written Inquiry

AMOUNT: Salary + travel & living expenses
for summer
DEADLINE(S): December 1
FIELD(S): Engineering; Math; Sciences;
Computer Science

Program offers minority students & women
students technical employment experience
at Bell Laboratories. Students should have
completed their third year of study at an
accredited college or university. USA citizen or permanent resident.
Selection is based partially on academic
achievement and personal motivation.
Write special programs manager—SRP for
complete information.

207

DEVRY INC.
(Scholarship Program)
One Tower Lane
Oakbrook Terrace IL 60181
708/571-7700; 800/323-4256

AMOUNT: Full tuition (40); 1/2 tuition (80)
DEADLINE(S): March 22
FIELD(S): Electronics Engineering
Technology; Computer Information
Systems; Business Operations;
Telecommunications Management;
Accounting

40 full-tuition & 80 1/2-tuition undergraduate
scholarships. Open to US high school graduates who wish to enroll in a fully-accredited bachelor of science degree program at
one of the Devry Institutes located throughout North America.
Awards renewable provided 2.5 GPA is maintained. Contact your guidance counselor;
nearest Devry Institute or address above
for complete information.

208

ELECTRONIC INDUSTRIES
FOUNDATION
(Scholarship Fund)
919 18th St.; Suite 900
Washington DC 20006
202/955-5814

AMOUNT: $2000
DEADLINE(S): February 1
FIELD(S): Aeronautics; Computer Science;
Electrical Engineering; Engineering
Technology; Applied Mathematics;
Microbiology

Open to disabled students who are pursuing
careers in high-tech areas through academic
or technical training. Awards tenable at recognized undergraduate & graduate colleges
& universities. Must be US citizen.
Financial need is considered.
6 awards per year. Renewable. Write for complete information.

209

INSTITUTE OF INDUSTRIAL
ENGINEERS
(IIE Scholarships)
25 Technology Park/Atlanta
Norcross GA 30092
404/449-0460

AMOUNT: Varies

DEADLINE(S): November 15 (nominations);
February 15 (applications)

FIELD(S): Industrial Engineering

Undergraduate & graduate scholarships open to active IIE members with at least 1 full year of study remaining at an accredited college or university in North America. A GPA of 3.4 or better is required.

Applications will be mailed ONLY to students nominated by their department head. Write for nomination forms & complete information.

210

**JAMES F. LINCOLN ARC WELDING
FOUNDATION**
(Awards Program)
P.O. Box 17035
Cleveland OH 44117
216/481-4300

AMOUNT: Up to $2000

DEADLINE(S): June 15

FIELD(S): Arc Welding Technology

Open to undergraduate & graduate engineering & technology students who solve design engineering or fabrication problems involving the knowledge or application of arc welding.

Total of 29 awards; 17 for undergraduate and 12 for graduate students. Write for complete information.

211

LADIES OF NORTHANTS
(Scholarship)
P.O. Box 6609
Coddingtown CA 95406
Written inquiry

AMOUNT: $250

DEADLINE(S): February 8

FIELD(S): Nuclear Engineering

The Ladies of Northants offers a scholarship to a women over 40 who immigrates to the United States from Northamptonshire, England, and is committed to a career in nuclear engineering. For undergraduate or graduate study.

Preference to natives of the village of Podington who have a 3.75 or better grade point average (4.0 scale) and can demonstrate financial need. Write for complete information.

212

**NATIONAL ASSOCIATION OF
PLUMBING-HEATING-COOLING
CONTRACTORS**
**(NAPHCC Educational Foundation
Scholarship Program)**
P.O. Box 6808
Falls Church VA 22046
703/237-8100 or 800/533-7694; FAX 703/237-7442

AMOUNT: $2500

DEADLINE(S): April 1

FIELD(S): Plumbing; Heating; Cooling

Open to NAPHCC members in good standing or family members/friends/employees sponsored by NAPHCC member. Must be high school senior or college freshman planning to attend a 4-year accredited college in the USA. Must maintain a "C" average.

Scholarships renewable for four years. Write for complete information.

213

**NATIONAL ASSOCIATION OF WATER
COMPANIES—NEW JERSEY CHAPTER**
(Scholarship)
c/o NJ-American Water Co.
66 Shrewsbury Ave.
Shrewsbury NJ 07702
908/842-6900; FAX 908/842-7541

AMOUNT: $2500

DEADLINE(S): April 1 (postmark)

FIELD(S): Business Administration; Biology;
Chemistry; Engineering

Open to USA citizens who have lived in NJ at least 5 years and plan a career in the investor-owned water utility industry in disciplines such as those above. Must be undergrad or graduate student in a 2- or 4-year NJ college or university.

GPA of 3.0 or better required. Write for complete information.

214

NCSU PULP & PAPER FOUNDATION
(Scholarships); Attn: J. Ben Chilton;
Executive Director
P.O. Box 8005
Raleigh NC 27695-8005
919/515-5661

AMOUNT: $1200–$3700
DEADLINE(S): January 15
FIELD(S): Pulp & Paper Science & Technology

Open to undergraduate students enrolled in North Carolina State University and majoring in pulp and paper science technology. USA citizen.

NC residents receive $1200; out-of-state students receive $3700. Awards renewable annually. Write for complete information.

215

NORTH AMERICAN DIE CASTING
ASSOCIATION
(David Laine Memorial Scholarships)
9701 W. Higgins Rd.; Suite 880
Rosemont IL 60018
708/292-3600

AMOUNT: varies
DEADLINE(S): May 1
FIELD(S): Die Casting Technology

Open to students enrolled at an engineering college affiliated with The Foundry Educational Foundation (FEF) & registered with FEF for the current year. USA citizen.

For undergraduate or graduate study. Write for complete information.

216

SOCIETY OF MANUFACTURING
ENGINEERING EDUCATION
FOUNDATION
(William E. Weisel Scholarship Fund)
One SME Drive
P.O. Box 930
Dearborn MI 48121
313/271-1500 ext 512

AMOUNT: $1000
DEADLINE(S): March 1
FIELD(S): Manufacturing Engineering; Engineering Technology

Open to full-time undergraduate students at accredited schools who are seeking a career in manufacturing/robotics/automated systems; have completed 30 credit hours in this area & have at least 2.75 GPA (4.0 scale). USA or Canadian citizen.

Write for complete information.

217

SOCIETY OF WOMEN ENGINEERS
(General Motors Foundation Scholarships)
120 Wall St.; 11th Floor
New York NY 10005
800/666-ISWE; FAX 212/509-0224

AMOUNT: $1000
DEADLINE(S): February 1
FIELD(S): Mechanical; Electrical; Chemical; Industrial; Materials; Automotive or Manufacturing Engineering or Engineering Technology

Open to women entering their junior year at selected universities having a declared major in one of the fields listed above. Recipients must demonstrate leadership characteristics.

Renewable for senior year. Applications available October–January only. Send self-addressed stamped envelope for complete information.

218

SOCIETY OF WOMEN ENGINEERS
(Hewlett-Packard Scholarships)
120 Wall St.; 11th Floor
New York NY 10005
800/666-ISWE; FAX 212/509-0224

AMOUNT: $1000
DEADLINE(S): February 1
FIELD(S): Electrical Engineering; Computer Science

Open to women who are juniors or seniors majoring in electrical engineering or computer science at an accredited school. Applicants must be active supporters and contributors to SWE.

Applications available October–January only. Send self-addressed stamped envelope for complete information.

219

SOCIETY OF WOMEN ENGINEERS
(Texaco Foundation Scholarships)
120 Wall St.; 11th Floor
New York NY 10005
800/666-ISWE; FAX 212/509-0224

AMOUNT: $1000
DEADLINE(S): February 1
FIELD(S): Chemical or Mechanical Engineering

Open to women in their junior year in mechanical or chemical engineering who are in the top 20% of their class at selected universities. Must be USA citizen or permanent resident and a student member of SWE.

Renewable with continued ranking in top 20% of class. Applications available October–January only. Send self-addressed stamped envelope for complete information.

220

SPIE—THE INTERNATIONAL SOCIETY FOR OPTICAL ENGINEERING
(Scholarships & Grants)
P.O. Box 10
Bellingham WA 98227
206/676-3290

AMOUNT: $500–$5000
DEADLINE(S): April 1
FIELD(S): Optical Engineering

Open to college students at all levels for study of optical or optoelectronic applied science and engineering. May be awarded to students in community colleges or technical institutes; undergraduate and graduate schools at universities.

Write to the SPIE Scholarship Committee Chair (address above) for complete information.

221

TECHNOLOGY STUDENT ASSOCIATION
(Scholarships)
1914 Association Dr.
Reston VA 22091
703/860-9000

AMOUNT: $250 to $500
DEADLINE(S): May 1
FIELD(S): Technology Education

Open to student members of the Technology Student Association who can demonstrate financial need. Grade point average is NOT a consideration but applicants must be accepted to a 4-year college or university.

Funds are sent to and administered by the recipient's college or university. Write for complete information.

222

UNIVERSITY OF MAINE PULP & PAPER FOUNDATION
(Scholarships)
5737 Jenness Hall
Orono ME 04469-5737
207/581-2296

AMOUNT: $1000; tuition
DEADLINE(S): February 15
FIELD(S): Engineering

Open to undergraduate students accepted to or enrolled in the University of Maine at Orono who have demonstrated an interest in a paper-related career. USA or Canadian citizen.

Twenty-five $1000 scholarships are awarded to 1st-year students; also 100 tuition scholarships (equal to Maine resident tuition). Write for complete information.

223

US AIR FORCE ROTC
(4-Year Scholarship Program)
AFROTC/RROO; Recruiting Operations Branch
Maxwell AFB AL 36112
205/953-2091

AMOUNT: Tuition; fees & books + $100 per month stipend
DEADLINE(S): December 1
FIELD(S): Aeronautical Engineering; Civil Engineering; Mechanical Engineering; Mathematics; Physics; Nursing & some Liberal Arts

Open to USA citizens who are at least 17 and will graduate from college before age 25. Must complete application, furnish SAT/ACT scores, high school transcripts, and record of extracurricular activities.

Must qualify on Air Force medical examination. About 1600 scholarships awarded each year at campuses which offer Air Force ROTC.

224

WASHINGTON PULP & PAPER FOUNDATION
(Scholarship Program)
c/o Univ. of Washington; Box 352100
Seattle WA 98195-2100
206/543-2763

AMOUNT: $2000 to $6000

DEADLINE(S): February 1
FIELD(S): Paper Science & Engineering

Awards are undergraduate tuition scholarships at the Univ. of Washington. Open to students who are accepted to or enrolled in the paper science & engineering curriculum at the university. US citizenship or legal residency required.

Approximately 50 awards per year. Renewable. Write for complete information.

MECHANICAL ENGINEERING

225

AMERICAN SOCIETY OF MECHANICAL ENGINEERS
(Auxiliary Student Loans)
345 E. 47th St.
New York NY 10017
212/705-7375

AMOUNT: Up to $2500
DEADLINE(S): April 1; November 1
FIELD(S): Mechanical Engineering; Engineering Technology

Loans to student members of ASME who are undergrad or grad students enrolled in schools with accredited mechanical engineering or engineering technology curricula. Minimum 2.2 GPA for undergrads; 3.2 GPA for grads. US citizenship required.

First preference given to undergraduate juniors and seniors. Write for complete information.

226

AMERICAN SOCIETY OF MECHANICAL ENGINEERS AUXILIARY INC.
(Sylvia W. Farny Scholarship)
345 E. 47th St.
New York NY 10017-2392
212/705-7746

AMOUNT: $1500
DEADLINE(S): February 15

FIELD(S): Mechanical Engineering

Open to US citizens enrolled in junior year of undergraduate study in school with accredited mechanical engineering curricula in USA. Award is for senior year of study. Must be student member of ASME.

4–6 scholarships per year. Send inquiries to Mrs. Sue Flanders; 3556 Stevens Way; Martinez GA 30907. Requests for applications must be received by chairman by February 1.

227

ASM FOUNDATION FOR EDUCATION & RESEARCH
Scholarship Program
Materials Park OH 44073
216/338-5151

AMOUNT: 34 $500 awards; 3 $2000 awards; 1 full tuition award
DEADLINE(S): June 15
FIELD(S): Metallurgy; Materials Science

Open to undergraduate students who are majoring in metallurgy/materials and have completed at least 1 year of study. For citizens of USA, Canada, or Mexico who are enrolled in a recognized college or university in one of those countries.

For full tuition award must be in junior or senior year and demonstrate financial need. Write for complete information.

228

AT&T BELL LABORATORIES
(Summer Research Program for Minorities & Women)
101 Crawfords Corner Rd.; RM 1B-222
Holmdel NJ 07733
Written Inquiry

AMOUNT: Salary + travel & living expenses for summer
DEADLINE(S): December 1
FIELD(S): Engineering; Math; Sciences; Computer Science

Program offers minority students & women students technical employment experience at Bell Laboratories. Students should have completed their third year of study at an accredited college or university. USA citizen or permanent resident.

Selection is based partially on academic achievement and personal motivation. Write special programs manager—SRP for complete information.

229

NATIONAL ASSOCIATION OF WATER COMPANIES—NEW JERSEY CHAPTER (Scholarship)
c/o NJ-American Water Co.
66 Shrewsbury Ave.
Shrewsbury NJ 07702
908/842-6900; FAX 908/842-7541

AMOUNT: $2500
DEADLINE(S): April 1 (postmark)
FIELD(S): Business Administration; Biology; Chemistry; Engineering

Open to USA citizens who have lived in NJ at least 5 years and plan a career in the investor-owned water utility industry in disciplines such as those above. Must be undergrad or graduate student in a 2- or 4-year NJ college or university.

GPA of 3.0 or better required. Write for complete information.

230

SOCIETY OF WOMEN ENGINEERS
(General Motors Foundation Scholarships)
120 Wall St.; 11th Floor
New York NY 10005
800/666-ISWE; FAX 212/509-0224

AMOUNT: $1000
DEADLINE(S): February 1
FIELD(S): Mechanical; Electrical; Chemical; Industrial; Materials; Automotive or Manufacturing Engineering or Engineering Technology

Open to women entering their junior year at selected universities having a declared major in one of the fields listed above. Recipients must demonstrate leadership characteristics.

Renewable for senior year. Applications available October–January only. Send self-addressed stamped envelope for complete information.

231

SOCIETY OF WOMEN ENGINEERS
(Texaco Foundation Scholarships)
120 Wall St.; 11th Floor
New York NY 10005
800/666-ISWE; FAX 212/509-0224

AMOUNT: $1000
DEADLINE(S): February 1
FIELD(S): Chemical or Mechanical Engineering

Open to women in their junior year in mechanical or chemical engineering who are in the top 20% of their class at selected universities. Must be USA citizen or permanent resident and a student member of SWE.

Renewable with continued ranking in top 20% of class. Applications available October–January only. Send self-addressed stamped envelope for complete information.

232

US AIR FORCE ROTC
(4-Year Scholarship Program)
AFROTC/RROO; Recruiting Operations Branch
Maxwell AFB AL 36112
205/953-2091

AMOUNT: Tuition; fees & books + $100 per month stipend
DEADLINE(S): December 1
FIELD(S): Aeronautical Engineering; Civil Engineering; Mechanical Engineering; Mathematics; Physics; Nursing & some Liberal Arts

Open to USA citizens who are at least 17 and will graduate from college before age 25. Must complete application, furnish SAT/ACT scores, high school transcripts and record of extracurricular activities.

Must qualify on Air Force medical examination. About 1600 scholarships awarded each year at campuses which offer Air Force ROTC.

233

VERTICAL FLIGHT FOUNDATION
(Undergraduate/Graduate Scholarships)
217 N. Washington St.
Alexandria VA 22314
703/684-6777

AMOUNT: Up to $2000
DEADLINE(S): February 1
FIELD(S): Mechanical Engineering; Electrical Engineering; Aerospace Engineering

Annual scholarships open to undergraduate & graduate students in the above areas who are interested in pursuing careers in some aspect of helicopter or vertical flight. For full-time study at accredited school of engineering.

Write for complete information.

234

WEBB INSTITUTE
(Naval Architecture Scholarships)
Crescent Beach Rd.
Glen Cove NY 11542
516/671-2213

AMOUNT: Full tuition for 4 years
DEADLINE(S): February 15
FIELD(S): Naval Architecture; Marine Engineering

Open to high school students aged 16–24 who are in the top 10% of their class & have at least a 3.2 GPA (4.0 scale). Selection based on college boards, SAT scores, demonstrated interest in above areas, & interview. US citizenship required.

20 to 25 four-year full tuition undergrad scholarships per year to Webb Institute. Write for complete information.

235

WOMEN'S AUXILIARY TO THE AMERICAN INSTITUTE OF MINING METALLURGICAL & PETROLEUM ENGINEERS
(WAAIME Scholarship Loan Fund)
345 E. 47th St.; 14th Floor
New York NY 10017
Written inquiry only

AMOUNT: Varies
DEADLINE(S): March 15
FIELD(S): Earth Sciences; Mining Engineering; Petroleum Engineering

Open to undergraduate juniors & seniors and grad students. Eligible applicants receive a scholarship loan for all or part of their education. Recipients repay only 50% with no interest charges.

Repayment to begin by 6 months after graduation and be completed within 6 years. Write to WAAIME Scholarship Loan Fund (address above) for complete information.

SCHOOL OF HUMANITIES

236

ASSOCIATION FOR EDUCATION IN JOURNALISM & MASS COMMUNICATION
(Correspondents Fund Scholarships)
University of SC College of Journalism
Columbia SC 29208
803/777-2005

AMOUNT: Up to $3000
DEADLINE(S): April 30
FIELD(S): Journalism; Mass Communications; Liberal Arts

Open to children of print or broadcast journalists who are foreign correspondents for a USA news medium. For undergraduate, graduate, or post-graduate study at any accredited college or university in the USA.

Preference to journalism or communications majors. 8–15 renewable awards per year. Write for complete information.

237

CAPE CANAVERAL CHAPTER RETIRED OFFICERS ASSOC.
(Scholarships)
P.O. Box 4186
Patrick AFB FL 32925
Written inquiry

AMOUNT: Approximately $1500 per year
DEADLINE(S): May 31
FIELD(S): Science; Mathematics; Engineering; Liberal Arts; Chemistry

Open ONLY to Brevard County Florida residents who are undergraduate juniors or seniors at any 4-year college in the USA and the son or daughter of active duty or retired military personnel. Must be US citizen.

Awards renewable for one year. Write to the scholarship program committee (address above) for complete information.

238

CHAUTAUQUA INSTITUTION
(Scholarships)
Schools Office; Box 1098; Dept. 6
Chautauqua NY 14722
716/357-6233

AMOUNT: Varies
DEADLINE(S): April 1
FIELD(S): Art; Music; Dance; Theater

Scholarships for summer school only. Awards are based on auditions (portfolio in art) indicating proficiency; financial need is a consideration.

Some auditions are required in person but taped auditions also are acceptable. 250 awards per year. Write or call for complete information.

239

CIVIL AIR PATROL
(CAP Undergraduate Scholarships)
　National Headquarters
　Maxwell AFB AL 36112
　205/293-5315

AMOUNT: $750

DEADLINE(S): October 1

FIELD(S): Humanities; Science; Engineering;
　Education

Open to CAP members who have received the
　Billy Mitchell Award or the senior rating in
　level II of the senior training program. For
　undergraduate study in the above areas.

Write for complete information.

240

**NATIONAL LEAGUE OF AMERICAN
PEN WOMEN INC.**
(Scholarship Grants for Mature Women)
　1300 Seventeenth St. NW
　Washington DC 20036
　202/785-1997

AMOUNT: $1000

DEADLINE(S): January 15

FIELD(S): Art; Music; Creative Writing

The National League of American Pen
　Women gives three $1000 grants in even-
　numbered years to women aged 35 and
　over. Should submit slides, manuscripts, or
　musical compositions suited to the criteria
　for that year.

Write for complete information.

241

UNITARIAN UNIVERSALIST ASSN.
(Stanfield Scholarship Program)
　25 Beacon Street
　Boston MA 02108
　617/742-2100

AMOUNT: $1000–$3000

DEADLINE(S): February 15

FIELD(S): Art; Law; Music

Art scholarships for undergraduate or gradu-
　ate study. Law scholarships for graduates
　only. Applicants must be Unitarian
　Universalists.

Send a self-addressed stamped envelope to the
　above address for complete information. No
　phone calls please.

AREA STUDIES

242

**AMERICAN ASSOCIATION OF
TEACHERS OF FRENCH**
(National French Contest)
　Sidney L. Teitelbaum; Box 1178
　Long Beach NY 11561
　516/897-8119; FAX 516/938-2273

AMOUNT: Varies

DEADLINE(S): February 1

FIELD(S): French Language; French Studies

National French contest is an examination
　taken throughout the country. Students are
　ranked regionally and nationally and are
　eligible for both regional and national
　awards.

Not a scholarship. Winners receive trips,
　medals, and books. Write for complete
　information.

243

**COMMITTEE ON INSTITUTIONAL
COOPERATION**
(CIC Pre-doctoral Fellowships)
　Indiana University; 803 East 8th St.
　Bloomington IN 47408
　812/855-0823

AMOUNT: $11,000 + tuition (4 years)

DEADLINE(S): December 1

FIELD(S): Humanities; Social Sciences;
　Natural Sciences; Mathematics; Engineering

Pre-doctoral fellowships for US citizens of
　African American, American Indian;
　Mexican American, or Puerto Rican her-
　itage. Must hold or expect to receive bache-

lor's degree by late summer from a regionally accredited college or unviersity.

Awards for specified universities in IL, IN, IA,
MI, MN, OH, WI, PA. Write for details.

244

CREOLE-AMERICAN GENEALOGICAL SOCIETY INC.
(Creole Scholarships)
P.O. Box 3215; Church Street Station
New York NY 10008
Written inquiry only

AMOUNT: $1500

DEADLINE(S): Apply between January 1
and April 30

FIELD(S): Genealogy or language or Creole
culture

Awards in the above areas open to individuals
of mixed racial ancestry who submit a four-
generation genealogical chart attesting to
Creole ancestry and/or inter-racial parentage. For undergraduate or graduate
study/research.

For scholarship/award information send $2
money order and self-addressed stamped
envelope to address above. Cash and personal checks are not accepted. Letters without SASE and handling charge will not be
answered.

245

DUMBARTON OAKS
(The Bliss Prize Fellowship in Byzantine Studies)
1703 32nd St. NW
Washington DC 20007
202/342-3232

AMOUNT: Up to $31,000

DEADLINE(S): November 1

FIELD(S): Byzantine Studies

Open to outstanding college seniors who plan
to enter the field of Byzantine studies. Must
be in last year of studies or already hold BA
and have completed at least one year of
Greek by the end of the senior year.

Students must be nominated by their advisors
by October 15 and attend grad school in the
USA or Canada. Write for complete information.

246

EAST-WEST CENTER
(Undergraduate Fellowships for Pacific Islanders)
1777 East-West Rd.; Room 2066
Honolulu HI 96848
Written inquiry

AMOUNT: Varies

DEADLINE(S): January 14

FIELD(S): Asian Pacific Studies

Open to Pacific Islanders who wish to pursue
studies relevant to development needs in
the Pacific Islands region. Applicants
should have a strong academic record and a
desire to broaden their knowledge of the
Pacific, Asia, and the USA.

Write for complete information.

247

IRISH AMERICAN CULTURAL INSTITUTE
(Irish Way Scholarships)
Plaza Building; Suite 204
3 Elm St.
Morristown NJ 07960
609/647-5678

AMOUNT: $250 - $1000

DEADLINE(S): April

FIELD(S): Irish Studies

A summer study & recreation program in the
Republic of Ireland. Open to 9th–11th
grade high school students who have an
interest in Irish culture & are USA citizens.
This is NOT a scholarship.

30–40 awards per year. Write for complete
information.

248

MEMORIAL FOUNDATION FOR JEWISH CULTURE
(International Scholarship Program for Community Service)
15 East 26th St.; Room 1903
New York NY 10010
212/679-4074

AMOUNT: Varies
DEADLINE(S): November 30
FIELD(S): Jewish Studies

Open to any individual regardless of country of origin for undergrad study that leads to careers in the Rabbinate, Jewish education, social work, or as religious functionaries in Diaspora Jewish communities outside the USA, Israel, & Canada.

Must commit to serve in a community of need for 3 years. Those planning to serve in the USA, Canada, or Israel are excluded from this program. Write for complete information.

249

MEMORIAL FOUNDATION FOR JEWISH CULTURE
(Soviet Jewry Community Service Scholarship Program)
15 East 26th St.; Room 1901
New York NY 10010
212/679-4074

AMOUNT: Not specified
DEADLINE(S): November 30
FIELD(S): Jewish studies

Open to Soviet Jews enrolled or planning to enroll in recognized institutions of higher Jewish learning. Must agree to serve a community of Soviet Jews anywhere in the world for a minimum of three years.

Grants are to help prepare well qualified Soviet Jews to serve in the USSR or wherever the foundation deems necessary. Write for complete information.

250

MINISTRY OF EDUCATION OF THE REPUBLIC OF CHINA
(Scholarships for Foreign Students)
5 South Chung-Shan Road
Taipei; Taiwan R.O.C.
321-6375; 321-7644

AMOUNT: $8000
DEADLINE(S): Between February 1 and April 30
FIELD(S): Chinese Studies

Undergrad and graduate scholarships are available to foreign students wishing to study in Taiwan who have already studied in R.O.C. for at least one academic year. Must study full time.

Scholarships are renewable. 300 awards per year. Write for complete information.

251

MONGOLIA SOCIETY
(Dr. Gombojab Hangin Memorial Scholarship)
321-322 Goodbody Hall; Indiana Univ.
Bloomington IN 47405
812/855-4078

AMOUNT: $2500
DEADLINE(S): January 1
FIELD(S): Mongolian Studies

Open to students of Mongolian nationality (permanent resident of Mongolia, China, or the former Soviet Union) to pursue Mongolian studies in the USA: Recipient will receive money in one lump sum upon arrival in the USA.

Report on recipient's activities is due at conclusion of the award year. Write for complete information.

252

NELLIE MARTIN CARMAN SCHOLARSHIP TRUST
(Scholarships)
18223 73rd Ave. NE; #B101
Bothell WA 98011
206/486-6575

AMOUNT: Up to $1000

DEADLINE(S): March 15

FIELD(S): All fields of study except those noted below

Open to high school seniors in King, Pierce, & Snohomish Counties (WA). For undergraduate study in the state of Washington in all fields EXCEPT music, sculpting, drawing, interior design, & home economics. US citizenship required.

Applications available only through high schools & nomination by counselor is required. Awards are renewable. Write for complete information.

253

RADIO FREE EUROPE/RADIO LIBERTY
(Media & Opinion Research on Eastern Europe & the Former Soviet Union)
Personnel Division; 1201 Connecticut Ave. NW
Washington DC 20036
Written inquiry

AMOUNT: Daily stipend of 48 German marks plus accommodations

DEADLINE(S): February 22

FIELD(S): Communications; Market Research; Statistics; Sociology; Social Psychology; East European Studies

Internship open to graduate students or exceptionally qualified undergrads in the above areas who can demonstrate knowledge of quantitative research methods; computer applications and public opinion survey techniques.

East European language skills would be an advantage. Write for complete information.

254

SONS OF NORWAY FOUNDATION
(King Olav V. Norwegian-American Heritage Fund)
1455 West Lake Street
Minneapolis MN 55408
612/827-3611

AMOUNT: $250 - $3000

DEADLINE(S): March 1

FIELD(S): Norwegian Studies

Open to USA citizens 18 or older who have demonstrated a keen and sincere interest in the Norwegian heritage. The student must be enrolled in a recognized educational institution and be studying a subject related to the Norwegian heritage.

Financial need is a consideration but it is secondary to scholarship. 12 awards per year. Write for complete information.

ART

255

ACADEMY OF MOTION PICTURE ARTS AND SCIENCES
(Student Academy Awards Competition)
8949 Wilshire Blvd.
Beverly Hills CA 90211
310/247-3000

AMOUNT: $2000; $1500; $1000

DEADLINE(S): April 3

FIELD(S): Filmmaking

Student academy awards competition is open to student filmmakers who have no professional experience and are enrolled in accredited colleges and universities. Awards are for COMPLETED film projects ONLY.

Write for complete information.

256

AMERICAN COLLEGE FOR THE APPLIED ARTS
(Emilio Pucci Scholarships)
3330 Peachtree Rd. NE; Admissions Office
Atlanta GA 30326
404/231-9000

AMOUNT: $1800 (distributed over 6 quarters)

DEADLINE(S): May 1

FIELD(S): Fashion Design; Fashion Marketing; Interior Design; Commercial Art; Business Administration; Video Production

Scholarships are for high school seniors who are interested in either a 2-year or 4-year program at one of the American Colleges for the Applied Arts in Atlanta, Los Angeles, or London. Scholarship is applied toward tuition.

Write for applications and complete information.

257

AMERICAN WOMEN IN RADIO & TELEVISION
(Houston Internship Program)
Aprille Meek; AWRT—Houston; P.O. Box 980908
Houston TX 77098
Written inquiry

AMOUNT: $500 per year

DEADLINE(S): March 1

FIELD(S): Radio; Television; Film & Video; Advertising; Marketing

Internships open to students who are juniors, seniors, or graduate students at greater Houston-area colleges & universities.

Write for complete information.

258

ARTS INTERNATIONAL; INSTITUTE OF INTERNATIONAL EDUCATION
(Cintas Fellowship Program)
809 United Nations Plaza
New York NY 10017
212/984-5370

AMOUNT: $10,000

DEADLINE(S): March 1

FIELD(S): Architecture; Painting; Photography; Sculpture; Printmaking; Music Composition; Creative Writing

Fellowships open to artists who are of Cuban ancestry or Cuban citizens living outside of Cuba. They are intended to foster &

encourage the professional development & recognition of talented creative artists in the above areas.

Fellowships are not awarded for furtherance of academic study. 5–10 awards per year. Write for complete information.

259

BLACK AMERICAN CINEMA SOCIETY
(Filmmakers Grants Program)
3617 Montclair Street
Los Angeles CA 90018
213/737-3292; FAX 213/737-2842

AMOUNT: Up to $3000

DEADLINE(S): February 27

FIELD(S): Filmmaking

Open to Black filmmakers. Applications accepted only from the individual(s) who has primary creative responsibility for the film. Project (1 per grant cycle) may be submitted in 16mm film or 3/4" video. US citizenship or legal residency.

Projects must be made in the US. Write for complete information.

260

BUSH FOUNDATION
(Bush Artist Fellowships)
E900 First National Bank Bldg.
322 Minnesota St.
St. Paul MN 55101
612/227-5222 or 899/605-7315

AMOUNT: Up to $36,000 fellowship

DEADLINE(S): Late October/early November

FIELD(S): Literature; Music Composition; Choreography; Visual Arts; Scriptworks; Film/Video

Open to writers, visual artists, composers, & choreographers who are residents of MN, ND, SD, or western WI & who are at least 25 years old. Awards are to help artists work full-time in their chosen field—NOT for academic study!

Students are NOT eligible to apply! 15 fellowships per year; 12–18 months in duration. Write for complete information.

261

CALIFORNIA COLLEGE OF ARTS & CRAFTS
(Undergraduate and Graduate Scholarships)
5212 Broadway
Oakland CA 94618
510/653-8118

AMOUNT: Varies
DEADLINE(S): March 1
FIELD(S): Art

Open to undergraduate and graduate students accepted to or enrolled in a degree program at the California College of Arts and Crafts. Must be a US citizen or legal resident and demonstrate financial need.
Approximately 600 awards per year. Renewble. Contact Office of Enrollment Services for complete information.

262

DISTRICT OF COLUMBIA COMMISSION ON THE ARTS & HUMANITIES
(Grants)
410 Eighth St. NW; 5th Floor
Washington DC 20004
202/724-5613; TDD 202/727-318; FAX 202/727-4135

AMOUNT: $5000
DEADLINE(S): March 1
FIELD(S): Arts; Performing Arts; Literature

Applicants for grants must be professional artists and residents of Washington DC for at least one year prior to submitting application. Awards intended to generate art endeavors within the Washington DC community.
Open also to art organizations that train, exhibit, or perform within DC. 150 grants per year. Write for complete information.

263

FLORIDA ARTS COUNCIL
(Individual Artists' Fellowships)
FL Dept. of State; Div. of Cultural Affairs; State Capitol
Tallahassee FL 32399-0250
904/487-2980

AMOUNT: $5000
DEADLINE(S): January 25
FIELD(S): Visual Arts; Dance; Folk Arts; Media; Music; Theater; Literary Arts; Interdisciplinary

Fellowships awarded to individual artists in the above areas. Must be Florida residents, US citizens, and over 18 years old. May NOT be a degree-seeking student—funding is for support of artistic endeavors only.
Forty awards per year. Write for complete information.

264

FOUNDATION OF FLEXOGRAPHIC TECHNICAL ASSN.
(Flexography Scholarships)
900 Marconi Ave.
Ronkonkoma NY 11779
516/737-6026

AMOUNT: $500
DEADLINE(S): March 20
FIELD(S): Flexography/Graphic Arts

Open to students with at least a 3.0 GPA interested in a career in Flexography. Must be presently enrolled in a college which offers Flexography. Students in 2-year colleges may apply.
Must be a sophomore or junior. Approx 14 renewable scholarships per year.

265

FRANCES HOOK SCHOLARSHIP FUND
(2-Dimensional Art Contest)
Box 597346
Chicago IL 60659-7346
708/673-ARTS; FAX 708/673-2782

AMOUNT: $350 to $3000

DEADLINE(S): March 1

FIELD(S): Art

Open to full-time undergraduate art students age 24 or younger. Awards are intended to pay for art supplies and/or tuition for art classes.

Total prize money is $55,000. 74 awards per year. Write for complete information.

266

GEORGIA COUNCIL FOR THE ARTS
(Individual Artist Grants)
530 Means St. NW; Suite 115
Atlanta GA 30318-5793
404/651-7920

AMOUNT: Up to $5000

DEADLINE(S): April 1

FIELD(S): The Arts

Grants to support artistic projects by professional artists who have been Georgia residents at least one year prior to application. Selection is based on project's artistic merit and its potential for career development.

Grants do NOT support academic study. Write for complete information.

267

HAYSTACK MOUNTAIN SCHOOL OF CRAFTS
(Scholarship Program)
Admissions Office; P.O. Box 518
Deer Isle ME 04627
207/348-2306

AMOUNT: Varies

DEADLINE(S): March 25

FIELD(S): Crafts

Scholarships are for study in graphics, ceramics, weaving, jewelry, glass, blacksmithing, fabric, & wood. Limited work scholarships also are available.

Scholarships are tenable at the school of crafts for the six summer sessions. Each session is two or three weeks long. Write for complete information.

268

HOME FASHION PRODUCTS ASSN.
(Design Competition)
355 Lexington Ave.
New York NY 10017
212/661-4261

AMOUNT: $1000

DEADLINE(S): June 30

FIELD(S): Interior Design; Fashion Design

Annual textile or home furnishings design competition open to any undergraduate student who is enrolled in an accredited 2-year or 4-year school of art or design.

Application accepted from department chairman only—NOT individuals. Write for complete information.

269

ILLINOIS ARTS COUNCIL
(Artists Fellowship Awards)
100 W. Randolph; Suite 10-500
Chicago IL 60601
312/814-6750

AMOUNT: $500; $5000; $10,000

DEADLINE(S): September 1

FIELD(S): Choreography; Visual Arts; Poetr;y Prose; Film; Video; Playwriting; Music Composition; Crafts; Ethnic & Folk Arts; Performance Art; Photography; Audio Art.

Open to professional artists who are Illinois residents. Awards are in recognition of work in the above areas; they are not for continuing study. Students are NOT eligible.

Write to address above for application form.

270

LADIES AUXILIARY TO THE VETERANS OF FOREIGN WARS OF THE UNITED STATES
(Young American Patriotic Art Award)
Attn Judy Millick; Admin. of Programs
406 W. 34th St.
Kansas City MO 64111
816/561-8655

AMOUNT: $300–$2500
DEADLINE(S): April 15
FIELD(S): Art competition

This program gives high school students an opportunity to display their artistic talents and ideas on America and at the same time be eligible for funds to further their art education. US citizenship required.

Contact local VFW auxiliary office or address above for complete information.

271

MEMPHIS COLLEGE OF ART
(Portfolio Awards)
Overton Park
1930 Poplar Ave.
Memphis TN 38104
Written inquiry

AMOUNT: $200–$4275 (half tuition) per year
DEADLINE(S): November 15–June 15
FIELD(S): Visual Arts

Awards are given to excellent visual art portfolios submitted by either high school students or transfer students. Awards to be used for full-time enrollment at Memphis College of Art. International students are welcome.

Awards are renewable for four years. Write for complete information.

272

METROPOLITAN MUSEUM OF ART
(Internships)
1000 Fifth Avenue
New York NY 10028-0198
212/570-3710

AMOUNT: $2750 (grads); $8000 (minority grads); $12,000 (disadvantaged NYers); $2500 (college juniors & seniors)
DEADLINE(S): January & February
FIELD(S): Art History & related fields

Internships open to undergraduates & graduates who intend to pursue careers in art museums. Programs vary in length & requirements. Interns work in curatorial, education; conservation, administration, or library department of museum.
Write for complete information.

273

MINNESOTA STATE ARTS BOARD
(Grants Program)
432 Summit Ave.
St. Paul MN 55102
612/297-2603

AMOUNT: Fellowships $6000; Career Opportunity Grants $100_$1000 or Special Residency Stipend.
DEADLINE(S): August—Visual Arts; September—Music & Dance; October—Literature & Theater
FIELD(S): Literature; Music; Theater; Dance; Visual Arts

Fellowship grants open to professional artists who are residents of Minnesota. Grants are not intended for support of tuition or work toward any degree.

Career opportunity grants and fellowships are available.

274

NATIONAL ENDOWMENT FOR THE ARTS
(Visual Artists Fellowships)
1100 Pennsylvania Ave. NW
Washington DC 20506
202/682-5448

AMOUNT: $15,000–$20,000
DEADLINE(S): Various in January, February, & March
FIELD(S): Visual Arts

Fellowships open to practicing professional artists of exceptional talent in all areas of the visual arts. Awards are to assist creative development. They will not support academic study. USA citizen or legal resident.

Students are NOT eligible to apply. Write for complete information.

275

NATIONAL FOUNDATION FOR ADVANCEMENT IN THE ARTS (Arts Recognition and Talent Search)
   800 Brickell Ave.; #500
   Miami FL 33131
   305/377-1147

AMOUNT: $100–$3000
DEADLINE(S): October 1
FIELD(S): Creative Arts; Performing Arts

Open to high school seniors with talent in such arts as dance, music, music/jazz, theater, visual arts, film, video, and writing. Awards can be used anywhere for any purpose. For US citizens or residents. Entry fee is required.

Approximately 300 awards per year. Write for complete information.

276

NATIONAL SCHOLARSHIP TRUST FUND OF THE GRAPHIC ARTS
   4615 Forbes Ave.
   Pittsburgh PA 15213
   412/621-6941

AMOUNT: $500–$1500 (scholarships); $1500–$4000 (fellowships)
DEADLINE(S): January 10—Fellowships; March 1—High School Seniors; April 1—College Students
FIELD(S): Graphic Communications

Open to students enrolled full time in a two- or four-year program in graphic communications and related fields. Fellowships also are available for post-graduate studies. Scholarships are renewed if student maintains a 3.0 yearly GPA.

Approx 100 awards per year. Write for complete information.

277

NATIONAL SCULPTURE SOCIETY (Young Sculptor Awards Competition)
   1177 Avenue of the Americas
   New York NY 10036
   212/764-5645

AMOUNT: $1000; $750; $500; $250
DEADLINE(S): May 31
FIELD(S): Sculpture

Competition is open to sculptors under age 36 who are residents of the USA. A jury of professional sculptors will make their selections based upon 5–10 black & white 8×10 photos of each entrant's works.

In addition to cash awards & prizes, photos of winners' works will be published in Sculpture Review magazine. Please send SASE for complete information.

278

OHIO ARTS COUNCIL (OAC Scholarship Program)
   727 E. Main St.
   Columbus OH 43205-1796
   614/466-2613

AMOUNT: $1000
DEADLINE(S): April 15 (senior year of high school)
FIELD(S): Dance; Music; Theater Arts; Visual Arts; Writing

Open to Ohio residents who are high school seniors wishing to continue their arts training and education at an accredited college or university in the State of Ohio.
Write for complete information.

279

PASTEL SOCIETY OF AMERICA (PSA Scholarships)
   15 Gramercy Park South
   New York NY 10003
   212/533-6931

AMOUNT: Tuition only for PSA-sponsored classes (no cash awards)

DEADLINE(S): May 30 (for submission of slides)

FIELD(S): Painting (pastels only)

Open to talanted pastel artists at all levels of study. Awards are for the study of pastel arts at the Art Students League, PSA studio, or with a private PSA teacher. Duration ranges from 1 week to 1 class per week for 1 year.

30–40 awards per year. Write for complete information.

280

SAN FRANCISCO FOUNDATION
(James D. Phelan Art Awards)
685 Market St.; Suite 910
San Francisco CA 94105
415/495-3100 or 510/436-3100

AMOUNT: $2500

DEADLINE(S): Early fall

FIELD(S): Printmaking; Photography; Film & Video

Open to California-born artists in the above areas. Printmaking & photography awards in odd-numbered years and film & video awards in even-numbered years. US citizenship required.

Awards will be presented at a public reception and screening of winners' works. Write for complete information.

281

SCRIPPS HOWARD FOUNDATION
(Charles M. Schulz Award)
312 Walnut St.; 28th Floor; P.O. Box 5380
Cincinnati OH 45201-5380
513/977-3035

AMOUNT: $2000

DEADLINE(S): January 14

FIELD(S): College Cartoonist

Award to honor outstanding college cartoonists & to encourage them to launch post-graduate professional careers. Open to any student cartoonist at a college newspaper or magazine in the US or its territories.

Applications available during the fall months. Write for complete information.

282

SCRIPPS HOWARD FOUNDATION
(Robert P. Scripps Graphic Arts Scholarships)
312 Walnut St.; 28th Floor; P.O. Box 5380
Cincinnati OH 45201-5380
513/977-3035

AMOUNT: Up to $3000

DEADLINE(S): February 25

FIELD(S): Graphic Arts (as applied to newspaper industry)

Open to full-time undergrad students majoring in graphic arts as applied to the newspaper industry, who (in the opinion of college authorities) have the potential of becoming administrators in newspaper production. US citizenship required.

Renewable with reapplication. Submit letter with request for scholarship application by December 20 stating college major, academic year, & career goal. Write or call for complete information.

283

SMITHSONIAN INSTITUTION
(Cooper-Hewitt Museum of Design Summer Internships)
Cooper-Hewitt Museum; 2 East 91st St.
New York NY 10128
212/860-6868; FAX 212/860-6909

AMOUNT: Varies

DEADLINE(S): March 31

FIELD(S): Art; Design; Architecture; Museum Studies

10-week summer internships at the Cooper-Hewitt Museum open to undergraduate and graduate students.

Write for complete information.

284

**SMITHSONIAN INSTITUTION
(Minority Undergraduate & Graduate
Internship)**
    Office of Fellowships & Grants
    955 L'Enfant Plaza; Suite 7000
    Washington DC 20560
    202/287-3271
AMOUNT: $250 to $300/week stipend +
    travel
DEADLINE(S): February 15; June 15;
    October 15
FIELD(S): Design; Architecture; Art;
    Museum Studies
Internships open to minority students for
    research & study at the Smithsonian or
    Cooper-Hewitt Museum of Design in New
    York City. The museum's collection spans
    3000 years of design from ancient pottery to
    modern fashion & advertising.
Undergraduates receive $250 per week
    stipend & graduate students receive $300
    per week stipend. Write for complete infor-
    mation.

285

**SMITHSONIAN INSTITUTION
(Peter Krueger Summer Internship Program)**
    Cooper-Hewitt Museum; 2 East 91st St.
    New York NY 10128
    212/860-6868; FAX 212/860-6909

AMOUNT: $2500
DEADLINE(S): March 31
FIELD(S): Art History; Architectural History;
    Design
Ten-week summer internships open to gradu-
    ate and undergraduate students considering
    a career in the museum profession. Interns
    will assist on special research or exhibition
    projects and participate in daily museum
    activities.
Internship commences in June and ends in
    August. Housing is not provided. Write for
    complete information.

286

**SOCIETY FOR IMAGING SCIENCE AND
TECHNOLOGY
(Raymond Davis Scholarship)**
    7003 Kilworth Lane
    Springfield VA 22151
    703/642-9090; FAX 703/642-9094

AMOUNT: $1000
DEADLINE(S): December 15
FIELD(S): Photographic Science or
    Engineering
Scholarships for undergraduate juniors or
    seniors or graduate students for full-time con-
    tinuing studies in the theory or practice of
    photographic science, including any kind of
    image formation initiated by radiant energy.
Write for complete information.

287

**SOLOMON R. GUGGENHEIM MUSEUM
(Fellowship and Voluntary Internship
Programs)**
    1071 Fifth Ave.
    New York NY 10128
    212/423-3600

AMOUNT: Stipends vary (some positions
    non-paid)
DEADLINE(S): August 15; December 15;
    March 15
FIELD(S): Arts Administration; Art History
Ten-week internship open to students in the
    above fields who have completed at least
    two years of undergraduate study; fellow-
    ships open to graduate students holding
    B.A. or M.A. in Art History.
Direct inquiries to address above, Attn:
    internship program.

288

**TENNESSEE ARTS COMMISSION
(Individual Artists' Fellowships)**
    404 James Robertson Parkway; Suite 160
    Nashville TN 37243-0780
    615/741-1701

AMOUNT: $2500 to $5000
DEADLINE(S): January 11
FIELD(S): Visual Arts; Performing Arts;
Creative Arts
Open to artists who are residents of
Tennessee. Duration of award is one year.
Applicants must be professional artists.
FULL-TIME STUDENTS ARE NOT ELI-
GIBLE.
Write for complete information.

289

THE SCHOLASTIC ART & WRITING
AWARDS
555 Broadway
New York NY 10012
212/343-6493

AMOUNT: Varied
DEADLINE(S): Apply September 15–
January 1
FIELD(S): Art; Photography; Writing
Open to students in grades 7–12. Finalists in
regional competitions go on to the national
level.
More than 100 undergraduate scholarships are
offered per year. Send requests for information between September 15th & January
1st.

290

UNIVERSITY FILM AND VIDEO ASSN.
(Grants)
Professor Julie Simon; University of
Baltimore; Communication Design; 1420 N.
Charles St.
Baltimore MD 21201
Written inquiry only

AMOUNT: $5000
DEADLINE(S): January 15
FIELD(S): Film & Video
Open to undergraduate & graduate students
who are sponsored by a faculty member
who is active in the film and video associa-

tion. $4000 grants for student film or video
productions. $1000 for research projects.
Research projects may be in historical, critical,
theoretical, or experimental studies of film
or video. Write for complete information.

291

UNIVERSITY OF ILLINOIS AT URBANA-
CHAMPAIGN
(Lydia E. Parker Bates Scholarship)
Student Services Bldg.
610 East John Street
Champaign IL 61820
217/333-0100

AMOUNT: Varies
DEADLINE(S): March 15
FIELD(S): Art; Architecture; Landscape
Architecture; Urban Planning; Dance;
Theater
Open to undergraduate students in the
College of Fine & Applied Arts who are
attending the University of Illinois at
Urbana-Champaign. Must demonstrate
financial need and have 3.85 GPA.
175 awards per year. Recipients must carry at
least 14 credit hours per semester. Contact
office of student financial aid.

292

VIRGINIA MUSEUM OF FINE ARTS
(Undergrad/Graduate & Professional
Fellowships)
2800 Grove Ave.
Richmond VA 23221-2466
804/367-0824

AMOUNT: Up to $4000 (undergrads); $5000
(grads); $800 (professionals)
DEADLINE(S): March 1
FIELD(S): Art; Fine Arts; Art History
(graduate only); Crafts; Drawing;
Filmmaking; Painting; Photography;
Printmaking; Sculpture; Video.
Open to Virginia residents (minimum 1-year
residency prior to deadline) who are US cit-
izens or legal residents. Professional artist

fellowships are also available. Financial need is considered.

Art, Fine Arts, & Art History are for grad students only. Write for complete information.

293

WAVERLY COMMUNITY HOUSE INC.
(F. Lammont Belin Arts Scholarships)
Scholarships Selection Committee
P.O. Box 142
Waverly PA 18471
717/586-8191

AMOUNT: $9000

DEADLINE(S): December 15

FIELD(S): Painting; Sculpture; Music; Drama; Dance; Literature; Architecture; Photography

Applicants must reside in the Abington or Pocono regions of Northeastern Pennsylvania. They must furnish proof of exceptional ability in their chosen field but need no formal training in any academic or professional program.

USA citizenship required. Finalists must appear in person before the selection committee. Write for complete information.

294

WELLESLEY COLLEGE
(Harriet A. Shaw Fellowships)
Career Center; Secretary Graduate Fellowships
Wellesley MA 02181-8200
617/283-3525

AMOUNT: Up to $3000 stipend per year

DEADLINE(S): Mid-December

FIELD(S): Music; Allied Arts

Open to women who hold a BA degree from Wellesley College for research in music and allied arts in the USA or abroad. Preference given to music candidates; undergrad work in art history is required for other candidates.

Write for complete information.

ENGLISH LANGUAGE/ LITERATURE

295

ALPHA MU GAMMA NATIONAL OFFICE
(Goddard, Indovina, and Krakowski Scholarships)
c/o Los Angeles City College; 855 N. Vermont Ave.
Los Angeles CA 90029
213/664-8742

AMOUNT: $500 (3-ea.); $400 & $200 (1-ea.)

DEADLINE(S): January 4

FIELD(S): Language

Scholarships open to college or university students who are MEMBERS OF ALPHA MU GAMMA CHAPTERS. Students must have completed at least 1-1/2 semesters of college work and have two 'A' grades in a foreign language.

Renewable. Write for complete information.

296

AMERICAN FOUNDATION FOR THE BLIND
(R.L. Gillette Scholarship Fund)
15 West 16th St.
New York NY 10011
212/620-2000; TDD 212/620-2158

AMOUNT: $1000

DEADLINE(S): April 1

FIELD(S): Creative Writing; Literature; Music Performance

Open to legally blind women who are enrolled in or can provide proof of acceptance to a 4-year bachelor program at a recognized school or university. Writing sample or music performance tape will be required. Must be USA citizen.

Write for complete information.

297

AMERICAN LEGION
(National High School Oratorical Contest)
P.O. Box 1055
Indianapolis IN 46206
317/635-8411

AMOUNT: $12,000 to $18,000 (national);
$3000 (sectional); $1000 (regional)
DEADLINE(S): Varies
FIELD(S): Oratory

Competition open to high school students.
Undergraduate scholarship awards go to
the top 4 contestants; also regional & sec-
tional awards. US citizenship required.
Write to the American Legion headquarters in
your state of residence for contest procedures.

298

ARTS INTERNATIONAL; INSTITUTE OF
INTERNATIONAL EDUCATION
(Cintas Fellowship Program)
809 United Nations Plaza
New York NY 10017
212/984-5370

AMOUNT: $10,000
DEADLINE(S): March 1
FIELD(S): Architecture; Painting;
Photography; Sculpture; Printmaking;
Music Composition; Creative Writing

Fellowships open to artists who are of Cuban
ancestry or Cuban citizens living outside of
Cuba. They are intended to foster and
encourage the professional development
and recognition of talented creative artists
in the above areas.
Fellowships are not awarded for furtherance
of academic study. 5–10 awards per year.
Write for complete information.

299

BEVERLY HILLS THEATRE GUILD
(Julie Harris Playwright Award Competition)
2815 N. Beachwood Dr.
Los Angeles CA 90068
213/465-2703

AMOUNT: $5000 (first prize); $2000 (second
prize); $1000 (third prize)
DEADLINE(S): November 1 (entries
accepted Aug. 1 to Nov. 1)
FIELD(S): Playwriting competition

Annual competition of full-length (90 minutes) unproduced & unpublished plays.
Musicals, short one-act plays, adaptations,
translations, & plays having won other competitions or entered in previous BHTG
competitions not eligible.
Must be US citizen to enter. Co-authorship is
allowed. Send SASE for complete information & applications which must be submitted with entry.

300

BUSH FOUNDATION
(Bush Artist Fellowships)
E900 First National Bank Bldg.
322 Minnesota St.
St. Paul MN 55101
612/227-5222 or 899/605-7315

AMOUNT: Up to $36,000 fellowship
DEADLINE(S): Late October/early
November
FIELD(S): Literature; Music Composition;
Choreography; Visual Arts; Scriptworks;
Film/Video

Open to writers, visual artists, composers, &
choreographers who are residents of MN,
ND, SD, or western WI & who are at least
25 years old. Awards are to help artists
work full-time in their chosen field—NOT
for academic study!
Students are NOT eligible to apply! 15 fellowships per year, 12–18 months in duration.
Write for complete information.

301

CALIFORNIA LIBRARY ASSOCIATION
(Reference Service Press Fellowship)
717 K St.; Suite 300
Sacramento CA 95814-3477
916/447-8541

AMOUNT: $2000
DEADLINE(S): May 31
FIELD(S): Library science

Open to college seniors or graduates who
have been accepted in an accredited MLS
program. For California residents attending
library school in any state OR resident of
any state attending a library school in
California.

Students pursuing an MLS on a part-time or
full-time basis are equally eligible. Write for
complete information.

302

CATHOLIC LIBRARY ASSOCIATION
(World Book Inc. Grant)
St. Joseph Central High School Library
22 Maplewood Ave.
Pittsfield MA 01201-4780
413/443-2CLA

AMOUNT: $1500
DEADLINE(S): March 15
FIELD(S): Library Science

Open to members of national Catholic Library
Association. Purpose of award is continuing
education in school or children's librarianship; may not be used for library science
degree.

Write for complete information. Include
SASE.

303

CONNECTICUT LIBRARY
ASSOCIATION
(Program for Education Grants)
P.O. Box 1046
Norwich CT 06360
860/885-2758

AMOUNT: Varies
DEADLINE(S): None
FIELD(S): Librarianship

Continuing education grants for library
employees, volunteer trustees, or friends of
the library in the state of Connecticut. Must
join CLA to be eligible. Tuition cost is not
covered.

4–5 grants per year. Write for complete information.

304

CREOLE-AMERICAN GENEALOGICAL
SOCIETY INC.
(Creole Scholarships)
P.O. Box 3215; Church Street Station
New York NY 10008
Written inquiry only

AMOUNT: $1500
DEADLINE(S): Apply between January 1
and April 30
FIELD(S): Genealogy or language or Creole
culture

Awards in the above areas open to individuals
of mixed racial ancestry who submit a four-
generation genealogical chart attesting to
Creole ancestry and/or interracial parentage. For undergraduate or graduate
study/research.

For scholarship/award information send $2
money order and self-addressed stamped
envelope to address above. Cash and personal checks are not accepted. Letters without SASE and handling charge will not be
answered.

305

DISTRICT OF COLUMBIA COMMISSION
ON THE ARTS & HUMANITIES
(Grants)
410 Eighth St. NW; 5th Floor
Washington DC 20004
*202/724-5613; TDD 202/727-318; FAX
202/727-4135*

AMOUNT: $5000

DEADLINE(S): March 1

FIELD(S): Arts; Performing Arts; Literature

Applicants for grants must be professional artists and residents of Washington DC for at least one year prior to submitting application. Awards intended to generate art endeavors within the Washington DC community.

Open also to art organizations that train, exhibit, or perform within DC. 150 grants per year. Write for complete information.

306

FLORIDA ARTS COUNCIL
(Individual Artists' Fellowships)
FL Dept. of State; Div. of Cultural Affairs; State Capitol
Tallahassee FL 32399-0250
904/487-2980

AMOUNT: $5000

DEADLINE(S): January 25

FIELD(S): Visual Arts; Dance; Folk Arts; Media; Music; Theater; Literary Arts; Interdisciplinary

Fellowships awarded to individual artists in the above areas. Must be Florida residents, US citizens, and over 18 years old. May NOT be a degree-seeking student—funding is for support of artistic endeavors only.

Forty awards per year. Write for complete information.

307

GEORGE MASON UNIVERSITY
(Mary Roberts Rinehart Fund)
Mail Stop 3E4; English Dept.; George Mason University; 4400 University Dr.
Fairfax VA 22030
703/993-1185

AMOUNT: $900 (approx.)

DEADLINE(S): November 30

FIELD(S): Creative Writing

Grants awarded to unpublished creative writers who need financial aid to complete works of fiction, poetry, drama, biography, autobiography, or history. Only works written in English will be considered, but USA citizenship not required.

Candidate must be nominated by writing program faculty member or a sponsoring writer, agent, or editor. Write to William Miller at address above for complete information.

308

GEORGE WASHINGTON UNIVERSITY
(Maud E. McPherson Scholarship in English)
GWU Office of Student Financial Aid
Washington DC 20052
202/994-6180

AMOUNT: Up to full tuition

DEADLINE(S): May 1

FIELD(S): English

Need-based scholarships up to full tuition at George Washington University for continuing or transfer students majoring in English. GPA of 3.0 or better (4.0 scale) is required. Must be US citizen.

Write for complete information.

309

ILLINOIS ARTS COUNCIL
(Artists Fellowship Awards)
100 W. Randolph; Suite 10-500
Chicago IL 60601
312/814-6750

AMOUNT: $500; $5000; $10,000

DEADLINE(S): September 1

FIELD(S): Choreography; Visual Arts; Poetry; Prose; Film; Video; Playwriting; Music Composition; Crafts; Ethnic & Folk Arts; Performance Art; Photography; Audio Art.

Open to professional artists who are Illinois residents. Awards are in recognition of work in the above areas; they are not for continuing study. Students are NOT eligible.

Write to address above for application form.

310

IOWA SCHOOL OF LETTERS
(Award for Short Fiction)
Department of English; University of Iowa
308 English Philosophy Bldg.
Iowa City IA 52242
Written inquiry

AMOUNT: Winners' manuscripts will be published by University of Iowa under standard press contract.

DEADLINE(S): Apply between August 1 & September 30

FIELD(S): Creative Writing (fiction)

Any writer who has not previously published a volume of prose fiction is eligible to enter the competition. Revised manuscripts which have been previously entered may be resubmitted.

The manuscript must be a collection of short stories of at least 150 typewritten pages. Writers who have published a volume of poetry are eligible.

311

MINNESOTA STATE ARTS BOARD
(Grants Program)
432 Summit Ave.
St. Paul MN 55102
612/297-2603

AMOUNT: Fellowships $6000; Career Opportunity Grants $100–$1000 or Special Residency Stipend

DEADLINE(S): August—Visual Arts; September—Music & Dance; October—Literature & Theater

FIELD(S): Literature; Music; Theater; Dance; Visual Arts

Fellowship grants open to professional artists who are residents of Minnesota. Grants are not intended for support of tuition or work toward any degree.

Career opportunity grants and fellowships are available.

312

NATIONAL FEDERATION OF STATE POETRY SOCIETIES INC.
(Scholarship Fund for Poets)
Golda F. Walker; 915 Aberdeen Ave.
Baton Rouge LA 70808
504/344-9932

AMOUNT: $500

DEADLINE(S): February 15

FIELD(S): Poetry

Scholarships open to undergraduate juniors and seniors at accredited colleges and universities in the USA. 10 original poems to be submitted with completed application form and a bio of the applicant.

Send SASE (#10 envelope) for application form and complete information. Inquiries without SASE will not be acknowledged.

313

NATIONAL FOUNDATION FOR ADVANCEMENT IN THE ARTS
(Arts Recognition and Talent Search)
800 Brickell Ave.; #500
Miami FL 33131
305/377-1147

AMOUNT: $100–$3000

DEADLINE(S): October 1

FIELD(S): Creative Arts; Performing Arts

Open to high school seniors with talent in such arts as dance, music, music/jazz, theater, visual arts, film, video, and writing. Awards can be used anywhere for any purpose. For US citizens or residents. Entry fee is required.

Approximately 300 awards per year. Write for complete information.

314

NATIONAL JUNIOR CLASSICAL LEAGUE
(Scholarships)
Miami University
Oxford OH 45056
513/529-7741

AMOUNT: $500 to $1000

DEADLINE(S): May 1

FIELD(S): Classics

Open to NJCL members who are high school seniors and plan to study Classics (though Classics major is not required). Preference will be given to a student who plans to pursue a teaching career in the Classics (also not a requirement).

Must be a member of a National Junior Classical League club. Write for complete information.

315

NATIONAL SPEAKERS ASSOCIATION
(NSA Scholarship)
1500 S. Priest Dr.
Tempe AZ 85281
602/968-2552; fax 968-0911

AMOUNT: $2500

DEADLINE(S): June 3

FIELD(S): Oral Communications

Open to college juniors, seniors, or graduate students who are majoring or minoring in speech or a directly related field. Must be full time student in an accredited college or university. Need at least 3.0 GPA.

Four awards per year to well-rounded students capable of leadership and having potential to make an impact by using oral communications.

316

NELLIE MARTIN CARMAN SCHOLARSHIP TRUST
(Scholarships)
18223 73rd Ave. NE; #B101
Bothell WA 98011
206/486-6575

AMOUNT: Up to $1000

DEADLINE(S): March 15

FIELD(S): All fields of study except those noted below

Open to high school seniors in King, Pierce, & Snohomish Counties (WA). For undergraduate study in the state of Washington in all fields EXCEPT music, sculpting, drawing, interior design, & home economics. US citizenship required.

Applications available only through high schools & nomination by counselor is required. Awards are renewable. Write for complete information.

317

OHIO ARTS COUNCIL
(OAC Scholarship Program)
727 E. Main St.
Columbus OH 43205-1796
614/466-2613

AMOUNT: $1000

DEADLINE(S): April 15 (senior year of high school)

FIELD(S): Dance; Music; Theater Arts; Visual Arts; Writing

Open to Ohio residents who are high school seniors wishing to continue their arts training and education at an accredited college or university in the State of Ohio.

Write for complete information.

318

PLAYWRIGHTS' CENTER
(McKnight Advancement Grant)
2301 Franklin Ave. East
Minneapolis MN 55406
612/332-7481; FAX 612/332-6037

AMOUNT: $8500

DEADLINE(S): February 1

FIELD(S): Playwriting

Open to playwrights whose primary residence is Minnesota & whose work demonstrates exceptional artistic merit & potential. Two works by applicant must have been fully produced by professional theatres.

Recipients must designate two months of the grant year for active participation in center programs. Applications available December 1. Write for complete information.

319

PLAYWRIGHTS' CENTER
(PlayLabs)
2301 Franklin Ave. East
Minneapolis MN 55406
612/332-7481; FAX 612/332-6037

AMOUNT: Honoraria; travel expenses; room and board

DEADLINE(S): December 15

FIELD(S): Playwriting

Two-week workshop open to US citizens who are authors of unproduced, unpublished full-length plays (no one-acts). Each play receives a public reading followed by audience discussion of the work.

4 to 6 playwrights chosen by open script competition. Conference is intended to allow playwrights to take risks free of artistic restraint. Applications available by Oct 1. Send SASE for complete information.

320

POETRY SOCIETY OF AMERICA
(Cash Awards)
15 Gramercy Park
New York NY 10003
212/254-9628

AMOUNT: $100

DEADLINE(S): December 31

FIELD(S): Poetry

Awards competition "aimed at advancing excellence in poetry and encouraging skill in traditional forms as well as experimentation." These are cash awards, not scholarships.

This is a contest, NOT a scholarship; write for complete deatils.

321

POETRY SOCIETY OF AMERICA
(Contests open to PSA members)
15 Gramercy Park
New York NY 10003
Written inquiry

AMOUNT: Varies with award

DEADLINE(S): October 1—December 31

FIELD(S): Poetry

Various contests open to PSA members. Only one submission allowed per contest. All submissions must be unpublished on the date of entry and not scheduled for publication by the date of the PSA awards ceremony held in the spring.

This is a contest, NOT a scholarship; write for complete details.

322

RIPON COLLEGE
(Music & Debate-Forensics Scholarships)
P.O. Box 248
300 Seward St.; Admissions Office
Ripon WI 54971
414/748-8102 or 1-800/94RIPON

AMOUNT: $500–1500

DEADLINE(S): March 1

FIELD(S): Music; Debate-Forensic

Scholarships recognize & encourage academic potential & accomplishment in above fields. Renewable up to 3 years provided recipient maintains good academic standing.

Must apply and be accepted for admission to Ripon College. Write for complete information.

323

SAN FRANCISCO FOUNDATION
(James D. Phelan Literary Award)
685 Market St.; Suite 910
San Francisco CA 94105
415/495-3100 or 510/436-3100

AMOUNT: $2000

DEADLINE(S): January 15

FIELD(S): Literature

Open to California-born authors of unpublished works-in-progress (fiction, non-fiction, or poetry) who are between the ages of 20 & 35 and are US citizens.

Writers of non-fiction are also eligible for the $1000 Joseph Henry Jackson Honorable Mention Award. Write for complete information.

324

SAN FRANCISCO FOUNDATION
(Joseph Henry Jackson Literary Award)
685 Market St.; Suite 910
San Francisco CA 94105
415/495-3100 OR 510/436-3100

AMOUNT: $2000

DEADLINE(S): January 15

FIELD(S): Literature

Open to N. California or Nevada residents (for 3 consecutive years immediately prior to closing date of the competition) who are authors of unpublished work-in-progress (fiction, non-fiction, poetry) & 20–35 years of age.

Writers of non-fiction are also eligible for the $1000 Joseph Henry Jackson Honorable Mention Award. Write for complete information.

325

SONS OF THE AMERICAN REVOLUTION
(Joseph S. Rumbaugh Historical Oration Contest)
1000 South 4th St.
Louisville KY 40203
Written inquiry

AMOUNT: $2000 1st prize; $1000 2nd prize; $500 3rd prize

DEADLINE(S): State deadline February 1

FIELD(S): Oratory

Competition open to high school sophomores, juniors, & seniors who submit an original 5 to 6 minute oration on a personality, event, or document of the American Revolutionary War & how it relates to the USA today.

Oration must be delivered from memory without props or charts. Applicants must be US citizens. Write for complete information.

326

STANLEY DRAMA AWARD
(Playwriting/Musical Awards Competition)
Department of Humanities; Wagner College; Howard Ave. & Campus Rd.
Staten Island NY 10301
718/390-3256

AMOUNT: $2000

DEADLINE(S): September 1

FIELD(S): Playwriting; Music Composition

Annual award for an original full-length play or musical which has not been professionally produced or received tradebook publication.

Submit musical works on cassette tape w/ book & lyrics. A series of 2–3 thematically related one-act plays will also be considered. Send script with SASE large enough to accommodate script. Write for complete information.

327

TENNESSEE ARTS COMMISSION
(Individual Artists' Fellowships)
404 James Robertson Parkway; Suite 160
Nashville TN 37243-0780
615/741-1701

AMOUNT: $2500 to $5000

DEADLINE(S): January 11

FIELD(S): Visual Arts; Performing Arts; Creative Arts

Open to artists who are residents of Tennessee. Duration of award is one year. Applicants must be professional artists. FULL-TIME STUDENTS ARE NOT ELIGIBLE.

Write for complete information.

328

US MARINE CORPS HISTORICAL CENTER
(College Internships)
Building 58; Washington Navy Yard
Washington DC 20374
202/433-3839

AMOUNT: Stipend to cover daily expenses
DEADLINE(S): None specified
FIELD(S): US Military History; Library Science; History; Museum Studies

Open to undergraduate students at a college or university which will grant academic credit for work experience as interns at the address above or at the Marine Corps Airground Museum in Quantico, Virginia.

All internships are regarded as beginning professional-level historian, curator, librarian, or archivist positions. Write for complete information.

329

VETERANS OF FOREIGN WARS OF THE UNITED STATES
(Voice of Democracy Audio-Essay Competition)
VFW Bldg; 406 W. 34th St.
Kansas City MO 64111
816/968-1117

AMOUNT: $1000 to $20,000
DEADLINE(S): November 15
FIELD(S): Creative writing

Open to sophomores, juniors, & seniors in public, private, & parochial high schools. Contestants will be judged on their treatment of an annual theme. They may not refer to their race, national origin, etc.; as a means of identification.

47 awards per year. Contact local VFW post or high school for details.

330

WAVERLY COMMUNITY HOUSE INC.
(F. Lammont Belin Arts Scholarships)
Scholarships Selection Committee
P.O. Box 142
Waverly PA 18471
717/586-8191

AMOUNT: $9000
DEADLINE(S): December 15
FIELD(S): Painting; Sculpture; Music; Drama; Dance; Literature; Architecture; Photography

Applicants must reside in the Abington or Pocono regions of Northeastern Pennsylvania. They must furnish proof of exceptional ability in their chosen field but need no formal training in any academic or professional program.

US citizenship required. Finalists must appear in person before the selection committee. Write for complete information.

FOREIGN LANGUAGE

331

AMERICAN ASSOCIATION OF TEACHERS OF FRENCH
(National French Contest)
Sidney L. Teitelbaum; Box 1178
Long Beach NY 11561
516/897-8119; FAX 516/938-2273

AMOUNT: Varies
DEADLINE(S): February 1
FIELD(S): French Language; French Studies

National French contest is an examination taken throughout the country. Students are ranked regionally and nationally and are eligible for both regional and national awards.

Not a scholarship. Winners receive trips, medals, and books. Write for complete information.

332

AMERICAN ASSOCIATION OF TEACHERS OF GERMAN
(National AATG/PAD Awards)
112 Haddontowne Ct. #104
Cherry Hill NJ 08034
609/795-5553

AMOUNT: Costs of travel & study

DEADLINE(S): December 1 (deadline for teachers to order test)

FIELD(S): German Language

This summer-study trip award to Germany is open to high school students aged 16 or older who score at or above the 90th percentile on the AATG National German Test. US citizenship or permanent residency is required.

Up to 54 travel-study awards per year. Tests are administered by high school German teachers—write to address above for complete information or inquire with your German teacher. FINANCIAL AID FOR POST-SECONDARY EDUCATION IS NOT AVAILABLE.

333

AMERICAN COUNCIL OF LEARNED SOCIETIES
(East European Summer Language Training Grants)
Office of Fellowships & Grants
228 E. 45th St.
New York NY 10017
Written inquiry

AMOUNT: $2500

DEADLINE(S): February 1

FIELD(S): East European Languages

Grants of $2500 each offered for intensive summer study of an East European language (except Russian) at the intermediate or advanced level in Eastern Europe.

US citizen or legal resident. For graduating seniors; grad or postgrad study. Write for complete information.

334

AMERICAN INSTITUTE OF INDIAN STUDIES
(AIIS 9-month Language Program)
c/o University of Chicago
Foster Hall
1130 E. 59th St.
Chicago IL 60637
312/702-8638

AMOUNT: $3000 plus travel

DEADLINE(S): January 31

FIELD(S): Languages of India

Fellowships held in India open to graduate students who have a minimum of 2 years or 240 hours of classroom instruction in a language of India. US citizenship required.

10 fellowships per year. Write for complete information.

335

AUSTRIAN CULTURAL INSTITUTE
(Grants for American Students to Study German in Austria)
11 East 52nd St.
New York NY 10022
212/759-5165; FAX 212/319-9636

AMOUNT: Austrian 10.000 (approx. US $830) + tuition allowance

DEADLINE(S): January 31

FIELD(S): German Language

Open to US citizens between 20 and 35 who have completed at least 2 years of college and have studied German for at least 2 years. Grants also may be used for research at an Austrian library or research institution archive.

Three one-month grants available for use between July 1 and September 30. Call for complete information.

336

LUSO-AMERICAN EDUCATION FOUNDATION
(General Scholarships)
P.O. Box 2967
Dublin CA 94568
510/828-3883

AMOUNT: Varies
DEADLINE(S): March 1
FIELD(S): Portuguese Language or Portuguese Descent-related fields

Open to Calif. high school seniors (under 21) of Portuguese descent who will enroll full-time in a 4-year program that includes Portuguese language classes. Also open to members of Luso-American Fraternal Federation.

Write for complete information.

337

NELLIE MARTIN CARMAN SCHOLARSHIP TRUST
(Scholarships)
18223 73rd Ave. NE; #B101
Bothell WA 98011
206/486-6575

AMOUNT: Up to $1000
DEADLINE(S): March 15
FIELD(S): All fields of study except those noted below

Open to high school seniors in King, Pierce, & Snohomish Counties (WA). For undergraduate study in the state of Washington in all fields EXCEPT music, sculpting, drawing, interior design, & home economics. US citizenship required.

Applications available only through high schools & nomination by counselor is required. Awards are renewable. Write for complete information.

338

NORWICH JUBILEE ESPERANTO FOUNDATION
(Travel Grants)
37 Granville Court
Oxford 0X3 0HS England
0865-245509

AMOUNT: 1000 pounds sterling (maximum award)
DEADLINE(S): None
FIELD(S): Esperanto

Travel grants open to those who speak Esperanto and wish to improve their use of the language through travel in the U.K. Candidates must be under the age of 26 and be able to lecture in Esperanto.

Inquiries without indication of fluency and interest in Esperanto will not be acknowledged. Up to 25 awards per year. Renewable. Write for complete information.

PERFORMING ARTS

339

AMERICAN ACCORDION MUSICOLOGICAL SOCIETY
(Contest)
334 South Broadway
Pitman NJ 08071
609/854-6628

AMOUNT: $100–$250
DEADLINE(S): September 10
FIELD(S): Music Composition

Annual competition open to amateur or professional music composers who write a serious piece of music (of six minutes or more) for the accordion.

Write for complete information.

340

AMERICAN FOUNDATION FOR THE BLIND
(Gladys C. Anderson Memorial Scholarship)
15 West 16th St.
New York NY 10011
212/620-2000; TDD 212/620-2158

AMOUNT: $1000
DEADLINE(S): April 1
FIELD(S): Music performance or singing
Undergrad scholarships open to legally blind women studying religious or classical music at the college level. Sample performance tape of voice or instrumental selection will be required. USA citizen.
Write for complete information.

341

AMERICAN FOUNDATION FOR THE BLIND
(R.L. Gillette Scholarship Fund)
15 West 16th St.
New York NY 10011
212/620-2000; TDD 212/620-2158

AMOUNT: $1000
DEADLINE(S): April 1
FIELD(S): Creative Writing; Literature; Music Performance
Open to legally blind women who are enrolled in or can provide proof of acceptance to a 4-year bachelor program at a recognized school or university. Writing sample or music performance tape will be required. Must be US citizen.
Write for complete information.

342

AMERICAN SYMPHONY ORCHESTRA LEAGUE
(Music Assistance Fund)
1156 15th St. NW; Suite 800
Washington DC 20005-1704
202/628-0099 (FAX 202/783-7228)

AMOUNT: Up to $2500
DEADLINE(S): January 14
FIELD(S): Orchestral Music Study
Open to US citizens of African descent who are pursuing degrees at conservatories and university schools of music. For orchestral instruments only. Voice,; piano, sax, composition, & conducting NOT included.
Scholarships are based on live auditions, recommendations, and financial need. Applicants must apply and audition each year. For more information, please write.

343

ARTS INTERNATIONAL; INSTITUTE OF INTERNATIONAL EDUCATION
(Cintas Fellowship Program)
809 United Nations Plaza
New York NY 10017
212/984-5370

AMOUNT: $10,000
DEADLINE(S): March 1
FIELD(S): Architecture; Painting; Photography; Sculpture; Printmaking; Music Composition; Creative Writing
Fellowships open to artists who are of Cuban ancestry or Cuban citizens living outside of Cuba. They are intended to foster & encourage the professional development & recognition of talented creative artists in the above areas.
Fellowships are not awarded for furtherance of academic study. 5–10 awards per year. Write for complete information.

344

ASCAP FOUNDATION, THE
(Music Composition Awards Program)
ASCAP Building; 1 Lincoln Plaza
New York NY 10023
212/621-6219

AMOUNT: $250–$1500
DEADLINE(S): March 15
FIELD(S): Music Composition Competition

Competition is open to young composers who are under 30 years of age as of March 15 of the year of application. Winning compositions selected by panel of judges.

Awards help young composers continue their studies and develop their skills. 15 awards per year. Write for complete information.

345

BALTIMORE OPERA COMPANY
(Vocal Competition for North American Operatic Artists)
1202 Maryland Ave.
Baltimore MD 21201
410/625-1600

AMOUNT: $1000–$12,000
DEADLINE(S): March 1
FIELD(S): Singing

Biannual contest for operatic singers between the ages of 20 & 35 who are US, Canadian, or Mexican citizens & who can present 2 letters of recommendation from recognized musical authorities.

Eight awards biannually renewable by competition. There is a $45 application fee. Write for complete information.

346

BARNUM FESTIVAL
(Jenny Lind Competition for Sopranos)
1070 Main St.
Bridgeport CT 06604
Written inquiry

AMOUNT: $2000 scholarship & ticket to Sweden
DEADLINE(S): Competition held May 30
FIELD(S): Singing

Open to women between 18 and 25 who have had formal training in operatic or concert singing but have not reached professional status. Only residents or students from the state of Connecticut may apply.

Application forms, copies of the information memo, and other materials on the Jenny Lind contest may be obtained from the Barnum Festival office.

347

BRYAN INTERNATIONAL STRING COMPETITION
(Music Performance Awards)
North Carolina Symphony; P.O. Box 28026
Raleigh NC 27611
919/733-2750

AMOUNT: $12,000 1st prize; $6000 2nd prize; $3000 3rd prize
DEADLINE(S): January 2 (1996) and every four years thereafter
FIELD(S): Music Performance Competition (Violin; Viola; Cello)

Auditions for competition open to violinists, violists, cellists between the ages of 18 and 30. Competition is open to all nationalities and is held every four years. NEXT COMPETITION will be in 1996.

Write for complete information.

348

BUSH FOUNDATION
(Bush Artist Fellowships)
E900 First National Bank Bldg.
322 Minnesota St.
St. Paul MN 55101
612/227-5222 or 899/605-7315

AMOUNT: Up to $36,000 fellowship
DEADLINE(S): Late October/early November
FIELD(S): Literature; Music Composition; Choreography; Visual Arts; Scriptworks; Film/Video

Open to writers, visual artists, composers, & choreographers who are residents of MN, ND, SD, or western WI, & who are at least 25 years old. Awards are to help artists work full-time in their chosen field—NOT for academic study!

Students are NOT eligible to apply! 15 fellowships per year; 12–18 months in duration. Write for complete information.

349

CHATHAM COLLEGE
(Minna Kaufmann Ruud Fund)
Woodland Rd.; Office of Admissions
Pittsburgh PA 15232
412/365-1290

AMOUNT: $3500/year (average) + fees &
private accompanist
DEADLINE(S): January 31
FIELD(S): Vocal Music

Women only. Awards for full-time undergraduate study at Chatham College.
Scholarships open to promising young
female vocalists who are accepted for
admission, pass an audition, & plan to
major in music.
Awards renewable. Write for complete information.

350

COLUMBIA UNIVERSITY
(Joseph H. Bearns Prize in Music)
Dept. of Music; 703 Dodge Hall
New York NY 10027
212/854-3825

AMOUNT: $3000; $2000
DEADLINE(S): February 1 (of odd-
numbered years)
FIELD(S): Music Composition

Competition open to young composers aged
18–25. There are two categories for music
composition. One award of $3000 for larger
forms & one award of $2000 for smaller
forms. No more than one entry should be
sent. US citizenship required.
Write to Attn of Bearns Prize Committee at
address above for complete details.

351

CURTIS INSTITUTE OF MUSIC
(Tuition Scholarships)
Admissions Office; 1726 Locust St.
Philadelphia PA 19103
215/893-5252

AMOUNT: Full tuition
DEADLINE(S): January 15
FIELD(S): Music; Voice; Opera

Full-tuition scholarships open to students in
the above areas who are accepted for full-
time study at the Curtis Institute of Music.
(Opera is for master of music only.)
Approx 50 awards per year. Scholarships are
renewable. Write for complete information.

352

DELTA OMICRON INTERNATIONAL
MUSIC FRATERNITY
(Triennial Composition Competition)
12297 W. Tennessee Pl.
Lakewood CO 80228-3325
606/266-1215

AMOUNT: $500 and premiere
DEADLINE(S): March 20
FIELD(S): Music Composition

Sacred choral anthem for 3- or 4-part voices:
SSA, SAB, or SATB with keyboard accom-
paniment or a capella with optional obliga-
to. Competition open to composers of college age or over. No music fraternity affiliation required.
Prior publication or public performance of
entry is NOT allowed. Entry fee of $10 is
required. Contact Judith Eidson at above
address for complete information.

353

DISTRICT OF COLUMBIA COMMISSION
ON THE ARTS & HUMANITIES
(Grants)
410 Eighth St. NW; 5th Floor
Washington DC 20004
202/724-5613; TDD 202/727-318;
FAX 202/727-4135

AMOUNT: $5000
DEADLINE(S): March 1
FIELD(S): Arts; Performing Arts; Literature

Applicants for grants must be professional
artists and residents of Washington DC for

at least one year prior to submitting application. Awards intended to generate art endeavors within the Washington, DC community.

Open also to art organizations that train, exhibit, or perform within DC. 150 grants per year. Write for complete information.

354

ETUDE MUSIC CLUB OF SANTA ROSA
(Music Competition for Instrumentalists)
P.O. Box 823
Santa Rosa CA 95402
707/538-1370

AMOUNT: $600 first (3); $300 second (3)

DEADLINE(S): March 2 (competition is March 16)

FIELD(S): Classical Instrumental Music

Competition is open to any high school student (grades 9–12) who is a resident of Sonoma, Napa, or Mendocino Counties & is studying music with a private teacher of music or is recommended by his/her school's music department.

Write for complete information.

355

ETUDE MUSIC CLUB OF SANTA ROSA
(Music Competition for Vocalists)
P.O. Box 823
Santa Rosa CA 95402
707/538-1370

AMOUNT: $600 first (1); $300 second (1)

DEADLINE(S): March 2 (competition is March 16)

FIELD(S): Classical Vocalists

Competition is open to high school vocalists in grades 9–12 who are residents of Sonoma, Napa, or Mendocino Counties & are studying music with a private teacher of music or are recommended by their school's music department.

Write for complete information.

356

FARGO-MOORHEAD SYMPHONY ORCHESTRAL ASSOCIATION
(Sigwald Thompson Composition Award Competition)
P.O. Box 1753
Fargo ND 58107
218/233-8397

AMOUNT: $2500

DEADLINE(S): September 30 of even-numbered years

FIELD(S): Music Composition

This award was established to biennially select American composers for the commissioning of a work to be premiered by the Fargo-Moorhead Symphony Orchestra during its concert season. US citizen.

Write for more information.

357

FLORIDA ARTS COUNCIL
(Individual Artists' Fellowships)
FL Dept. of State; Div. of Cultural Affairs; State Capitol
Tallahassee FL 32399-0250
904/487-2980

AMOUNT: $5000

DEADLINE(S): January 25

FIELD(S): Visual Arts; Dance; Folk Arts; Media; Music; Theater; Literary Arts; Interdisciplinary

Fellowships awarded to individual artists in the above areas. Must be Florida residents, US citizens, and over 18 years old. May NOT be a degree-seeking student—funding is for support of artistic endeavors only.

Forty awards per year. Write for complete information.

358

GEORGIA COUNCIL FOR THE ARTS
(Individual Artist Grants)
530 Means St. NW; Suite 115
Atlanta GA 30318-5793
404/651-7920

AMOUNT: Up to $5000
DEADLINE(S): April 1
FIELD(S): The Arts

Grants to support artistic projects by professional artists who have been Georgia residents at least one year prior to application. Selection is based on project's artistic merit and its potential for career development.

Grants do NOT support academic study. Write for complete information.

359

GLENN MILLER BIRTHPLACE SOCIETY
(Scholarship Competition)
711 N. 14th St.
Clarinda IA 51632
712/542-4439

AMOUNT: $1000 & $500 vocal; $1250 & $500 instrumental
DEADLINE(S): March 15
FIELD(S): Music Performance

Instrumental & vocal music competitions open to high school seniors & undergraduate freshmen at recognized colleges & music schools. Audition tape required with application. Finalists perform at Clarinda's Glenn Miller Festival in June.

College music major is not required. All facets of competition are reviewed after each competition. Early inquiry is recommended. Write for complete information.

360

HONOLULU SYMPHONY ASSOCIATES
(Orchestra Scholarships)
1441 Kapiolani Blvd.; Suite 1515
Honolulu HI 96814
808/942-2200

AMOUNT: $288 (36 lessons @ $8 each)
DEADLINE(S): Auditions during spring school break
FIELD(S): Orchestra

Open to residents of Hawaii who are in the 7th through 12th grades. Scholarships are for partial payment for music lessons with a member of the Hawaii symphony orchestra. Awards are based on student's talent and progress.

22 awards per year. Renewable for 4 years. Contact Marilyn Trankle, Volunteer Coordinator, for complete information.

361

HOWARD UNIVERSITY
(Debbie Allen & Phylicia Rashad's Dr. Andrew Allen Creative Arts Scholarship)
College of Fine Arts; Dept. Theatre Arts
6th & Fairmont NW
Washington DC 20059
202/806-7050

AMOUNT: $5000
DEADLINE(S): April 1
FIELD(S): Drama; Singing; Dancing

Scholarship open to all undergraduate juniors & seniors at Howard University who display excellence & versatility in all 3 areas of theatre—acting, singing, & dancing.

Write for complete information.

362

ILLINOIS ARTS COUNCIL
(Artists Fellowship Awards)
100 W. Randolph; Suite 10-500
Chicago IL 60601
312/814-6750

AMOUNT: $500; $5000; $10,000
DEADLINE(S): September 1
FIELD(S): Choreography; Visual Arts; Poetry; Prose; Film; Video; Playwriting; Music Composition; Crafts; Ethnic & Folk Arts; Performance Art; Photography; Audio Art.

Open to professional artists who are Illinois residents. Awards are in recognition of work in the above areas; they are not for continuing study. Students are NOT eligible.

Write to address above for application form.

363

INTERNATIONAL COMPETITION FOR SYMPHONIC COMPOSITION
(Premio Citta Di Trieste)
Piazza Dell'unita D'Italia 4
Palazzo municipale
34121 Trieste Italy
040-366030

AMOUNT: 10 mil. lira (1st)
DEADLINE(S): April 30
FIELD(S): Music Composition

Open to anyone who submits an original composition for full orchestra (normal symphonic instrumentation). Composition must never have been performed and be unpublished.

Previous first-prize winners are excluded from competition. Write to secretariat of the music award at address above for complete information.

364

INTERNATIONAL VOCAL COMPETITION 'S-HERTOGENBOSCH
P.O. Box 1225
5200 BG 'S-Hertogenbosch
The Netherlands
0/73-136569

AMOUNT: $20,000 total prizes
DEADLINE(S): July 1
FIELD(S): Singing Competition

Annual vocal competition to reward exceptional singing talent of all nationalities (up to 32 years old). Prizes for opera, oratorio, and lied categories; various other prizes. Entry fee of 175 Dutch guilders is required.

This is a contest, NOT A SCHOLARSHIP. Write for complete information.

365

LIEDERKRANZ FOUNDATION
(Scholarship Awards)
6 East 87th Street
New York NY 10128
212/534-0880

AMOUNT: $1000–$5000
DEADLINE(S): December 1
FIELD(S): Vocal Music

20 scholarships awarded by competition each year. Awards can be used anywhere. There is a $30 application fee and a lower age limit of 20.

Contact competition director John Balme at address above for application regulations, audition schedules, and other details.

366

LOREN L. ZACHARY SOCIETY FOR THE PERFORMING ARTS
(Annual National Vocal Competition for Young Opera Singers)
2250 Gloaming Way
Beverly Hills CA 90210
310/276-2731

AMOUNT: $1000–$3000 + round-trip air transportation for auditions in Europe
DEADLINE(S): February 2 (NY); April 6 (LA); May (final competition)
FIELD(S): Opera Singing

Annual vocal competition open to young (aged 21–33 females; 21–35 males) Opera singers. The competition is geared toward finding employment for them in European Opera houses.

Approx 10 awards per year. Applications available in November. Send self-addressed stamped envelope to address above for application & complete information.

367

MERCYHURST COLLEGE
(D'Angelo School of Music Scholarships)
Glenwood Hills
Erie PA 16546
814/825-0363

AMOUNT: Varies
DEADLINE(S): April
FIELD(S): Music

Music scholarships at the D'Angelo School of Music of Mercyhurst College are awarded to talented young musicians who are ready to start their college education. Awards are for full-time undergraduate study.

35 awards per year. Renewable. Write for complete information.

368

MERCYHURST COLLEGE
(D'Angelo Young Artist Competition)
  Glenwood Hills
  Erie PA 16546
  814/825-0363

AMOUNT: $10,000; $5000; $3000
DEADLINE(S): January 15
FIELD(S): Voice; Strings; Piano

For musicians aged 18–30. Rotating cycle of areas (piano 1995). Dollar awards & performance contracts. Write for application & repertoire requirements in the fall of the year preceding year of competition.
Write for complete information.

369

MILWAUKEE MUSIC SCHOLARSHIP
FOUNDATION
(Music Scholarships)
  Lisa Sivanich; Firstar Trust Co.;
  P.O. Box 2054
  Milwaukee WI 53201
  Written inquiry

AMOUNT: $300 to $1000
DEADLINE(S): February 1
FIELD(S): Music

Open to Wisconsin residents age 16 to 26 for undergraduate study. Applicants compete in recitals for awards.
Write for complete information.

370

MINNESOTA STATE ARTS BOARD
(Grants Program)
  432 Summit Ave.
  St. Paul MN 55102
  612/297-2603

AMOUNT: Fellowships $6000; Career Opportunity Grants $100–$1000; or Special Residency Stipend.
DEADLINE(S): August—Visual Arts; September—Music & Dance; October–Literature & Theater
FIELD(S): Literature; Music; Theater; Dance; Visual Arts

Fellowship grants open to professional artists who are residents of Minnesota. Grants are not intended for support of tuition or work toward any degree.
Career opportunity grants and fellowships are available.

371

NAPA VALLEY SYMPHONY
ASSOCIATION
(Robert Mondavi International Music
Achievement Awards)
  Elle Wheeler; 2407 California Blvd.
  Napa CA 94558
  707/226-6872

AMOUNT: $2000, $1000, and $500 cash prizes
DEADLINE(S): February 12
FIELD(S): Music Performance

Contest held in odd-numbered years for musicians aged 18 to 25. Competition is in the following sequence of instruments—1995 strings; 1997 piano; 1999 strings; 2001 piano.
Applicants submit audition cassette recording and a non-refundable $25 entrance fee with the application. Write for complete information.

372

NATIONAL ASSOCIATION OF
TEACHERS OF SINGING
(Artist Awards Competition)
  2800 University Blvd. North
  Jacksonville FL 32211
  904/744-9022

AMOUNT: $2500 to $5000
DEADLINE(S): Varies
FIELD(S): Singing

Purpose of the program is to select young singers who are ready for professional careers and to encourage them to carry on the tradition of fine singing.

Applicants should be between 21 and 35 years old and have studied with a NATS teacher for at least one academic year. Six awards every 18 months. Write for complete information.

373

NATIONAL FEDERATION OF MUSIC CLUBS SCHOLARSHIP AND AWARDS PROGRAM
(Student Awards)
1336 N. Delaware St
Indianapolis IN 46202
317/638-4003

AMOUNT: $100–$5000

DEADLINE(S): Various

FIELD(S): Music Performance; Music Composition

Numerous scholarship & award programs open to young musicians aged 16-35 who are either group or individual members of the National Federation of Music Clubs. The programs provide opportunities for students interested in professional music careers.

Request scholarship & awards chart from the address above. Include check for $1 to cover costs.

374

NATIONAL FOUNDATION FOR ADVANCEMENT IN THE ARTS
(Arts Recognition and Talent Search)
800 Brickell Ave.; #500
Miami FL 33131
305/377-1147

AMOUNT: $100–$3000

DEADLINE(S): October 1

FIELD(S): Creative Arts; Performing Arts

Open to high school seniors with talent in such arts as dance, music, music/jazz, theater, visual arts, film, video, and writing. Awards can be used anywhere for any purpose. For US citizens or residents. Entry fee is required.

Approximately 300 awards per year. Write for complete information.

375

NATIONAL GUILD OF COMMUNITY SCHOOLS OF THE ARTS
(Young Composers Awards)
40 North Van Brunt St.; Suite 32
Englewood NJ 07631
201/871-3337

AMOUNT: $1000; $750; $500; $250

DEADLINE(S): May 1

FIELD(S): Music Composition

Competition open to students aged 13-18 (as of June 30 of award year) who are enrolled in a public or private secondary school, recognized musical school, or engaged in private study of music with an established teacher in the US or Canada.

US or Canadian citizenship or legal residency required. Write for complete information.

376

NEW JERSEY STATE OPERA
(Cash Awards)
50 Park Pl.
Robert Treat Center
Newark NJ 07102
201/623-5757

AMOUNT: Awards total $10,000

DEADLINE(S): Varies each year

FIELD(S): Opera

Professional singers between the ages of 22 and 34 can apply for this competition. Singers competing should have been represented by an artists' management firm for no more than one year. Management representation not required for entry.

Contact address above for complete information.

377

NEW YORK CITY OPERA
(Julius Rudel Award)
New York State Theater; 20 Lincoln Center
New York NY 10023
212/870-5600

AMOUNT: $12,000
DEADLINE(S): None
FIELD(S): Opera & Music Management
(career support)

Applicants should present evidence of artistic accomplishments along with a resume and letters of recommendation; also a statement outlining how affiliation with the NYC Opera will further applicant's artistic and career goals.

Award recipient performs administrative tasks for NYC Opera but recipient is encouraged to continue outside artistic work. Write for complete information.

378

OHIO ARTS COUNCIL
(OAC Scholarship Program)
727 E. Main St.
Columbus OH 43205-1796
614/466-2613

AMOUNT: $1000
DEADLINE(S): April 15 (senior year of high school)
FIELD(S): Dance; Music; Theater Arts;
Visual Arts; Writing

Open to Ohio residents who are high school seniors wishing to continue their arts training and education at an accredited college or university in the State of Ohio.
Write for complete information.

379

PITTSBURGH NEW MUSIC ENSEMBLE
(Harvey Gaul Bi-annual Composition Contest)
600 Forbes Ave.
Pittsburgh PA 15219
412/261-0554

AMOUNT: $3000
DEADLINE(S): April 15
FIELD(S): Music Composition

Open to US citizens. Prizes are given for new works scored for six to fifteen instruments. An entry fee of $10 must accompany each composition submitted. Composers may enter more than one composition.
Write for complete information.

380

QUEEN MARIE JOSE
(Musical Prize Contest)
Box 19; CH-1252 Meinier
Geneva Switzerland
Written inquiry

AMOUNT: 10,000 Swiss francs
DEADLINE(S): May 31
FIELD(S): Music Composition

This competition is open to composers of all nationalities without age limit. The subject for the 1996 competition is a work for percussion (maximum 4 players) & 1 singing and/or speaking voice. Two scores & a recording are required.
Write for complete information.

381

RIPON COLLEGE
(Music & Debate-Forensics Scholarships)
P.O. Box 248; 300 Seward St.
Admissions Office
Ripon WI 54971
414/748-8102 or 1-800/94RIPON

AMOUNT: $500-1500
DEADLINE(S): March 1
FIELD(S): Music; Debate-Forensics

Scholarships recognize & encourage academic potential & accomplishment in above fields. Renewable up to 3 yrs provided recipient maintains good academic standing.
Must apply and be accepted for admission to Ripon College. Write for complete information.

382

SANTA BARBARA FOUNDATION
(Mary & Edith Pillsbury Foundation Scholarships)
15 E. Carrillo St.
Santa Barbara CA 93101
805/963-1873

AMOUNT: Varies

DEADLINE(S): May 15

FIELD(S): Music Performance; Music Composition

Open to talented music students who are Santa Barbara county residents or have strong Santa Barbara ties. Awards may be used for music lessons, camps, or college tuition. US citizen. Financial need is a consideration.

Approximately 30 scholarships per year; renewable. Write for complete information.

383

TENNESSEE ARTS COMMISSION
(Individual Artists' Fellowships)
404 James Robertson Parkway; Suite 160
Nashville TN 37243-0780
615/741-1701

AMOUNT: $2500 to $5000

DEADLINE(S): January 11

FIELD(S): Visual Arts; Performing Arts; Creative Arts

Open to artists who are residents of Tennessee. Duration of award is one year. Applicants must be professional artists. FULL-TIME STUDENTS ARE NOT ELIGIBLE.

Write for complete information.

384

THE QUEEN SONJA INTERNATIONAL MUSIC COMPETITION
(Piano/Voice Competition)
P.O. Box 5190 Majorstua
N-0302 Oslo Norway
+47/22464055 ext. 430; FAX +47/22463630

AMOUNT: $40,000 approximate total prize money

DEADLINE(S): March 15—every 3 years

FIELD(S): Piano; Voice

The next competition will be for pianists in 1997. In addition to cash awards for the 4 finalists (places 1–4) the Board of Directors will endeavor to provide them with solo engagements in Norway.

Write for complete information.

385

UNIVERSITY OF ALABAMA AT BIRMINGHAM
(Theatre Scholarships)
UAB Station; School Of Arts & Humanities; Dept. of Theatre
Birmingham AL 35294-3340
205/934-3236

AMOUNT: $1000

DEADLINE(S): Spring

FIELD(S): Theatre

Scholarships open to high school seniors with above-average GPAs & theatre talent. For undergraduate study at the University of Alabama/Birmingham. Winners will appear in various shows & touring groups. Must be enrolled in UAB.

Approximately 20 awards per year. Renewable. Write to the department chairman for complete information.

386

UNIVERSITY OF ILLINOIS AT URBANA-CHAMPAIGN
(Lydia E. Parker Bates Scholarship)
Student Services Bldg.
610 East John Street
Champaign IL 61820
217/333-0100

AMOUNT: Varies

DEADLINE(S): March 15

FIELD(S): Art; Architecture; Landscape Architecture; Urban Planning; Dance; Theater

Open to undergraduate students in the college of fine & applied arts who are attending the University of Illinois at Urbana-Champaign. Must demonstrate financial need and have 3.85 GPA.

175 awards per year. Recipients must carry at least 14 credit hours per semester. Contact office of student financial aid.

387

VIRGIN ISLANDS BOARD OF EDUCATION
(Music Scholarships)
P.O. Box 11900
St. Thomas VI 00801
809/774-4546

AMOUNT: $2000
DEADLINE(S): March 31
FIELD(S): Music

Open to bona fide residents of the Virgin Islands who are enrolled in an accredited music program at an institution of higher learning.

This scholarship is granted for the duration of the course provided the recipients maintain at least a 'C' average. Write for complete information.

388

WAMSO
(Young Artist Competition)
1111 Nicollet Mall
Minneapolis MN 55403
612/371-5654

AMOUNT: $2500 1st prize plus performance with MN Orchestra
DEADLINE(S): November 1 (competition usually held in January)
FIELD(S): Piano & Orchestral Instruments

Competition offers 4 prizes & possible scholarships to H.S. & college students in schools in IA, MN, MO, NE, ND, SD, WI, & the Canadian provinces of Manitoba & Ontario. Entrants may not have passed their 26th birthday on date of competition.

For list of repertoires & complete information, specify your instrument & write to address above.

389

WAVERLY COMMUNITY HOUSE INC.
(F. Lammont Belin Arts Scholarships)
Scholarships Selection Committee; P.O. Box 142
Waverly PA 18471
717/586-8191

AMOUNT: $9000
DEADLINE(S): December 15
FIELD(S): Painting; Sculpture; Music; Drama; Dance; Literature; Architecture; Photography

Applicants must reside in the Abington or Pocono regions of Northeastern Pennsylvania. They must furnish proof of exceptional ability in their chosen field but need no formal training in any academic or professional program.

USA citizenship required. Finalists must appear in person before the selection committee. Write for complete information.

390

WELLESLEY COLLEGE
(Harriet A. Shaw Fellowships)
Career Center; Secretary Graduate Fellowships
Wellesley MA 02181-8200
617/283-3525

AMOUNT: Up to $3000 stipend per year
DEADLINE(S): Mid-December
FIELD(S): Music; Allied Arts

Open to women who hold a BA degree from Wellesley College for research in music and allied arts in the USA or abroad. Preference given to music candidates; undergrad work in art history is required for other candidates.

Write for complete information.

PHILOSOPHY

391

AMERICAN CATHOLIC HISTORICAL ASSOCIATION
(The John Gilmary Shea Prize)
c/o Catholic University of America
Washington DC 20064
201/635-5079

AMOUNT: $300
DEADLINE(S): October 1
FIELD(S): Creative Writing; Catholic Church

Prize for the book published within last year judged to have made the most significant contribution to the history of the Catholic church. Must be citizen or permanent resident of the US or Canada.

Publishers or authors should send 3 copies of the work to the judges at the address above.

392

AMERICAN SOCIETY OF CHURCH HISTORY
(Albert C. Outler Prize in Ecumenical Church History)
P.O. Box 8517
Red Bank NJ 07701
Written Inquiry

AMOUNT: $1000–$3000
DEADLINE(S): June 1
FIELD(S): Creative writing; theology

Award of $1000 to the author of a book-length manuscript on Ecumenical church history & a possible grant of up to $3000 for publication. Should be chiefly concerned with the problems of Christian unity & disunity in any period.

Write for complete information.

393

CHRISTIAN CHURCH
(Disciples of Christ—Black 'Star Supporter' Scholarship Fund)
P.O. Box 1986
Indianapolis IN 46206
317/353-1491

AMOUNT: Varies
DEADLINE(S): April 15
FIELD(S): Theology

Open to Christian Church (Disciples of Christ) members who are Black or African American and are enrolled in an accredited bachelor's degree or graduate program in preparation for the ministry. Above average GPA & financial need considered.

Renewable. Write for complete information.

394

CLEM JAUNICH EDUCATION TRUST
(Scholarships)
5353 Gamble Dr.; Suite 110
Minneapolis MN 55416
612/546-1555

AMOUNT: $750 to $3000
DEADLINE(S): July 1
FIELD(S): Theology; Medicine

Open to students who have attended public or parochial school in the Delano (MN) school district or currently reside within 7 miles of the city of Delano, MN. Awards support undergraduate or graduate study in theology or medicine.

4–6 scholarships per year. Write for complete information.

395

ELMER O. & IDA PRESTON EDUCATIONAL TRUST
(Grants & Loans)
801 Grand Ave.; Suite 3700
Des Moines IA 50309
515/243-4191

AMOUNT: Varies

DEADLINE(S): June 30

FIELD(S): Christian Ministry

Open to male residents of Iowa who are pursuing collegiate or professional studies at an Iowa college or university. Applicants must provide recommendation from a minister commenting on student's potential in his chosen church vocation.

Awards are one-half grant and one-half loan. The loan is repayable at 6% per annum. Write for complete information.

396

**FITZGERALD MEMORIAL FUND
(Scholarships)**
First of America Trust Company; 301 S.W. Adams St.
Peoria IL 61652
309/655-5000

AMOUNT: Varies

DEADLINE(S): None specified

FIELD(S): Theology

Undergraduate scholarships available for students preparing for priesthood at a Catholic University or college.

Write for complete information.

397

**J. HUGH & EARLE W. FELLOWS
MEMORIAL FUND
(Scholarship Loans)**
Pensacola Junior College Exec VP
1000 College Blvd.
Pensacola FL 32504
904/484-1706

AMOUNT: Each is negotiated individually

DEADLINE(S): None

FIELD(S): Medicine; Nursing; Medical Technology; Theology

Open to bona fide residents of the Florida counties of Escambia, Santa Rosa, Okaloosa, or Walton. For undergraduate study in the fields listed above. US citizenship required.

Loans are interest-free until graduation. Write for complete information.

398

**JIMMIE ULLERY CHARITABLE TRUST
(Scholarship Grant)**
Scholarship Committee
Christian Education Dept.
First Presbyterian Church
709 S. Boston
Tulsa OK 74193
918/584-4701

AMOUNT: $1000–$1200

DEADLINE(S): June 1

FIELD(S): Theology

Open to Presbyterian students in full-time Christian service. Scholarships are usually (but not always) awarded for study at Presbyterian theological seminaries. US citizen or legal resident.

6–8 Scholarships per year. Write for complete information.

399

**NELLIE MARTIN CARMAN
SCHOLARSHIP TRUST
(Scholarships)**
18223 73rd Ave. NE; #B101
Bothell WA 98011
206/486-6575

AMOUNT: Up to $1000

DEADLINE(S): March 15

FIELD(S): All fields of study except those noted below

Open to high school seniors in King, Pierce, & Snohomish Counties (WA). For undergraduate study in the state of Washington in all fields EXCEPT music, sculpting, drawing, interior design, & home economics. US citizenship required.

Applications available only through high schools & nomination by counselor is required. Awards are renewable. Write for complete information.

400

NORTH AMERICAN BAPTIST SEMINARY
(Financial Aid Grants)
1525 S. Grange Ave.
Sioux Falls SD 57105
605/336-6588

AMOUNT: Up to $2100
DEADLINE(S): None
FIELD(S): Theology

Financial aid grants are open to students who are enrolled full time at North American Baptist seminary. Financial need is a consideration.

Approx. 70 awards per year. Write for complete information.

401

ROBERT SCHRECK MEMORIAL FUND
(Grants)
c/o Texas Commerce Bank—Trust Dept
P.O. Drawer 140
El Paso TX 79980
915/546-6515

AMOUNT: $500–$1500
DEADLINE(S): July 15; November 15
FIELD(S): Medicine; Veterinary Medicine; Physics; Chemistry; Architecture; Engineering; Episcopal Clergy

Grants to undergraduate juniors or seniors or graduate students who have been residents of El Paso county for at least two years. Must be US citizen or legal resident and have a high grade point average. Financial need is a consideration.

Write for complete information.

402

UNITED METHODIST CHURCH
(Youth Ministry—David W. Self & Richard S. Smith Scholarships)
P.O. Box 840
Nashville TN 37202
Written inquiry

AMOUNT: Up to $1000
DEADLINE(S): June 1
FIELD(S): Church-Related Vocation

Open to United Methodist church youth who have at least a 2.0 high school GPA, been active in local church at least 1 year, are entering college as freshmen in pursuit of a church career, and can demonstrate financial need.

Richard S. Smith award is for ethnic minorities ONLY. Obtain application between November 1 & May 15. Write for complete information.

403

VIRGINIA BAPTIST GENERAL BOARD
(Virginia Baptist Ministerial Undergraduate student aid)
P.O. Box 8568
Richmond VA 23226
Written inquiry

AMOUNT: Varies
DEADLINE(S): August 1
FIELD(S): Theology

Open to residents of Virginia who are enrolled full time as an undergrad college student and are studying to become a Southern Baptist minister. Must be a member of a church associated with the Baptist General Association of Virginia.

50 awards per year. Loans are non-repayable if recipient works for a Christian-related service for 2 years. Write for complete information.

SCHOOL OF NATURAL RESOURCES

404

EXPLORERS CLUB
(Youth Activity Fund)
46 East 70th St.
New York NY 10021
212/628-8383; fax 212/288-4449

AMOUNT: $200–$1000

DEADLINE(S): April 15

FIELD(S): Natural Sciences

Open to high school and undergraduate college students to help them participate in field research in the Natural Sciences anywhere in the world. Grants are to help with travel costs & expences; joint funding is strongly recommended.

US citizen or legal resident. Applications available in February before April deadline. Write for complete information.

405

GENERAL LEARNING CORPORATION
(Dupont & GLC Science Essay Awards Program)

60 Revere Dr.
Northbrook IL 60062-1562
708/205-3000

AMOUNT: Up to $1500

DEADLINE(S): January 27

FIELD(S): Sciences

Annual essay competition open to students in grades 7–12 in USA & Canada. Cash awards for 1st, 2nd, 3rd, & honorable mention. 1st-place essayists, their science teacher, & 1 parent receive trip to space center Houston; April 27–29

Contact your science teacher or address above for complete information. Official entry blank must accompany essay entry.

406

NATIONAL FEDERATION OF THE BLIND
(Howard Brown Rickard Scholarship)

814 4th Ave.; Suite #200
Grinnell IA 50112
515/236-3366

AMOUNT: $2500

DEADLINE(S): March 31

FIELD(S): Natural Sciences; Architecture; Engineering; Medicine; Law

Scholarships for undergraduate or graduate study in the above areas. Open to legally blind students enrolled full time at accredited post-secondary institutions.

Awards based on academic excellence, service to the community, and financial need. Write for complete information.

407

NELLIE MARTIN CARMAN SCHOLARSHIP TRUST
(Scholarships)

18223 73rd Ave. NE; #B101
Bothell WA 98011
206/486-6575

AMOUNT: Up to $1000

DEADLINE(S): March 15

FIELD(S): All fields of study except those noted below

Open to high school seniors in King, Pierce, & Snohomish Counties (WA). For undergraduate study in the state of Washington in all fields EXCEPT music, sculpting, drawing, interior design, & home economics. US citizenship required.

Applications available only through high schools & nomination by counselor is required. Awards are renewable. Write for complete information.

408

SLOCUM-LUNZ FOUNDATION
(Scholarships & Grants)

P.O. Box 12559; 205 Fort Johnson
Charleston SC 29422
803/762-5052

AMOUNT: Up to $2000

DEADLINE(S): April 1

FIELD(S): Natural Sciences; Marine Sciences

Open to beginning graduate students & Ph.D. candidates enrolled at institutions located in South Carolina. Awards support research studies in the above areas.

Academic work must be performed in South Carolina. Write for complete information.

AGRICULTURE

409

**ABBIE SARGENT MEMORIAL
SCHOLARSHIP INC.**
(Scholarships)
 295 Sheep Davis Road
 Concord NH 03301
 603/224-1934

AMOUNT: $200
DEADLINE(S): March 15
FIELD(S): Agriculture; Veterinary Medicine;
 Home Economics

Open to New Hampshire residents who are
 high school graduates with good grades and
 character. For undergraduate or graduate
 study. Must be legal resident of US and
 demonstrate financial need.
Renewable with reapplication. Write for complete information.

410

**AMERICAN JUNIOR BRAHMAN
ASSOCIATION**
(Ladies of the ABBA Scholarship)
 1313 La Concha Lane
 Houston TX 77054-1890
 Written inquiry

AMOUNT: $500 to $1000
DEADLINE(S): April 30
FIELD(S): Agriculture

Open to graduating high school seniors who
 are members of the Junior Brahman
 Association. For full-time undergraduate
 study. US citizenship required.
1–4 awards per year. Write for complete information.

411

BEDDING PLANTS FOUNDATION INC.
(Carl Dietz Memorial Scholarship)
 P.O. Box 27241
 Lansing MI 48909
 517/694-8537

AMOUNT: $1000
DEADLINE(S): April 1
FIELD(S): Horticulture

Open to undergrads entering sophomore,
 junior, or senior year who are enrolled in
 accredited 4-year college/university in the
 US or Canada. Must be a horticulture
 major with a specific interest in bedding
 plants. Minimum 3.0 GPA required.
Write for complete information.

412

BEDDING PLANTS FOUNDATION INC.
(Earl J. Small Growers Inc. Scholarships)
 P.O. Box 27241
 Lansing MI 48909
 517/694-8537

AMOUNT: $2000
DEADLINE(S): April 1
FIELD(S): Horticulture

Open to US & Canadian citizens who are
 undergrads entering sophomore, junior, or
 senior year. Must be enrolled in accredited
 4-year college or university program in the
 US or Canada & intend to pursue a career
 in greenhouse production.
Write for complete information.

413

BEDDING PLANTS FOUNDATION INC.
(Harold Bettinger Memorial Scholarship)
 P.O. Box 27241
 Lansing MI 48909
 517/694-8537

AMOUNT: $1000
DEADLINE(S): April 1
FIELD(S): Horticulture &
 Business/Marketing

Open to sophomore/junior/senior undergrads
 as well as grad students enrolled in an
 accredited 4-year college or university in
 the US or Canada. Minimum 3.0 GPA
 required.

Must be horticulture major with a business and/or marketing emphasis or business/marketing major with horticulture emphasis. Write for complete information.

414

BEDDING PLANTS FOUNDATION INC.
(James K. Rathmell Jr. Memorial Scholarship)
P.O. Box 27241
Lansing MI 48909
517/694-8537

AMOUNT: Up to $2000
DEADLINE(S): April 1
FIELD(S): Horticulture/Floriculture

Open to upper-level undergrad or grad students for work/study programs outside of the US or Canada in the fields of floriculture or horticulture. Preference to those planning programs of 6 months or more.
US citizen. Write for complete information.

415

BEDDING PLANTS FOUNDATION INC.
(Jerry Baker/America's Master Gardener College Freshman Scholarship)
P.O. Box 27241
Lansing MI 48909
517/694-8537

AMOUNT: $1000
DEADLINE(S): April 1
FIELD(S): Horticulture; Landscaping; Gardening

Open to undergraduates entering their freshman year who are interested in careers in horticulture, landscaping, or gardening.
Two awards per year. Write for complete information.

416

BEDDING PLANTS FOUNDATION INC.
(Jerry Wilmot Scholarship)
P.O. Box 27241
Lansing MI 48909
517/694-8537

AMOUNT: $2000
DEADLINE(S): April 1
FIELD(S): Horticulture

Open to undergrads entering sophomore, junior, or senior year. Must be enrolled in accredited 4-year college/university in the US or Canada & be pursuing a career in garden center management. Open to horticulture or business/finance majors.
Write for complete information.

417

BEDDING PLANTS FOUNDATION INC.
(Vocational Scholarships)
P.O. Box 27241
Lansing MI 48909
517/694-8537

AMOUNT: $500–$1000
DEADLINE(S): April 1
FIELD(S): Horticulture

Open to undergrads accepted in a 1- or 2-year vocational program. Must be US or Canadian citizen enrolled for the entire academic year & intend to become a floriculture plant producer and/or operations manager. Minimum 3.0 GPA required.
2–4 awards per year. Write for complete information.

418

CALIFORNIA FARM BUREAU
SCHOLARSHIP FOUNDATION
(Scholarships)
1601 Exposition Blvd.
Sacramento CA 95815
916/924-4052

AMOUNT: $1250–$1750
DEADLINE(S): March 1
FIELD(S): Agriculture

Open to US citizens who are students entering or attending an accredited 4-year college or university in California. Must be majoring in a field related to agriculture; however, membership in a county farm bureau is NOT required.

Renewable. Write for complete information.

419

CDS INTERNATIONAL INC.
(Congress-Bundestag Youth Exchange Program)
330 Seventh Ave.; 19th Floor
New York NY 10001
212/760-1400; FAX 212/268-1288

AMOUNT: Airfare; partial domestic travel & host family payment
DEADLINE(S): December 15
FIELD(S): Business; Vo-tech Fields; Agricultural Fields

Year-long work/study programs in Germany for US citizens aged 18–24 & in the USA for German citizens aged 18–21. Program for Americans includes 2-month language study, 4-month tech or professional school study, & 6-month internship.

Professional target and applicable work experience is required. Participants must provide their own spending money of $300–$350/month. Write or call for complete information.

420

COMMITTEE ON INSTITUTIONAL COOPERATION
(CIC Pre-doctoral Fellowships)
Indiana University
803 East 8th St.
Bloomington IN 47408
812/855-0823

AMOUNT: $11,000 + tuition (4 years)
DEADLINE(S): December 1
FIELD(S): Humanities; Social Sciences; Natural Sciences; Mathematics; Engineering

Pre-doctoral fellowships for US citizens of African American, American Indian, Mexican American, or Puerto Rican heritage. Must hold or expect to receive bache-

lor's degree by late summer from a regionally accredited college or unviersity.

Awards for specified universities in IL, IN, IA, MI, MN, OH, WI, PA. Write for details.

421

DAIRY RECOGNITION EDUCATION FOUNDATION
(Low-interest Loans)
6245 Executive Blvd.
Rockville MD 20852
301/984-1444

AMOUNT: Up to $1500
DEADLINE(S): None
FIELD(S): Dairy Science; Food Science

Low-interest loans (currently 4%) for citizens of the US & Canada who are in good academic standing in the above areas. Awards support undergraduate study. Preference given to students who have completed at least one year of college.

10–20 awards per year. Write for complete information.

422

DAIRY SHRINE
(Dairy Student Recognition Program Scholarship Awards)
Jim Leuenberger
100 MBC Drive
Shawano WI 54166
715/526-2141

AMOUNT: $200 to $1000
DEADLINE(S): March 15
FIELD(S): Dairy Science

Scholarships for college juniors and seniors majoring in dairy science and related fields who plan to work with dairy cattle and/or within the dairy industry after graduation. Must be nominated by college dairy science department.

5 awards per year. Contact your dairy science department or write for complete information.

423

DOG WRITERS' EDUCATIONAL TRUST
(Scholarships)
Berta I. Pickett
P.O. Box 2220
Payson AZ 85547
602/474-8867

AMOUNT: $1000
DEADLINE(S): December 31
FIELD(S): Veterinary Medicine; Animal Behavior; Journalism

Open to applicants whose parents, grandparents, or other close relatives (or the applicant) are or have been involved in the world of dogs as exhibitors, breeders, handlers, judges, club officers, or other activities.

Scholarships support undergraduate or graduate study. 10 awards per year. Send self-addressed stamped envelope for complete information and application.

424

GOLF COURSE SUPERINTENDENTS
ASSOCIATION OF AMERICA
(O. M. Scott Scholarship Program)
1421 Research Park Dr.
Lawrence KS 66049
913/841-2240

AMOUNT: $1000–$5000
DEADLINE(S): March 15
FIELD(S): Green Industry

Internship/scholarship program offers work experience and an opportunity to compete for financial aid awards. Students are selected for paid summer internships based on academic ability and interest in a "green industry" career.

Write for complete information.

425

MOORMAN COMPANY FUND
(Scholarships in Agriculture)
1000 N. 30th St.
Quincy IL 62301
217/222-7100

AMOUNT: Varies
DEADLINE(S): Varies
FIELD(S): Agriculture

Moorman scholarships open to sophomores, juniors, and seniors at 30 Land Grant colleges of Agriculture in the US. Awards based on scholarship record, leadership qualities, & Ag major.

Recipients should reside in the same state as the University awarding the scholarship. Contact the Dean of your University's College of Agriculture for further information.

426

NATIONAL COUNCIL OF FARMER
COOPERATIVES
(Undergraduate Awards)
50 F Street NW; Suite 900
Washington DC 20001
202/626-8700

AMOUNT: $200
DEADLINE(S): June 1 (postmark)
FIELD(S): US Farming Cooperatives

Award is for an outstanding term paper on topics related to the operations of American cooperatives. Open to undergrads in their junior or senior year or 2nd year students at a junior/community college or voc-tech school.

Five awards per year. Write or call for complete information.

427

NATIONAL JUNIOR HORTICULTURAL
ASSOCIATION
(Scottish Gardening Scholarship)
401 N. 4th
Durant OK 74701
Written inquiry

AMOUNT: Transportation; stipend; food and lodging
DEADLINE(S): October 1
FIELD(S): Horticulture

Program provides a 1-year horticultural study & work experience program in Scotland at the Threave School of Practical Gardening. Previous work in horticulture is essential. Must be 18 or older and a US citizen.

Write for program outline and complete information.

428

SAFEWAY STORES INC.
(Grand National Junior Livestock Exposition Scholarships)
   c/o Cow Palace
   P.O. Box 34206
   San Francisco CA 94134
   415/469-6000

AMOUNT: $800
DEADLINE(S): February 1
FIELD(S): Animal Science

Open to California high school seniors who are 4-H or FFA members, "participate" in the Junior Grand National & plan to enroll in any accredited 2- or 4-year agricultural program of study in the US.

Write for complete information.

429

SAN MATEO COUNTY FARM BUREAU
(Scholarship)
   765 Main Street
   Half Moon Bay CA 94019
   415/726-4485

AMOUNT: Varies
DEADLINE(S): April 1
FIELD(S): All areas of study

Open to entering college freshmen and continuing students who are members of the San Mateo county farm bureau or the dependent child of a member.

Write for complete information.

430

SOIL AND WATER CONSERVATION SOCIETY
(Donald A. Williams Soil Conservation Scholarship)
   7515 Northeast Ankeny Road
   Ankeny IA 50021-9764
   515/289-2331 or 1-800-THE-SOIL;
   FAX 515/289-1227

AMOUNT: $1500
DEADLINE(S): April 1
FIELD(S): Conservation-related (technical or administrative course work)

Open to SWCS members who are currently employed in a related field & have completed at least 1 year of natural resource conservation work with a governmental agency, organization, or business firm. Must show reasonable financial need.

Applicants who have not received a bachelor's degree will be given preference. Attainment of degree not required. Write for complete information.

431

THERESA CORTI FAMILY AGRICULTURAL TRUST
(Scholarship Program)
   Wells Fargo Bank Trust Dept.
   2222 W. Shaw Ave.; Suite 11
   Fresno CA 93711
   209/445-7732

AMOUNT: Varies
DEADLINE(S): February 28
FIELD(S): Agriculture

Open to students who are agriculture majors and graduates of Kern County High Schools. For undergraduate study at accredited colleges and universities. Must carry at least 12 units and have a 2.0 or better GPA.

Financial need is a consideration. Write for complete information.

432

TOWER HILL BOTANIC GARDEN
(Scholarship Program)
Worcester County Horticultural Society
Boylston MA 01505
508/869-6111

AMOUNT: $500–$2000
DEADLINE(S): May 1
FIELD(S): Horticulture

Open to undergraduates in their junior or
senior year and to graduate students who
reside in New England or attend a New
England college or university and are
majoring in horticulture or a horticulture-
related field.

Selections based on interest in horticulture,
sincerity of purpose, academic performance,
financial need. Write for complete information.

433

TYSON FOUNDATION INC.
(Scholarship Program)
2210 W. Oaklawn
Springdale AR 72762-6999
501/290-4955

AMOUNT: Up to $1200/semester
DEADLINE(S): June 21
FIELD(S): Business; Agriculture;
Engineering; Computer Science; Nursing

Open to a US citizen who was raised in and
still lives in the vicinity of a Tyson Food's
facility. Must maintain a 2.5 GPA while
working and going to school full time. For
undergrad study at schools in USA.

Recipients sign a pledge either to repay the
scholarship money or help another deserving student not related by blood or marriage to attend college. Write for complete
information.

434

UNITED AGRIBUSINESS LEAGUE
(UAL Scholarship Program)
54 Corporate Park
Irvine CA 92714
714/975-1424

AMOUNT: $1500–$3500
DEADLINE(S): May 1
FIELD(S): Agriculture; Agribusiness

Open ONLY to UAL member employees &
their dependent children. Awards support
undergraduate or graduate study in the
above areas at recognized colleges & universities.

Awards renewable. Write for complete information.

435

UNITED DAIRY INDUSTRY
ASSOCIATION
(Dairy Shrine-UDIA Milk Marketing
Scholarships)
10255 W. Higgins Rd. #900
Rosemont IL 60018
708/803-2000

AMOUNT: Varies
DEADLINE(S): April 1
FIELD(S): Dairy Marketing

Open to undergraduate sophomores, juniors,
& seniors enrolled in an accredited agricultural program in the US. At least 2.5 GPA
on 4.0 scale. Purpose is to encourage qualified applicants to pursue a career in dairy
marketing.

Write for complete information.

436

WELLS FARGO BANK
(Grand National Stock Show Scholarships)
c/o Cow Palace
P.O. Box 34206
San Francisco CA 94134
415/469-6000

AMOUNT: $1000

DEADLINE(S): Varies

FIELD(S): Animal Science

Open to California high school seniors who are 4-H or FFA members, "participate" in the Grand National, & plan to enroll in any accredited 2- or 4-year agricultural program in the US.

Write for complete information.

EARTH SCIENCE

437

AMERICAN GEOLOGICAL INSTITUTE
(AGI Minority Geoscience Scholarships)
4220 King St.
Alexandria VA 22302-1507
703/379-2480; FAX 703/379-7563

AMOUNT: Up to $10,000/year undergrad; $4000/year grad

DEADLINE(S): February 1

FIELD(S): Geoscience

Open to full-time undergrads or grads majoring in geology, geophysics, geochemistry, hydrology, meteorology, physical oceanography, planetary geology, or earth-science education (NOT for engineering, mathematic,s or natural science majors).

Must be ethnic minority & US citizen. Financial need must be demonstrated. Write for complete information.

438

AMERICAN METEOROLOGICAL SOCIETY
(AMS Undergraduate Scholarships)
45 Beacon Street
Boston MA 02108
617/227-2426 ext. 235

AMOUNT: $2000 (Orville); $700 (Hanks Jr.); $5000 (Kutschenreuter); $2500 (Grau); $2000 (75th Anniversary)

DEADLINE(S): June 16

FIELD(S): Atmospheric or Related Oceanic & Hydrologic Sciences

Five different scholarships for the final year of undergrad study in the field of atmospheric or related oceanic & hydrologic sciences at an accredited US institution. GPA of 3.0 or better & US citizenship or permanent residency required.

Financial need must be demonstrated for the Kutschenreuter Scholarship. All scholarships are for full-time students only. Write for complete information (send SASE to receive application).

439

AMERICAN METEOROLOGICAL SOCIETY
(Father James B. MacElwane Annual Awards)
45 Beacon St.
Boston MA 02108
617/227-2425

AMOUNT: $300 (1st); $200 (2nd); $100 (3rd)

DEADLINE(S): June 15

FIELD(S): Meteorology

Awards are for original papers on meteorology. Open to all undergraduate students enrolled in colleges & universities in the Americas at the time paper is written. Purpose is to stimulate interest in meteorology among collge students.

Write for complete information.

440

ARTHUR & DOREEN PARRETT SCHOLARSHIP TRUST FUND
(Scholarships)
c/o US Bank of Washington; P.O. Box 720; Trust Dept.; 8th Floor
Seattle WA 98111-0720
206/344-4653

AMOUNT: Up to $3500

DEADLINE(S): July 31

FIELD(S): Engineering; Science; Medicine; Dentistry

Washington state resident who has completed her/his first year of college by July 31. Open to students enrolled in above schools.

Awards tenable at any accredited undergrad college or university.

Approximately 15 awards per year. Write for complete information.

441

PENN STATE UNIVERSITY—COLLEGE OF EARTH & MINERAL SCIENCES
(Scholarships)
Committee on Scholarships & Awards
116 Deike Bldg.
University Park PA 16802
814/865-6546

AMOUNT: $500–$2500

DEADLINE(S): None

FIELD(S): Geosciences; Meteorology; Mineral Economics; Materials Science; Mineral Engineering; Geography; Earth Science

Scholarship program open to outstanding undergraduate students accepted to or enrolled in Penn State's College of Earth & Mineral Sciences. Minimum GPA of 3.15 on 4.0 scale.

290 awards per year. Renewable. Contact Dean's office for complete information.

442

SOCIETY OF EXPLORATION GEOPHYSICISTS FOUNDATION
(Scholarship Program)
P.O. Box 702740
Tulsa OK 74170
918/493-3516

AMOUNT: $500–$3000

DEADLINE(S): March 1

FIELD(S): Geophysics & Related Earth Sciences

Undergraduate & graduate scholarships open to students who are accepted to or enrolled in an accredited program in the USA or its possessions & intend to pursue a career in exploration geophysics.

60–100 awards per year. Renewable. Interest and an aptitude for physics, mathematics,

and geology required. Write for complete information.

443

US AIR FORCE ROTC
(4-Year Scholarship Program)
AFROTC/RROO; Recruiting Operations Branch
Maxwell AFB AL 36112
205/953-2091

AMOUNT: Tuition; fees & books + $100 per month stipend

DEADLINE(S): December 1

FIELD(S): Aeronautical Engineering; Civil Engineering; Mechanical Engineering; Mathematics; Physics; Nursing; & some Liberal Arts

Open to USA citizens who are at least 17 and will graduate from college before age 25. Must complete application, furnish SAT/ACT scores, high school transcripts, and record of extracurricular activities.

Must qualify on Air Force medical examination. About 1600 scholarships awarded each year at campuses which offer Air Force ROTC.

444

WOMEN'S AUXILIARY TO THE AMERICAN INSTITUTE OF MINING METALLURGICAL & PETROLEUM ENGINEERS
(WAAIME Scholarship Loan Fund)
345 E. 47th St.; 14th Floor
New York NY 10017
Written inquiry only

AMOUNT: Varies

DEADLINE(S): March 15

FIELD(S): Earth Sciences; Mining Engineering; Petroleum Engineering

Open to undergraduate juniors & seniors and grad students. Eligible applicants receive a scholarship loan for all or part of their education. Recipients repay only 50% with no interest charges.

Repayment to begin by 6 months after graduation and be completed within 6 years. Write to WAAIME Scholarship Loan Fund (address above) for complete information.

ENVIRONMENTAL STUDIES

445

EDMUND NILES HUYCK PRESERVE
(Graduate and Postgraduate Research Grants)
Main St.
Rensselaerville NY 12147
518/797-3440

AMOUNT: Up to $2500
DEADLINE(S): February 1
FIELD(S): Ecology; Behavior; Evolution; Natural History

Grants to support graduate and postgraduate scientists conducting research on the natural resources of the Huyck Preserve. Funds are NOT available to help students defray college expenses.

Housing and lab space are provided at the preserve. Write for complete information.

446

GARDEN CLUB OF AMERICA
(GCA Awards for Summer Environmental Studies)
598 Madison Ave.
New York NY 10022
212/753-8287; FAX 212/753-0134

AMOUNT: $1500
DEADLINE(S): February 15
FIELD(S): Ecology and Related Fields

Two summer scholarships open to students who have demonstrated a keen interest in the betterment of the environment and opportunity for summer study in the fields of ecology. Preference is given to college students.

Write to Mrs. Monica Freeman at above address for complete information (include SASE for application request).

447

NATIONAL ENVIRONMENTAL HEALTH ASSOC.
(NEHA/AAS Scholarship)
720 South Colorado Blvd.; Suite 970
South Tower
Denver CO 80222
303/756-9090

AMOUNT: $750 to $1500
DEADLINE(S): February 1
FIELD(S): Environmental Health

Open to undergraduate juniors & seniors as well as grad students enrolled in an environmental health curriculum at an approved US college or university.

Financial need is not a consideration. Three awards. Write for complete information.

448

SMITHSONIAN INSTITUTION ENVIRONMENTAL RESEARCH CENTER
(Work/Learn Program)
P.O. Box 28
Edgewater MD 21037
301/798-4424; 202/287-3321

AMOUNT: Stipend
DEADLINE(S): March 1; December 1
FIELD(S): Environmental Studies; Biology

Work/learn internships at the center open to undergraduate & graduate students. Competitive program which offers unique opportunity to gain exposure to & experience in environmental research.

Projects generally coincide with academic semesters & summer sessions and are normally 12–15 weeks in duration. Write for complete information. E-mail for application EDUCATION@SERC.SI.EDU.

449

SOIL AND WATER CONSERVATION SOCIETY
(Donald A. Williams Soil Conservation Scholarship)
7515 Northeast Ankeny Road
Ankeny IA 50021-9764
515/289-2331 or 1-800-THE-SOIL; FAX 515/289-1227

AMOUNT: $1500
DEADLINE(S): April 1
FIELD(S): Conservation-related (technical or administrative course work)

Open to SWCS members who are currently employed in a related field & have completed at least 1 year of natural resource conservation work with a governmental agency, organization, or business firm. Must show reasonable financial need.

Applicants who have not received a bachelor's degree will be given preference. Attainment of degree not required. Write for complete information.

450

WATER ENVIRONMENT FEDERATION
(Student Paper Competition)
Liza Clark; 601 Wythe St.
Alexandria VA 22314
703/684-2407

AMOUNT: $1000 (1st prize); $500 (2nd); $250 (3rd) in each of 4 categories
DEADLINE(S): January 1
FIELD(S): Water Pollution

Awards for 500 to 1000-word abstracts dealing with water pollution control, water quality problems, water related concerns or hazardous wastes. Open to operations students (AA degree candidates) as well as undergrad and grad students.

Also open to recently graduated students (within 1 calendar year of January 1 deadline). Write for complete information.

MARINE SCIENCE

451

SEASPACE SCHOLARSHIPS
P.O. Box 3753
Houston TX 77253-3753
Written inquiry

AMOUNT: $1000 (average)
DEADLINE(S): March 15
FIELD(S): Marine Sciences; Marine Biology or Geology; Nautical Archeology; Biological Oceanography; Ocean & Fishery Sciences; Naval/Marine Engineering

Open to college juniors, seniors, and graduate students who aspire to a career in the marine sciences and attend a USA school. Undergrads should have at least a 3.5 GPA; graduates at least 3.0. Must demonstrate financial need.

Average of 15 awards per year. Applications must be received by March 15 deadline to be considered. Write for complete information by November 30.

452

WOODS HOLE OCEANOGRAPHIC INSTITUTION
(Summer Student Fellowship)
Fellowships Coordinator
Woods Hole MA 02543
508/457-2000 ext 2709

AMOUNT: $3900 stipend for 12-week program & possible travel allowance
DEADLINE(S): March 1
FIELD(S): Oceanography

Summer fellowships to study oceanography at the Woods Hole Oceanographic Institution. Open to undergraduates who have completed their junior year and beginning graduate students.

Applicants must be studying in any fields of science or engineering and have at least a tentative interest in oceanography. Write for complete information.

NATURAL HISTORY

453

COMMITTEE ON INSTITUTIONAL COOPERATION
(CIC Pre-doctoral Fellowships)
Indiana University
803 East 8th St.
Bloomington IN 47408
812/855-0823

AMOUNT: $11,000 + tuition (4 years)
DEADLINE(S): December 1
FIELD(S): Humanities; Social Sciences; Natural Sciences; Mathematics; Engineering

Pre-doctoral fellowships for US citizens of African American, American Indian, Mexican American, or Puerto Rican heritage. Must hold or expect to receive bachelor's degree by late summer from a regionally accredited college or unviersity.

Awards for specified universities in IL, IN, IA, MI, MN, OH, WI, PA. Write for details.

454

CREOLE-AMERICAN GENEALOGICAL SOCIETY INC.
(Creole Scholarships)
P.O. Box 3215
Church Street Station
New York NY 10008
Written inquiry only

AMOUNT: $1500
DEADLINE(S): Apply between January 1 and April 30
FIELD(S): Genealogy or language or Creole culture

Awards in the above areas open to individuals of mixed racial ancestry who submit a four-generation genealogical chart attesting to Creole ancestry and/or interracial parentage. For undergraduate or graduate study/research.

For scholarship/award information send $2 money order and self-addressed stamped envelope to address above. Cash and per-sonal checks are not accepted. Letters without SASE and handling charge will not be answered.

455

EDMUND NILES HUYCK PRESERVE
(Graduate and Postgraduate Research Grants)
Main St.
Rensselaerville NY 12147
518/797-3440

AMOUNT: Up to $2500
DEADLINE(S): February 1
FIELD(S): Ecology; Behavior; Evolution; Natural History

Grants to support graduate and postgraduate scientists conducting research on the natural resources of the Huyck Preserve. Funds are NOT available to help students defray college expenses.

Housing and lab space are provided at the preserve. Write for complete information.

456

SMITHSONIAN INSTITUTION
(Cooper-Hewitt Museum of Design Summer Internships)
Cooper-Hewitt Museum
2 East 91st St.
New York NY 10128
212/860-6868; FAX 212/860-6909

AMOUNT: Varies
DEADLINE(S): March 31
FIELD(S): Art; Design; Architecture; Museum Studies

10-week summer internships at the Cooper-Hewitt Museum open to undergraduate and graduate students.

Write for complete information.

457

SMITHSONIAN INSTITUTION
(Minority Undergraduate & Graduate
Internship)
    Office of Fellowships & Grants
    955 L'Enfant Plaza; Suite 7000
    Washington DC 20560
    202/287-3271

AMOUNT: $250 to $300/week stipend +
    travel
DEADLINE(S): February 15; June 15;
    October 15
FIELD(S): Design; Architecture; Art;
    Museum Studies

Internships open to minority students for
    research & study at the Smithsonian or
    Cooper-Hewitt Museum of Design in New
    York City. The museum's collection spans
    3000 years of design from ancient pottery to
    modern fashion & advertising.
Undergraduates receive $250 per week
    stipend & graduate students receive $300
    per week stipend. Write for complete infor-
    mation.

458

SMITHSONIAN INSTITUTION
(Peter Krueger Summer Internship Program)
    Cooper-Hewitt Museum
    2 East 91st St.
    New York NY 10128
    212/860-6868; FAX 212/860-6909

AMOUNT: $2500
DEADLINE(S): March 31
FIELD(S): Art history; Architectural History;
    Design

Ten-week summer internships open to gradu-
    ate and undergraduate students considering
    a career in the museum profession. Interns
    will assist on special research or exhibition
    projects and participate in daily museum
    activities.
Internship commences in June and ends in
    August. Housing is not provided. Write for
    complete information.

459

US MARINE CORPS HISTORICAL
CENTER
(College Internships)
    Building 58; Washington Navy Yard
    Washington DC 20374
    202/433-3839

AMOUNT: Stipend to cover daily expenses
DEADLINE(S): None specified
FIELD(S): US Military History; Library
    Science; History; Museum Studies

Open to undergraduate students at a college
    or university which will grant academic
    credit for work experience as interns at the
    address above or at the Marine Corps
    Airground Museum in Quantico Virginia.
All internships are regarded as beginning pro-
    fessional-level historian, curator, librarian,
    or archivist positions. Write for complete
    information.

SCHOOL OF SCIENCE

460

ALEXANDER GRAHAM BELL
ASSOCIATION FOR THE DEAF
(Robert H. Weitbrecht Scholarship Award)
    3417 Volta Place
    Washington DC 20007
    202/337-5220

AMOUNT: $750
DEADLINE(S): April 1
FIELD(S): Engineering/Science

Open to oral deaf students who were born
    with a profound hearing impairment or who
    suffered such a loss before acquiring lan-
    guage. Must be accepted into a full-time
    academic program for hearing students.
    Preference to N. American citizens.
Write for complete information.

461

AMERICAN INDIAN SCIENCE & ENGINEERING SOCIETY
(Santa Fe Pacific Foundation Scholarships)
1630 30th St.; Suite 301
Boulder CO 80301
303/939-0023

AMOUNT: Up to $2500 per year for 4 years
DEADLINE(S): March 31
FIELD(S): Business; Engineering; Science; Health Administration

Open to graduating high school seniors with 1/4 or more Indian blood. Must reside in KS, OK, CO, AZ, NM, or San Bernardino County, CA (AT&SF Railway service area). Two of the five scholarships are designated for Navajo tribe members.

Must plan to attend a 4-year post-secondary accredited educational institution. Write for complete information.

462

CAPE CANAVERAL CHAPTER RETIRED OFFICERS ASSOC.
(Scholarships)
P.O. Box 4186
Patrick AFB FL 32925
Written inquiry

AMOUNT: Approximately $1500 per year
DEADLINE(S): May 31
FIELD(S): Science; Mathematics; Engineering; Liberal Arts; Chemistry

Open ONLY to Brevard County, Florida, residents who are undergraduate juniors or seniors at any 4-year college in the USA and the son or daughter of active duty or retired military personnel. Must be US citizen.

Awards renewable for one year. Write to the scholarship program committee (address above) for complete information.

463

CIVIL AIR PATROL
(CAP Undergraduate Scholarships)
National Headquarters
Maxwell AFB AL 36112
205/293-5315

AMOUNT: $750
DEADLINE(S): October 1
FIELD(S): Humanities; Science; Engineering; Education

Open to CAP members who have received the Billy Mitchell Award or the senior rating in level II of the senior training program. For undergraduate study in the above areas. Write for complete information.

464

GENERAL LEARNING CORPORATION
(Dupont & GLC Science Essay Awards Program)
60 Revere Dr.
Northbrook IL 60062-1562
708/205-3000

AMOUNT: Up to $1500
DEADLINE(S): January 27
FIELD(S): Sciences

Annual essay competition open to students in grades 7–12 in USA & Canada. Cash awards for 1st, 2nd, 3rd, & honorable mention. 1st-place essayists, their science teacher, & 1 parent receive trip to space center Houston; April 27–29

Contact your science teacher or address above for complete information. Official entry blank must accompany essay entry.

465

JOSEPH BLAZEK FOUNDATION
(Scholarships)
8 South Michigan Ave.
Chicago IL 60603
312/372-3880

AMOUNT: $750 per year for 4 years

DEADLINE(S): February 1

FIELD(S): Science; Chemistry; Engineering; Mathematics; Physics

Open to residents of Cook County (Illinois) who are high school seniors planning to study in the above fields at a four-year college or university.

20 scholarships per year. Renewable. Write for complete information.

466

NATIONAL FEDERATION OF THE BLIND
(Howard Brown Rickard Scholarship)
814 4th Ave.; Suite #200
Grinnell IA 50112
515/236-3366

AMOUNT: $2500

DEADLINE(S): March 31

FIELD(S): Natural Sciences; Architecture; Engineering; Medicine; Law

Scholarships for undergraduate or graduate study in the above areas. Open to legally blind students enrolled full time at accredited post secondary institutions.

Awards based on academic excellence, service to the community, and financial need. Write for complete information.

467

NORTH CAROLINA STUDENT LOAN PROGRAM FOR HEALTH, SCIENCE, & MATHEMATICS
(Loans)
3824 Barrett Dr.; Suite 304
Raleigh NC 27619
919/733-2164

AMOUNT: $2500 to $7500 per year

DEADLINE(S): January 8 to May 5

FIELD(S): Health Professions; Sciences; Engineering

Low-interest scholarship loans open to North Carolina residents of at least 1 year who are pursuing an associates, undergraduate, or

graduate degree in the above fields at an accredited institution in the US.

Loans may be retired after graduation by working (1 year for each year funded) at designated institutions. Write for complete details.

468

SOCIETY OF HISPANIC PROFESSIONAL ENGINEERS FOUNDATION
(SHPE Scholarships)
5400 E. Olympic Blvd.; Suite 210
Los Angeles CA 90022
213/888-2080

AMOUNT: $500 to $3000

DEADLINE(S): April 15

FIELD(S): Engineering & Science

Open to deserving students of Hispanic descent who are seeking careers in engineering and science. For full-time undergraduate or graduate study at a college or university. Academic achievement and financial need are considerations.

Write for complete information.

469

TANDY TECHNOLOGY SCHOLARS
(Student Awards; Teacher Awards)
TCU Station; Box 32897
Fort Worth TX 76129
817/924-4087

AMOUNT: $1000 students; $2500 teachers

DEADLINE(S): October 14

FIELD(S): Mathematics; Science; Computer Science

Program recognizes academic performance and outstanding achievements by Mathematics, Science, and Computer Science students and teachers. Students and teachers receive cash awards.

Must be a senior in an enrolled high school located in one of the 50 states. 100 of each awarded each year. Nomination packets sent to high schools.

470

THOMAS ALVA EDISON FOUNDATION
(Edison/McGraw Scholarship Program)
3000 Book Building
Detroit MI 48226
313/965-1149

AMOUNT: $3000; $5000; $1500; $1000
DEADLINE(S): December 1
FIELD(S): Science; Engineering &
Technology

Outstanding high school students. No formal
application. Submit a proposal not to
exceed 1000 words on a completed experiment or a project idea which would have
"practical application" in fields of science
and/or engineering.

Include letter of recommendation from a
teacher or sponsor which describes how you
exemplify creativity & ingenuity demonstrated by life & work of Thomas Edison &
Max McGraw. Mail entry to Dr. K.R. Roy;
P.O. Box 380057; E. Hartford CT 06138.

471

WILLIAM M. GRUPE FOUNDATION INC.
(Scholarships)
P.O. Box 775
Livingston NJ 07039
201/428-1190

AMOUNT: $2000 to $3000
DEADLINE(S): March 1
FIELD(S): Medicine; Nursing

For residents of Bergen, Essex, or Hudson
County NJ. Annual scholarship aid to good
students in need of financial support in the
above fields. Must be US citizen.

20–30 awards per year. Students may apply
every year. Write for complete information.

BIOLOGY

472

**AMERICAN SOCIETY FOR ENOLOGY
AND VITICULTURE**
(Scholarship)
P.O. Box 1855
Davis CA 95617
916/753-3142

AMOUNT: No predetermined amounts
DEADLINE(S): March 1
FIELD(S): Enology (Wine Making);
Viticulture (Grape Growing)

For college juniors, seniors, or grad students
enrolled in an accredited North American
college or university in a science curriculum
basic to the wine and grape industry. Must
be resident of North America.

GPA requirements of 3.0 or better for undergrads; 3.2 or better for grads. Scholarships
are renewable. Financial need is considered.
Write for complete information.

473

**ARTHUR & DOREEN PARRETT
SCHOLARSHIP TRUST FUND**
(Scholarships)
c/o US Bank of Washington
P.O. Box 720
Trust Dept.; 8th Floor
Seattle WA 98111-0720
206/344-4653

AMOUNT: Up to $3500
DEADLINE(S): July 31
FIELD(S): Engineering; Science; Medicine;
Dentistry

Washington state resident who has completed
her/his first year of college by July 31. Open
to students enrolled in above schools.
Awards tenable at any accredited undergrad
college or university.

Approximately 15 awards per year. Write for
complete information.

474

BUSINESS & PROFESSIONAL WOMEN'S FOUNDATION
(Career Advancement Scholarships)
2012 Massachusetts Ave. NW
Washington DC 20036
202/293-1200

AMOUNT: $500–$1000

DEADLINE(S): April 15 (postmark)

FIELD(S): Computer Science; Education; Paralegal; Engineering; Science; Law; Dentistry; Medicine

Open to women (30 or older) within 12–24 months of completing undergrad or grad study in US (including Puerto Rico & Virgin Islands). Studies should lead to entry/reentry in work force or improve career advancement chances.

Not for doctoral study. Must demonstrate financial need. Send self-addressed stamped ($.64) #10 envelope for complete info. Applications available October 1–April 1.

475

COMMITTEE ON INSTITUTIONAL COOPERATION
(CIC Pre-doctoral Fellowships)
Indiana University; 803 East 8th St.
Bloomington IN 47408
812/855-0823

AMOUNT: $11,000 + tuition (4 years)

DEADLINE(S): December 1

FIELD(S): Humanities; Social Sciences; Natural Sciences; Mathematics; Engineering

Pre-doctoral fellowships for US citizens of African American, American Indian, Mexican American, or Puerto Rican heritage. Must hold or expect to receive bachelor's degree by late summer from a regionally accredited college or unviersity.

Awards for specified universities in IL, IN, IA, MI, MN, OH, WI, PA. Write for details.

476

ELECTRONIC INDUSTRIES FOUNDATION
(Scholarship Fund)
919 18th St.; Suite 900
Washington DC 20006
202/955-5814

AMOUNT: $2000

DEADLINE(S): February 1

FIELD(S): Aeronautics; Computer Science; Electrical Engineering; Engineering Technology; Applied Mathematics; Microbiology

Open to disabled students who are pursuing careers in high-tech areas through academic or technical training. Awards tenable at recognized undergraduate & graduate colleges & universities. Must be US citizen. Financial need is considered.

6 awards per year. Renewable. Write for complete information.

477

ENTOMOLOGICAL SOCIETY OF AMERICA
(Undergraduate Scholarships)
9301 Annapolis Road; Suite 300
Lanham MD 20706
Written inquiry only

AMOUNT: $1500

DEADLINE(S): May 31

FIELD(S): Entomology; Biology (or related science)

For undergraduate study in the above fields. Must be enrolled in a recognized college or university in the USA, Canada, or Mexico. Applicants must have accumulated at least 30 semester hours by the time award is presented.

Send SASE for complete information.

478

NATIONAL ASSOCIATION OF WATER COMPANIES—NEW JERSEY CHAPTER
(Scholarship)

c/o NJ-American Water Co.
66 Shrewsbury Ave.
Shrewsbury NJ 07702
908/842-6900; FAX 908/842-7541

AMOUNT: $2500

DEADLINE(S): April 1 (postmark)

FIELD(S): Business Administration; Biology; Chemistry; Engineering

Open to USA citizens who have lived in NJ at least 5 years and plan a career in the investor-owned water utility industry in disciplines such as those above. Must be undergrad or graduate student in a 2- or 4-year NJ college or university.

GPA of 3.0 or better required. Write for complete information.

479

NATIONAL RESEARCH COUNCIL
(Howard Hughes Medical Institute Pre-doctoral Fellowships in Biological Sciences)

Fellowship Office; 2101 Constitution Ave. NW
Washington DC 20418
202/334-2872

AMOUNT: $14,500 annual stipend + $14,000 cost of education allowance

DEADLINE(S): November 14

FIELD(S): Biological Sciences

Open to college seniors or graduates at or near the beginning of their study toward a Ph.D. or SC.D. in Biological Sciences. US citizens may study in the USA or abroad; foreign nationals may study only in the USA.

Write for complete information.

480

NELLIE MARTIN CARMAN SCHOLARSHIP TRUST
(Scholarships)

18223 73rd Ave. NE; #B101
Bothell WA 98011
206/486-6575

AMOUNT: Up to $1000

DEADLINE(S): March 15

FIELD(S): All fields of study except those noted below

Open to high school seniors in King, Pierce, & Snohomish Counties (WA). For undergraduate study in the state of Washington in all fields EXCEPT music, sculpting, drawing, interior design, & home economics. US citizenship required.

Applications available only through high schools & nomination by counselor is required. Awards are renewable. Write for complete information.

481

TERATOLOGY SOCIETY
(Student Travel Grants)

9650 Rockville Pike
Bethesda MD 20814
301/571-1841

AMOUNT: $400

DEADLINE(S): May 1

FIELD(S): Teratology

Travel assistance grants open to graduates & post-grads for attendance at the Teratology Society's annual meeting for abstract presentation. Purpose is to promote interest in & advance study of Biological Abnormalities.

35–40 awards per year. Write for complete information.

482

WILSON ORNITHOLOGICAL SOCIETY
(Fuertes; Nice & Stewart Grants)
c/o Museum of Zoology
University of Michigan
Ann Arbor MI 48109
Written inquiry only

AMOUNT: $600 (Fuertes); $200 (Nice &
Stewart)
DEADLINE(S): January 15
FIELD(S): Ornithology

Grants to support research on birds only—
NOT for general college funding. Open to
anyone presenting a suitable research prob-
lem in ornithology. Research proposal
required.
5–6 grants per year. NOT renewable. Write
for complete information.

CHEMISTRY

483

ARTHUR & DOREEN PARRETT
SCHOLARSHIP TRUST FUND
(Scholarships)
c/o US Bank of Washington
P.O. Box 720
Trust Dept.; 8th Floor
Seattle WA 98111-0720
206/344-4653

AMOUNT: Up to $3500
DEADLINE(S): July 31
FIELD(S): Engineering; Science; Medicine;
Dentistry

Washington state resident who has completed
her/his first year of college by July 31. Open
to students enrolled in above schools.
Awards tenable at any accredited undergrad
college or university.
Approximately 15 awards per year. Write for
complete information.

484

AT&T BELL LABORATORIES
(Summer Research Program for Minorities &
Women)
101 Crawfords Corner Rd.; RM 1B-222
Holmdel NJ 07733
Written Inquiry

AMOUNT: Salary + travel & living expences
for summer
DEADLINE(S): December 1
FIELD(S): Engineering; Math; Sciences;
Computer Science

Program offers minority students & women
students technical employment experience
at Bell Laboratories. Students should have
completed their third year of study at an
accredited college or university. USA citizen or permanent resident.
Selection is based partially on academic
achievement and personal motivation.
Write special programs manager—SRP for
complete information.

485

BUSINESS & PROFESSIONAL WOMEN'S
FOUNDATION
(Career Advancement Scholarships)
2012 Massachusetts Ave. NW
Washington DC 20036
202/293-1200

AMOUNT: $500–$1000
DEADLINE(S): April 15 (postmark)
FIELD(S): Computer Science; Education;
Paralegal; Engineering; Science; Law;
Dentistry; Medicine

Open to women (30 or older) within 12–24
months of completing undergrad or grad
study in US (including Puerto Rico &
Virgin Islands). Studies should lead to
entry/reentry in work force or improve
career advancement chances.
Not for doctoral study. Must demonstrate
financial need. Send self-addressed stamped
($.64) #10 envelope for complete info.
Applications available October 1–April 1.

486

**CAPE CANAVERAL CHAPTER
RETIRED OFFICERS ASSOC.**
(Scholarships)
P.O. Box 4186
Patrick AFB FL 32925
Written inquiry

AMOUNT: Approximately $1500 per year
DEADLINE(S): May 31
FIELD(S): Science; Mathematics;
Engineering; Liberal Arts; Chemistry

Open ONLY to Brevard County, Florida, residents who are undergraduate juniors or seniors at any 4-year college in the USA and the son or daughter of active duty or retired military personnel. Must be US citizen.

Awards renewable for one year. Write to the scholarship program committee (address above) for complete information.

487

H. FLETCHER BROWN FUND
(Scholarships)
c/o PNC Bank; Trust Dept.
P.O. Box 791
Wilmington DE 19899
302/429-2827

AMOUNT: Varies
DEADLINE(S): April 15
FIELD(S): Medicine; Dentistry; Law;
Engineering; Chemistry

Open to US citizens born and still residing in Delaware. For 4 years of study (undergrad or grad) leading to a degree that enables applicant to practice in chosen field.

Scholarships are based on need, scholastic achievement, and good moral character. Applications available in February. Write for complete information.

488

**INTERNATIONAL ORDER OF THE
KING'S DAUGHTERS AND SONS**
(Health Careers Scholarships)
c/o Mrs. Merle Raber
6024 E. Chicago Rd.
Jonesville MI 49250
716/357-4951

AMOUNT: Up to $1000
DEADLINE(S): April 1
FIELD(S): Medicine; Dentistry; Nursing;
Physical Therapy; Occupational Therapy;
Medical Technologies; Pharmacy

Open to students accepted to/enrolled in an accredited USA or Canadian 4-yr or graduate school. RN candidates must have completed 1st year; BA candidates in at least 3rd year. Pre-med students -NOT- eligible.

USA or Canadian citizen. Those seeking MD OR DDS degrees must be in 2nd yr of Medical or Dental school.

489

**NATIONAL ASSOCIATION OF WATER
COMPANIES—NEW JERSEY CHAPTER**
(Scholarship)
c/o NJ-American Water Co.
66 Shrewsbury Ave.
Shrewsbury NJ 07702
908/842-6900; FAX 908/842-7541

AMOUNT: $2500
DEADLINE(S): April 1 (postmark)
FIELD(S): Business Administration; Biology;
Chemistry; Engineering

Open to USA citizens who have lived in NJ at least 5 years and plan a career in the investor-owned water utility industry in disciplines such as those above. Must be undergrad or graduate student in a 2- or 4-year NJ college or university.

GPA of 3.0 or better required. Write for complete information.

490

NELLIE MARTIN CARMAN SCHOLARSHIP TRUST
(Scholarships)

18223 73rd Ave. NE; #B101
Bothell WA 98011
206/486-6575

AMOUNT: Up to $1000
DEADLINE(S): March 15
FIELD(S): All fields of study except those noted below

Open to high school seniors in King, Pierce, & Snohomish Counties (WA). For undergraduate study in the state of Washington in all fields EXCEPT music, sculpting, drawing, interior design, & home economics. US citizenship required.

Applications available only through high schools & nomination by counselor is required. Awards are renewable. Write for complete information.

491

ROBERT SCHRECK MEMORIAL FUND
(Grants)

c/o Texas Commerce Bank—Trust Dept.
P.O. Drawer 140
El Paso TX 79980
915/546-6515

AMOUNT: $500–$1500
DEADLINE(S): July 15; November 15
FIELD(S): Medicine; Veterinary Medicine; Physics; Chemistry; Architecture; Engineering; Episcopal Clergy

Grants to undergraduate juniors or seniors or graduate students who have been residents of El Paso county for at least two years. Must be US citizen or legal resident and have a high grade point average. Financial need is a consideration.

Write for complete information.

492

SALES ASSOCIATION OF THE CHEMICAL INDUSTRY
(One-year Scholarship)

66 Morris Ave.
Springfield NJ 07081-1450
201/379-1100

AMOUNT: $500
DEADLINE(S): May 30
FIELD(S): Chemistry or Pharmaceuticals

Open to residents of CT, NY, NJ, PA, or DE who are entering freshmen at an accredited college or university. US legal residency required. Academic achievement & extracurricular activities are considered.

Send self-addressed stamped envelope (business size) for complete information.

MATHEMATICS

493

AMERICAN PHYSICAL SOCIETY
(Scholarships for Minority Undergraduate Students in Physics)

One Physics Ellipse
College Park; MD 20740
301/209-3232

AMOUNT: $2000
DEADLINE(S): Early February
FIELD(S): Physics

Open to any Black, Hispanic, or American Indian US citizen who is majoring or plans to major in physics and is a high school senior, college freshman, or sophomore.

Each scholarship is sponsored by a corporation. Write for complete information.

494

AT&T BELL LABORATORIES
(Summer Research Program for Minorities & Women)
101 Crawfords Corner Rd.; RM 1B-222
Holmdel NJ 07733
Written inquiry

AMOUNT: Salary + travel & living expenses for summer

DEADLINE(S): December 1

FIELD(S): Engineering; Math; Sciences; Computer Science

Program offers minority students & women students technical employment experience at Bell Laboratories. Students should have completed their third year of study at an accredited college or university. US citizen or permanent resident.

Selection is based partially on academic achievement and personal motivation. Write special programs manager—SRP for complete information.

495

BUSINESS & PROFESSIONAL WOMEN'S FOUNDATION
(Career Advancement Scholarships)
2012 Massachusetts Ave. NW
Washington DC 20036
202/293-1200

AMOUNT: $500–$1000

DEADLINE(S): April 15 (postmark)

FIELD(S): Computer Science; Education; Paralegal; Engineering; Science; Law; Dentistry; Medicine

Open to women (30 or older) within 12–24 months of completing undergrad or grad study in US (including Puerto Rico & Virgin Islands). Studies should lead to entry/reentry in work force or improve career advancement chances.

Not for doctoral study. Must demonstrate financial need. Send self-addressed stamped ($.64) #10 envelope for complete info. Applications available October 1–April 1.

496

CAPE CANAVERAL CHAPTER RETIRED OFFICERS ASSOC.
(Scholarships)
P.O. Box 4186
Patrick AFB FL 32925
Written inquiry

AMOUNT: Approximately $1500 per year

DEADLINE(S): May 31

FIELD(S): Science; Mathematics; Engineering; Liberal Arts; Chemistry

Open ONLY to Brevard County, Florida, residents who are undergraduate juniors or seniors at any 4-year college in the USA and the son or daughter of active duty or retired military personnel. Must be US citizen.

Awards renewable for one year. Write to the scholarship program committee (address above) for complete information.

497

COMMITTEE ON INSTITUTIONAL COOPERATION
(CIC Pre-doctoral Fellowships)
Indiana University; 803 East 8th St.
Bloomington IN 47408
812/855-0823

AMOUNT: $11,000 + tuition (4 years)

DEADLINE(S): December 1

FIELD(S): Humanities; Social Sciences; Natural Sciences; Mathematics; Engineering

Pre-doctoral fellowships for US citizens of African American, American Indian, Mexican American, or Puerto Rican heritage. Must hold or expect to receive bachelor's degree by late summer from a regionally accredited college or unviersity.

Awards for specified universities in IL, IN, IA, MI, MN, OH, WI, PA. Write for details.

498

ELECTRONIC INDUSTRIES FOUNDATION (Scholarship Fund)
919 18th St.; Suite 900
Washington DC 20006
202/955-5814

AMOUNT: $2000

DEADLINE(S): February 1

FIELD(S): Aeronautics; Computer Science; Electrical Engineering; Engineering Technology; Applied Mathematics; Microbiology

Open to disabled students who are pursuing careers in high-tech areas through academic or technical training. Awards tenable at recognized undergraduate & graduate colleges & universities. Must be US citizen. Financial need is considered.

6 awards per year. Renewable. Write for complete information.

499

NELLIE MARTIN CARMAN SCHOLARSHIP TRUST (Scholarships)
18223 73rd Ave. NE; #B101
Bothell WA 98011
206/486-6575

AMOUNT: Up to $1000

DEADLINE(S): March 15

FIELD(S): All fields of study except those noted below

Open to high school seniors in King, Pierce, & Snohomish Counties (WA). For undergraduate study in the state of Washington in all fields EXCEPT music, sculpting, drawing, interior design, & home economics. US citizenship required.

Applications available only through high schools & nomination by counselor is required. Awards are renewable. Write for complete information.

500

PACIFIC GAS & ELECTRIC CO. (Scholarships for High School Seniors)
77 Beale St.; Room 2837
San Francisco CA 94106
415/973-1338

AMOUNT: $1000–$4000

DEADLINE(S): November 15

FIELD(S): Engineering; Computer Science; Mathematics; Marketing; Business; Economics

High school seniors in good academic standing who reside in or attend high school in areas served by PG&E are eligible to compete for scholarships awarded on a regional basis. Not open to children of PG&E employees.

36 awards per year. Applications & brochures are available in all high schools within PG&E's service area and at PG&E offices.

501

RADIO FREE EUROPE/RADIO LIBERTY (Media & Opinion Research on Eastern Europe & the Former Soviet Union)
Personnel Division
1201 Connecticut Ave. NW
Washington DC 20036
Written inquiry

AMOUNT: Daily stipend of 48 German marks plus accommodations

DEADLINE(S): February 22

FIELD(S): Communications; Market Research; Statistics; Sociology; Social Psychology; East European Studies

Internship open to graduate students or exceptionally qualified undergrads in the above areas who can demonstrate knowledge of quantitative research methods,; computer applications, and public opinion survey techniques.

East European language skills would be an advantage. Write for complete information.

502

SOCIETY OF PHYSICS STUDENTS
(SPS Scholarships)
National Office
One Physics Ellipse
College Park MD 20740
202/232-6688

AMOUNT: $4000 1st place; $2000 second; $1000 all others
DEADLINE(S): January 31
FIELD(S): Physics

SPS members. For final year of full-time study leading to a BS degree in physics. Consideration given to high scholastic performance, potential for continued scholastic development in physics, and active SPS participation.

Nonrenewable. 10 scholarships per year. Write for complete information.

503

STATE FARM COMPANIES FOUNDATION
(Exceptional Student Fellowship)
1 State Farm Plaza
Bloomington IL 61710
309/766-2039

AMOUNT: $3000
DEADLINE(S): February 15 (applications available November 1)
FIELD(S): Accounting; Business Administration; Actuarial Science; Computer Science; Economics; Finance; Insurance; Investments; Marketing; Mathematics; Statistics; & Related Fields

Open to current full-time college juniors and seniors majoring in any of the fields above. Only students nominated by the college dean or a department head qualify as candidates. Applications without nominations will NOT be considered.

US citizen. 3.4 or better GPA (4.0 scale) required. 50 fellowships per year. Write for complete information.

504

STATE FARM COMPANIES FOUNDATION
(Exceptional Student Fellowship Awards)
One State Farm Plaza; SC-3
Bloomington IL 61710
309/766-2039

AMOUNT: $3000
DEADLINE(S): February 15
FIELD(S): Business-related fields; Computer Science; Mathematics; Accounting; Actuarial Science; Business Admin.; Economics; Finance; Insurance; Investments; Marketing; Management, & Statistics

Must be junior or senior undergrad at time of application & have at least a 3.4 GPA (on 4.0 scale). Nominations by Dean or department head only. USA citizenship required.

50 fellowships per academic year. Applications and nominations available November 1. Write for complete information and state your current year in college.

505

TANDY TECHNOLOGY SCHOLARS
(Student Awards; Teacher Awards)
TCU Station; Box 32897
Fort Worth TX 76129
817/924-4087

AMOUNT: $1000 students; $2500 teachers
DEADLINE(S): October 14
FIELD(S): Mathematics; Science; Computer Science

Program recognizes academic performance and outstanding achievements by Mathematics, Science, and Computer Science students and teachers. Students and teachers receive cash awards.

Must be a senior in an enrolled high school located in one of the 50 states. 100 of each awarded each year. Nomination packets sent to high schools.

506

US AIR FORCE ROTC
(4-Year Scholarship Program)
AFROTC/RROO
Recruiting Operations Branch
Maxwell AFB AL 36112
205/953-2091

AMOUNT: Tuition; fees & books + $100 per month stipend
DEADLINE(S): December 1
FIELD(S): Aeronautical Engineering; Civil Engineering; Mechanical Engineering; Mathematics; Physics; Nursing; & some Liberal Arts

Open to US citizens who are at least 17 and will graduate from college before age 25. Must complete application, furnish SAT/ACT scores, high school transcripts and record of extracurricular activities.

Must qualify on Air Force medical examination. About 1600 scholarships awarded each year at campuses which offer Air Force ROTC.

MEDICAL DOCTOR

507

AMERICAN INDIAN SCIENCE &
ENGINEERING SOCIETY
(Santa Fe Pacific Foundation Scholarships)
1630 30th St.; Suite 301
Boulder CO 80301
303/939-0023

AMOUNT: Up to $2500 per year for 4 years
DEADLINE(S): March 31
FIELD(S): Business; Engineering; Science; Health Administration

Open to graduating high school seniors with 1/4 or more Indian blood. Must reside in KS, OK, CO, AZ, NM, or San Bernardino County CA (AT&SF Railway service area). Two of the five scholarships are designated for Navajo tribe members.

Must plan to attend a 4-year post-secondary accredited educational institution. Write for complete information.

508

AMERICAN MEDICAL ASSOCIATION
(Rock Sleyster Memorial Scholarship)
Div. of Undergraduate Medical Education
515 N. State St.
Chicago IL 60610
312/645-4691

AMOUNT: $2500
DEADLINE(S): May 1
FIELD(S): Psychiatry

Open to USA citizens enrolled in USA or Canadian medical schools that grant an MD degree and who aspire to specialize in psychiatry. Candidates must be nominated by their medical school. Nominees must be rising seniors.

Approx. 20 scholarships per year based on demonstrated interest in psychiatry, scholarship, & financial need. Write for complete information.

509

AMERICAN OSTEOPATHIC
ASSOCIATION AUXILIARY
(Scholarship Program)
Scholarship Chairman
142 E. Ontario St.
Chicago IL 60611
312/280-5819

AMOUNT: $3000 maximum
DEADLINE(S): June 1
FIELD(S): Osteopathic Medicine

Open to citizens of US or Canada who are entering sophomore year in approved college of osteopathic medicine. Must be in top 20% or have honors from 1st year and show evidence of financial need and motivation towards osteopathic medicine.

Unspecified number of scholarships per year. Write for complete information.

510

**ARTHUR & DOREEN PARRETT
SCHOLARSHIP TRUST FUND**
(Scholarships)
 c/o US Bank of Washington
 P.O. Box 720; Trust Dept.; 8th Floor
 Seattle WA 98111-0720
 206/344-4653

AMOUNT: Up to $3500
DEADLINE(S): July 31
FIELD(S): Engineering; Science; Medicine;
 Dentistry

Washington state resident who has completed
 her/his first year of college by July 31. Open
 to students enrolled in above schools.
 Awards tenable at any accredited undergrad
 college or university.
Approximately 15 awards per year. Write for
 complete information.

511

BOYS & GIRLS CLUBS OF SAN DIEGO
(Spence Reese Scholarship Fund)
 3760 Fourth Ave.; Suite 1
 San Diego CA 92103
 619/298-3520

AMOUNT: $2000 per year for 4 years
DEADLINE(S): May 15
FIELD(S): Medicine; Law; Engineering;
 Political Science

Open to male high school seniors planning a
 career in above fields. Preference to students within a 250-mile radius of San Diego.
 Boys Club affiliation is not required.
Applications are available in January. Must
 enclose a self-addressed stamped envelope
 to receive application. A $10 processing fee
 is required with completed application.
 Write for complete information.

512

**BUSINESS & PROFESSIONAL WOMEN'S
FOUNDATION**
(Career Advancement Scholarships)
 2012 Massachusetts Ave. NW
 Washington DC 20036
 202/293-1200

AMOUNT: $500–$1000
DEADLINE(S): April 15 (postmark)
FIELD(S): Computer Science; Education;
 Paralegal; Engineering; Science; Law;
 Dentistry; Medicine

Open to women (30 or older) within 12–24
 months of completing undergrad or grad
 study in US (including Puerto Rico &
 Virgin Islands). Studies should lead to
 entry/reentry in work force or improve
 career advancement chances.
Not for doctoral study. Must demonstrate
 financial need. Send self-addressed stamped
 ($.64) #10 envelope for complete info.
 Applications available October 1–April 1.

513

**BUSINESS & PROFESSIONAL WOMEN'S
FOUNDATION**
**(New York Life Foundation Scholarships for
Women in the Health Professions)**
 2012 Massachusetts Ave. NW
 Washington DC 20036
 202/293-1200

AMOUNT: $500–$1000
DEADLINE(S): April 15 postmark (Applica-
 tions available only October 1–April 1
FIELD(S): Health Related Professions

Open to women (25 or older) who are within
 12–24 months of completing their undergraduate program of study in USA. Studies
 should lead to entry or reentry into the
 work force or improve career advancement
 chances. US citizen.
Must be accepted into an accredited program
 and demonstrate financial need. Send self-
 addressed stamped ($.64) #10 envelope for
 application and complete information.

514

CLEM JAUNICH EDUCATION TRUST
(Scholarships)
5353 Gamble Dr.; Suite 110
Minneapolis MN 55416
612/546-1555

AMOUNT: $750 to $3000
DEADLINE(S): July 1
FIELD(S): Theology; Medicine

Open to students who have attended public or parochial school in the Delano (MN) school district or currently reside within 7 miles of the city of Delano MN. Awards support undergraduate or graduate study in theology or medicine.

4–6 scholarships per year. Write for complete information.

515

COMMUNITY FOUNDATION OF
GREATER LORAIN COUNTY
(A.C. Siddall Educational Trust Fund
Scholarship)
1865 N. Ridge Road E.; Suite A
Lorain OH 44055
216/277-0142 or 216/323-4445

AMOUNT: $1000
DEADLINE(S): May 1
FIELD(S): Health Care

Open to those who wish to pursue or further their education in health care, who have been or are now employed and reside in or work for a health care facility within the Allen Memorial Hospital District in Lorain county.

Must have work experience and demonstrate financial need. Applications available beginning January 1 from Administrator; Allen Memorial Hospital; 200 W. Lorain St; Oberlin OH 44074.

516

CUYAHOGA COUNTY MEDICAL
FOUNDATION
(Scholarship Grant Program)
6000 Rockside Woods Blvd.; Suite 150
Cleveland OH 44131-2352
216/520-1000

AMOUNT: $500–$1500
DEADLINE(S): June 1
FIELD(S): Medicine; Dentistry; Pharmacy; Nursing; Osteopathy

Grants open to residents of Cuyahoga County who are accepted to or enrolled in an accredited professional school in one of the above areas.

Approx 40 awards per year. Write for complete information.

517

EDWARD BANGS AND ELZA KELLEY
FOUNDATION
(Scholarship Program)
243 South St.; Box M
Hyannis MA 02601
508/775-3117

AMOUNT: Up to $4000
DEADLINE(S): April 30
FIELD(S): Medicine; Nursing; Health Sciences; & Related Fields

Open to residents of Barnstable County (MA). Scholarships are intended to benefit health and welfare of Barnstable County residents. Awards support study at recognized undergraduate, graduate, and professional institutions.

Financial need is a consideration. Write for complete information.

518

FAIRFAX COUNTY MEDICAL SOCIETY
FOUNDATION
(Scholarships)
8100 Oak St.
Dunn Loring VA 22027
703/560-4855

AMOUNT: $1000
DEADLINE(S): May 30
FIELD(S): Medical Doctor; Medical-related Disciplines; Medical Technologies; Nursing

Open to undergraduate and graduate students who are US citizens and are residents of Fairfax County, VA. For studies related to human health. Must demonstrate financial need.
10 awards per year; renewable. Write for complete information.

519

H. FLETCHER BROWN FUND
(Scholarships)
c/o PNC Bank; Trust Dept.
P.O. Box 791
Wilmington DE 19899
302/429-2827

AMOUNT: Varies
DEADLINE(S): April 15
FIELD(S): Medicine; Dentistry; Law; Engineering; Chemistry

Open to US citizens born and still residing in Delaware. For 4 years of study (undergrad or grad) leading to a degree that enables applicant to practice in chosen field.
Scholarships are based on need, scholastic achievement, and good moral character. Applications available in February. Write for complete information.

520

INTERNATIONAL ORDER OF THE KING'S DAUGHTERS AND SONS
(Health Careers Scholarships)
c/o Mrs. Merle Raber
6024 E. Chicago Rd.
Jonesville MI 49250
716/357-4951

AMOUNT: Up to $1000
DEADLINE(S): April 1
FIELD(S): Medicine; Dentistry; Nursing; Physical Therapy; Occupational Therapy; Medical Technologies; Pharmacy

Open to students accepted to/enrolled in an accredited USA or Canadian 4-yr or graduate school. RN candidates must have completed 1st year; BA candidates in at least 3rd year. Pre-med students NOT eligible.
US or Canadian citizen. Those seeking MD or DDS degrees must be in 2nd yr of Medical or Dental school.

521

J. HUGH & EARLE W. FELLOWS MEMORIAL FUND
(Scholarship Loans)
Pensacola Junior College Exec VP
1000 College Blvd.
Pensacola FL 32504
904/484-1706

AMOUNT: Each is negotiated individually
DEADLINE(S): None
FIELD(S): Medicine; Nursing; Medical Technology; Theology

Open to bona fide residents of the Florida counties of Escambia, Santa Rosa, Okaloosa, or Walton. For undergraduate study in the fields listed above. US citizenship required.
Loans are interest-free until graduation. Write for complete information.

522

JEWISH VOCATIONAL SERVICE
(Marcus & Theresa Levie Educational Fund Scholarships)
1 S. Franklin St.
Chicago IL 60606
312/346-6700 Ext. 2214

AMOUNT: $5000
DEADLINE(S): March 1
FIELD(S): Social Work; Medicine; Dentistry; Nursing; & other related professions & vocations

Open to Cook County residents of the Jewish faith who plan careers in the helping professions. For undergraduate juniors and seniors and for graduate and vocational students.

Applications available December 1 from Scholarship Secretary.

Must show financial need. 85–100 awards per year. Renewal possible with reapplication. Write for complete information.

523

MARYLAND HIGHER EDUCATION COMMISSION
(Professional School Scholarships)
State Scholarship Administration
16 Francis St.
Annapolis MD 21401
410/974-5370

AMOUNT: $200–$1000
DEADLINE(S): March 1
FIELD(S): Dentistry; Pharmacy; Medicine; Law; Nursing

Open to Maryland residents who have been admitted as full-time students at a participating graduate institution of higher learning in Maryland or an undergraduate nursing program.

Renewable up to 4 years. Write for complete information and a list of participating Maryland institutions.

524

MINNESOTA HEART ASSOCIATION
(Helen N. and Harold B. Shapira Scholarship)
4701 West 77th Street
Minneapolis MN 55435
612/835-3300

AMOUNT: $1000
DEADLINE(S): May 1
FIELD(S): Medicine

Open to pre-med undergraduate students & medical students who are accepted to or enrolled in an accredited Minnesota college or university. Medical students should be in a curriculum that is related to the heart and circulatory system.

May be renewed once. US citizenship or legal residency required. Write for complete information.

525

NATIONS BANK TRUST DEPT.
(Minne L. Maffett Scholarship Trust)
P.O. Box 831515
Dallas TX 75283
214/559-6476

AMOUNT: $50–$1000
DEADLINE(S): April 1
FIELD(S): All fields of study

Open to US citizens who graduated from Limestone County, Texas, high schools. Scholarships for full time study at an accredited Texas institution.

30 scholarships per year. Write to Debra Hitzelberger, Vice President, and Trust Officer, address above, for complete information.

526

NELLIE MARTIN CARMAN SCHOLARSHIP TRUST
(Scholarships)
18223 73rd Ave. NE; #B101
Bothell WA 98011
206/486-6575

AMOUNT: Up to $1000
DEADLINE(S): March 15
FIELD(S): All fields of study except those noted below

Open to high school seniors in King, Pierce, & Snohomish Counties (WA). For undergraduate study in the state of Washington in all fields EXCEPT music, sculpting, drawing, interior design, & home economics. US citizenship required.

Applications available only through high schools & nomination by counselor is required. Awards are renewable. Write for complete information.

527

**PENNSYLVANIA MEDICAL SOCIETY—
EDUCATIONAL AND SCIENTIFIC
TRUST**
(Loan Program)
777 East Park Drive
P.O. Box 8820
Harrisburg PA 17105
717/558-7750 Ext. 424

AMOUNT: $1500–$3000
DEADLINE(S): April 1 to July 1
FIELD(S): Medicine and Allied Health Fields

Open to Pennsylvania residents with demonstrated financial need who are seeking a
Medical degree or are enrolled in 4-year or
2-year programs in the health field. Medical
loan only in USA. Allied health:
Pennsylvania-based institutions only

Approx 200 loans per year. Write for complete information.

528

ROBERT SCHRECK MEMORIAL FUND
(Grants)
c/o Texas Commerce Bank—Trust Dept
P.O. Drawer 140
El Paso TX 79980
915/546-6515

AMOUNT: $500–$1500
DEADLINE(S): July 15; November 15
FIELD(S): Medicine; Veterinary Medicine;
Physics; Chemistry; Architecture;
Engineering; Episcopal Clergy

Grants to undergraduate juniors or seniors or
graduate students who have been residents
of El Paso county for at least two years.
Must be US citizen or legal resident and
have a high grade point average. Financial
need is a consideration.

Write for complete information.

529

**US DEPT. OF HEALTH & HUMAN
SERVICES**
**(Indian Health Service's Health Scholarship
Program; Public Law 94-437)**
Twinbrook Metro Plaza; Suite 100
12300 Twinbrook Pkwy.
Rockville MD 20852
301/443-6197

AMOUNT: Tuition + fees & monthly stipend
DEADLINE(S): April 1
FIELD(S): Health professions

Open to American Indians or Alaska natives
who enroll in courses leading to a baccalaureate degree (preparing them for acceptance into health professions schools). US
citizenship required. Renewable annually
with reapplication.

Scholarship recipients must intend to serve the
Indian people as a health care provider.
They incur a 1-year service obligation to the
IHS for each year of support. Write for
complete information.

530

**VIRGIN ISLANDS BOARD OF
EDUCATION**
(Nursing & Other Health Scholarships)
P.O. Box 11900
St. Thomas VI 00801
809/774-4546

AMOUNT: Up to $1800
DEADLINE(S): March 31
FIELD(S): Nursing; Medicine; Health-related
Areas

Open to bona fide residents of the Virgin
Islands who are accepted by an accredited
school of nursing or an accredited institution offering courses in one of the health-
related fields.

This scholarship is granted for one academic
year. Recipients may reapply with at least a
"C" average. Write for complete information.

MEDICAL-RELATED DISCIPLINES

531

ABBIE SARGENT MEMORIAL SCHOLARSHIP INC.
(Scholarships)
295 Sheep Davis Road
Concord NH 03301
603/224-1934

AMOUNT: $200
DEADLINE(S): March 15
FIELD(S): Agriculture; Veterinary Medicine; Home Economics

Open to New Hampshire residents who are high school graduates with good grades and character. For undergraduate or graduate study. Must be legal resident of US and demonstrate financial need.

Renewable with reapplication. Write for complete information.

532

AMERICAN ASSOCIATION OF WOMEN DENTISTS
(Gillette Hayden Memorial Foundation)
95 W. Broadway
Salem NJ 08079
609/935-0467

AMOUNT: $2000
DEADLINE(S): August 1
FIELD(S): Dentistry

Loans available to women who are 3rd and 4th year pre-dental students or are graduate degree candidates. Scholarship; need for assistance and amount of debt currently accumulated are main points considered.

Write for complete information.

533

AMERICAN COLLEGE OF HEALTHCARE EXECUTIVES
(Albert W. Dent Scholarship)
1 N. Franklin St.; Suite 1700
Chicago IL 60606
312/424-2800

AMOUNT: $3000
DEADLINE(S): March 31
FIELD(S): Health Care Administration

Open to ACHE student associates who are handicapped or are members of a minority group and have been accepted to or are enrolled full time in an accredited graduate program. US or Canadian citizen. Previous recipients are not eligible.

Must demonstrate financial need. Apply between January 1 and March 31. Write for complete information.

534

AMERICAN FOUNDATION FOR PHARMACEUTICAL EDUCATION
(Gateway Scholarship Program)
618 Somerset St.
P.O. Box 7126
North Plainfield NJ 07060
908/561-8077

AMOUNT: $9250
DEADLINE(S): October 1
FIELD(S): Pharmacy

Open to undergraduates in the last three years of a bachelor's program in a college of pharmacy. US citizen or permanent resident. $4250 is awarded for an undergraduate research project; then $5000 when student enrolls in a graduate program.

Purpose is to encourage undergraduates to pursue the Ph.D. in a pharmacy college graduate program. Write for complete information.

535

AMERICAN FOUNDATION FOR VISION AWARENESS
(Education/Research Grants)
243 North Lindbergh Blvd.
St. Louis MO 63141
314/991-1949

AMOUNT: $5000 to $10,000 (research grants); $1000 (scholarships)
DEADLINE(S): February 1
FIELD(S): Optometry

Scholarships open to optometry students. Research grants open to scientists doing research in the field of vision.

Write for complete information.

536

AMERICAN INDIAN SCIENCE & ENGINEERING SOCIETY
(Santa Fe Pacific Foundation Scholarships)
1630 30th St.; Suite 301
Boulder CO 80301
303/939-0023

AMOUNT: Up to $2500 per year for 4 years
DEADLINE(S): March 31
FIELD(S): Business; Engineering; Science; Health Administration

Open to graduating high school seniors with 1/4 or more Indian blood. Must reside in KS, OK, CO, AZ, NM, or San Bernardino County, CA (AT&SF Railway service area). Two of the five scholarships are designated for Navajo tribe members.

Must plan to attend a 4-year post-secondary accredited educational institution. Write for complete information.

537

AMERICAN PODIATRIC MEDICAL ASSN (FPME) SCHOLARSHIPS
9312 Old Georgetown Rd.
Bethesda MD 20814
301/571-9200

AMOUNT: $1000-$3000

DEADLINE(S): June 1
FIELD(S): Podiatric Medicine

Scholarships and loans open to 3rd and 4th year podiatry students or graduate students who wish to continue their studies full time. Recipient must take at least 12 credits per semester at one of the podiatric medical colleges.

Selection is based on financial need, scholastic ability, and community service. Available only through school's financial aid office.

538

AMERICAN VETERINARY MEDICAL ASSOCIATION FOUNDATION
(AMVA Auxiliary Student Loan Fund)
1931 N. Meacham Rd.; Suite 100
Schaumburg IL 60173
708/925-8070 Ext. 208

AMOUNT: Up to $4000
DEADLINE(S): Continual
FIELD(S): Veterinary Medicine

Loans available to worthy students in AMVA-accredited colleges of veterinary medicine who need financial aid to complete their schooling. Preference to seniors but sophomores and juniors may be considered. US citizenship required.

Applicants must be members of AVMA student chapter. Write for complete information.

539

ARTHUR & DOREEN PARRETT SCHOLARSHIP TRUST FUND
(Scholarships)
c/o US Bank of Washington
P.O. Box 720; Trust Dept.; 8th Floor
Seattle WA 98111-0720
206/344-4653

AMOUNT: Up to $3500
DEADLINE(S): July 31
FIELD(S): Engineering; Science; Medicine; Dentistry

Washington state resident who has completed her/his first year of college by July 31. Open to students enrolled in above schools. Awards tenable at any accredited undergrad college or university.

Approximately 15 awards per year. Write for complete information.

540

AUXILIARY TO THE MICHIGAN OPTOMETRIC ASSOCIATION
(Scholarship Program)
Linda Moleski
3440 Williamson NE
Grand Rapids MI 49505
906/635-0861

AMOUNT: $400–$1000

DEADLINE(S): March 1

FIELD(S): Optometry

Michigan resident & student member of Michigan Optometric Assn. Apply in 3rd year of study at a recognized school of optometry. Maintain "B" average. US citizen.

2–5 scholarships per year. Applications available in November at all optometric colleges. Write for complete information.

541

BUSINESS & PROFESSIONAL WOMEN'S FOUNDATION
(Career Advancement Scholarships)
2012 Massachusetts Ave. NW
Washington DC 20036
202/293-1200

AMOUNT: $500–$1000

DEADLINE(S): April 15 (postmark)

FIELD(S): Computer Science; Education; Paralegal; Engineering; Science; Law; Dentistry; Medicine

Open to women (30 or older) within 12–24 months of completing undergrad or grad study in US (including Puerto Rico & Virgin Islands). Studies should lead to entry/reentry in work force or improve career advancement chances.

Not for doctoral study. Must demonstrate financial need. Send self-addressed stamped

($.64) #10 envelope for complete info. Applications available October 1–April 1.

542

BUSINESS & PROFESSIONAL WOMEN'S FOUNDATION
(New York Life Foundation Scholarships for Women in the Health Professions)
2012 Massachusetts Ave. NW
Washington DC 20036
202/293-1200

AMOUNT: $500–$1000

DEADLINE(S): April 15 postmark (Applications available only October 1–April 1

FIELD(S): Health-Related Professions

Open to women (25 or older) who are within 12–24 months of completing their undergraduate program of study in USA. Studies should lead to entry or reentry into the work force or improve career advancement chances. US citizen.

Must be accepted into an accredited program and demonstrate financial need. Send self-addressed stamped ($.64) #10 envelope for application and complete information.

543

CHARLES E. SAAK TRUST
(Educational Grants)
Wells Fargo Bank Trust Dept.
5262 N. Blackstone
Fresno CA 93710
Written Inquiry Only

AMOUNT: Varies

DEADLINE(S): March 31

FIELD(S): Education; Dental

Undergraduate grants for residents of the Porterville-Poplar area of Tulare County, Calif. Must carry a minimum of 12 units; have at least a 2.0 GPA, be under age 21, and demonstrate financial need.

Approximately 100 awards per year; renewable with reapplication. Write for complete information.

544

COMMUNITY FOUNDATION OF GREATER LORAIN COUNTY
(A.C. Siddall Educational Trust Fund Scholarship)
  1865 N. Ridge Road E.; Suite A
  Lorain OH 44055
  216/277-0142 or 216/323-4445

AMOUNT: $1000
DEADLINE(S): May 1
FIELD(S): Health Care

Open to those who wish to pursue or further their education in health care and have been or are now employed and reside in or work for a health care facility within the Allen Memorial Hospital District in Lorain County.

Must have work experience and demonstrate financial need. Applications available beginning January 1 from Administrator; Allen Memorial Hospital; 200 W. Lorain St.; Oberlin OH 44074.

545

CUYAHOGA COUNTY MEDICAL FOUNDATION
(Scholarship Grant Program)
  6000 Rockside Woods Blvd.; Suite 150
  Cleveland OH 44131-2352
  216/520-1000

AMOUNT: $500–$1500
DEADLINE(S): June 1
FIELD(S): Medicine; Dentistry; Pharmacy; Nursing; Osteopathy

Grants open to residents of Cuyahoga County who are accepted to or enrolled in an accredited professional school in one of the above areas.

Approx. 40 awards per year. Write for complete information.

546

DOG WRITERS' EDUCATIONAL TRUST
(Scholarships)
  Berta I. Pickett
  P.O. Box 2220
  Payson AZ 85547
  602/474-8867

AMOUNT: $1000
DEADLINE(S): December 31
FIELD(S): Veterinary Medicine; Animal Behavior; Journalism

Open to applicants whose parents, grandparents, or other close relatives (or the applicant) are or have been involved in the world of dogs as exhibitors, breeders, handlers, judges, club officers, or other activities.

Scholarships support undergraduate or graduate study. 10 awards per year. Send self addressed stamped envelope for complete information and application.

547

EDWARD BANGS AND ELZA KELLEY FOUNDATION
(Scholarship Program)
  243 South St.; Box M
  Hyannis MA 02601
  508/775-3117

AMOUNT: Up to $4000
DEADLINE(S): April 30
FIELD(S): Medicine; Nursing; Health Sciences; & related fields

Open to residents of Barnstable County (MA). Scholarships are intended to benefit health and welfare of Barnstable County residents. Awards support study at recognized undergraduate, graduate, and professional institutions.

Financial need is a consideration. Write for complete information.

548

FAIRFAX COUNTY MEDICAL SOCIETY FOUNDATION
(Scholarships)
8100 Oak St.
Dunn Loring VA 22027
703/560-4855

AMOUNT: $1000
DEADLINE(S): May 30
FIELD(S): Medical Doctor; Medical-related Disciplines; Medical Technologies; Nursing

Open to undergraduate and graduate students who are US citizens and are residents of Fairfax County, VA. For studies related to human health. Must demonstrate financial need.

10 awards per year; renewable. Write for complete information.

549

H. FLETCHER BROWN FUND
(Scholarships)
c/o PNC Bank; Trust Dept.
P.O. Box 791
Wilmington DE 19899
302/429-2827

AMOUNT: Varies
DEADLINE(S): April 15
FIELD(S): Medicine; Dentistry; Law; Engineering; Chemistry

Open to US citizens born and still residing in Delaware. For 4 years of study (undergrad or grad) leading to a degree that enables applicant to practice in chosen field.

Scholarships are based on need, scholastic achievement, and good moral character. Applications available in February. Write for complete information.

550

INDIANA DENTAL ASSOCIATION
(Loan Program)
P.O. Box 2467
Indianapolis IN 46202
317/845-0490

AMOUNT: Up to $3000
DEADLINE(S): None specified
FIELD(S): Dentistry

Loans are made to dental students (undergraduate and graduate) who are residents of Indiana, are enrolled in the Indiana University School of Dentistry, and have demonstrated a need for financial assistance.

Contact Robert D. Godfrey, Branch Officer, at above address for complete information.

551

INTERNATIONAL CHIROPRACTORS ASSOCIATION
(Scholarships)
1110 N. Glebe Rd.; Suite 1000
Arlington VA 22201
703/528-5000

AMOUNT: Varies
DEADLINE(S): Check with college financial office
FIELD(S): Chiropractic

Open to student members of ICA who have a minimum 2.5 GPA & who are enrolled in a chiropractic college. Awards are based on academic achievement and do not cover the total cost of tuition.

Additional requirements are determined by the individual SICA chapter scholarship committee. Contact ICA chapter officer or representative at your chiropractic college or write to address above for complete information & application.

552

INTERNATIONAL ORDER OF THE KING'S DAUGHTERS AND SONS
(Health Careers Scholarships)
c/o Mrs. Merle Raber
6024 E. Chicago Rd.
Jonesville MI 49250
716/357-4951

AMOUNT: Up to $1000
DEADLINE(S): April 1

FIELD(S): Medicine; Dentistry; Nursing; Physical Therapy; Occupational Therapy; Medical Technologies; Pharmacy

Open to students accepted to/enrolled in an accredited USA or Canadian 4-yr or graduate school. RN candidates must have completed 1st year; BA candidates in at least 3rd year. Pre-med students NOT eligible.

US or Canadian citizen. Those seeking MD or DDS degrees must be in 2nd yr of Medical or Dental school.

553

JEWISH VOCATIONAL SERVICE
(Marcus & Theresa Levie Educational Fund Scholarships)
1 S. Franklin St.
Chicago IL 60606
312/346-6700 Ext. 2214

AMOUNT: $5000

DEADLINE(S): March 1

FIELD(S): Social Work; Medicine; Dentistry; Nursing & other related professions & vocations

Open to Cook County residents of the Jewish faith who plan careers in the helping professions. For undergraduate juniors and seniors and for graduate and vocational students. Applications available December 1 from Scholarship Secretary.

Must show financial need. 85–100 awards per year. Renewal possible with reapplication. Write for complete information.

554

MARYLAND HIGHER EDUCATION COMMISSION
(Professional School Scholarships)
State Scholarship Administration
16 Francis St.
Annapolis MD 21401
410/974-5370

AMOUNT: $200–$1000

DEADLINE(S): March 1

FIELD(S): Dentistry; Pharmacy; Medicine; Law; Nursing

Open to Maryland residents who have been admitted as full-time students at a participating graduate institution of higher learning in Maryland or an undergraduate nursing program.

Renewable up to 4 years. Write for complete information and a list of participating Maryland institutions.

555

NATIONAL STRENGTH & CONDITIONING ASSN.
(Challenge Scholarships)
P.O. Box 38909
Colorado Springs CO 80937
719/632-6772

AMOUNT: $1000

DEADLINE(S): March 1

FIELD(S): Fields related to Strength & Conditioning

Open to National Strength & Conditioning Association members. Awards are for undergraduate or graduate study.

Write for complete information.

556

NELLIE MARTIN CARMAN SCHOLARSHIP TRUST
(Scholarships)
18223 73rd Ave. NE; #B101
Bothell WA 98011
206/486-6575

AMOUNT: Up to $1000

DEADLINE(S): March 15

FIELD(S): All fields of study except those noted below

Open to high school seniors in King, Pierce, & Snohomish Counties (WA). For undergraduate study in the state of Washington in all fields EXCEPT music, sculpting, drawing, interior design, & home economics. US citizenship required.

Applications available only through high schools & nomination by counselor is required. Awards are renewable. Write for complete information.

557

ROBERT SCHRECK MEMORIAL FUND
(Grants)
c/o Texas Commerce Bank—Trust Dept
P.O. Drawer 140
El Paso TX 79980
915/546-6515

AMOUNT: $500–$1500
DEADLINE(S): July 15; November 15
FIELD(S): Medicine; Veterinary Medicine; Physics; Chemistry; Architecture; Engineering; Episcopal Clergy

Grants to undergraduate juniors or seniors or graduate students who have been residents of El Paso county for at least two years. Must be US citizen or legal resident and have a high grade point average. Financial need is a consideration.
Write for complete information.

558

US DEPT. OF HEALTH & HUMAN SERVICES
(Indian Health Service's Health Scholarship Program; Public Law 94-437)
Twinbrook Metro Plaza; Suite 100
12300 Twinbrook Pkwy.
Rockville MD 20852
301/443-6197

AMOUNT: Tuition + fees & monthly stipend
DEADLINE(S): April 1
FIELD(S): Health professions

Open to American Indians or Alaska natives who enroll in courses leading to a baccalaureate degree (preparing them for acceptance into health professions schools). US citizenship required. Renewable annually with reapplication.
Scholarship recipients must intend to serve the Indian people as a health care provider.

They incur a 1-year service obligation to the IHS for each year of support. Write for complete information.

MEDICAL RESEARCH

559

THE HAN'T FOUNDATION
(J. Quest Award in Micro-Meteorites)
288 San Marin Dr.
Navato CA 94945
Written inquiries only

AMOUNT: $2001
DEADLINE(S): June 5
FIELD(S): Medical Research in Geoscience

Open to full-time undergraduate or graduate students majoring in bio-physical effects of micro-meteorites in all geophysical environments.
Must be ethnic minority and a US citizen. Must have been born on June 5th and demonstrate financial need.

560

BUSINESS & PROFESSIONAL WOMEN'S FOUNDATION
(New York Life Foundation Scholarships for Women in the Health Professions)
2012 Massachusetts Ave. NW
Washington DC 20036
202/293-1200

AMOUNT: $500–$1000
DEADLINE(S): April 15 postmark (Applications available only October 1–April 1
FIELD(S): Health-Related Professions

Open to women (25 or older) who are within 12-24 months of completing their undergraduate program of study in USA. Studies should lead to entry or reentry into the work force or improve career advancement chances. US citizen.
Must be accepted into an accredited program and demonstrate financial need. Send self-

addressed stamped ($.64) #10 envelope for application and complete information.

561

COMMUNITY FOUNDATION OF GREATER LORAIN COUNTY
(A.C. Siddall Educational Trust Fund Scholarship)
1865 N. Ridge Road E.; Suite A
Lorain OH 44055
216/277-0142 or 216/323-4445

AMOUNT: $1000
DEADLINE(S): May 1
FIELD(S): Health Care

Open to those who wish to pursue or further their education in health care and have been or are now employed and reside in or work for a health care facility within the Allen Memorial Hospital District in Lorain County.

Must have work experience and demonstrate financial need. Applications available beginning January 1 from Administrator; Allen Memorial Hospital; 200 W. Lorain St.; Oberlin OH 44074.

562

EPILEPSY FOUNDATION OF AMERICA
(Behavioral Sciences Student Fellowships)
4351 Garden City Dr.; Suite 406
Landover MD 20785
301/459-3700

AMOUNT: $1500
DEADLINE(S): March 2
FIELD(S): Epilepsy-related study or training projects

Open to undergrad and grad students in nursing, psychology, and related areas who propose a 3-month epilepsy-related project to be carried out in a US institution at which there are ongoing epilepsy research, service, or training programs.

Fellowship must be undertaken during a free period in the student's year. Write for complete information.

563

INTERMURAL RESEARCH TRAINING AWARD
(Summer Intern Program)
Office of Education; Bldg. 10
Room 1C-129
Bethesda MD 20892
301/496-2427

AMOUNT: Stipend
DEADLINE(S): February 1
FIELD(S): Research Training (Biomedical Research)

Summer intern program is designed to provide "academically talented" undergraduate, graduate, or medical students a unique opportunity to acquire valuable hands-on research training and experience in the neurosciences.

Write for complete information.

564

LUPUS FOUNDATION OF AMERICA
(Student Summer Fellowship Program)
4 Research Place; Suite 180
Rockville MD 20850
310/670-9292

AMOUNT: $2000
DEADLINE(S): February 1
FIELD(S): Lupus Erythematosus Research

Summer fellowships open to undergrads, grads, & post-grads but applicants already having college degree are preferred. Applications are evaluated NIH-style. Purpose is to encourage students to pursue research careers in above areas.

Research may be conducted at any recognized institution in the USA. Application materials available in November. 10 awards per year. Write for complete information.

565

NATIONAL INSTITUTES OF HEALTH— NATIONAL CENTER FOR RESEARCH RESOURCES
(Minority High School Research Apprentice Program)
Westwood Bldg.; Room 10A11
5333 Westbard Ave.
Bethesda MD 20892
301/496-6743

AMOUNT: $2000
DEADLINE(S): January 31
FIELD(S): Health Sciences Research

Summer program designed to offer minority high school students a meaningful experience in various aspects of health-related research. Its aim is to stimulate students' interest in science. US citizen or permanent resident.

NIH supports this program at over 350 research institutions. Students must apply through program director at the institution. NOT a scholarship.

566

PREVENT BLINDNESS AMERICA
(Student Research Fellowship)
500 East Remington Rd.
Schaumburg IL 60173
708/843-2020

AMOUNT: $1500 Maximum ($500/month)
DEADLINE(S): March 1
FIELD(S): Ophthalmology and Visual Sciences

Stipend open to undergraduates, medical students, or graduate students for full-time extracurricular eye-related research during the summer months.

Write administrator for brochure and application.

MEDICAL TECHNOLOGIES

567

AMERICAN ART THERAPY ASSOCIATION
(Gladys Agell Award for Excellence in Research)
1202 Allanson Road
Mundelein IL 60060
708/949-6064

AMOUNT: Not specified
DEADLINE(S): September 15
FIELD(S): Art Therapy

Open to AATA student members. Award is designed to encourage student research and goes to the most outstanding project completed within the past year in the area of applied art therapy.

US citizenship required. Write for complete information.

568

AMERICAN ASSOCIATION OF MEDICAL ASSISTANTS ENDOWMENT
(Maxine Williams Scholarship Fund)
20 N. Wacker Dr. #1575
Chicago IL 60606
312/899-1500

AMOUNT: $500
DEADLINE(S): February 1; June 1
FIELD(S): Medical Assistant

Undergraduate scholarships open to high school graduates who submit a written statement expressing interest in a career as a medical assistant.

3–7 scholarships per year. Renewable. Write for complete information.

569

AMERICAN DENTAL HYGIENISTS ASSN.
(Certificate Scholarship Program; Baccalaureate Scholarship Program; Minority Scholarship Fund)
444 North Michigan Ave; Suite 3400
Chicago IL 60611
312/440-8900

AMOUNT: $1500 maximum
DEADLINE(S): June 1
FIELD(S): Dental Hygiene

Open to students entering their final year in an associates/certificate program or who have completed at least 1 year in a bachelors program & will receive a degree to practice dental hygiene in the current year or year the award is made.
20–25 awards per year. Minimum GPA of 3.0 (4.0 scale) is required. Write for complete information.

570

AMERICAN FOUNDATION FOR THE BLIND
(Rudolph Dillman Memorial Scholarship)
15 West 16th St.
New York NY 10011
212/620-2000; TDD 212/620-2158

AMOUNT: $2500
DEADLINE(S): April 1
FIELD(S): Rehabilitation; Education of Blind & Visually Impaired

Open to legally blind undergrad or graduate students accepted to or enrolled in an accredited program within the broad areas of rehabilitation and/or education of the blind and visually impaired. USA citizen.
Three awards per year. Write for complete information.

571

AMERICAN FOUNDATION FOR THE BLIND
(TeleSensory Scholarship)
15 West 16th St.
New York NY 10011
212/620-2000; TDD 212/620-2158

AMOUNT: $1000
DEADLINE(S): April 1
FIELD(S): None specified

Open to full-time undergrad students who are legally blind and do not meet the criteria for other AFB scholarships. Must be US citizen; provide proof of acceptance to a college or university and three letters of recommendation.
Write for complete information.

572

AMERICAN FUND FOR DENTAL HEALTH
(Dental Laboratory Technology Scholarships)
211 E. Chicago Ave.; Suite 820
Chicago IL 60611
312/787-6270

AMOUNT: Up to $500
DEADLINE(S): June 1
FIELD(S): Dental Lab Technology

Open to high school graduates enrolled or planning to enroll in accredited dental laboratory technology program. Basic criteria are academic record, financial need & letter of acceptance. For first or second year of study.
Must be US citizen. 10–12 scholarships annually. Renewable upon reapplication. Write for complete information.

573

AMERICAN MEDICAL TECHNOLOGISTS
(AMT Scholarships)
710 Higgins Road
Park Ridge IL 60068
708/823-5169

AMOUNT: $250

DEADLINE(S): April 1

FIELD(S): Medical Technology; Dental Assistant; Medical Assistant

Open to high school graduates or high school seniors who are residents of the USA and plan to enroll or are enrolled in an accredited program in the above fields in the USA. Financial need is a consideration.

Write for complete information include a legal-sized SASE and a listing of your educational and career goals with your request.

574

AMERICAN RESPIRATORY CARE FOUNDATION
(Student Scholarship Programs)
11030 Ables Lane
Dallas TX 75229
214/243-2272

AMOUNT: $500; $1000; $1250; $2500

DEADLINE(S): June 30

FIELD(S): Respiratory Therapy

Scholarships for accredited respiratory therapy programs. Must have medical or technical director's sponsorship,; maintain a 3.0 or better GPA, and be a citizen of the US.

Eligibility requirements vary. Minority scholarship offered. Write for complete information.

575

AMERICAN SOCIETY OF CLINICAL PATHOLOGISTS
(Scholarship Program)
2100 W. Harrison St.
Chicago IL 60612-3798
1-800-621-4142

AMOUNT: $1000

DEADLINE(S): October 28

FIELD(S): Cytotechnology; Histologic Technician; Medical Laboratory Technician; Medical Technology

Open to undergraduates in their final clinical year of training in a CAHEA-accredited program in the above fields. Official transcripts and three letters of recommendation are required.

Write for complete information.

576

BUSINESS & PROFESSIONAL WOMEN'S FOUNDATION
(New York Life Foundation Scholarships for Women in the Health Professions)
2012 Massachusetts Ave. NW
Washington DC 20036
202/293-1200

AMOUNT: $500–$1000

DEADLINE(S): April 15 postmark (Applications available only October 1–April 1

FIELD(S): Health-Related Professions

Open to women (25 or older) who are within 12-24 months of completing their undergraduate program of study in USA. Studies should lead to entry or reentry into the work force or improve career advancement chances. US citizen.

Must be accepted into an accredited program and demonstrate financial need. Send self-addressed stamped ($.64) #10 envelope for application and complete information.

577

COMMUNITY FOUNDATION OF GREATER LORAIN COUNTY
(A.C. Siddall Educational Trust Fund Scholarship)
1865 N. Ridge Road E.; Suite A
Lorain OH 44055
216/277-0142 or 216/323-4445

AMOUNT: $1000

DEADLINE(S): May 1

FIELD(S): Health Care

Open to those who wish to pursue or further their education in health care who have been or are now employed and reside in or work for a health care facility within the Allen Memorial Hospital District in Lorain County.

Must have work experience and demonstrate financial need. Applications available beginning January 1 from Administrator; Allen Memorial Hospital; 200 W. Lorain St.; Oberlin OH 44074.

578

DAUGHTERS OF THE AMERICAN REVOLUTION
(NSDAR Occupational Therapy Scholarships)
Office of the Committee/Scholarships
National Society DAR
1776 'D' St. NW
Washington DC 20006-5392
202/879-3292

AMOUNT: $500 to $1000 (one-time award)
DEADLINE(S): February 15; August 15
FIELD(S): Occupational Therapy; Physical Therapy

Open to graduate and undergrad students enrolled in an accredited therapy program in the USA. Must be sponsored by a local DAR chapter. Biannual award is based on academic excellence, recommendation, need, & commitment to field of study.
US citizenship required. Send SASE for complete information.

579

EASTER SEAL SOCIETY OF IOWA
(Scholarships & Awards)
P.O. Box 4002
Des Moines IA 50333
515/289-1933

AMOUNT: $400–$600
DEADLINE(S): April 15
FIELD(S): Physical Rehabilitation; Mental Rehabilitation; & related areas

Open to Iowa residents who are full-time undergraduate sophomores, juniors, seniors, or graduate students at accredited institutions, planning a career in the broad field of rehabilitation, financially needy, & in top 40% of their class.

6 scholarships per year. Must re-apply each year.

580

EDWARD BANGS AND ELZA KELLEY FOUNDATION
(Scholarship Program)
243 South St.; Box M
Hyannis MA 02601
508/775-3117

AMOUNT: Up to $4000
DEADLINE(S): April 30
FIELD(S): Medicine; Nursing; Health Sciences, & related fields

Open to residents of Barnstable County (MA). Scholarships are intended to benefit health and welfare of Barnstable County residents. Awards support study at recognized undergraduate, graduate, and professional institutions.
Financial need is a consideration. Write for complete information.

581

EMPIRE COLLEGE
(Dean's Scholarship)
3033 Cleveland Ave.
Santa Rosa CA 95403
707/546-4000

AMOUNT: $250–$1500
DEADLINE(S): April 15
FIELD(S): Court Reporting; Accounting; Secretarial; Legal; Medical (Clinical & Administrative); Travel & Tourism; General Business

Open to high school seniors who meet admission requirements and want to attend Empire college in Santa Rosa California. US citizenship required.
Ten scholarships per year. Contact Ms. Carole A. Bratton at the above address for complete information.

582

FAIRFAX COUNTY MEDICAL SOCIETY FOUNDATION
(Scholarships)
8100 Oak St.
Dunn Loring VA 22027
703/560-4855

AMOUNT: $1000
DEADLINE(S): May 30
FIELD(S): Medical Doctor; Medical-related Disciplines; Medical Technologies; Nursing

Open to undergraduate and graduate students who are US citizens and are residents of Fairfax County VA. For studies related to human health. Must demonstrate financial need.

10 awards per year; renewable. Write for complete information.

583

FLORIDA DENTAL ASSOCIATION
(Dental Hygiene Scholarship Program)
1111 E. Tennessee St.; Suite 102
Tallahassee FL 32308
904/681-3620

AMOUNT: Varies
DEADLINE(S): May 1 & November 1
FIELD(S): Dental Hygiene

Open to Florida residents who have been accepted for enrollment in an accredited dental hygiene school in Florida. Preference to applicants from areas in Florida with dental hygienist shortages.

Write for complete information.

584

INTERNATIONAL ORDER OF THE KING'S DAUGHTERS AND SONS
(Health Careers Scholarships)
c/o Mrs. Merle Raber
6024 E. Chicago Rd.
Jonesville MI 49250
716/357-4951

AMOUNT: Up to $1000

DEADLINE(S): April 1
FIELD(S): Medicine; Dentistry; Nursing; Physical Therapy; Occupational Therapy; Medical Technologies; Pharmacy

Open to students accepted to/enrolled in an accredited USA or Canadian 4-yr or graduate school. RN candidates must have completed 1st year; BA candidates in at least 3rd year. Pre-med students NOT eligible.

USA or Canadian citizen. Those seeking MD or DDS degrees must be in 2nd yr of Medical or Dental school.

585

J. HUGH & EARLE W. FELLOWS MEMORIAL FUND
(Scholarship Loans)
Pensacola Junior College Exec VP
1000 College Blvd.
Pensacola FL 32504
904/484-1706

AMOUNT: Each is negotiated individually
DEADLINE(S): None
FIELD(S): Medicine; Nursing; Medical Technology; Theology

Open to bona fide residents of the Florida counties of Escambia, Santa Rosa, Okaloosa, or Walton. For undergraduate study in the fields listed above. US citizenship required.

Loans are interest-free until graduation. Write for complete information.

586

JEWISH VOCATIONAL SERVICE
(Marcus & Theresa Levie Educational Fund Scholarships)
1 S. Franklin St.
Chicago IL 60606
312/346-6700 Ext. 2214

AMOUNT: $5000
DEADLINE(S): March 1
FIELD(S): Social Work; Medicine; Dentistry; Nursing; & other related professions & vocations

Open to Cook County residents of the Jewish faith who plan careers in the helping professions. For undergraduate juniors and seniors and for graduate and vocational students. Applications available December 1 from Scholarship Secretary.

Must show financial need. 85–100 awards per year. Renewal possible with reapplication. Write for complete information.

587

MARYLAND HIGHER EDUCATION COMMISSION
(Physical & Occupational Therapists & Assistants Scholarships)
State Scholarship Administration
16 Francis St.
Annapolis MD 21401
410/974-5370

AMOUNT: $2000
DEADLINE(S): July 1
FIELD(S): Occupational Therapy; Physical Therapy

Open to Maryland residents who enroll full-time in post-secondary institutions having approved occupational or physical therapy programs that lead to Maryland licensing as a therapist or assistant.

Recipients agree to one year of service at a public school, state hospital, or other approved site for each year of award. Write for complete information.

588

MARYLAND HIGHER EDUCATION COMMISSION
(Reimbursement of Firefighter & Rescue Squad Members)
State Scholarship Administration
16 Francis St.
Annapolis MD 21401
410/974-5370

AMOUNT: Tuition reimbursement up to $2600
DEADLINE(S): July 1

FIELD(S): Fire service or Emergency Medical Technology

Open to Maryland residents affiliated with an organized fire department or rescue squad in Maryland. For full or part-time study at a Maryland institution. Reimbursement made one year after successful completion of course(s).

For undergraduate or graduate study in Maryland. Renewable. Write for complete information.

589

NATIONAL ASSOCIATION OF AMERICAN BUSINESS CLUBS (AMBUCS)
P.O. Box 5127
High Point NC 27262
910/869-2166

AMOUNT: $500–$1500
DEADLINE(S): April 15
FIELD(S): Physical Therapy; Music Therapy; Occupational Therapy; Speech-Language Pathology; Hearing-Audiology; Therapeutic Recreation.

Open to undergraduate juniors, seniors, & graduate students who have good scholastic standing & plan to enter practice in his or her field in the USA. GPA of 3.0 or better (4.0 scale) and US citizenship required.

Please include a self-addressed stamped envelope; scholarships are mailed in December; incomplete applications will not be considered.

590

NATIONAL ATHLETIC TRAINERS ASSOCIATION
(NATA Undergraduate & Graduate Scholarship Program)
2952 Stemmons
Dallas TX 75247
214/637-6282

AMOUNT: $1500
DEADLINE(S): February 1

FIELD(S): Athletic Trainer

Scholarship program open to student members of NATA who have excellent academic record, have excelled as student athletic trainer, & have completed at least their freshman year of study at an accredited college or university in the USA.

44 Awards in 1994. Write to Jan Martin (address above) for complete information.

591

NATIONAL STRENGTH & CONDITIONING ASSN.
(Challenge Scholarships)
P.O. Box 38909
Colorado Springs CO 80937
719/632-6772

AMOUNT: $1000
DEADLINE(S): March 1
FIELD(S): Fields related to Strength & Conditioning

Open to National Strength & Conditioning Association members. Awards are for undergraduate or graduate study.

Write for complete information.

592

NELLIE MARTIN CARMAN SCHOLARSHIP TRUST
(Scholarships)
18223 73rd Ave. NE; #B101
Bothell WA 98011
206/486-6575

AMOUNT: Up to $1000
DEADLINE(S): March 15
FIELD(S): All fields of study except those noted below

Open to high school seniors in King, Pierce, & Snohomish Counties (WA). For undergraduate study in the state of Washington in all fields EXCEPT music, sculpting, drawing, interior design, & home economics. US citizenship required.

Applications available only through high schools & nomination by counselor is

required. Awards are renewable. Write for complete information.

593

NORTH CAROLINA SOCIETY FOR CLINICAL LABORATORY SCIENCE
(Scholarship Award)
The University of NC at Chapel Hill
Medical School Wing E; CB #7145
Chapel Hill NC 27599-7145
Written inquiry only

AMOUNT: Approximately $300 to $700 (amounts approved annually)
DEADLINE(S): June 1
FIELD(S): Medical Technology/Medical Laboratory Technician

Open to North Carolina residents who have been accepted in an approved clinical laboratory science program. Must meet North Carolina residency requirements.

Renewable. Write to NCSCLS Scholarship Chair Rebecca J. Laudicina, Ph.D., CLS(NCA), for complete information.

594

UNITED CEREBRAL PALSY ASSOCIATIONS OF NEW YORK STATE
(Physical Therapy Scholarship)
330 W. 34th St.
New York NY 10001
212/947-5770; Fax 212/594-4538

AMOUNT: $5000
DEADLINE(S): December 1
FIELD(S): Physical Therapy; Occupational Therapy

Open to qualifying senior physical therapy students. Recipients must agree to accept employment by UCP of NY full time for 18 consecutive months. Applicants are judged on academic record, references, personal interview.

Applicants must be eligible to sit for New York State physical therapy licensing exam upon graduation. Write for complete information.

NURSING

595

AMERICAN ASSOCIATION OF CRITICAL CARE NURSES
(Educational Advancement Scholarship Program)
101 Columbia
Aliso Viejo CA 92656
714/362-2000 or 800/899-2226 Ext. 376

AMOUNT: $1500
DEADLINE(S): January 15 (postmark)
FIELD(S): Critical Care Nursing

Open to AACCN members who are RNs and are working or have worked in a critical care unit. For undergraduate (junior or senior status) or graduate study. Should have worked in critical care for 1 year of the last 3 & have 3.0 or better GPA.

37 awards for baccalaureate study and 17 for graduate study per year. At least 20% of the awards will go to ethnic minorities. Write for complete information.

596

AMERICAN ASSOCIATION OF NURSE ANESTHETISTS
(Educational Loans)
222 S. Prospect Ave.
Park Ridge IL 60068
708/692-7050

AMOUNT: $500–$2500
DEADLINE(S): None
FIELD(S): Nurse Anesthetist

Loans available to AANA members & associate members enrolled in a school of anesthesia approved by the Council on Accreditation of Nurse Anesthesia Educational Programs. Loans are intended to cover unexpected events of an emergency nature.

Contact the finance director, address above, for complete information.

597

AMERICAN COLLEGE OF NURSE-MIDWIVES FOUNDATION
(Scholarships Program)
818 Connecticut Ave. NW; Suite 900
Washington DC 20006
202/728-9865

AMOUNT: $1500 maximum per year (varies)
DEADLINE(S): February 15
FIELD(S): Nurse-Midwifery

Scholarships open to students enrolled in ACNM-accredited certificate or graduate nurse-midwifery programs. Student membership in ACNM and completion of one clinical module or semester also required.

5–10 awards per year. Applications and information available from directors of nurse-midwifery programs at accredited schools.

598

AMERICAN LEGION AUXILIARY
(Past Presidents Parley Nursing Scholarship)
State Veterans Service Building
St. Paul MN 55155
612/224-7634

AMOUNT: $500
DEADLINE(S): March 15
FIELD(S): Nursing

Minnesota resident who is a member of the Dept. of Minnesota American Legion Auxiliary and has a 2.0 or better GPA. To help needy & deserving students or adults commence or further their education in nursing at a Minnesota school.
Write for complete information.

599

ASSOCIATION OF OPERATING ROOM NURSES
(AORN Scholarship Program)
Scholarship Board
2170 S. Parker Rd.; Suite 300
Denver CO 80231
303/755-6300

AMOUNT: Tuition & fees

DEADLINE(S): March 1

FIELD(S): Nursing

Open to active & associate AORN members for at least 12 consecutive months prior to deadline date. Awards support BSN, master's, & doctoral degree programs accredited by the NLN or other acceptable accrediting body.

For full or part-time study in the USA. Minimum 3.0 GPA on 4.0 scale. Renewable. Write for complete information.

600

BUSINESS & PROFESSIONAL WOMEN'S FOUNDATION
(New York Life Foundation Scholarships for Women in the Health Professions)
2012 Massachusetts Ave. NW
Washington DC 20036
202/293-1200

AMOUNT: $500–$1000

DEADLINE(S): April 15 postmark (Applications available only October 1–April 1

FIELD(S): Health Related Professions

Open to women (25 or older) who are within 12–24 months of completing their undergraduate program of study in USA. Studies should lead to entry or reentry into the work force or improve career advancement chances. USA citizen.

Must be accepted into an accredited program and demonstrate financial need. Send self-addressed stamped ($.64) #10 envelope for application and complete information.

601

COMMUNITY FOUNDATION OF GREATER LORAIN COUNTY
(A.C. Siddall Educational Trust Fund Scholarship)
1865 N. Ridge Road E.; Suite A
Lorain OH 44055
216/277-0142 or 216/323-4445

AMOUNT: $1000

DEADLINE(S): May 1

FIELD(S): Health Care

Open to those who wish to pursue or further their education in health care and have been or are now employed and reside in or work for a health care facility within the Allen Memorial Hospital District in Lorain County.

Must have work experience and demonstrate financial need. Applications available beginning January 1 from Administrator; Allen Memorial Hospital; 200 W. Lorain St.; Oberlin OH 44074.

602

CONNECTICUT LEAGUE FOR NURSING
(CLN Scholarships)
P.O. Box 365
Wallingford CT 06492
203/265-4248

AMOUNT: $500 undergrads (2); $1000 graduate

DEADLINE(S): October 1

FIELD(S): Nursing

Two undergrad scholarships open to Connecticut residents in their final year of study at a Connecticut school of nursing. One graduate award for student having completed 20 credits in nursing school. School must be agency member of CLN.

Awards are based on merit & need. Write for complete information.

603

CUYAHOGA COUNTY MEDICAL FOUNDATION
(Scholarship Grant Program)
6000 Rockside Woods Blvd.; Suite 150
Cleveland OH 44131-2352
216/520-1000

AMOUNT: $500–$1500

DEADLINE(S): June 1

FIELD(S): Medicine; Dentistry; Pharmacy; Nursing; Osteopathy

Grants open to residents of Cuyahoga County who are accepted to or enrolled in an accredited professional school in one of the above areas.

Approx 40 awards per year. Write for complete information.

604

DAUGHTERS OF THE AMERICAN REVOLUTION
(Caroline Holt Nursing Scholarships)
Office of the Committee/Scholarships
National Society DAR
1776 'D' St. NW
Washington DC 20006-5392
202/879-3292

AMOUNT: $500 (one-time award)
DEADLINE(S): February 15; August 15
FIELD(S): Nursing

Open to undergrad students enrolled in an accredited nursing program in the USA. No affiliation or relation to DAR is required but applicants must be sponsored by a local DAR chapter. US citizenship required.

Awards are based on academic excellence, financial need, and recommendations. Send SASE for complete information.

605

EDWARD BANGS AND ELZA KELLEY FOUNDATION
(Scholarship Program)
243 South St.; Box M
Hyannis MA 02601
508/775-3117

AMOUNT: Up to $4000
DEADLINE(S): April 30
FIELD(S): Medicine; Nursing; Health Sciences; & related fields

Open to residents of Barnstable County (MA). Scholarships are intended to benefit health and welfare of Barnstable County residents. Awards support study at recognized undergraduate, graduate, and professional institutions.

Financial need is a consideration. Write for complete information.

606

EPILEPSY FOUNDATION OF AMERICA
(Behavioral Sciences Student Fellowships)
4351 Garden City Dr.; Suite 406
Landover MD 20785
301/459-3700

AMOUNT: $1500
DEADLINE(S): March 2
FIELD(S): Epilepsy-related study or training projects

Open to undergrad and grad students in nursing, psychology, and related areas who propose a 3-month epilepsy-related project to be carried out in a US institution at which there are ongoing epilepsy research, service, or training programs.

Fellowship must be undertaken during a free period in the student's year. Write for complete information.

607

FAIRFAX COUNTY MEDICAL SOCIETY FOUNDATION
(Scholarships)
8100 Oak St.
Dunn Loring VA 22027
703/560-4855

AMOUNT: $1000
DEADLINE(S): May 30
FIELD(S): Medical Doctor; Medical-related Disciplines; Medical Technologies; Nursing

Open to undergraduate and graduate students who are US citizens and are residents of Fairfax County, VA. For studies related to human health. Must demonstrate financial need.

10 awards per year; renewable. Write for complete information.

608

GENERAL HOSPITAL #2 NURSES ALUMNAE
(Scholarship Fund)
P.O. Box 413657
Kansas City MO 64141
Written Inquiry

AMOUNT: $500
DEADLINE(S): March 31
FIELD(S): Nursing

Open to any black student enrolled in a registered nursing program at any accredited school of nursing in the USA. Must show financial need and furnish copy of acadenic record.

Applicants are to provide statement of why field of nursing was chosen and what the award would mean to them. Write for complete information.

609

HARVEY AND BERNICE JONES FOUNDATION
P.O. Box 233
Springdale AR 72765
501/756-0611

AMOUNT: Varies
DEADLINE(S): None specified
FIELD(S): Nursing

Scholarships available to residents of Springdale AR who want to pursue a career in nursing. Must be US citizen and demonstrate financial need.

Number of awards per year varies. Contact address above for complete information.

610

INDIANA STATE STUDENT ASSISTANCE COMMISSION
(Nursing Scholarship Fund)
150 W. Market St.; 5th Floor
Indianapolis IN 46204
317/232-2350

AMOUNT: Up to $5000
DEADLINE(S): Varies with college
FIELD(S): Nursing

Open to Indiana residents enrolled in an undergraduate nursing program at an Indiana college or university. Applicants must have a GPA of 2.0 or better (4.0 scale).

Must demonstrate financial need. Write for complete information.

611

INTERNATIONAL ORDER OF THE KING'S DAUGHTERS AND SONS
(Health Careers Scholarships)
c/o Mrs. Merle Raber
6024 E. Chicago Rd.
Jonesville MI 49250
716/357-4951

AMOUNT: Up to $1000
DEADLINE(S): April 1
FIELD(S): Medicine; Dentistry; Nursing; Physical Therapy; Occupational Therapy; Medical Technologies; Pharmacy

Open to students accepted to/enrolled in an accredited USA or Canadian 4-yr or graduate school. RN candidates must have completed 1st year; BA candidates in at least 3rd year. Pre-med students NOT eligible.

US or Canadian citizen. Those seeking MD or DDS degrees must be in 2nd yr of Medical or Dental school.

612

J. HUGH & EARLE W. FELLOWS MEMORIAL FUND
(Scholarship Loans)
Pensacola Junior College Exec VP
1000 College Blvd.
Pensacola FL 32504
904/484-1706

AMOUNT: Each is negotiated individually
DEADLINE(S): None
FIELD(S): Medicine; Nursing; Medical Technology; Theology

Open to bona fide residents of the Florida counties of Escambia, Santa Rosa, Okaloosa, or Walton. For undergraduate study in the fields listed above. US citizenship required.

Loans are interest-free until graduation. Write for complete information.

613

JEWISH VOCATIONAL SERVICE
(Marcus & Theresa Levie Educational Fund Scholarships)
1 S. Franklin St.
Chicago IL 60606
312/346-6700 Ext. 2214

AMOUNT: $5000

DEADLINE(S): March 1

FIELD(S): Social Work; Medicine; Dentistry; Nursing; & other related professions & vocations

Open to Cook County residents of the Jewish faith who plan careers in the helping professions. For undergraduate juniors and seniors and for graduate and vocational students. Applications available December 1 from Scholarship Secretary.

Must show financial need. 85–100 awards per year. Renewal possible with reapplication. Write for complete information.

614

MARYLAND HIGHER EDUCATION COMMISSION
(Professional School Scholarships)
State Scholarship Administration
16 Francis St.
Annapolis MD 21401
410/974-5370

AMOUNT: $200–$1000

DEADLINE(S): March 1

FIELD(S): Dentistry; Pharmacy; Medicine; Law; Nursing

Open to Maryland residents who have been admitted as full-time students at a participating graduate institution of higher learning in Maryland or an undergraduate nursing program.

Renewable up to 4 years. Write for complete information and a list of participating Maryland institutions.

615

MARYLAND HIGHER EDUCATION COMMISSION
(State Nursing Scholarship & Living Grant)
State Scholarship Administration
16 Francis St.
Annapolis MD 21401-1781
410/974-5370

AMOUNT: $2400/year (scholarship); $2400/year (grant)

DEADLINE(S): June 15 (scholarship); March 1 (grant)

FIELD(S): Nursing

For full or part-time grad or undergrad study in MD. Must be MD resident & agree to serve as full-time nurse in MD after graduation & have 3.0 or better GPA. Must hold nursing scholarship & show financial need for living expenses grant.

Renewable. Write for complete information.

616

MATERNITY CENTER ASSOCIATION
(Hazel Corbin Assistance Fund/Stipend Awards)
48 East 92nd St.
New York NY 10128
212/369-7300

AMOUNT: Monthly stipend—amount varies

DEADLINE(S): Varies

FIELD(S): Nurse-Midwifery

Monthly stipend for nurse-midwifery students (they must be nurses already) who are enrolled in an accredited school of midwifery and who plan to practice nurse-midwifery in the USA for at least 1 year upon certification.

Write for complete information.

617

**MCFARLAND CHARITABLE
FOUNDATION TRUST
(Nursing Scholarships)**
   L.M. Butler, VP; Havana Nat'l Bank
   112 S. Orange; POB 200
   Havana IL 62644
   309/543-3361

AMOUNT: $3000–$12000
DEADLINE(S): April 1
FIELD(S): Registered Nursing

Open to IL residents who are US citizens &
   undergrad RN degree candidates enrolled
   in accredited institutions. Recipients must
   agree to return to Havana IL area to work
   as RN for an agreed-upon number of years
   upon completion of education.
Written contract with co-signers is required.
   Penalty for breach of contract is severe.
   6–10 awards per year. Write for complete
   information.

618

**MISSISSIPPI BOARD OF TRUSTEES OF
STATE INSTITUTIONS OF HIGHER
LEARNING
(Nursing Education Scholarship Grants)**
   3825 Ridgewood Road
   Jackson MS 39211
   601/982-6570

AMOUNT: $50–$3000
DEADLINE(S): None specified
FIELD(S): Nursing

Open to registered nurses who have lived in
   Mississippi at least one year and are
   enrolled in a nursing program at an accredited Mississippi institution in pursuit of a
   BS or graduate degree.
Scholarships are renewable. Write for complete information.

619

**MISSOURI LEAGUE FOR NURSING
(Scholarships)**
   P.O. Box 104476
   Jefferson City MO 65110
   314/635-5355

AMOUNT: $100–$5000
DEADLINE(S): September 30
FIELD(S): Nursing

Open to nursing students who reside in
   Missouri and are attending a NLN accredited school in Missouri. For course work
   leading to licensing as an LPN or RN or to
   a BSN or MSN degree. Financial need must
   be demonstrated.
Application must be made through the director of nursing at the student's school.

620

**NATIONAL BLACK NURSES'
ASSOCIATION INC.
(Dr. Lauranne Sams Scholarship)**
   P.O. Box 1823
   Washington DC 20013
   202/393-6870

AMOUNT: $1000
DEADLINE(S): April 15
FIELD(S): Nursing

Scholarships for students enrolled in a nursing
   program (A.D., diploma, BSN, LPN/LVN)
   who are in good scholastic standing and are
   members of the association.
Write for complete information.

621

**NATIONAL FOUNDATION FOR LONG-
TERM HEALTH CARE
(James D. Durante Nurse Scholarship
Program)**
   1201 'L' Street N.W.
   Washington DC 20005
   202/842-4444

AMOUNT: $500

DEADLINE(S): Early June

FIELD(S): Nursing

Open to LPN and RN students who seek to continue or further their education and are interested in long-term care.

Twenty $500 scholarships per year. Send a self-addressed stamped legal size envelope with request for application in late winter.

622

NATIONAL STUDENT NURSES' ASSN. FOUNDATION
(Scholarship Program)
555 West 57th Street; Suite 1327
New York NY 10019
212/581-2215

AMOUNT: $1000 to $2500

DEADLINE(S): February 1

FIELD(S): Nursing

Open to students enrolled in state-approved schools of nursing or pre-nursing in associate degree, baccalaureate, diploma, generic doctorate, or generic master's programs. Financial need, grades, & community activities are considerations.

Applications available August through January 15. Write for complete information. Include self-addressed stamped (64 cents) business size envelope for application.

623

NELLIE MARTIN CARMAN SCHOLARSHIP TRUST
(Scholarships)
18223 73rd Ave. NE; #B101
Bothell WA 98011
206/486-6575

AMOUNT: Up to $1000

DEADLINE(S): March 15

FIELD(S): All fields of study except those noted below

Open to high school seniors in King, Pierce, & Snohomish Counties (WA). For undergraduate study in the state of Washington in all fields EXCEPT music, sculpting, drawing,

interior design, & home economics. US citizenship required.

Applications available only through high schools & nomination by counselor is required. Awards are renewable. Write for complete information.

624

NEW HAMPSHIRE POST-SECONDARY EDUCATION COMMISSION
(Nursing Education Assistance Grants)
Two Industrial Park Dr.
Concord NH 03301-8512
603/271-2555

AMOUNT: $600 to $2000

DEADLINE(S): June 1; December 15

FIELD(S): Nursing

Open to New Hampshire residents who are accepted to or enrolled in an approved nursing program in the state of New Hampshire. US citizenship or legal residency required. Financial need must be demonstrated.

Approximately 110 grants per year. Write for complete information.

625

OHIO LEAGUE FOR NURSING
(Grants and Loans)
Student Aid Committee
2800 Euclid Ave.; Suite 235
Cleveland OH 44115
216/781-7222

AMOUNT: Varies

DEADLINE(S): May 15

FIELD(S): Nursing

Open to nursing students who are residents of Greater Cleveland area (Cuyahoga, Grauga, Lake, Lorain Counties) & will agree to work in a health care facility in that area for at least one year after graduation. US citizen or legal resident.

20–25 awards per year. Write for complete information.

626

ONCOLOGY NURSING FOUNDATION
(Scholarships)
501 Holiday Drive
Pittsburgh PA 15220
412/921-7373

AMOUNT: $2000 undergrad (18); $3000 graduate (18); $3000 doctoral (5); $1000 post-master's nurse practitioner (2)
DEADLINE(S): February 1
FIELD(S): Nursing (Cancer)

Open to registered nurses who are seeking a bachelor's, master's, or doctoral degree in an NLN accredited nursing program & have an interest in oncology nursing.
Write for complete information.

627

TYSON FOUNDATION INC.
(Scholarship Program)
2210 W. Oaklawn
Springdale AR 72762-6999
501/290-4955

AMOUNT: Up to $1200/semester
DEADLINE(S): June 21
FIELD(S): Business; Agriculture; Engineering; Computer Science; Nursing

Open to a US citizen who was raised in and still lives in the vicinity of a Tyson Food's facility. Must maintain a 2.5 GPA while working and going to school full time. For undergrad study at schools in USA.
Recipients sign a pledge either to repay the scholarship money or help another deserving student not related by blood or marriage to attend college. Write for complete information.

628

US AIR FORCE ROTC
(4-Year Scholarship Program)
AFROTC/RROO
Recruiting Operations Branch
Maxwell AFB AL 36112
205/953-2091

AMOUNT: Tuition; fees & books + $100 per month stipend
DEADLINE(S): December 1
FIELD(S): Aeronautical Engineering; Civil Engineering; Mechanical Engineering; Mathematics; Physics; Nursing; & some Liberal Arts

Open to US citizens who are at least 17 and will graduate from college before age 25. Must complete application, furnish SAT/ACT scores, high school transcripts, and record of extracurricular activities.
Must qualify on Air Force medical examination. About 1600 scholarships awarded each year at campuses which offer Air Force ROTC.

629

US DEPT. OF HEALTH & HUMAN SERVICES
(Indian Health Service's Health Scholarship Program; Public Law 94-437)
Twinbrook Metro Plaza; Suite 100
12300 Twinbrook Pkwy.
Rockville MD 20852
301/443-6197

AMOUNT: Tuition + fees & monthly stipend
DEADLINE(S): April 1
FIELD(S): Health professions

Open to American Indians or Alaska natives who enroll in courses leading to a baccalaureate degree (preparing them for acceptance into health professions schools). US citizenship required. Renewable annually with reapplication.
Scholarship recipients must intend to serve the Indian people as a health care provider. They incur a 1-year service obligation to the IHS for each year of support. Write for complete information.

630

VIRGIN ISLANDS BOARD OF EDUCATION
(Nursing & Other Health Scholarships)
P.O. Box 11900
St. Thomas VI 00801
809/774-4546

AMOUNT: Up to $1800

DEADLINE(S): March 31

FIELD(S): Nursing; Medicine; Health-related Areas

Open to bona fide residents of the Virgin Islands who are accepted by an accredited school of nursing or an accredited institution offering courses in one of the health-related fields.

This scholarship is granted for one academic year. Recipients may reapply with at least a "C" average. Write for complete information.

631

VIRGINIA DEPT. OF HEALTH—OFFICE OF PUBLIC HEALTH NURSING
(Mary Marshall Nursing Scholarships)
P.O. Box 2448
Richmond VA 23218
804/371-4090

AMOUNT: $150 to $4000

DEADLINE(S): July 30 (postmark)

FIELD(S): Nursing

Practical & registered nursing program scholarships open to Virginia residents enrolled or accepted in a VA school of nursing. For full-time study leading to undergrad or grad nursing degree. GPA of 3.0 or better in required courses.

Must agree to engage in full-time nursing practice in VA upon graduation (1 month for every $100 received). Financial need must be demonstrated. Applications accepted after April 30. Write or call for complete information.

632

WISCONSIN LEAGUE FOR NURSING INC.
(Scholarship)
2121 East Newport Ave.
Milwaukee WI 53211
414/332-6271

AMOUNT: $500

DEADLINE(S): February 28

FIELD(S): Nursing

Open to Wisconsin residents enrolled in National League for Nursing (NLN) accredited program in WI. Categories—RN seeking BSN/student seeking RN (ADN diploma or BSN)/BSN-RN seeking MSN. Must be halfway through academic program.

Must have 3.0 or better GPA & demonstrate financial need. Must be recommended by dean or director at your NLN accredited school. Contact financial aid or nursing department for application/information.

NUTRITION

633

ABBIE SARGENT MEMORIAL SCHOLARSHIP INC.
(Scholarships)
295 Sheep Davis Road
Concord NH 03301
603/224-1934

AMOUNT: $200

DEADLINE(S): March 15

FIELD(S): Agriculture; Veterinary Medicine; Home Economics

Open to New Hampshire residents who are high school graduates with good grades and character. For undergraduate or graduate study. Must be legal resident of US and demonstrate financial need.

Renewable with reapplication. Write for complete information.

634

AMERICAN ASSOCIATION OF CEREAL CHEMISTS
(Undergraduate Scholarships and Graduate Fellowships)
Scholarship Dept.
3340 Pilot Knob Rd.
St. Paul MN 55121
612/454-7250

AMOUNT: $1000–$2000 undergrad; $1000–$3000 grad

DEADLINE(S): April 1

FIELD(S): Food Science

Open to undergrads & grads majoring or interested in a career in cereal science or technology (incl. baking or related area). Undergrads must have completed at least 1 quarter or semester of college/university work at time of application.

AACC membership is helpful but not necessary. Strong academic record & career interest are important criteria. Write for complete information.

635

AMERICAN DIETETIC ASSOCIATION
(Dietetic Technician)
216 W. Jackson Blvd.; Suite 800
Chicago IL 60606
800/877-1600 Ext. 4876

AMOUNT: $250 - $1000

DEADLINE(S): February 15 (request application by January 15)

FIELD(S): Dietetic Technician

Open to students in their first year of study in an ADA-approved dietetic technician program. If selected student may use the scholarship for study during second year. Must be US citizen and show evidence of leadership & academic ability.

Financial need, professional potential, & scholarship are considerations. Write for complete information.

636

AMERICAN DIETETIC ASSOCIATION
FOUNDATION
(Baccalaureate or Coordinated Program)
216 W. Jackson Blvd.; Suite 800
Chicago IL 60606
800/877-1600 Ext. 4876

AMOUNT: $250–$1000

DEADLINE(S): February 13 (request application by January 15)

FIELD(S): Dietetics

Open to students who have completed the academic requirements in an ADA-accredited or approved college or university program for minimum standing as a junior. Must be US citizen and show promise of value to the profession.

Financial need; professional potential, & scholarship are considerations. Write for complete information.

637

AMERICAN DIETETIC ASSOCIATION
FOUNDATION
(Dietetic Internships)
216 West Jackson Blvd.; Suite 800
Chicago IL 60606
800/877-1600 Ext. 4876

AMOUNT: $250 - $2500

DEADLINE(S): February 15 (request application by January 15)

FIELD(S): Dietetics

Open to students who have applied to an ADA-accredited dietetic internship and who show promise of being a valuable contributing member to the profession. US citizenship required.

Financial need, professional potential, & scholarship are considerations. Write for complete information.

638

AMERICAN DIETETIC ASSOCIATION
FOUNDATION
(Kraft General Foods Fellowship Program)
216 West Jackson; Suite 800
Chicago IL 60606
312/899-0040

AMOUNT: $10,000 per year

DEADLINE(S): June 1

FIELD(S): Nutrition

Open to senior undergraduate & graduate students who propose to pursue graduate work related to nutrition research or nutrition education & consumer awareness at recognized institutions in the USA. For citizens of USA, Mexico, & Canada.

Fellowships renewable for up to 3 years. Write for complete information.

639

AMERICAN DIETETIC ASSOCIATION FOUNDATION
(Pre-professional Practice Program—AP4)
216 W. Jackson Blvd.; Suite 800
Chicago IL 60606
800/877-1600 Ext. 4876

AMOUNT: $250 - $2500
DEADLINE(S): February 13 (request application by January 15)
FIELD(S): Dietetics

Open to students who are enrolled or have applied to an ADA-approved preprofessional practice program and who show promise of being a valuable contributing member of the profession. US citizenship required.

Financial need, professional potential, & scholarship are considerations. Write for complete information.

640

BUSINESS & PROFESSIONAL WOMEN'S FOUNDATION
(New York Life Foundation Scholarships for Women in the Health Professions)
2012 Massachusetts Ave. NW
Washington DC 20036
202/293-1200

AMOUNT: $500–$1000
DEADLINE(S): April 15 postmark (Applications available only October 1–April 1
FIELD(S): Health-Related Professions

Open to women (25 or older) who are within 12–24 months of completing their undergraduate program of study in USA. Studies should lead to entry or reentry into the work force or improve career advancement chances. US citizen.

Must be accepted into an accredited program and demonstrate financial need. Send self-addressed stamped ($.64) #10 envelope for application and complete information.

641

COMMUNITY FOUNDATION OF GREATER LORAIN COUNTY
(A.C. Siddall Educational Trust Fund Scholarship)
1865 N. Ridge Road E.; Suite A
Lorain OH 44055
216/277-0142 or 216/323-4445

AMOUNT: $1000
DEADLINE(S): May 1
FIELD(S): Health Care

Open to those who wish to pursue or further their education in health care who have been or are now employed and reside in or work for a health care facility within the Allen Memorial Hospital District in Lorain County.

Must have work experience and demonstrate financial need. Applications available beginning January 1 from Administrator; Allen Memorial Hospital; 200 W. Lorain St; Oberlin OH 44074.

642

DAIRY RECOGNITION EDUCATION FOUNDATION
(Low-interest Loans)
6245 Executive Blvd.
Rockville MD 20852
301/984-1444

AMOUNT: Up to $1500
DEADLINE(S): None
FIELD(S): Dairy Science; Food Science

Low-interest loans (currently 4%) for citizens of the US & Canada who are in good academic standing in the above areas. Awards support undergraduate study. Preference given to students who have completed at least one year of college.

10–20 awards per year. Write for complete information.

643

EDUCATIONAL FOUNDATION OF NATIONAL RESTAURANT ASSOC.
(Undergraduate Scholarship Program)
  250 S. Wacker Dr.; Suite 1400
  Chicago IL 60606
  312/715-1010

AMOUNT: $1000–$10,000
DEADLINE(S): March 1
FIELD(S): Foodservice; Hospitality

Open to full time undergrads in a foodservice/hospitality degree granting program beginning with the fall term. Must have worked in food service industry and demonstrated consistent academic achievement.

More than 100 undergrad awards per year. Write for complete information.

644

GOLDEN GATE RESTAURANT ASSN.
(David Rubenstein Memorial Scholarship Foundation Awards)
  720 Market St.; Suite 200
  San Francisco CA 94102
  415/781-5348

AMOUNT: $1000 - $1500
DEADLINE(S): March 31
FIELD(S): Hotel & Restaurant Management/Food Science

Open to students who have completed the first semester of college as a foodservice major and have a 2.75 or better GPA (4.0 scale) in hotel and restaurant courses.

Seven awards per year. Write for complete information.

645

HOTEL EMPLOYEES & RESTAURANT EMPLOYEES INTERNATIONAL UNION
(Edward T. Hanley Scholarship)
  1219 28th Street NW
  Washington DC 20007
  202/393-4373

AMOUNT: Tuition; fees; room & board; value over $6500 per year
DEADLINE(S): April 1
FIELD(S): Culinary Arts

Two-year scholarship to Culinary Institute of America in NY. Open to HERE union members (minimum 1 year) and candidates recommended by union members. Applications are by the vice-presidential district in which the member lives.

Residents of odd-numbered districts apply in odd-numbered years; even-numbered districts in even years. Applications are published in January, February, & March editions of "Catering Industry Employee." Write for complete information.

646

ILLINOIS RESTAURANT ASSN.
(Scholarship Fund)
  350 West Ontario; 7th Floor
  Chicago IL 60610
  312/787-4000

AMOUNT: Varies
DEADLINE(S): Varies
FIELD(S): Food Management; Food Science; Culinary Arts

Open to Illinois residents for undergraduate study of food service management, culinary arts, food processing, and related subjects at accredited institutions in the USA.

Write for complete information.

647

INSTITUTE OF FOOD TECHNOLOGISTS
(Junior/Senior Scholarships)
  221 N. LaSalle St.
  Chicago IL 60601
  312/782-8424; FAX 312/782-8348

AMOUNT: $750 to $2000
DEADLINE(S): February 1
FIELD(S): Food Science; Food Technology

Open to undergraduate sophomores and juniors pursuing an approved program in food science/technology in a US or

Canadian institution. Applicants should be scholastically outstanding & have a well-rounded personality.

For junior or senior year of study. 65 junior/senior awards per year (8 @ $2000; 3 @ $1500; 44 @ $1000 & 10 @ $750). Write for complete information.

648

NELLIE MARTIN CARMAN SCHOLARSHIP TRUST
(Scholarships)
18223 73rd Ave. NE; #B101
Bothell WA 98011
206/486-6575

AMOUNT: Up to $1000
DEADLINE(S): March 15
FIELD(S): All fields of study except those noted below

Open to high school seniors in King, Pierce, & Snohomish Counties (WA). For undergraduate study in the state of Washington in all fields EXCEPT music, sculpting, drawing, interior design, & home economics. US citizenship required.

Applications available only through high schools & nomination by counselor is required. Awards are renewable. Write for complete information.

649

PHI UPSILON OMICRON NATIONAL OFFICE
(Janice Cory Bullock Scholarship)
208 Mount Hall
1050 Carmack Road
Columbus OH 43210
614/421-7860

AMOUNT: $500
DEADLINE(S): March 1
FIELD(S): Home Economics

Open ONLY to Phi Upsilon Omicron homemakers who want to continue their undergraduate or graduate education so they are able to be gainfully employed.

Write for complete information.

650

PHI UPSILON OMICRON NATIONAL OFFICE
(Undergraduate Scholarships)
208 Mount Hall
1050 Carmack Road
Columbus OH 43210
614/421-7860

AMOUNT: $500
DEADLINE(S): March 1
FIELD(S): Home Economics

Open ONLY to Phi Upsilon Omicron members working toward a baccalaureate degree. Selection based on scholastic record, participation in PUO/AHEA and other collegiate activities, statement of professional goals, & personal considerations.

Write for complete information.

651

SCHOOL FOOD SERVICE FOUNDATION
(Scholarships)
1600 Duke St.; 7th Floor
Alexandria VA 22314
703/739-3900 or 800-877-8822

AMOUNT: Up to $1000
DEADLINE(S): April 15
FIELD(S): Food Science & Nutrition; Food Service Management

Must be an ASFSA member and/or the child of an ASFSA member who plans to study in the above field(s). Must express a desire to make school food service a career & be pursuing an AA degree or higher for this undergraduate scholarship.

Must have satisfactory academic record. Write for complete information.

652

STATLER FOUNDATION
(Scholarships)
107 Delaware Ave.; Suite 508
Buffalo NY 14202
716/852-1104

AMOUNT: $500 per year

DEADLINE(S): April 15

FIELD(S): Food Management; Culinary Arts; Hotel-Motel Management

Open to undergraduate or graduate students who are accepted to or enrolled full-time at a US institution in an accredited program of study in any of the above areas.

Approximately 900 awards per year. Renewable. Write for complete information.

653

TEXAS ELECTRIC COOPERATIVES INC.
(Ann Lane Homemaker Scholarship)
P.O. Box 9589
Austin TX 78766
512/454-0311

AMOUNT: $1000

DEADLINE(S): March 1

FIELD(S): Home Economics

Open to Texas residents who are graduating high school seniors and active members of a local Future Homemakers of America chapter. Award tenable at accredited undergraduate colleges or universities. Must be USA citizen.

Write for complete information.

654

WOMEN GROCERS OF AMERICA
(Mary Macey Scholarship Program)
1825 Samuel Morse Dr.
Reston VA 22090-5317
703/437-5300

AMOUNT: $1000 (minimum)

DEADLINE(S): June 1

FIELD(S): Food Management/Science

Open to undergraduate & graduate students pursuing a course of study leading to a food industry-related career. Awards are tenable at recognized colleges & universities.

Write for complete information.

SCHOOL OF SOCIAL SCIENCE

655

CAPE CANAVERAL CHAPTER
RETIRED OFFICERS ASSOC.
(Scholarships)
P.O. Box 4186
Patrick AFB FL 32925
Written inquiry

AMOUNT: Approximately $1500 per year

DEADLINE(S): May 31

FIELD(S): Science; Mathematics; Engineering; Liberal Arts; Chemistry

Open ONLY to Brevard County, Florida residents who are undergraduate juniors or seniors at any 4-year college in the USA and the son or daughter of active duty or retired military personnel. Must be US citizen.

Awards renewable for one year. Write to the scholarship program committee (address above) for complete information.

656

NELLIE MARTIN CARMAN
SCHOLARSHIP TRUST
(Scholarships)
18223 73rd Ave. NE; #B101
Bothell WA 98011
206/486-6575

AMOUNT: Up to $1000

DEADLINE(S): March 15

FIELD(S): All fields of study except those noted below

Open to high school seniors in King, Pierce, & Snohomish Counties (WA). For undergraduate study in the state of Washington in all fields EXCEPT music, sculpting, drawing, interior design, & home economics. US citizenship required.

Applications available only through high schools & nomination by counselor is required. Awards are renewable. Write for complete information.

COMMUNICATIONS

657

AMERICAN INSTITUTE OF POLISH CULTURE INC.
(Scholarships)
1440 79th Street Causeway; Suite 117
Miami FL 33141
305/864-2349

AMOUNT: $2500
DEADLINE(S): January 15
FIELD(S): Journalism/Public Relations

Scholarships to encourage young Americans of Polish descent to pursue the above professions. Award can be used at any accredited American college. The ruling criteria for selection are achievement/talent & involvement in public life.

For full-time study only. Renewable. Contact Prof. Zdzislaw Wesolowski at address above for complete information.

658

AMERICAN WOMEN IN RADIO & TELEVISION
(Houston Internship Program)
Aprille Meek; AWRT—Houston
P.O. Box 980908
Houston TX 77098
Written inquiry

AMOUNT: $500 per year
DEADLINE(S): March 1
FIELD(S): Radio; Television; Film & Video; Advertising; Marketing

Internships open to students who are juniors, seniors, or graduate students at greater Houston area colleges & universities.

Write for complete information.

659

ASIAN AMERICAN JOURNALISTS ASSOCIATION
(Scholarship Awards)
1765 Sutter St.; Room 1000
San Francisco CA 94115
415/346-2051

AMOUNT: Up to $2000
DEADLINE(S): April 15
FIELD(S): Journalism; Mass Communications

Open to students with a demonstrated ability & serious career interest in print, photo, or broadcast journalism. Awards based on scholastic achievement; commitment to journalism & to the Asian Pacific American community, & financial need.

For undergraduate or graduate study. Write for complete information.

660

ASSOCIATED PRESS TELEVISION-RADIO ASSOCIATION OF CALIFORNIA/NEVADA
(APTRA-CLETE Roberts Memorial Journalism Scholarship Awards)
Rachel Ambrose
Associated Press
221 S. Figueroa St. #300
Los Angeles CA 90012
213/626-1200

AMOUNT: $1500
DEADLINE(S): December 16
FIELD(S): Broadcast Journalism

Open to students with a broadcast journalism career objective who are studying in California or Nevada. For undergraduate or graduate study.

Write for complete information.

661

ASSOCIATION FOR EDUCATION IN JOURNALISM & MASS COMMUNICATIONS
(Correspondents Fund Scholarships)
University of SC College of Journalism
Columbia SC 29208
803/777-2005

AMOUNT: Up to $3000
DEADLINE(S): April 30
FIELD(S): Journalism; Mass Communications; Liberal Arts

Open to children of print or broadcast journalists who are foreign correspondents for a USA news medium. For undergraduate, graduate, or post-graduate study at any accredited college or university in the USA.

Preference to journalism or communications majors. 8–15 renewable awards per year. Write for complete information.

662

ASSOCIATION FOR EDUCATION IN JOURNALISM & MASS COMMUNICATIONS
(Mary A. Gardner Scholarship)
Jennifer McGill
1621 College St.; USC
Columbia SC 29208-0251
803/777-2005

AMOUNT: $500
DEADLINE(S): April 15
FIELD(S): Journalism

Open to undergraduate students having at least one year of study remaining who are enrolled full time in an accredited news-editorial program & have at least a 3.0 GPA (4.0 scale).

Write for complete information.

663

ASSOCIATION FOR EDUCATION IN JOURNALISM AND MASS COMMUNICATIONS
(Summer Journalism Internship for Minorities)
NYU Institute of Afro-American Affairs
269 Mercer; Suite 601
New York NY 10003
212/998-2130

AMOUNT: Salary of at least $200 per week
DEADLINE(S): November 3 (application request); December 15 (completed application)
FIELD(S): Journalism; Mass Communications; Advertising; Public Relations; Photo Journalism; Broadcasting

Open to members of ethnic minorities whose credentials reflect an interest in and commitment to journalism. Interns will be placed for 10 weeks in an entry-level position with participating companies, primarily in the NY/NJ area.

Write for complete information.

664

BALL STATE UNIVERSITY
(David Letterman Telecommunications Scholarship Program)
Dept. of Telecommunications
Muncie IN 47306
317/285-1480

AMOUNT: Full tuition (1st); 1/2 tuition (2nd); 1/3 tuition (3rd)
DEADLINE(S): April 1
FIELD(S): Telecommunications

Open to undergraduate juniors at Ball State who have demonstrated reasonable expectations of becoming professionals in the telecommunications industry. Scholarships are based on creativity; grades are NOT considered.

Any creative effort connected with the telecommunications field will be considered. Write for complete information.

665

**BROADCAST EDUCATION
ASSOCIATION**
(Scholarships in Broadcasting)
1771 N Street NW
Washington DC 20036
202/429-5354

AMOUNT: $1250 to $3000
DEADLINE(S): January 15
FIELD(S): Broadcasting

Scholarships are awarded for one scholastic
year of degree work at the junior, senior, or
graduate level. Applicants must show evidence of superior academic performance
and potential. Applications will not be sent
out after December 15.

Scholarship winners must study at a campus
where at least one department is a BEA
institutional member. Write for complete
information.

666

**CALIFORNIA CHICANO NEWS MEDIA
ASSOCIATION**
**(Joel Garcia Memorial Scholarship
Competition)**
c/o USC School of Journalism (GFS 315)
Los Angeles CA 90089
213/743-7158

AMOUNT: Up to $2000
DEADLINE(S): April 15
FIELD(S): Journalism; Communications

Open to all Latino undergraduate students
interested in pursuing careers in the above
areas. It is not necessary to be a journalism
or communications major. Awards tenable
at accredited colleges and universities in
California.

US residency required. 10–30 awards per year.
Write for complete information.

667

CENTRAL NEWSPAPERS INC.
(Pulliam Journalism Fellowships)
Russell B. Pulliam; Editor
The Indianapolis News
P.O. Box 145
Indianapolis IN 46206-0145
317/633-9121

AMOUNT: $4500 stipend
DEADLINE(S): March 1 (postmark)
FIELD(S): Journalism

Open to recent graduates & to undergraduate
seniors who will receive their bachelor's
degree by June. Award is for a 10-week
work & study internship at one of CNI's
newspapers in Indianapolis or Phoenix.

Includes sessions with a writing coach & semi-
nars with local & national journalists. 20
awards per year. Contact Mr. Russ Pulliam,
Editor, for complete information.

668

COX ENTERPRISES INC.
(Cox Minority Journalism Scholarship)
1400 Lake Hearn Drive
Atlanta GA 30302
404/843-5000

AMOUNT: Varies
DEADLINE(S): April 30
FIELD(S): Newspaper-Related

Each year a Cox-owned newspaper is chosen
to administer the program; applicant must
plan to attend college in that city. Open to
high school seniors who are members of a
racial minority, US citizen, and pursuing a
career in the newspaper industry.

Contact your senior guidance office in
February for information & application for
the upcoming school year.

669

DAYTON FOUNDATION
(Larry Fullerton Photojournalism
Scholarship)
2100 Kettering Tower
Dayton OH 45423
513/222-0410

AMOUNT: $1000
DEADLINE(S): January 31
FIELD(S): Photojournalism

Open to Ohio residents who are full-time
undergrad students at an Ohio college,
junior college, or school with a structured
curriculum & who plan to pursue a photojournalism career. Financial need & personal circumstances are considered.

Portfolio must be submitted following guidelines established by Ohio News
Photographers Association. Write for complete information.

670

DOG WRITERS' EDUCATIONAL TRUST
(Scholarships)
Berta I. Pickett
P.O. Box 2220
Payson AZ 85547
602/474-8867

AMOUNT: $1000
DEADLINE(S): December 31
FIELD(S): Veterinary Medicine; Animal
Behavior; Journalism

Open to applicants whose parents, grandparents, or other close relatives (or the applicant) are or have been involved in the
world of dogs as exhibitors, breeders, handlers, judges, club officers, or other activities.

Scholarships support undergraduate or graduate study. 10 awards per year. Send self-
addressed stamped envelope for complete
information and application.

671

DOW JONES NEWSPAPER FUND INC.
(Editing Intern Program for College Juniors,
Seniors, and Graduate Students)
P.O. Box 300
Princeton NJ 08543
609/452-2820

AMOUNT: $1000
DEADLINE(S): November 15
FIELD(S): Journalism

Open to college juniors, seniors, & graduate
students with a sincere desire for career in
journalism. Recipients receive $1000 schol-
arship, free 2-week pre-internship residency,
& summer copy editor job on daily paper at
regular wages.

Journalism major not required. Up to 45
awards per year. Applications available
from September 1 to November 1. Write for
complete information.

672

FUND FOR AMERICAN STUDIES
(Institutes on Political Journalism, Business &
Government Affairs, & Comparative Political
& Economic Systems)
1526 18th St. NW
Washington DC 20036
202/986-0384

AMOUNT: Up to $3500
DEADLINE(S): January 31 (early decision);
March 15 (general application deadline)
FIELD(S): Political Science; Economics;
Journalism; Business Administration

Scholarships cover cost to attend annual 6-
week summer institute at Georgetown Univ.
Courses are worth 6 credits & include foreign policy lectures, media dialogue series,
and site briefings. Open to college sophomores, juniors, and seniors.

Approx 100 awards per year. For Fund's programs only. Write for complete information.

673

INTERNATIONAL RADIO & TELEVISION SOCIETY FOUNDATION
(IRTS Summer Fellowship Program)
Ms. Maria De Leon
420 Lexington Ave.; Suite 1714
New York NY 10170
212/867-6650

AMOUNT: Housing; stipend; travel
DEADLINE(S): November 23
FIELD(S): Broadcasting; Communications; Sales

Annual 9-week summer fellowship program in New York City open to outstanding full-time undergraduate juniors & seniors with a demonstrated interest in a career in communications.
Write for complete information.

674

JOHN BAYLISS BROADCAST FOUNDATION
(Scholarship)
P.O. Box 221070
Carmel CA 93922
408/624-1536

AMOUNT: $2000
DEADLINE(S): April 30
FIELD(S): Radio Broadcasting

Open to undergrads in their junior or senior year and to graduate students who aspire to a career in radio. Applicants should have a 3.0 or better GPA. Financial need is a consideration. US citizen or legal resident.
Enclose a self-addressed stamped envelope for more information.

675

JOURNALISM FOUNDATION OF METROPOLITAN ST. LOUIS
(Scholarships)
c/o Patrick Gaven
900 N. Tucker Blvd.
St. Louis MO 63101
314/340-8000

AMOUNT: $750 to $2500
DEADLINE(S): February 28
FIELD(S): Journalism/Communications

Open to St. Louis metro residents entering their junior/senior year of college or graduate school. Must have a desire to pursue a career in journalism & have writing talent (samples).
17 or more scholarships per year. Contact Patricia Rice (chairman) at the above address for complete information.

676

KNTV TELEVISION
(Minority Scholarship)
645 Park Ave.
San Jose CA 95110
408/286-1111

AMOUNT: 2 @ $1000 each
DEADLINE(S): April 1
FIELD(S): Television Broadcasting

Open to Black, Hispanic, Asian/Pacific Islander, or American Indian students who are residents of Santa Clara, Santa Cruz, Monterey, or San Benito Counties (Calif.) & attend or plan to attend an accredited 4-year institution in California.
Must enroll in at least 12 semester units each semester. Considerations include interest in TV, financial need, community involvement, academics, and carrer aspirations. Write for complete information.

677

MIAMI INTERNATIONAL PRESS CLUB
(Scholarship Program)
c/o Miami Herald
One Herald Plaza
Miami FL 33132
305/376-2784

AMOUNT: $500 to $2500
DEADLINE(S): April 15
FIELD(S): Journalism; Broadcasting

Dade County (FL) residents who are deserving high school seniors are eligible for scholarships for undergraduate study at any accredited college or university in the above fields.

Scholarships are renewable. Write for complete information or call the club's secretary-treasurer at the number above.

678

NATIONAL ASSN. OF HISPANIC JOURNALISTS
(Mark Zambrano Scholarship Fund)
National Press Building; Suite 1193
Washington DC 20045
202/622-7145

AMOUNT: $1000

DEADLINE(S): January 31

FIELD(S): Print or Broadcast Journalism; Photojournalism

Open to undergrad juniors & seniors and grad students who are committed to pursuing a career in print or broadcast journalism or photojournalism. It is not necessary to be a journalism or broadcast major, nor is Hispanic ancestry required.

Awards tenable at accredited institutions in the USA & its territories. Write for complete information.

679

NATIONAL ASSN. OF HISPANIC JOURNALISTS
(NAHJ Scholarship Program)
National Press Building; Suite 1193
Washington DC 20045
202/622-7145

AMOUNT: Varies

DEADLINE(S): January 31

FIELD(S): Print or Broadcast Journalism; Photojournalism

Open to high school seniors, undergraduate, & graduate students who are committed to a career in print or broadcast journalism or photojournalism. It is NOT required to be of Hispanic ancestry.

Awards tenable at accredited 2-year or 4-year schools in the USA & its territories. Send a self-addressed stamped envelope and a letter of request for information.

680

NATIONAL ASSOCIATION OF BLACK JOURNALISTS
(NABJ Scholarship Program)
11600 Sunrise Valley Dr.
Reston VA 22091
703/648-1270

AMOUNT: $2500

DEADLINE(S): March 31

FIELD(S): Journalism

Open to African American undergraduate or graduate students who are accepted to or enrolled in an accredited journalism program majoring in print, photo, radio, or television. GPA of 2.5 or better (4.0 scale) is required.

12 awards per year. Write for complete information.

681

NATIONAL FEDERATION OF PRESS WOMEN INC.
(Helen M. Malloch Scholarship)
4510 W. 89th St.
Prairie Village KS 66207-2282
913/341-0165

AMOUNT: $1000

DEADLINE(S): May 1

FIELD(S): Journalism

Open to women who are undergraduate juniors/seniors or grad students majoring in journalism at a college or university of the student's choice.

Send SASE for complete information.

682

NATIONAL FEDERATION OF PRESS WOMEN INC.
(Professional Education Scholarship)
4510 W. 89th St.; Suite 110
Prairie Village KS 66207-2282
913/341-0165

AMOUNT: $1000
DEADLINE(S): May 1
FIELD(S): Journalism

For members of the National Federation of
Press Women who want to continue or
return to college as a journalism major.
Financial need is a consideration but is not
paramount.
Send SASE for complete information.

683

**NATIONAL RIGHT TO WORK
COMMITTEE**
(William B. Ruggles Journalism Scholarship)
8001 Braddock Rd.; Suite 500
Springfield VA 22160
703/321-9820

AMOUNT: $2000
DEADLINE(S): March 31
FIELD(S): Journalism

Scholarships are open to undergraduate and
graduate students majoring in journalism at
accredited USA institutions of higher learning who exemplify the dedication to princi-
ple & high journalistic standards of the late
William B. Ruggles.
Write for complete information.

684

**NEW YORK FINANCIAL WRITERS'
ASSOCIATION**
(Scholarship Program)
P.O. Box 21
Syosset NY 11791-0021
516/921-7766

AMOUNT: $2000

DEADLINE(S): Late December
FIELD(S): Financial Journalism

Open to undergraduate & graduate students
who are enrolled in an accredited college or
university in metropolitan New York City &
are pursuing a course of study leading to a
financial or business journalism career.
Write for complete information.

685

NEW YORK UNIVERSITY
**(Gallatin Division Special Awards &
Scholarships)**
715 Broadway; 6th Floor
New York NY 10003
212/598-7077

AMOUNT: Varies with award
DEADLINE(S): None specified
FIELD(S): Publishing

Various special awards and scholarships are
available to undergraduate and graduate
students enrolled in the Gallatin Division of
New York University.
104 special awards and scholarships per year.
Contact address above for complete information.

686

PEORIA JOURNAL STAR
(Scholarship Program)
1 News Plaza
Peoria IL 61643
309/686-3027

AMOUNT: $1000 per year for 4 years
DEADLINE(S): May 1
FIELD(S): Newspaper Journalism

Open to high school seniors who reside in
Bureau, Fulton, Henderson, Knox, LaSalle,
Marshall-Putnam, Mason, McDonough,
Peoria, Schuyler, Stark, Tazewell, Warren,
or Woodford Counties in Illinois.
Scholarship renewable annually for four years.
Write for complete information.

687

QUILL & SCROLL
(Edward J. Nell Memorial Scholarship)
 University of Iowa School of Journalism &
 Mass Communications
 Iowa City IA 52242-1528
 319/335-5795

AMOUNT: $500

DEADLINE(S): May 10

FIELD(S): Journalism

Open to high school seniors who are winners
 in the national writing/photo or yearbook
 excellence contest sponsored by Quill &
 Scroll and who plan to enroll in an accredited journalism program. Must be US citizen
 or legal resident.

Candidates should ask journalism teacher to
 write to address above for information on
 administration of the contest.

688

RADIO AND TELEVISION NEWS
DIRECTORS FOUNDATION
(Electronic Journalism Scholarship Awards)
 1000 Connecticut Ave. NW; Suite 615
 Washington DC 20036
 202/659-6510

AMOUNT: $1000; $2000; $5000

DEADLINE(S): March 15

FIELD(S): Radio & Television Journalism

Open to undergraduate sophomores and
 above and master's degree candidates
 whose career objective is electronic journalism. Awards are for 1 year of undergraduate or graduate study.

13 scholarships and 4 fellowships per year. Not
 renewable. Write for complete information.

689

RADIO FREE EUROPE/RADIO
LIBERTY
(Media & Opinion Research on Eastern
Europe & the Former Soviet Union)
 Personnel Division
 1201 Connecticut Ave. NW
 Washington DC 20036
 Written inquiry

AMOUNT: Daily stipend of 48 German
 marks plus accommodations

DEADLINE(S): February 22

FIELD(S): Communications; Market
 Research; Statistics; Sociology; Social
 Psychology; East European Studies

Internship open to graduate students or
 exceptionally qualified undergrads in the
 above areas who can demonstrate knowledge of quantitative research methods, computer applications, and public opinion survey techniques.

East European language skills would be an
 advantage. Write for complete information.

690

SCRIPPS HOWARD FOUNDATION
(Scripps Howard Foundation Scholarships)
 312 Walnut St.; 28th Floor
 P.O. Box 5380
 Cincinnati OH 45201-5380
 513/977-3035

AMOUNT: $1000 to $3000

DEADLINE(S): February 25

FIELD(S): Journalism

Scholarships are available to full-time undergraduate students attending 4-year colleges
 to prepare for careers in print & electronic
 journalism. US citizenship required.
 Financial need must be demonstrated.

Renewable with reapplication. Submit letter
 with request for scholarship application
 before December 20 stating college major
 & career goal. SAT/ACT scores required of
 incoming freshmen. Write for complete
 information.

691

SOCIETY FOR TECHNICAL COMMUNICATION
(Undergraduate Scholarships)
901 N. Stuart St.; Suite 904
Arlington VA 22203
703/522-4114

AMOUNT: $2000
DEADLINE(S): February 15
FIELD(S): Technical Communication

Open to full-time undergraduate students who have completed at least 1 year of study & are enrolled in an accredited 2-year or 4-year degree program for career in any area of technical communication.

Awards tenable at recognized colleges & universities in USA & Canada. 7 awards per year. Write for complete information.

692

SOCIETY OF BROADCAST ENGINEERS
(Harold Ennes Scholarship Fund)
8445 Keystone Crossing; Suite 140
Indianapolis IN 46240-2454
317/253-1640

AMOUNT: $1000
DEADLINE(S): July 1
FIELD(S): Broadcasting

Open to undergraduate students interested in a career in broadcasting. Two references from SBE members are needed to confirm eligibility. Submit a statement of purpose and a brief biography.

Send self-addressed stamped envelope for application and complete information.

693

UNITED METHODIST COMMUNICATIONS
(Leonard M. Perryman Communications Scholarship for Ethnic Minority Students)
P.O. Box 320
Nashville TN 37202
615/742-5140

AMOUNT: $2500
DEADLINE(S): February 15
FIELD(S): Religious Journalism

Christian faith. Scholarship open to ethnic minority undergraduate juniors & seniors who are enrolled in accredited schools of communication or journalism (print, electronic, or audiovisual). USA citizen or legal resident.

Candidates should plan to pursue a career in religious communication. Write for complete information.

694

UNIVERSITY OF MARYLAND
(College of Journalism Scholarships)
Journalism Building; Room 1118
College Park MD 20742
301/405-2380

AMOUNT: $250 to $1500
DEADLINE(S): February 15
FIELD(S): Journalism

Variety of journalism scholarships; prizes and awards tenable at the University of Maryland. Application forms for all scholarships are available at the address above.

Write for complete information.

695

VANDERBILT UNIVERSITY
(Fred Russell—Grantland Rice Scholarship)
2305 West End Ave.
Nashville TN 37203-1700
615/322-2561

AMOUNT: $10,000/year ($40,000 total award)
DEADLINE(S): January 1
FIELD(S): Journalism

Four-year scholarship to Vanderbilt University open to high school seniors who want to become sports writers, have demonstrated outstanding potential in the field, & can meet entrance requirements of Vanderbilt's College of Arts & Science.

Write to Scholarship Coordinator at above address for complete information.

696

WILLIAM RANDOLPH HEARST FOUNDATION
(Journalism Awards Program)
90 New Montgomery St.; #1212
San Francisco CA 94105
415/543-6033

AMOUNT: $500–$3000

DEADLINE(S): Monthly contests at 95 accredited schools of journalism with a total of $317,600 awarded each year.

FIELD(S): Print Journalism; Photo Journalism; Broadcast News

Journalism awards program offers monthly competitions open to undergraduate college journalism majors who are currently enrolled in one of the 95 participating journalism schools.

Entry forms and details on monthly contests are only available through the Journalism department of participating schools.

HISTORY

697

COMMITTEE ON INSTITUTIONAL COOPERATION
(CIC Pre-doctoral Fellowships)
Indiana University
803 East 8th St.
Bloomington IN 47408
812/855-0823

AMOUNT: $11,000 + tuition (4 years)

DEADLINE(S): December 1

FIELD(S): Humanities; Social Sciences; Natural Sciences; Mathematics; Engineering

Pre-doctoral fellowships for US citizens of African American, American Indian, Mexican American, or Puerto Rican heritage. Must hold or expect to receive bachelor's degree by late summer from a regionally accredited college or unviersity.

Awards for specified universities in IL, IN, IA, MI, MN, OH, WI, PA. Write for details.

698

DAUGHTERS OF THE AMERICAN REVOLUTION
(American History Scholarships)
Office of the Committee/Scholarships
National Society DAR
1776 'D' St. NW
Washington DC 20006-5392
202/879-3292

AMOUNT: $2000 per year for up to 4 years

DEADLINE(S): February 1

FIELD(S): American History

Open to graduating high school seniors planning to major in American History. Must be USA citizen and attend an accredited USA college or university. Awards based on academic excellence, financial need, & commitment to American history.

DAR affiliation not required but must be sponsored by a local DAR chapter. Write for complete information (include a self-addressed stamped envelope).

699

DAUGHTERS OF THE AMERICAN REVOLUTION
(Enid Hall Griswold Memorial Scholarship Program)
Office of the Committee/Scholarships
National Society DAR
1776 'D' St. NW
Washington DC 20006-5392
202/879-3292

AMOUNT: $1000 (one-time award)

DEADLINE(S): February 15

FIELD(S): History; Political Science; Government; Economics

Open to undergraduate juniors & seniors attending an accredited college or university in the USA. Awards are judged on the basis of academic excellence, financial need, & commitment to field of study. Must be US citizen.

DAR affiliation is not required but applicants must be sponsored by a local DAR chapter.

Not renewable. Write for complete informtion (include SASE).

700

NATIONAL SPACE CLUB
(Dr. Robert H. Goddard Historical Essay Award)
655 15th St. NW; #300
Washington DC 20005
202/639-4210

AMOUNT: $1000

DEADLINE(S): December 1

FIELD(S): Aerospace History

Essay competition open to any US citizen on a topic dealing with any significant aspect of the historical development of rocketry and astronautics. Essays should not exceed 5000 words and should be fully documented. Write for complete information.

701

SOURISSEAU ACADEMY FOR STATE AND LOCAL HISTORY
(Research Grant)
c/o San Jose State University
San Jose CA 95192
408/924-6510 or 408/227-2657

AMOUNT: $500

DEADLINE(S): April 1; November 1

FIELD(S): California History

Grants are available to support undergraduate and graduate research on California history. Preference to research on Santa Clara County history.

5-10 awards per year are granted for project expences. Write for complete information.

702

US INSTITUTE OF PEACE
(National Peace Essay Contest)
1550 M St. NW; Suite 700
Washington DC 20005
202/457-1700

AMOUNT: $250 to $10,000

DEADLINE(S): January 23

FIELD(S): American History; American Foreign Policy

1500 word essay contest for college scholarships open to students in the 9th through 12th grades. US citizenship required for students attending school overseas. 1st, 2nd, and 3rd place winners receive scholarships.

First place state winners will receive all-expenses-paid trip to Washington for the 5-day awards program. 166 state winners; 3 national winners. Write for guidelines; topic changes yearly.

703

US MARINE CORPS HISTORICAL CENTER
(College Internships)
Building 58
Washington Navy Yard
Washington DC 20374
202/433-3839

AMOUNT: Stipend to cover daily expenses

DEADLINE(S): None specified

FIELD(S): US Military History; Library Science; History; Museum Studies

Open to undergraduate students at a college or university which will grant academic credit for work experience as interns at the address above or at the Marine Corps Airground Museum in Quantico, Virginia.

All internships are regarded as beginning professional-level historian, curator, librarian, or archivist positions. Write for complete information.

704

WILLIAM RANDOLPH HEARST FOUNDATION
(U.S. Senate Youth Program)
90 New Montgomery St.; Suite 1212
San Francisco CA 94105
415/543-4057; Fax 415/243-0760

AMOUNT: $2000 plus all-expenses-paid week
in Washington
DEADLINE(S): None specified
FIELD(S): U.S. Government; History;
Political Science; Economics

Open to any high school junior or senior who
is serving as an elected student body officer
at a USA high school. Student receives a
week's stay in Washington as guest of the
Senate and a $2000 scholarship.

Student must become a candidate for a degree
at an accredited USA college or university
within two years of high school graduation.
USA permanent resident. Contact high
school principal for complete information.

LAW

705

ASSOCIATION OF FORMER AGENTS OF
THE US SECRET SERVICE
(AFAUSS—Law Enforcement Career
Scholarship Program)
P.O. Box 848
Annandale VA 22003
Written inquiry

AMOUNT: $500–$1500
DEADLINE(S): May 1
FIELD(S): Law Enforcement; Police
Administration

Open to undergraduate students who have
completed at least one year of study and
graduate students working towards an
advanced degree in the above areas. US citizenship required.

Write for complete information; SASE (size
#10) required.

706

BOY SCOUTS OF AMERICA
(J. Edgar Hoover Foundation Scholarships)
1325 W. Walnut Hill Ln.
Irving TX 75015
214/580-2084

AMOUNT: $1000
DEADLINE(S): March 31
FIELD(S): Law Enforcement

Open to high school seniors who are registered Explorer Scouts, active in post spe-
cializing in law enforcement, & have
demonstrated a desire to pursue a career in
law enforcement. Awards for undergrad
tuition. US citizen.

Scholarship funds will remain available to winners for a 24-month period starting with
summer or fall semester of the year selected. Write for complete information.

707

BOYS & GIRLS CLUBS OF SAN DIEGO
(Spence Reese Scholarship Fund)
3760 Fourth Ave.; Suite 1
San Diego CA 92103
619/298-3520

AMOUNT: $2000 per year for 4 years
DEADLINE(S): May 15
FIELD(S): Medicine; Law; Engineering;
Political Science

Open to male high school seniors planning a
career in above fields. Preference to students within a 250-mile radius of San Diego.
Boys Club affiliation is not required.

Applications are available in January. Must
enclose a self-addressed stamped envelope
to receive application. A $10 processing fee
is required with completed application.
Write for complete information.

708

BUSINESS & PROFESSIONAL WOMEN'S FOUNDATION
(Career Advancement Scholarships)
2012 Massachusetts Ave. NW
Washington DC 20036
202/293-1200

AMOUNT: $500–$1000

DEADLINE(S): April 15 (postmark)

FIELD(S): Computer Science; Education; Paralegal; Engineering; Science; Law; Dentistry; Medicine

Open to women (30 or older) within 12–24 months of completing undergrad or grad study in US (including Puerto Rico & Virgin Islands). Studies should lead to entry/reentry in work force or improve career advancement chances.

Not for doctoral study. Must demonstrate financial need. Send self-addressed stamped ($.64) #10 envelope for complete info. Applications available October 1–April 1.

709

COUNCIL ON LEGAL EDUCATION OPPORTUNITY
(CLEO Stipends)
1420 N Street NW; Suite T-1
Washington DC 20005
202/785-4840

AMOUNT: $7000 per year maximum

DEADLINE(S): September 1; February 1

FIELD(S): Law

Open to pre-law students. Recipients must attend a summer institute. Graduates of the institute usually receive stipend for three years of law school. 150 awards annually. Must be US citizen or legal resident.

The institute helps students evaluate their potential for law study by exposing them to an intensive 6-week course of legal writing analysis and research. Write for complete information.

710

EARL WARREN LEGAL TRAINING PROGRAM
(Scholarships)
99 Hudson St.; 16th Floor
New York NY 10013
212/219-1900

AMOUNT: Varies

DEADLINE(S): March 15

FIELD(S): Law

Scholarships for entering Black law students. Emphasis on applicants who wish to enter law schools in the south. Must submit proof of acceptance to an accredited law school. US citizenship or legal residency required.

US citizens under 35 years of age preferred. Write for complete information.

711

H. FLETCHER BROWN FUND
(Scholarships)
c/o PNC Bank; Trust Dept.
P.O. Box 791
Wilmington DE 19899
302/429-2827

AMOUNT: Varies

DEADLINE(S): April 15

FIELD(S): Medicine; Dentistry; Law; Engineering; Chemistry

Open to US citizens born and still residing in Delaware. For 4 years of study (undergrad or grad) leading to a degree that enables applicant to practice in chosen field.

Scholarships are based on need, scholastic achievement, and good moral character. Applications available in February. Write for complete information.

712

INTERNATIONAL ASSN. OF ARSON INVESTIGATORS
(John Charles Wilson Scholarship Fund)
300 S. Broadway; Suite #100
St. Louis MO 63102
314/621-1966

AMOUNT: $1000

DEADLINE(S): February 15

FIELD(S): Police Science; Fire Science; & Affiliated Fields

Open to IAAI members, their immediate family, & non-members who are recommended & sponsored by members in good standing. Awards are for undergraduate study in above areas at accredited 2-year & 4-year institutions.

Write for complete information.

713

MARYLAND HIGHER EDUCATION COMMISSION
(Professional School Scholarships)
State Scholarship Administration
16 Francis St.
Annapolis MD 21401
410/974-5370

AMOUNT: $200–$1000

DEADLINE(S): March 1

FIELD(S): Dentistry; Pharmacy; Medicine; Law; Nursing

Open to Maryland residents who have been admitted as full-time students at a participating graduate institution of higher learning in Maryland or an undergraduate nursing program.

Renewable up to 4 years. Write for complete information and a list of participating Maryland institutions.

714

NATIONAL BLACK POLICE ASSOCIATION
(Alphonso Deal Scholarship Award)
3251 Mt. Pleasant St. NW; 2nd Floor
Washington DC 20010
202/986-2070

AMOUNT: $500

DEADLINE(S): June 1

FIELD(S): Law Enforcement; Criminal Justice

Open to minority high school graduates who have been accepted for enrollment in a two- or four-year college. Must have a GPA of 2.5 or better and demonstrate financial need. US citizenship required.

Write for complete information.

715

NATIONAL FEDERATION OF THE BLIND
(Howard Brown Rickard Scholarship)
814 4th Ave.; Suite #200
Grinnell IA 50112
515/236-3366

AMOUNT: $2500

DEADLINE(S): March 31

FIELD(S): Natural Sciences; Architecture; Engineering; Medicine; Law

Scholarships for undergraduate or graduate study in the above areas. Open to legally blind students enrolled full time at accredited post-secondary institutions.

Awards based on academic excellence, service to the community, and financial need. Write for complete information.

POLITICAL SCIENCE

716

AMERICAN JEWISH COMMITTEE
(Harold W. Rosenthal Fellowship)
1156 15th St. NW; Suite 1201
Washington DC 20005
202/785-4200

AMOUNT: $1800 stipend

DEADLINE(S): April

FIELD(S): Political Science; Government Service; Foreign Affairs

Open to college seniors & grad students. Fellowship provides opportunity for a student to spend a summer working in the office of a member of Congress or Executive Branch on Foreign Affairs and government service issues. US citizen.

Applications are available from the address above; however, they must be submitted with a recommendation from your dean. Selected fellows will also receive preferential treatment for a European community 3–5 week travel study.

717

BOYS & GIRLS CLUBS OF SAN DIEGO
(Spence Reese Scholarship Fund)
3760 Fourth Ave.; Suite 1
San Diego CA 92103
619/298-3520

AMOUNT: $2000 per year for 4 years
DEADLINE(S): May 15
FIELD(S): Medicine; Law; Engineering;
Political Science

Open to male high school seniors planning a career in above fields. Preference to students within a 250-mile radius of San Diego. Boys Club affiliation is not required.

Applications are available in January. Must enclose a self-addressed stamped envelope to receive application. A $10 processing fee is required with completed application. Write for complete information.

718

COMMITTEE ON INSTITUTIONAL COOPERATION
(CIC Pre-doctoral Fellowships)
Indiana University; 803 East 8th St.
Bloomington IN 47408
812/855-0823

AMOUNT: $11,000 + tuition (4 years)
DEADLINE(S): December 1
FIELD(S): Humanities; Social Sciences;
Natural Sciences; Mathematics; Engineering

Pre-doctoral fellowships for US citizens of African American, American Indian, Mexican American, or Puerto Rican heritage. Must hold or expect to receive bachelor's degree by late summer from a regionally accredited college or unviersity.

Awards for specified universities in IL, IN, IA, MI, MN, OH, WI, PA. Write for details.

719

DAUGHTERS OF THE AMERICAN REVOLUTION
(Enid Hall Griswold Memorial Scholarship Program)
Office of the Committee/Scholarships
National Society DAR
1776 'D' St. NW
Washington DC 20006-5392
202/879-3292

AMOUNT: $1000 (one-time award)
DEADLINE(S): February 15
FIELD(S): History; Political Science;
Government; Economics

Open to undergraduate juniors & seniors attending an accredited college or university in the USA. Awards are judged on the basis of academic excellence, financial need, & commitment to field of study. Must be US citizen.

DAR affiliation is not required but applicants must be sponsored by a local DAR chapter. Not renewable. Write for complete informtion (include SASE).

720

FUND FOR AMERICAN STUDIES
(Institutes on Political Journalism, Business & Government Affairs, & Comparative Political & Economic Systems)
1526 18th St. NW
Washington DC 20036
202/986-0384

AMOUNT: Up to $3500
DEADLINE(S): January 31 (early decision);
March 15 (general application deadline)
FIELD(S): Political Science; Economics;
Journalism; Business Administration

Scholarships cover cost to attend annual 6-week summer institute at Georgetown Univ. Courses are worth 6 credits & include foreign policy lectures, media dialogue series, site briefings. Open to college sophomores, juniors, and seniors.

Approx 100 awards per year. For Fund's programs only. Write for complete information.

721

HARRY S. TRUMAN SCHOLARSHIP FOUNDATION
(Scholarships)
712 Jackson Place NW
Washington DC 20006
202/395-4831

AMOUNT: Up to $30,000 over 4 years
DEADLINE(S): December 1
FIELD(S): Public Service; Government

Open to full-time students who are juniors in a 4-year college and committed to a career in government public service. Must be in upper 1/4 of class and have outstanding leadership potential.

Candidates must be US citizens nominated by their schools. Up to 80 scholarships per year. Send SASE for complete information.

722

ILLINOIS GOVERNOR'S MICHAEL CURRY SUMMER INTERNSHIP PROGRAM
2 1/2 State House
Springfield IL 62706
217/782-4921

AMOUNT: $1000 per month
DEADLINE(S): February 1
FIELD(S): Public Service

Illinois resident. Governor's summer internship program is open to undergraduate students who have completed at least 2 years of study. Interns are placed with various state agencies in Chicago & Springfield. US citizen.

Academic credit may be arranged. 140 internships per summer. Write for complete information.

723

JUNIATA COLLEGE
(Baker Peace and Conflict Studies Merit Scholarship and Lingenfelter Peace Studies Scholarship)
Baker Institute
Huntingdon PA 16652
814/643-4310

AMOUNT: $1000
DEADLINE(S): March 1
FIELD(S): International Affairs

Awards are made based on merit to students who are accepted as incoming freshmen at Juniata College and intend to pursue the peace and conflict studies curriculum.

Student should rank in upper 20% of graduating H.S. class and have above-average SAT scores. Scholarship is renewable for up to 3 years if 3.0 GPA is maintained.

724

LAVINIA ENGLE SCHOLARSHIP
(Undergraduate Women Scholarships)
c/o Judith Heimann
6900 Marbury Rd.
Bethesda MD 20817
301/229-4647

AMOUNT: Varies
DEADLINE(S): April 15
FIELD(S): Political Science/Government/ Public Administration

Open to women residing in Montgomery County, Maryland. For undergraduate study at a college or university in Maryland.

Send self-addressed stamped envelope for application and complete information.

725

NEW YORK CITY DEPT. OF PERSONNEL
(Government Scholars Internship Program)
2 Washington St.; 15th Floor
New York NY 10004
212/487-5698

AMOUNT: $3000 stipend

DEADLINE(S): January 13

FIELD(S): Public Administration; Urban Planning; Government; Public Service; Urban Affairs

10-week summer intern program open to undergraduate sophomores, juniors, & seniors. Program provides students with unique opportunity to learn about NY City government. Internships available in virtually every city agency & mayoral office. Write for complete information.

726

NEW YORK CITY DEPT. OF PERSONNEL
(Urban Fellows Program)
2 Washington St.; 15th Floor
New York NY 10004
212/487-5698

AMOUNT: $18,000 stipend

DEADLINE(S): January 20

FIELD(S): Public Administration; Urban Planning; Government; Public Service; Urban Affairs

Fellowship program provides one academic year (9 months) of full-time work experience in urban government. Open to graduating college seniors and recent college graduates. US citizenship required. Write for complete information.

727

US INSTITUTE OF PEACE
(National Peace Essay Contest)
1550 M St. NW; Suite 700
Washington DC 20005
202/457-1700

AMOUNT: $250 to $10,000

DEADLINE(S): January 23

FIELD(S): American History; American Foreign Policy

1500-word essay contest for college scholarships open to students in the 9th through 12th grades. US citizenship required for students attending school overseas. 1st, 2nd, and 3rd place winners receive scholarships. First place state winners will receive all-expenses-paid trip to Washington for the 5-day awards program. 166 state winners; 3 national winners. Write for guidelines; topic changes yearly.

728

WASHINGTON CROSSING FOUNDATION
(Scholarship Fund)
Eugene C. Fish Esq.; Vice Chairman
P.O. Box 17
Washington Crossing PA 18977-0017
215/493-6577

AMOUNT: $5000 to $10,000

DEADLINE(S): January 15

FIELD(S): Government; Public Service

Open to USA high school seniors planning a career in government service (local/state/federal). $2000 for 1st year; $1000/year for the following 3 years. Tenable at any accredited USA college or university. USA citizenship required.

A 200-word essay on why student is considering a career in government (including any inspiration to be derived from the leadership of George Washington crossing the Delaware) will be considered. Write for complete information.

729

WILLIAM RANDOLPH HEARST FOUNDATION
(U.S. Senate Youth Program)
90 New Montgomery St.; Suite 1212
San Francisco CA 94105
415/543-4057; Fax 415/243-0760

AMOUNT: $2000 plus all-expenses-paid week in Washington

DEADLINE(S): None specified

FIELD(S): US Government; History; Political Science; Economics

Open to any high school junior or senior who is serving as an elected student body officer at a USA high school. Student receives a week's stay in Washington as guest of the Senate and a $2000 scholarship.

Student must become a candidate for a degree at an accredited USA college or university within two years of high school graduation. USA permanent resident. Contact high school principal for complete information.

PSYCHOLOGY

730

AMERICAN FOUNDATION FOR THE BLIND
(Delta Gamma Foundation Florence Harvey Memorial Scholarship)
15 W. 16th St.
New York NY 10011
212/620-2000; TDD 212/620-2158

AMOUNT: $1000

DEADLINE(S): None specified

FIELD(S): Rehabilitation and/or Education of the Visually Impaired and Blind

Open to legally blind undergraduate and graduate college students of good character who have exhibited academic excellence and are studying in the field of education and/or rehabilitation of the visually impaired and blind.

Must be USA citizen. Write for complete information.

731

AMERICAN FOUNDATION FOR THE BLIND
(Rudolph Dillman Memorial Scholarship)
15 West 16th St.
New York NY 10011
212/620-2000; TDD 212/620-2158

AMOUNT: $2500

DEADLINE(S): April 1

FIELD(S): Rehabilitation; Education of Blind & Visually Impaired

Open to legally blind undergrad or graduate students accepted to or enrolled in an accredited program within the broad areas of rehabilitation and/or education of the blind and visually impaired. USA citizen.

Three awards per year. Write for complete information.

732

AMERICAN FOUNDATION FOR THE BLIND
(TeleSensory Scholarship)
15 West 16th St.
New York NY 10011
212/620-2000; TDD 212/620-2158

AMOUNT: $1000

DEADLINE(S): April 1

FIELD(S): None specified

Open to full-time undergrad students who are legally blind and do not meet the criteria for other AFB scholarships. Must be US citizen, provide proof of acceptance to a college or university and three letters of recommendation.

Write for complete information.

733

COMMITTEE ON INSTITUTIONAL COOPERATION
(CIC Pre-doctoral Fellowships)
Indiana University
803 East 8th St.
Bloomington IN 47408
812/855-0823

AMOUNT: $11,000 + tuition (4 years)

DEADLINE(S): December 1

FIELD(S): Humanities; Social Sciences; Natural Sciences; Mathematics; Engineering

Pre-doctoral fellowships for US citizens of African American, American Indian, Mexican American, or Puerto Rican heritage. Must hold or expect to receive bachelor's degree by late summer from a regionally accredited college or unviersity.

Awards for specified universities in IL, IN, IA, MI, MN, OH, WI, PA. Write for details.

734

EASTER SEAL SOCIETY OF IOWA
(Scholarships & Awards)
P.O. Box 4002
Des Moines IA 50333
515/289-1933

AMOUNT: $400–$600

DEADLINE(S): April 15

FIELD(S): Physical Rehabilitation; Mental Rehabilitation; & Related Areas

Open to Iowa residents who are full-time undergraduate sophomores, juniors, seniors, or graduate students at accredited institutions, planning a career in the broad field of rehabilitation, financially needy, & in top 40% of their class.

6 scholarships per year. Must re-apply each year.

735

EPILEPSY FOUNDATION OF AMERICA
(Behavioral Sciences Student Fellowships)
4351 Garden City Dr.; Suite 406
Landover MD 20785
301/459-3700

AMOUNT: $1500

DEADLINE(S): March 2

FIELD(S): Epilepsy-related study or training projects

Open to undergrad and grad students in nursing, psychology, and related areas who propose a 3-month epilepsy-related project to be carried out in a US institution at which there are ongoing epilepsy research, service, or training programs.

Fellowship must be undertaken during a free period in the student's year. Write for complete information.

736

NORTH CAROLINA STUDENT LOAN PROGRAM FOR HEALTH, SCIENCE, & MATHEMATICS
(Loans)
3824 Barrett Dr.; Suite 304
Raleigh NC 27619
919/733-2164

AMOUNT: $2500 to $7500 per year

DEADLINE(S): January 8 to May 5

FIELD(S): Health Professions; Sciences; Engineering

Low-interest scholarship loans open to North Carolina residents of at least 1 year who are pursuing an associates, undergraduate, or graduate degree in the above fields at an accredited institution in the US.

Loans may be retired after graduation by working (1 year for each year funded) at designated institutions. Write for complete details.

737

PARAPSYCHOLOGY FOUNDATION
(Eileen J. Garrett Research Scholarship)
228 East 71st Street
New York NY 10021
212/628-1550; FAX 212/628-1559

AMOUNT: $3000

DEADLINE(S): July 15

FIELD(S): Parapsychology

Open to any undergrad or grad student wishing to pursue the academic study of the science of parapsychology. Funding is for study, research, & experimentation only. Applicants must demonstrate previous academic interest in parapsycholgy.

Approximately 15 awards per year. Write for complete information.

738

**RADIO FREE EUROPE/RADIO
LIBERTY**
**(Media & Opinion Research on Eastern
Europe & the Former Soviet Union)**
 Personnel Division; 1201 Connecticut Ave.
 NW
 Washington DC 20036
 Written inquiry

AMOUNT: Daily stipend of 48 German
 marks plus accommodations
DEADLINE(S): February 22
FIELD(S): Communications; Market
 Research; Statistics; Sociology; Social
 Psychology; East European Studies
Internship open to graduate students or
 exceptionally qualified undergrads in the
 above areas who can demonstrate knowledge of quantitative research methods, computer applications, and public opinion survey techniques.
East European language skills would be an
 advantage. Write for complete information.

739

**SOCIETY FOR THE SCIENTIFIC STUDY
OF SEXUALITY**
(Student Research Grant)
 P.O. Box 208
 Mount Vernon IA 52314-0208
 319/895-8407

AMOUNT: $500
DEADLINE(S): February 1; September 1
FIELD(S): Human Sexuality
Open to students doing research in the area of
 human sexuality. Must be enrolled in a
 degree granting program at an accredited
 institution. Can be master's thesis or doctoral dissertation but this is not a requirement.
Write to Karen Polonko, Ph.D., at the above
 address for application & complete information.

SOCIOLOGY

740

B'NAI B'RITH YOUTH ORGANIZATION
(Scholarship Program)
 1640 Rhode Island Avenue NW
 Washington DC 20036
 202/857-6633

AMOUNT: $2500 per year
DEADLINE(S): Each spring
FIELD(S): Social Work
Open to US citizens of Jewish faith who are
 first- or second-year grad students attending
 accredited graduate schools of social work
 or who are college seniors planning to
 attend a graduate school of social work.
Must show evidence of good scholarship,
 interest in working for Jewish agencies, &
 have knowledge of Jewish communal struc-
 ture & institutions. Renewable. Write for
 complete information.

741

EASTER SEAL SOCIETY OF IOWA
(Scholarships & Awards)
 P.O. Box 4002
 Des Moines IA 50333
 515/289-1933

AMOUNT: $400–$600
DEADLINE(S): April 15
FIELD(S): Physical Rehabilitation; Mental
 Rehabilitation; & Related Areas
Open to Iowa residents who are full-time
 undergraduate sophomores, juniors, seniors,
 or graduate students at accredited institutions, planning a career in the broad field of
 rehabilitation, financially needy, & in top
 40% of their class.
6 scholarships per year. Must re-apply each
 year.

742

JEWISH VOCATIONAL SERVICE
(Marcus & Theresa Levie Educational Fund
Scholarships)
1 S Franklin St.
Chicago IL 60606
312/346-6700 Ext. 2214

AMOUNT: $5000
DEADLINE(S): March 1
FIELD(S): Social Work; Medicine; Dentistry;
Nursing; & other related professions &
vocations

Open to Cook County residents of the Jewish
faith who plan careers in the helping professions. For undergraduate juniors and seniors
and for graduate and vocational students.
Applications available December 1 from
Scholarship Secretary.

Must show financial need. 85–100 awards per
year. Renewal possible with reapplication.
Write for complete information.

743

NEW YORK CITY DEPT. OF
PERSONNEL
(Government Scholars Internship Program)
2 Washington St.; 15th Floor
New York NY 10004
212/487-5698

AMOUNT: $3000 stipend
DEADLINE(S): January 13
FIELD(S): Public Administration; Urban
Planning; Government; Public Service;
Urban Affairs

10-week summer intern program open to
undergraduate sophomores, juniors, &
seniors. Program provides students with
unique opportunity to learn about NY City
government. Internships available in virtually every city agency & mayoral office.
Write for complete information.

744

NEW YORK CITY DEPT. OF
PERSONNEL
(Urban Fellows Program)
2 Washington St.; 15th Floor
New York NY 10004
212/487-5698

AMOUNT: $18,000 stipend
DEADLINE(S): January 20
FIELD(S): Public Administration; Urban
Planning; Government; Public Service;
Urban Affairs

Fellowship program provides one academic
year (9 months) of full-time work experience in urban government. Open to graduating college seniors and recent college
graduates. US citizenship required.
Write for complete information.

745

RADIO FREE EUROPE/RADIO
LIBERTY
(Media & Opinion Research on Eastern
Europe & the Former Soviet Union)
Personnel Division
1201 Connecticut Ave. NW
Washington DC 20036
Written inquiry

AMOUNT: Daily stipend of 48 German
marks plus accommodations
DEADLINE(S): February 22
FIELD(S): Communications; Market
Research; Statistics; Sociology; Social
Psychology; East European Studies

Internship open to graduate students or
exceptionally qualified undergrads in the
above areas who can demonstrate knowledge of quantitative research methods, computer applications, and public opinion survey techniques.

East European language skills would be an
advantage. Write for complete information.

SCHOOL OF VOCATIONAL EDUCATION

746

AMERICAN BOARD OF FUNERAL SERVICE EDUCATION
(Scholarships)
13 Gurnet Rd.
P.O. Box 1305
Brunswick ME 04011
207/798-5801; FAX 207/798-5988

AMOUNT: $250; $500
DEADLINE(S): March 15; September 15
FIELD(S): Funeral Service

Open to students who have completed at least one term of study in an accredited program in funeral service. Applicants must submit IRS form 1040 to demonstrate need. Must be citizen of USA.

Approximately 70 scholarships per year. Address inquiries to the scholarship chairman at address above.

747

AMERICAN INSTITUTE OF BAKING
(Scholarships)
1213 Bakers Way
Manhattan KS 66502
913/537-4750

AMOUNT: Partial or full tuition
DEADLINE(S): November 1; May 1
FIELD(S): Baking Industry (Including Electrical & Electronic Maintenance)

Award is for tuition for a 16- or 10-week course in baking science & technology or maintenance engineering at the institute. Experience in baking or mechanics or an approved alternative is required. Must be US citizen.

Awards are intended for people who plan to seek new positions in the baking and maintenance engineering fields.

748

AVIATION DISTRIBUTORS AND MANUFACTURERS ASSOCIATION INTERNATIONAL
(ADMA International Scholarship Fund)
1900 Arch Street
Philadelphia PA 19103
215/564-3484

AMOUNT: Varies
DEADLINE(S): May 1
FIELD(S): Aviation Management; Professional Pilot

Open to students seeking a career in aviation management or as a professional pilot. Emphasis may be in general aviation, airway science management, aviation maintenance; flight engineering, or airway a/c systems management.

Applicants must be studying in the aviation field in a four-year school having an aviation program and must have completed at least two years of the program. Write for complete information.

749

AVIATION MAINTENANCE EDUCATION FUND
(AMEF Scholarship Program)
P.O. Box 2826
Redmond WA 98073
206/827-2295

AMOUNT: $250–$1000
DEADLINE(S): None
FIELD(S): Aviation Maintenance Technology

AMEF scholarship program open to any worthy applicant who is enrolled in a federal aviation administration (FAA) certified aviation maintenance technology program.

Write for complete information.

750

BUSINESS & PROFESSIONAL WOMEN'S FOUNDATION
(Career Advancement Scholarships)
2012 Massachusetts Ave. NW
Washington DC 20036
202/293-1200

AMOUNT: $500–$1000

DEADLINE(S): April 15 (postmark)

FIELD(S): Computer Science; Education; Paralegal; Engineering; Science; Law; Dentistry; Medicine

Open to women (30 or older) within 12–24 months of completing undergrad or grad study in US (including Puerto Rico & Virgin Islands). Studies should lead to entry/reentry in work force or improve career advancement chances.

Not for doctoral study. Must demonstrate financial need. Send self-addressed stamped ($.64) #10 envelope for complete info. Applications available October 1–April 1.

751

CALIFORNIA STUDENT AID COMMISSION
(Cal. Grant "C" Program)
P.O. Box 510845
Sacramento CA 94245-0845
916/445-0880

AMOUNT: Up to $2360 (tuition); up to $530 (training-related costs)

DEADLINE(S): March 2

FIELD(S): Vocational-Technical

Open to vocational-technical students enrolled in eligible 4-month to 2-year programs in California. Must be California resident and US citizen/legal resident/eligible non-citizen.

Approximately 1500 grants per year. Renewable. Contact your counselor, financial aid office, or address above for complete information.

752

CDS INTERNATIONAL INC.
(Congress-Bundestag Youth Exchange Program)
330 Seventh Ave.; 19th Floor
New York NY 10001
212/760-1400; FAX 212/268-1288

AMOUNT: Airfare; partial domestic travel & host family payment

DEADLINE(S): December 15

FIELD(S): Business; Vo-tech Fields; Agricultural Fields.

Year-long work/study programs in Germany for US citizens aged 18–24 & in the USA for German citizens aged 18–21. Program for Americans includes 2-month language study, 4-month tech or professional school study, & 6-month internship.

Professional target and applicable work experience is required. Participants must provide their own spending money of $300–$350/month. Write or call for complete information.

753

CIVIL AIR PATROL
(Vocational-Technical Grants)
CAP National Headquarters/ETTC
Maxwell Air Force Base AL 36112
205/293-5315

AMOUNT: $750

DEADLINE(S): October 1

FIELD(S): Vocational-Technical Aerospace Studies

Open to CAP members who are qualified and interested in furthering their education in special aerospace courses at accredited vocational-technical institutions.

Write for complete information.

754

EAA AVIATION FOUNDATION
(Scholarship Program)
P.O. Box 3065
Oshkosh WI 54903-3065
414/426-4888

AMOUNT: $200 to $1500
DEADLINE(S): April 1
FIELD(S): Aviation

Ten different scholarship programs open to well rounded individuals involved in school and community activities as well as aviation. Applicant's academic records should verify their ability to complete their educational program.

Financial need is a consideration; a financial need statement may be required.

755

EASTERN NEW ENGLAND NINETY-NINES INC.
(Marjorie VanVliet Aviation Memorial Scholarship)
P.O. Box 19
Waterford VT 05848
617/259-0222

AMOUNT: $2000
DEADLINE(S): January 31
FIELD(S): Aeronautics; Aviation Maintenance; Flight Training

Open to high school seniors or beyond who live in one of the New England states; plan a career in aviation and have applied to an aviation-related education or training program. Must demonstrate financial need.

Can use for tuition and/or flight training. Write for complete information.

756

EMPIRE COLLEGE
(Dean's Scholarship)
3033 Cleveland Ave.
Santa Rosa CA 95403
707/546-4000

AMOUNT: $250–$1500
DEADLINE(S): April 15
FIELD(S): Court Reporting; Accounting; Secretarial; Legal; Medical (Clinical & Administrative); Travel & Tourism; General Business

Open to high school seniors who meet admission requirements and want to attend Empire college in Santa Rosa California. US citizenship required.

Ten scholarships per year. Contact Ms. Carole A. Bratton at the above address for complete information.

757

GEMOLOGICAL INSTITUTE OF AMERICA
(Home Study and Resident Scholarships)
Financial Aid Office
1660 Stewart St.
Santa Monica CA 90404
310/829-2991

AMOUNT: $500–$700
DEADLINE(S): April 1
FIELD(S): Gemology

A variety of scholarships offered to US citizens or permanent residents who are at least 17 years of age and are employed in the jewelry industry or who plan to enter the field and enroll in a GIA educational course.

The Mary Abelson resident scholarship offers one full or partial tuition award for graduate jeweler programs every other year. Home study scholarships are for undergrads. Write for complete information.

758

HILGENFELD FOUNDATION FOR MORTUARY EDUCATION
(Scholarship Grants)
P.O. Box 4311
Fullerton CA 92634
Written Inquiry

AMOUNT: Varies

DEADLINE(S): None

FIELD(S): Funeral Service and Education

Grants available to qualified individuals and organizations with interest in funeral service. Preference given to Southern California residents.

Grant funds available for individuals entering the funeral service profession and for individuals pursuing advanced degrees to advance in the teaching profession.

759

INTERNATIONAL ASSN. OF ARSON INVESTIGATORS
(John Charles Wilson Scholarship Fund)
    300 S. Broadway; Suite #100
    St. Louis MO 63102
    314/621-1966

AMOUNT: $1000

DEADLINE(S): February 15

FIELD(S): Police Science; Fire Science; & Affiliated Fields

Open to IAAI members, their immediate family, & non-members who are recommended & sponsored by members in good standing. Awards are for undergraduate study in above areas at accredited 2-year & 4-year institutions.

Write for complete information.

760

MARYLAND HIGHER EDUCATION COMMISSION
(Reimbursement of Firefighter & Rescue Squad Members)
    State Scholarship Administration
    16 Francis St.
    Annapolis MD 21401
    410/974-5370

AMOUNT: Tuition reimbursement up to $2600

DEADLINE(S): July 1

FIELD(S): Fire Service or Emergency Medical Technology

Open to Maryland residents affiliated with an organized fire department or rescue squad in Maryland. For full- or part-time study at a Maryland institution. Reimbursement made one year after successful completion of course(s).

For undergraduate or graduate study in Maryland. Renewable. Write for complete information.

761

MARYLAND HIGHER EDUCATION COMMISSION
(Tolbert Grants)
    State Scholarship Administration
    16 Francis St.
    Annapolis MD 21401-1781
    410/974-5370

AMOUNT: $200 to $1500

DEADLINE(S): Rolling deadline

FIELD(S): Vocational-Technical (Private Career Schools)

Open to Maryland residents pursuing full-time study. Grants support training at Maryland private career (vocational-technical) schools. Must demonstrate financial need.

Renewable for one year. Applicants must be nominated by their schools. Write for complete information.

762

MINNESOTA FEDERATION OF TEACHERS
(Charlie Carpenter Vocational Scholarship)
    168 Aurora Ave.
    St. Paul MN 55103
    612/227-8583

AMOUNT: $1000

DEADLINE(S): First Friday in March

FIELD(S): Vocational-Technical

Candidate for this scholarship must be a current high school senior. He/she must be recommended by two senior high school instructors on the basis of financial need, academic achievement, promise of leadership ability, and character.

Tenable at any accredited vocational school. Write for complete information.

763

PROFESSIONAL AVIATION MAINTENANCE ASSOCIATION
(Careerquest Scholarships)
P.O. Box 410260
St. Louis MO 63141
314/739-2580

AMOUNT: $1000 per year

DEADLINE(S): Apply between January 1 & February 15 or September 1 & February 15

FIELD(S): Aviation Maintenance

Open to students pursuing airframe and powerplant (A&P) technician certification through an FAA Part 147 aviation maintenance technician school. Must have completed 25% of required curriculum & have a 3.0 or better GPA.

6 awards per year; 3 in spring; 3 in fall. Application must be submitted through student's school. Must demonstrate financial need. Write for complete information.

764

PROFESSIONAL AVIATION MAINTENANCE ASSOCIATION
(PAMA Scholarship Fund)
1200 18th St. NW; Suite 401
Washington DC 20036-2598
202/296-0545

AMOUNT: Varies

DEADLINE(S): Apply between July 1 & November 30

FIELD(S): Aviation Maintenance

Open to students enrolled in an institution to obtain an airframe and powerplant (A&P) license who have completed 25% of the required curriculum. Must have 3.0 or better GPA, demonstrate financial need, and be recommended by instructor.

Applications to be submitted through student's school. Write for complete information.

765

US DEPT. OF VETERANS AFFAIRS
(Vocational Rehabilitation)
810 Vermont Ave. NW (28)
Washington DC 20420
VA regional office in each state
or 1-800-827-1000

AMOUNT: Tuition; books; fees; equipment; subsistence allowance

DEADLINE(S): Within 12 years from date of notification of entitlement to VA comp

FIELD(S): Vocational-Technical

Open to US military veterans disabled during active duty, honorably discharged, & in need of rehab services to overcome an employment handicap. At least a 20% disability comp rating (or 10% with a serious employment handicap) required.

Program will provide college, trade, technical, on-job or on-farm training (at home or in a special rehab facility if vet's disability requires). Contact nearest VA office for complete information.

766

US DEPT. OF INTERIOR; BUREAU OF INDIAN AFFAIRS
(Indian Employment Assistance Grants)
18th and C St. NW
MS/1458 M1B
Washington DC 20240
202/208-2570

AMOUNT: $4800 to $5500

DEADLINE(S): None

FIELD(S): Vocational-Technical

Open to members of tribes or bands who reside on or near a reservation under the jurisdiction of BIA. Grants for adult vocational training and job placement services for individual Indians who are unemployed or under employed.

3500 grants per year. Applications are available through tribal contract office or home agency. Funds for vocational training and job placement only—NOT for a formal degree.

767

VERTICAL FLIGHT FOUNDATION
(Undergraduate/Graduate Scholarships)
217 N. Washington St.
Alexandria VA 22314
703/684-6777

AMOUNT: Up to $2000
DEADLINE(S): February 1
FIELD(S): Mechanical Engineering; Electrical Engineering; Aerospace Engineering

Annual scholarships open to undergraduate & graduate students in the above areas who are interested in pursuing careers in some aspect of helicopter or vertical flight. For full-time study at accredited school of engineering.

Write for complete information.

768

VIOLIN SOCIETY OF AMERICA
(Kaplan-Goodkind Memorial Scholarships)
85-07 Abingdon Rd.
Kew Gardens NY 11415
718/849-1373

AMOUNT: $500 (average)
DEADLINE(S): None
FIELD(S): Violin Making; Restoration & Repair

Scholarships to study the "art of violin making" at an accredited school in the US. Not limited by residence, color, race, religion, or sex. Talent & need are the main criteria for selection of recipients. US citizenship required.

Renewable. Write for complete information.

769

WHIRLY-GIRLS INC.
(International Women Helicopter Pilots Scholarships)
Executive Towers 10-D
207 West Clarendon Ave.
Phoenix AZ 85013
602/263-0190; FAX 602/264-5812

AMOUNT: Not specified
DEADLINE(S): November 15
FIELD(S): Helicopter Flight Training

Three scholarships available to licensed women pilots for flight training. Two are awarded to Whirly-Girls who are helicopter pilots; one is awarded to a licensed woman pilot holding a private license (airplane, balloon, or glider).

Applications are available April 15. Write, call, or FAX for complete information.

GENERAL

770

37TH DIVISION VETERANS ASSOCIATION
(37th Infantry Division Award)
183 E. Mound St.; Suite 103
Columbus OH 43215
614/228-3788

AMOUNT: Varies
DEADLINE(S): April 1
FIELD(S): All fields of study

Scholarship/grant open to high school seniors or college students who are dependents of children of the 37th Infantry Division Veterans who served in World War I, II, or the Korean conflict.

Financial need is a consideration particularly if the father is deceased. 2 scholarships per year. Write for complete information.

771

ABBIE M. GRIFFIN EDUCATIONAL FUND
(Scholarships)
c/o Winer & Bennett
111 Concord St.
Nashua NH 03060
603/882-5157

AMOUNT: $300–$2000
DEADLINE(S): May 1
FIELD(S): All areas of study

Open ONLY to residents of Merrimack NH. Awards ONLY to entering freshmen for full-time undergraduate study at an accredited college or university.

10–15 awards per year. Write for complete information.

772

ABE AND ANNIE SEIBEL FOUNDATION
(Interest-free Educational Loan Fund)
US National Bank
P.O. Box 179
Galveston TX 77553
409/763-1151

AMOUNT: Up to $3000 a year
DEADLINE(S): February 28
FIELD(S): All fields of study

Open to Texas residents who will be or are enrolled (for at least 12 credit hours per semester) as undergraduate students at a Texas college or university. Must maintain 3.0 or better GPA. For study leading to first 4-year degree.

Write for complete information.

773

AFS INTERCULTURAL PROGRAMS
(International Exchange Student Program)
220 E. 42nd St.; Third Floor
New York NY 10017
212/949-4242 or 800/AFS-INFO

AMOUNT: Varies
DEADLINE(S): Fall and spring
FIELD(S): High school studies

International exchange of high school students who will live with host families & attend local secondary schools. Students go to & come from 50 countries. Scholarship assistance for summer; school year & semester for AFS participants ONLY.

10,000 participants worldwide. Write for complete information.

774

AIR FORCE AID SOCIETY
(Grants Program)
1745 Jefferson Davis Hwy. #202
Arlington VA 22202
800/429-9475

AMOUNT: $1000
DEADLINE(S): March 22
FIELD(S): All fields of study

Open to undergrads who are dependent children of active duty, retired, or deceased members of the US Air Force or spouses of active duty members residing stateside only. US citizenship or legal residency required.

For full-time study at an accredited institution. Must maintain at least a 2.0 GPA. Write for complete information.

775

AIR FORCE SERGEANTS'
ASSOCIATION
(Scholarship Awards Program)
P.O. Box 50
Temple Hills MD 20757
301/899-3500

AMOUNT: $1000–$2500
DEADLINE(S): April 15
FIELD(S): All fields of study

Open to single dependent children (under 23) of AFSA members or its auxiliary. For undergraduate study at accredited institutions only. Awards are based on academic excellence.

For application and complete information send self-addressed stamped (75 cents) business size envelope to AFSA/AMF Scholarships Administrator; 5211 Auth Rd.; Suitland MD 20757.

776

AIRLINE PILOTS ASSOCIATION
(Scholarship Program)
1625 Massachusetts Ave. NW
Washington DC 20036
202/797-4050

AMOUNT: $3000 per year for up to 4 years

DEADLINE(S): April 1

FIELD(S): All fields of study

Open to undergraduate sons or daughters of medically retired or deceased pilot members of the Airline Pilots Association. Academic capability and financial need are considered. Renewable for up to 3 years.

Write for complete information ONLY if above qualifications are met.

777

AIRMEN MEMORIAL FOUNDATION
(AMF Scholarship Awards Program)
5211 Auth Road
Suitland MD 20746
800/638-0594

AMOUNT: $500–$3000

DEADLINE(S): April 15

FIELD(S): All fields of study

Open to unmarried dependent children (under 25) of Air Force enlisted personnel (active or retired) of all components, including Air National Guard & Reserves. For undergraduate study at any accredited academic or trade/technical school.

Send self-addressed stamped (75 cents) business size envelope to AFSA/AMF Scholarship Program; P.O. Box 50; Temple Hills MD 20746 for application and complete information. Applications available November 1 thru March 31.

778

ALABAMA COMMISSION ON HIGHER EDUCATION
(Scholarships; Grants; Loans; Work Study Programs)
3465 Norman Bridge Rd.
Montgomery AL 36105-2310
Written inquiry

AMOUNT: Varies

DEADLINE(S): Varies

FIELD(S): All fields of study

The commission administers a number of financial aid programs tenable at post-secondary institutions in Alabama. Some awards are need-based.

Write for the "Financial Aid Sources in Alabama" brochure or contact high school guidance counselor or college financial aid officer.

779

ALABAMA DEPARTMENT OF VETERANS AFFAIRS
(GI Dependents Scholarship Program)
P.O. Box 1509
Montgomery AL 36102-1509
334/242-5077

AMOUNT: Varies

DEADLINE(S): Prior to 26th birthday

FIELD(S): All fields of study

Open to dependent children (under age 26) of veterans who were permanent Alabama residents for at least 1 year prior to active duty and who died as a result of military service or was/is MIA or POW or became 20%–100% disabled.

Applicants must be Alabama residents. For attendance at state-supported Alabama institutions. Totally disabled vets who are not original Alabama residents may qualify after 5 years of Alabama residency. Write for complete information.

780

ALABAMA DEPARTMENT OF VETERANS AFFAIRS
(GI Dependents Scholarship Program)
P.O. Box 1509
Montgomery AL 36102-1509
334/242-5077

AMOUNT: Varies

DEADLINE(S): None

FIELD(S): All fields of study

Open to wife or widow (not remarried) of veteran who was an Alabama resident for at least 1 year prior to active duty and died as a result of military service, was/is MIA or a POW, or became 20%–100% disabled.

Vets who are not original Alabama residents but have a 100% service-connected disability may qualify after 5 years' residency in Alabama. Awards tenable at state-supported Alabama institutions. Write for complete information.

781

ALASKA COMMISSION ON POST-SECONDARY EDUCATION
(Student Loan Program; Family Loan Program)
3030 Vintage Blvd.
Juneau AK 99801-7109
907/465-2962

AMOUNT: $5500–$6500
DEADLINE(S): May 15
FIELD(S): All areas of study

Open to Alaska residents of at least 1 year. These low-interest loans (8% student; 5% family) support full-time study at any accredited vocational, undergraduate, or graduate institution.

Up to $5500 available for vocational or undergraduate study and up to $6500 for graduate study. Renewable. Write for complete information.

782

ALASKA COMMISSION ON POST-SECONDARY EDUCATION
(State Educational Incentive Grant Program)
3030 Vintage Blvd.
Juneau AK 99801-7109
907/465-6741

AMOUNT: $100 to $1500
DEADLINE(S): May 31
FIELD(S): All fields of study

Open to Alaska residents of at least 1 year who are accepted to or enrolled in their first undergraduate degree or comparable certificate program at an accredited institution (in-state or out-of-state). Need must be demonstrated.

315 grants per year. Write for complete information.

783

ALBERT BAKER FUND
(Student Loans)
5 Third St. #717
San Francisco CA 94103
415/543-7028

AMOUNT: $1600–$2500
DEADLINE(S): July 1
FIELD(S): All fields of study

Open to students who are members of the Mother Church—the First Church of Christ Scientist in Boston—and are active as Christian Scientists. Student must have other primary lender and be enrolled in an accredited college or university.

Foreign students must have cosigner who is a US citizen. Average of 160 awards per year. Write or call for complete information. Applicant must be the one who calls.

784

ALEXANDER GRAHAM BELL ASSOCIATION FOR THE DEAF
(Elsie Bell Grosvenor Scholarship Awards)
3417 Volta Place NW
Washington DC 20007
202/337-5220

AMOUNT: $500–$1000
DEADLINE(S): April 1
FIELD(S): All areas of study

Open to oral deaf students who were born with severe or profound hearing impairment or who suffered such impairment before acquiring language. Must be accepted into a full-time academic program for hearing students.

Must reside in or attend college in Washington DC metropolitan area. Write for complete information.

785

**ALEXANDER GRAHAM BELL
ASSOCIATION FOR THE DEAF
(Lucile A. Abt & Maude Winkler
Scholarships)**
3417 Volta Pl. NW
Washington DC 20007
202/337-5220

AMOUNT: $1000
DEADLINE(S): April 1
FIELD(S): All fields of study

Open to oral deaf students born with a severe or profound hearing impairment or who suffered such a loss before acquiring language. Must be accepted into a full-time academic program for hearing students.

5 awards per year. Preference to North American citizens. Write for complete information.

786

**ALEXANDER GRAHAM BELL
ASSOCIATION FOR THE DEAF
(Herbert P. Feibelman Jr. International
Parents' Organization Scholarship Awards)**
3417 Volta Pl. NW
Washington DC 20007
202/337-5220 (Voice or TDD)

AMOUNT: $1000
DEADLINE(S): April 1
FIELD(S): All fields of study

Open to oral deaf students born with severe or profound hearing impairment or who suffered such loss before acquiring language. Must be accepted into a full-time academic program for hearing students. Preference to North American citizens.

Write for complete information.

787

**ALEXANDER GRAHAM BELL
ASSOCIATION FOR THE DEAF
(Oral Hearing Impaired Section Scholarship
Award)**
3417 Volta Pl. NW
Washington DC 20007
202/337-5220

AMOUNT: $1000
DEADLINE(S): April 1
FIELD(S): All fields of study

Open to oral deaf undergraduate students who were born with a severe or profound hearing impairment or who have suffered hearing loss before acquiring language. Must be accepted into a full-time academic program for hearing students.

Preference to North American citizens. Write for complete information.

788

**ALEXANDER GRAHAM BELL
ASSOCIATION FOR THE DEAF**
3417 Volta Place NW
Washington DC 20007
202/337-5220

AMOUNT: $250–$1000
DEADLINE(S): April 15
FIELD(S): All areas of study

Open to students who are oral deaf or were born with a profound hearing impairment or suffered loss before acquiring language. Must be accepted into a full-time academic program for hearing students.

North American citizens given preference. Write for complete information.

789

**ALEXANDER GRAHAM BELL
ASSOCIATION FOR THE DEAF
(Volta Scholarship Awards)**
3417 Volta Place NW
Washington DC 20007
202/337-5220

AMOUNT: $500

DEADLINE(S): April 1

FIELD(S): All areas of study

Open to oral deaf students born with profound hearing impairment or who suffered such a loss before acquiring language. Must be accepted into a full-time academic program for hearing students. Preference to North American citizens.

Write for complete information.

790

ALPHA KAPPA ALPHA SORORITY INC.
(AKA/PIMS Summer Youth Mathematics & Science Camp)
5656 S. Stony Island Ave.
Chicago IL 60637
312/684-1282

AMOUNT: $1000 value (for room, board, & travel)

DEADLINE(S): May 1

FIELD(S): Mathematics; Science

Open to high school students grades 9–11 who have at least a "B" average. Essay required for entry. This 2-week camp includes AM classes, PM activities, & a minimum of 4 field trips. The site for 1995 is Michigan State Univ. in E. Lansing.

30 awards. Write for complete information.

791

AMERICAN ASSOCIATION OF UNIVERSITY WOMEN—HONOLULU BRANCH
(Ruth E. Black Scholarship)
1802 Keeaumoku Street
Honolulu HI 96822
808/537-4702

AMOUNT: Varies

DEADLINE(S): March 1

FIELD(S): All fields of study

Open to women who are legal residents of Hawaii. For undergraduate study at an accredited college or university in Hawaii.

Financial need must be demonstrated & US citizenship is required.

Write for complete information—applications are available October 1 - January 15 each year.

792

AMERICAN COUNCIL OF THE BLIND
(Scholarship Program)
Attn: Jessica L. Beach
1155 15th St. NW; Suite 720
Washington DC 20005
202/467-5081

AMOUNT: $500–$4000

DEADLINE(S): March 1

FIELD(S): All fields of study

Scholarships open to legally blind applicants who have been accepted to or are enrolled in an accredited institution for vocational, technical, undergraduate, graduate, or professional studies. US citizen or legal resident.

Write for complete information.

793

AMERICAN FEDERATION OF STATE, COUNTY, & MUNICIPAL EMPLOYEES
(AFSCME Family Scholarship Program)
1625 'L' Street NW
Education Dept.
Washington DC 20036
202/452-4800

AMOUNT: $2000 per year for 4 years

DEADLINE(S): December 31

FIELD(S): All areas of study

Open to high school seniors who are dependent children of active AFSCME members. Awards for full-time undergraduate study at any accredited 4-year college or university. US citizenship or legal residency required.

Renewable. Write for complete information.

794

AMERICAN FOUNDATION FOR THE BLIND
(Helen Keller Scholarship Fund)
15 West 16th St.
New York NY 10011
212/620-2000; TDD 212/620-2158

AMOUNT: $1000–$3000
DEADLINE(S): April 1
FIELD(S): All areas of study

Open to college or university students who are legally blind and deaf for help with their reading, tutoring, or equipment acquisition expenses. Student must be a US citizen and submit proof of both legal blindness & deafness.
Write for complete information.

795

AMERICAN LEGION AUXILIARY
(Dept. of Minnesota Scholarships)
Dept. of Minnesota
State Veterans Service Building
St. Paul MN 55155
612/224-7634

AMOUNT: $500
DEADLINE(S): March 5
FIELD(S): All fields of study

Open to MN residents who are children or grandchildren of US veterans of armed conflicts. Must be high school senior or grad w/ GPA of "C" or better, attend MN vocational/business school, college or university, & demonstrate financial need.
Write for complete information.

796

AMERICAN LEGION—DEPARTMENT OF NEW JERSEY
(Stutz Memorial Scholarship)
War Memorial Building
Trenton NJ 08608
Written inquiry

AMOUNT: $1000 per year (4 years)
DEADLINE(S): March 1
FIELD(S): All fields of study

Open to children of members or deceased members of the American Legion Department of New Jersey. Applicants must be a member of the graduating class of a senior high school and use the award the year it is received.
Financial need is a consideration. Write for complete information.

797

AMERICAN MENSA EDUCATION & RESEARCH FOUNDATION
(Scholarships)
2626 E. 14th St.
Brooklyn NY 11235
Written inquiry

AMOUNT: $200 to $1000
DEADLINE(S): January 31
FIELD(S): All fields of study

Open to students enrolled for the academic year following the award in a degree program in an accredited American institution of post-secondary education. Applicants must submit an essay describing career, vocational, and academic goals.
Essay should be fewer than 550 words and must be specific rather than general. It MUST be on an official application. Send self-addressed stamped envelope no later than January 1 for application.

798

AMERICAN NATIONAL CAN COMPANY
(Scholarship Program)
8770 W. Brynmawr Ave. #10-N
Chicago IL 60631
312/399-3000

AMOUNT: $500 to $3000
DEADLINE(S): March 15
FIELD(S): All fields of study

Must be high school senior to apply and the
son or daughter of an employee of the
American National Can Company with a
minimum of 3 years of service.

20 scholarships are available per year.
Renewable to 4 years. Write for complete
information.

799

**AMERICAN POSTAL WORKERS
UNION/AFL-CIO
(E.C. Hallbeck Memorial Scholarship
Program)**
1300 'L' Street NW
Washington DC 20005
202/842-4268

AMOUNT: $1000 per year for 4 years
DEADLINE(S): March 1
FIELD(S): All fields of study

Open to high school seniors who are depen-
dent children of American Postal Workers
Union Members (active or deceased).
Awards tenable at accredited colleges and
universities.
Write for complete information.

800

**AMERICAN RADIO RELAY LEAGUE
FOUNDATION
(New England Femara Scholarship)**
225 Main St.
Newington CT 06111
203/666-1541

AMOUNT: $600
DEADLINE(S): February 15
FIELD(S): All fields of study

Open to residents of the six New England
states who are radio amateurs holding at
least a technician's licence.
Write for complete information.

801

**AMERICAN RADIO RELAY LEAGUE
FOUNDATION INC.
(You've Got A Friend in Pennsylvania
Scholarship Fund)**
225 Main St.
Newington CT 06111
806/594-0230

AMOUNT: $1000
DEADLINE(S): February 15
FIELD(S): All fields of study

Open to ARRL members who hold a
"General" amateur radio license and have a
4.0 GPA in graded courses (sports and
physical education grades excluded).
Preference to Penn. residents.
Write for complete information.

802

**AMERICAN RADIO RELAY LEAGUE
FOUNDATION INC.
(Edward D. Jaikins Memorial Scholarship
Fund)**
225 Main St.
Newington CT 06111
806/594-0230

AMOUNT: $500
DEADLINE(S): February 15
FIELD(S): All fields of study

Open to residents of the FCC 8th call district
(Michigan, Ohio, W. Virginia) who attend
an accredited institution within that call district; have a 3.0 or better GPA, and hold at
least a "general" class amateur radio
license.
Write for complete information.

803

**AMERICAN SAMOA GOVERNMENT
(Financial Aid Program)**
Dept. of Education
Office of Student Financial Program
Pago Pago American Samoa 96799
684/633-4255

AMOUNT: $5000

DEADLINE(S): April 30

FIELD(S): All fields of study

Scholarships open to residents of American Samoa. Awards support undergraduate & graduate study at all accredited colleges & universities. Applicants from off islands may be eligible if their parents are citizens of American Samoa.

Approximately 50 awards per year. Renewable. Write for complete information.

804

AMVETS NATIONAL SCHOLARSHIP PROGRAM

Programs Dept.
4647 Forbes Blvd.
Lanham MD 20706
301/459-9600; FAX 301/459-7924

AMOUNT: $1000 per year for 4 years

DEADLINE(S): April 15

FIELD(S): All fields of study

Open to high school seniors who are the son/daughter of an American military veteran. Applicants must demonstrate academic achievement and financial need and be US citizens.

Veterans who have exhausted all government financial aid may apply under 'Special Consideration' category. Applications available beginning in December. Send stamped self-addressed envelope.

805

ANITA H. RICHARD TRUST
(David Carlyle III Scholarship)

353 Chicago Ave.
Savanna IL 61074
815/273-2839

AMOUNT: $2000 per semester for 4 years

DEADLINE(S): April 15 (every 4 years)

FIELD(S): All fields of study

Open to graduating seniors of Carrol County (IL) high schools. Awards tenable at accred-ited undergraduate colleges and universities. Must maintain at least a 2.0 GPA (4.0 scale), be a US citizen, and demonstrate financial need.

Award is given every 4 years and is advertised when it is available. Amount of award depends on interest rates. Write for complete information.

806

APPALOOSA YOUTH FOUNDATION
(Youth Educational Scholarships)

P.O. Box 8403
Moscow ID 83843
208/882-5578

AMOUNT: $1000

DEADLINE(S): June 10

FIELD(S): All fields of study

Open to members of the Appaloosa Youth Association or the Appaloosa Horse Club, children of Appaloosa Horse Club members, & individuals sponsored by a regional club or racing association.

11 scholarships per year. Renewable. Contact the Youth Coordinator at address above for complete information.

807

ARKANSAS DEPARTMENT OF HIGHER EDUCATION
(Student Assistance Grant Program)

114 E. Capitol
Little Rock AR 72201
501/342-9300

AMOUNT: $200–$624

DEADLINE(S): Awarded first-come-first-served until funds are exhausted

FIELD(S): All fields of study

Open to residents of Arkansas attending undergraduate institutions in Arkansas. Financial need & satisfactory academic progress must be demonstrated. US citizenship or legal residency required.

Approximately 9500 grants per year. Write for complete information.

808

ARLINE P. PADELFORD SCHOLARSHIP TRUST
(Scholarships)
c/o State Street Bank & Trust Co.
P.O. Box 351
Boston MA 02101
617/786-3000

AMOUNT: $600
DEADLINE(S): None specified
FIELD(S): All areas of study

Scholarships for worthy and deserving students at Taunton (MA) High School to pursue college or technical education.
12 scholarships per year. Contact Taunton High guidance counselor for complete information.

809

ARMENIAN RELIEF SOCIETY OF NORTH AMERICA INC.
(Grants)
80 Bigelow Ave.
Watertown MA 02172
617/926-3801

AMOUNT: $400–$1000
DEADLINE(S): April 1
FIELD(S): All fields of study

Open to undergrad and grad students of Armenian ancestry who are attending an accredited 4-year college or university in the USA and have completed at least one semester. Awards based on need, merit, & involvement in Armenian community.
Write to scholarship committee (address above) for complete information. Enclose self-addressed stamped envelope and indicate whether undergrad or grad student.

810

ARMENIAN STUDENTS' ASSOCIATION OF AMERICA INC.
(Scholarships; Fellowships)
Scholarship Adm.
395 Concord Ave.
Belmont MA 02178
Written inquiry

AMOUNT: $500 to $1500
DEADLINE(S): March 15 (request application by January 15)
FIELD(S): All fields of study

For full-time grads & undergrads attending a US 4-year accredited college or university. Must have completed or be in process of completing 1st year of college or higher and have good academic performance.
Financial need must be demonstrated. Participation in extra-curricular activities is required. 30–50 awards per year. Renewable. $10 application fee. Write for complete information.

811

ARTHUR C. & FLORENCE S. BOEHMER FUND
(Scholarships)
c/o Rinn & Elliot
P.O. Box 1827
Lodi CA 95241
209/369-2781

AMOUNT: Yearly income
DEADLINE(S): June 15 (Applications available March 1 to June 15)
FIELD(S): Medical

Open to students who are graduates of a high school within the Lodi (San Joaquin County, CA) Unified School District. For undergraduate, graduate, or post-graduate study in the field of medicine at an accredited California institution.
Grade point average of 2.9 or better required. Scholarships are renewable. Write for complete information.

812

ASSOCIATION FOR EDUCATION & REHABILITATION OF THE BLIND & VISUALLY IMPAIRED
(Ferrell Scholarship Fund)
206 N. Washington St.; Suite 320
Alexandria VA 22314
703/548-1884

AMOUNT: Varies

DEADLINE(S): April 15 of even-numbered years

FIELD(S): Career field in services to the blind

Open to legally blind students enrolled in a college or university program related to blind services such as orientation and mobility, special education, rehabilitation teaching, vision rehabilitation.

For undergraduate, graduate, or postgraduate study. Write for complete information.

813

ASSOCIATION ON AMERICAN INDIAN AFFAIRS INC.
(Emergency Aid & Health Profession Scholarships)
245 Fifth Avenue; Suite 1801
New York NY 10016
212/689-8270

AMOUNT: Up to $300

DEADLINE(S): None

FIELD(S): All fields of study

Open to US citizens with 1/4 or more American Indian or Alaskan Native blood. Must be a member of a federally recognized tribe in the US. First-come first-serve basis when funds are available. Inquire only after beginning classes.

Write for complete information—enclose self-addressed stamped envelope.

814

ASSOCIATION OF THE SONS OF POLAND
(Scholarship Program)
333 Hackensack St.
Carlstadt NJ 07072
201/935-2807

AMOUNT: $1000 Scholarship; $100 Achievement Award

DEADLINE(S): May 14

FIELD(S): All fields of study

Open to high school students who have been members of the Association of the Sons of Poland for at least 2 years and are insured by the association. Must be entering an accredited college in September of the year of high school graduation.

Must be US citizen. Write for complete information.

815

AUTOMOTIVE HALL OF FAME INC.
(Scholarship Program)
P.O. Box 1727
Midland MI 48641
517/631-5760

AMOUNT: $250 to $2000

DEADLINE(S): June 30

FIELD(S): All fields of study

Open to full-time undergraduate college students who have a sincere interest in pursuing an automotive career upon graduation from college. Must be at least a sophomore when scholarship is granted but freshmen may send in application.

16–24 awards per year. Renewable with reapplication. Write for complete information.

816

AYN RAND INSTITUTE
(Fountainhead Essay Contest)
P.O. Box 6004; Dept. DB
Inglewood CA 90312
310/306-9232; FAX 310/306-4925

AMOUNT: $5000—1st prize; $1000—2nd
   prize (5); $500—3rd prize (10)
DEADLINE(S): April 15
FIELD(S): All fields of study

Essay competition open to high school juniors
   & seniors. Contest is to encourage analyti-
   cal thinking and writing excellence & to
   introduce students to the philosophic and
   psychological meaning of Ayn Rand's novel
   "The Fountainhead".
16 awards per year. Write for complete information.

817

BAKERY, CONFECTIONERY, AND TOBACCO WORKERS INTERNATIONAL UNION
(Scholarship Program)
   10401 Connecticut Ave.
   Kensington MD 20895
   301/933-8600

AMOUNT: $1000 per year for a max of 4
   years
DEADLINE(S): December 31
FIELD(S): All fields of study

Undergraduate scholarships are awarded each
   year to winners of a competition that is
   open to members and children of members
   of BC&TWIU. Applicants must be high
   school students entering college for the first
   time.
8 scholarships per year. Write for complete
   information.

818

BALSO FOUNDATION
(Scholarships)
   493 West Main Street
   Cheshire CT 06410
   203/272-5381

AMOUNT: Varies
DEADLINE(S): April 15
FIELD(S): All fields of study
Open to residents of Cheshire CT.
   Scholarships are for full-time undergradu-

ate study & are awarded based on academic
   & financial need. US citizenship required.
10 to 15 awards per year. Renewable. Write
   for complete information.

819

BEMENT EDUCATIONAL GRANTS COMMITTEE
(Diocese of Western Massachusetts Undergraduate Grants)
   37 Chestnut St.
   Springfield MA 01103
   413/737-4786

AMOUNT: Up to $750
DEADLINE(S): February 15
FIELD(S): All fields of study

Undergraduate grants for unmarried students
   who are active Episcopalians in the Diocese
   of Western Massachusetts. High GPA.
   Financial need. Interview required as
   arranged.
60–70 awards per year. Renewable with reapplication. Write for complete information.

820

BERYL BUCK INSTITUTE FOR EDUCATION
(American Revolution Bicentennial Scholarships)
   Nancy Wright
   18 Commercial Blvd.
   Novato CA 94949
   415/883-0122

AMOUNT: $500 to $2000
DEADLINE(S): March 31
FIELD(S): All fields of study

Open to Marin County residents who have
   lived in the area since September 1 of the
   year prior to submitting an application.
   Scholarships tenable at accredited colleges
   & universities & vocational or trade programs.
Contact high school or college counselor or
   address above for complete information.

821

BETA THETA PI GENERAL FRATERNITY
(Scholarships & Fellowships)
Administrative Office
208 East High St.
Oxford OH 45056
513/523-7591

AMOUNT: $750 to $1500
DEADLINE(S): April
FIELD(S): All fields of study

Open to undergraduate and graduate students who are Beta Theta Pi members in good standing and have a competitive grade point average.

30 scholarships and 8 fellowships per year. Non-renewable. Write for complete information.

822

BLAINE HOUSE SCHOLARS PROGRAM
State House Station #119
Augusta ME 04333
207/287-2183 (in state 800/228-3734)

AMOUNT: $1500 per year
DEADLINE(S): April 1
FIELD(S): All fields of study; preference to Education majors

Maine residents. High school seniors, college students, & teachers are eligible to apply for interest, free loans. Loans are competitive & based on academic merit, relevance of field of study, etc.

400 new awards per year. Renewable. Write for complete information.

823

BLINDED VETERANS ASSOCIATION
(Kathern F. Gruber Scholarship Program)
477 H Street NW
Washington DC 20001-2694
202/371-8880 or 800/667-7079
FAX 202/371-8258

AMOUNT: $2000

DEADLINE(S): April 12
FIELD(S): All areas of study

Open to children & spouses of vets who are legally blind (service or non-service related). Must be accepted or already enrolled full-time in an accredited college or university or business/secretarial or vo-tech school & be a US citizen.

12 awards per year. Write for complete information.

824

BOETTCHER FOUNDATION
(Scholarships)
600 17th St.; Suite 2210 South
Denver CO 80202
303/534-1938

AMOUNT: Tuition + $2800 stipend
DEADLINE(S): February 1
FIELD(S): All fields of study

Open to Colorado residents presently in the top 7% of their high school class who have been accepted as an incoming freshman at a Colorado college or university. Minimim ACT score 27; SAT 1100. US citizen.

40 awards per year. Write for complete information or consult your high school counselor.

825

BRANCH-WILBUR FUND INC.
(Grants)
1600 East Avenue; Apt. 1101
Rochester NY 14610
Written inquiry

AMOUNT: $500–$5000
DEADLINE(S): Indefinite
FIELD(S): All areas of study

Open to foreign students who are already residing or studying in the Rochester area and who are ineligible for government loans. Grants are based on need and usually last until a degree is obtained.

NOT open to US citizens. Eight awards per year. Write for complete information.

826

BRITISH AMERICAN EDUCATIONAL FOUNDATION
(Scholars' Program)
Box 2482
Providence RI 02906
401/272-2438; FAX 401/273-6296

AMOUNT: Up to $10,000
DEADLINE(S): May 1
FIELD(S): Wide variety limited by British 'A' level offerings at each school.

Open to American high school seniors who are 18 or younger and want to spend a year at an independent boarding school in the United Kingdom prior to entering college. Financial need is used to evaluate financial aid.
Write for complete information.

827

BUCKNELL UNIVERSITY
(Gertrude J. Deppen & Voris Auten Teetotaling Non-athlete Scholarship Fund)
Financial Aid Office
Lewisburg PA 17837
717/524-1331

AMOUNT: Varies
DEADLINE(S): None
FIELD(S): All areas of study

Open to students who have lived in Mt. Carmel PA for the last 10 years, graduated from Mt. Carmel High School, and do not use alcohol, tobacco, narcotics, or engage in strenuous athletic contests.
Award tenable at Bucknell University.

828

BUFFALO FOUNDATION
(Scholarships)
237 Main St.
Buffalo NY 14203
716/852-2857

AMOUNT: Varies
DEADLINE(S): May 10

FIELD(S): All fields of study
Scholarships open to residents of Erie County NY. Awards are limited to one member per family per year and are tenable at recognized undergraduate colleges and universities.
Approximately 400 awards per year. Write for complete information.

829

C. BASCOM SLEMP FOUNDATION
(Scholarships)
Star Bank NA
P.O. Box 5208
Cincinnati OH 45201
513/632-4579

AMOUNT: $2000
DEADLINE(S): October 1
FIELD(S): All fields of study
Open ONLY to residents of Lee or Wise counties in Virginia. For undergraduate study.
30 awards per year. Write for complete information.

830

CALIFORNIA DEPARTMENT OF VETERANS AFFAIRS
(California Veterans Dependents Educational Act)
P.O. Box 942895
Sacramento CA 94295
916/653-2573

AMOUNT: California State University tuition & fee waiver
DEADLINE(S): Varies
FIELD(S): All fields of study
Open to spouses & dependent children of veterans who (as a result of military service) were disabled, killed in action, POW, or MIA, or whose death was service-related. Awards are for undergrad study at California public colleges.
Applicant's annual income cannot exceed $5000 per year (including support from parents). 2000 awards per year. Write for complete information.

831

CALIFORNIA GOVERNOR'S COMMITTEE FOR EMPLOYMENT OF DISABLED PERSONS
(Hal Connolly Scholar-Athlete Award)
  c/o EDD/MIC 41
  P.O. Box 826880
  Sacramento CA 94280
  916/323-2545

AMOUNT: $1000 (3 male; 3 female)
DEADLINE(S): March 1
FIELD(S): All fields of study

Must have competed during high school in varsity level or equivalent athletics and have a disabilty. Academic and athletic histories must demonstrate the qualities of leadership and accomplishment. Age 19 or under.

Must be a California resident; write for more information.

832

CALIFORNIA JUNIOR MISS PROGRAM
(Scholarships & Awards)
  P.O. Box 1863
  Santa Rosa CA 95402
  707/576-7505

AMOUNT: $10,000
DEADLINE(S): January 1
FIELD(S): All fields of study

Competition open to girls in their junior year of high school who are USA citizens and California residents. Winner receives $10,000 college scholarship; runners-up share up to $30,000 in awards. For undergraduate or graduate study.

Award can be used for books; fees & tuition at any college in the world. Write to C. (Ting) Guggiana; address above; for complete information.

833

CALIFORNIA MASONIC FOUNDATION
(General and Special Fund Scholarship Programs)
  1111 California St.
  San Francisco CA 94108
  415/776-7000

AMOUNT: $1000
DEADLINE(S): June 30
FIELD(S): All fields of study

Undergraduate scholarships open to California residents accepted to or enrolled in accredited colleges or technical schools in the USA. No religious or membership requirements. Must be USA citizen.

Special funds have been established with various restrictive conditions. Write for complete information.

834

CALIFORNIA STUDENT AID COMMISSION
(Cal. Grant 'A' Program)
  P.O. Box 510624
  Sacramento CA 94245
  916/445-0880

AMOUNT: Varies
DEADLINE(S): March 2
FIELD(S): All fields of study

Open to low & middle income undergraduate California residents attending eligible schools in California. Grants support tuition & fee costs. Selection based on need & grades. US citizenship or legal residency required.

Approximately 17,400 grants per year. Renewable. Contact your counselor, financial aid office, or address above for complete information.

835

CALIFORNIA STUDENT AID COMMISSION
(Cal. Grant 'B' Program)
P.O. Box 510845
Sacramento CA 94245-0845
916/445-0880

AMOUNT: $700 to $1410 (living allowance); $1584 (avg. state school tuition); $5250 (avg. independent school tuition)
DEADLINE(S): March 2
FIELD(S): All fields of study

Open to very low income undergrads with high potential attending eligible 2- & 4-year colleges in California. Grant supports living allowance & tuition/fee costs. Must be California resident & US citizen/legal resident/eligible non-citizen

Approximately 12,250 grants per year. Renewable. Contact your counselor, financial aid office, or address above for complete information.

836

CALIFORNIA STUDENT AID COMMISSION
(Law Enforcement Personnel Dependents Grant Program)
P.O. Box 510624
Sacramento CA 94245-0624
916/322-2294

AMOUNT: Up to $1500 per year
DEADLINE(S): None
FIELD(S): All fields of study

Open to the natural or adopted child of a California law enforcement officer killed or 100% disabled in the performance of duty. For undergrad or grad study at eligible California schools. Must be resident of California & US citizen.

Awards limited to a maximum of $6000 over six years. May be used for tuition, fees, books, supplie,s & living expenses. Write for complete information.

837

CALIFORNIA TEACHERS ASSN.
(CTA Scholarships)
P.O. Box 921
1705 Murchison Dr.
Burlingame CA 94011
415/697-1400

AMOUNT: $2000
DEADLINE(S): February 15
FIELD(S): All fields of study

Open to active CTA members or their dependent children for undergraduate or graduate study. Applications available each October from CTA Human Rights Department, address above, or regional offices.

20 scholarships per year. Write for complete information.

838

CAMP FOUNDATION
(Scholarship Grants)
P.O. Box 813
Franklin VA 23851
804/562-3439

AMOUNT: Not specified
DEADLINE(S): Not specified
FIELD(S): All fields of study

Open to graduating high school seniors in the city of Franklin and the counties of Isle of Wight and Southampton VA or to residents of these areas who graduated from high school elsewhere. For undergraduate study.

These awards are made locally—NOT on a nationwide basis. Only those who meet residency requirements should write for complete information.

839

CDR. WILLIAM S. STUHR SCHOLARSHIP FUND
1200 Fifth Ave.
New York NY 10029
Written inquiry

AMOUNT: $1000 per year for 4 years

DEADLINE(S): Varies according to service—usually April

FIELD(S): All fields of study

Open to high school seniors who are dependents of active duty or retired members of the US military. For study at an accredited 4-year college only.

Applicants should be in top 10% of their class and demonstrate leadership ability & financial need. Send self-addressed stamped envelope (business size) for complete information.

840

CENTRAL SCHOLARSHIP BUREAU
(Interest-free Loans)
4001 Clarks Lane
Baltimore MD 21215
301/358-8668

AMOUNT: $500–$8000 (max thru grad school)

DEADLINE(S): June 1; December 1

FIELD(S): All fields of study

Interest-free loans for residents of metropolitan Baltimore area who have exhausted all other available avenues of funding. Aid is offered for study at any accredited undergrad or graduate institution.

Awards are made on a non-competitive basis to anyone with a sound educational plan. 125 loans per year. Must apply first through government and school. Write for complete information.

841

CHARLES B. KEESEE EDUCATIONAL FUND INC.
(Scholarships)
P.O. Box 431
Martinsville VA 24114
703/632-2229

AMOUNT: Varies

DEADLINE(S): March 1

FIELD(S): All fields of study

Open to eligible residents of Virginia & North Carolina who attend a school or college in Virginia that is affiliated with Virginia Baptist General Association or a seminary of Southern Baptist convention. US citizenship required.

750 awards per year. Write for complete information.

842

CHATHAM COLLEGE
(Merit Scholarship Program)
Woodland Road
Office of Admissions and Financial Aid
Pittsburgh PA 15232
412/365-1290

AMOUNT: Up to $10,000 per year

DEADLINE(S): January 31

FIELD(S): All fields of study

Women only. Awards open to entering first-year students accepted at Chatham College. Selection based on high school record, SAT-ACT scores, teacher/counselor recommendations; interview, extra-curricular activities & essay.

Approximately 50 awards per year renewable for up to 4 years. Write for complete information.

843

CHAUTAUQUA REGION COMMUNITY FOUNDATION INC.
(Scholarships)
104-106 Hotel Jamestown Bldg.
Jamestown NY 14701
716/661-3390

AMOUNT: $100–$2000

DEADLINE(S): April 20

FIELD(S): All fields of study

Numerous scholarships with varying requirements open ONLY to students living in the vicinity of Jamestown NY. Preference to students in 12 school districts in Southern Chautauqua County. For full-time study.

Write for complete information.

844

CHEROKEE NATION
(Higher Education Need-based Grant Program)
P.O. Box 948
Tahlequah OK 74465
918/456-0671

AMOUNT: Varies
DEADLINE(S): April 1
FIELD(S): All areas of study

Grants available to members of the Cherokee Nation of Oklahoma. Awards are tenable at accredited undergraduate 2-year & 4-year colleges & universities in the USA. US citizenship required. Students must be eligible for Pell grants.

500 awards per year. Write for complete information.

845

CHRISTIAN RECORD SERVICES INC.
(Scholarships)
4444 South 52nd Street
Lincoln NE 68516
402/488-0981

AMOUNT: $500 to $1000
DEADLINE(S): April 1
FIELD(S): All fields of study

Undergraduate scholarships available to legally blind students who are attending school in the USA. Must demonstrate financial need. US citizenship required.

10–15 awards per year. Write for complete information.

846

CITIZEN'S SCHOLARSHIP
FOUNDATION OF AMERICA H&R
BLOCK
1505 Riverview Road
P.O. Box 297
St. Peter MN 56082
507/931-1682

AMOUNT: Varies

DEADLINE(S): April 1
FIELD(S): All areas of study

For children of eligible employees of H&R Block Inc./or one of its owned subsidiaries. Based on academic capability and financial need. Must be enrolled full time.

35 awards per year. Contact address above for complete information.

847

CLARK FOUNDATION
(Scholarship Program)
P.O. Box 427
Cooperstown NY 13326
607/547-9927

AMOUNT: $500 to $5000
DEADLINE(S): None
FIELD(S): All areas of study

Open to graduates of high schools in the districts of Cherry Valley, Cooperstown, Edmeston, Laurens, Milford, Richfield Springs, Scenevus, Springfield, Van Hornsville, West Winfield, & Worcester. 700 scholarships per year. Renewable.

Must have high school diploma, rank in the upper one-third of graduating class, and have a 3.0 or better GPA.

848

COCA-COLA SCHOLARS FOUNDATION
(Scholarships)
P.O. Box 442
Atlanta GA 30301
800/306-COKE

AMOUNT: $5000; $1000 (per year)
DEADLINE(S): October 31 of high school senior year
FIELD(S): All fields of study

Open to high school seniors in participating USA Coca-Cola bottlers territories (currently 90%+ are participating) who are planning to pursue a post-secondary degree at an accredited college or university in the USA.

Major selection criteria are leadership, character, and achievement. 50 4-year $20,000 scholarships & 100 4-year $4000 scholarships. Contact school guidance counselor or write to address above for complete information.

849

COLLEGE FOUNDATION INC.
(Federal Plus Loans Under NC Insured
Student Loan Program)
2100 Yonkers Rd.
P.O. Box 12100
Raleigh NC 27605
919/821-4771

AMOUNT: Difference between cost of attending and other financial aid received

DEADLINE(S): Varies

FIELD(S): All fields of study

For parent of student who is dependent (by Federal definition) and enrolled in eligible USA college. If the student is at a college not in NC, borrower must be legal NC resident. Must meet nationwide Federal Plus Loans requirements.

Approximately 2600 loans per year. Must reapply each year. Write for complete information.

850

COLLEGE FOUNDATION INC.
(North Carolina Insured Student Loan
Program; Stafford Loans—Subsidized &
Unsubsidized)
P.O. Box 12100
2100 Yonkers Rd.
Raleigh NC 27605
919/821-4771

AMOUNT: Max of $2625; $3500; $5500; or $8500 per year depending on level of study

DEADLINE(S): Varies

FIELD(S): All fields of study

Open to US citizens who are legal residents of NC enrolled in an eligible in-state or out-of-state college or an out-of-state student attending an eligible NC college. Must meet nationwide eligibility requirements of Stafford loans.

Approximately 56,000 loans per year. Financial need must be established for subsidized loan and new loan application is required yearly. Write for complete information.

851

COLLEGE FOUNDATION INC.
(North Carolina Student Incentive Grant)
P.O. Box 12100
2100 Yonkers Rd.
Raleigh NC 27605
919/821-4771

AMOUNT: $1500 max

DEADLINE(S): March 15

FIELD(S): All fields of study

Undergraduate grants to students who are US citizens, North Carolina residents, and attending or planning to attend college in North Carolina. Must demonstrate substantial financial need.

Approximately 4300 grants per year. Renewable to a maximum of 5 years of undergraduate study.

852

COLORADO MASONS BENEVOLENT
FUND ASSOCIATION
(Scholarship Program)
1130 Panorama Drive
Colorado Springs CO 80904
719/471-9587

AMOUNT: Up to $20,000 over four years

DEADLINE(S): March 15

FIELD(S): All fields of study

Open to seniors in Colorado public high schools who plan to attend a Colorado college or university. Must be Colorado resident but Masonic affiliation is not required. Need is considered but is not paramount.

Applications are mailed early in November to all Colorado public schools. Contact Colorado schools. DO NOT write address above.

853

COMMONWEALTH OF VIRGINIA DEPARTMENT OF VETERANS' AFFAIRS
(War Orphans Education Program)
  270 Franklin Rd. SW; Room 1012
  Poff Federal Building
  Roanoke VA 24011-2215
  703/857-7104

AMOUNT: Tuition + required fees
DEADLINE(S): None
FIELD(S): All fields of study

Open to surviving/dependent children (aged 16–25) of USA military personnel who were/are Virginia residents & as a result of war/armed conflict are deceased, disabled, a prisoner of war, or missing in action.

Must attend a state-supported secondary or post-secondary educational institution to pursue any vocational,; technical, under-graduate, or graduate program. Write for complete information.

854

COMMUNITY FOUNDATION OF GREATER LORAIN COUNTY
(Lorain Youth Center Scholarship Fund)
  1865 N. Ridge Rd. E.; Suite A
  Lorain OH 44055
  216/277-0142

AMOUNT: $1000
DEADLINE(S): March 1
FIELD(S): All fields of study

Open to students in the 4 Lorain High Schools who live in the city of Lorain and apply for the scholarship in the year of high school graduation. Must show financial need & academic ability and be active in extracur-ricular activities.

Application acceptance begins around Jan 1. Write for complete information.

855

COMMUNITY FOUNDATION OF GREATER LORAIN COUNTY
(Walter and Virginia Nord Scholarship Fund)
  1865 N. Ridge Rd. E.; Suite A
  Lorain OH 44055
  216/277-0142 OR 216/323-4445

AMOUNT: $1000
DEADLINE(S): March 1
FIELD(S): All fields of study

Open to residents of Lorain county who apply for scholarship in the year of graduation from a Lorain County high school. Must be in upper third of graduating class and demonstrate financial need.

Application acceptance begins around January 1. Write for complete information.

856

CONNECTICUT DEPT. OF HIGHER EDUCATION
(State Scholastic Grant Program)
  61 Woodland Street
  Hartford CT 06015
  203/566-2618

AMOUNT: $300 - $2000
DEADLINE(S): February 15
FIELD(S): All fields of study

Open to CT high school seniors & graduates who ranked in top 20% of their high school class or scored above 1100 on SAT exam. For undergraduate study at a New England college or university. US citizenship or legal residency required.

3000 awards per year. Write for complete information.

857

CONNECTICUT DEPT. OF HIGHER EDUCATION.
(Student Financial Assistance Programs)
  61 Woodland St.
  Hartford CT 06105
  203/566-2618

AMOUNT: Varies with program

DEADLINE(S): Varies

FIELD(S): All fields of study

Various state and federal programs providing financial aid to Connecticut students. Programs include tuition waivers for veterans and senior citizens, work study programs, loans and scholarships, and grants.

Most programs emphasize financial need. Write for brochure listing programs and application information.

858

CONRAIL-CONSOLIDATED RAIL CORPORATION
(Frank Thomson Scholarships for Males)
Attn: Nancy Hoernig
2001 Market St. (18B)
P.O. Box 41418
Philadelphia PA 19101-1418
215/209-1764

AMOUNT: $2000

DEADLINE(S): April 1

FIELD(S): Engineering

Open ONLY to high school seniors who are sons of ConRail or predecessor railroad company employees. Must take SAT and certain achievement tests.

Approximately 12 scholarships awarded on basis of both financial need and competitive exams. Renewable up to 4 years. Write for complete information.

859

CONRAIL-CONSOLIDATED RAIL CORPORATION
(Women's Aid Scholarships for Men and Women)
Attn: Nancy Hoernig
2001 Market St. (18B)
P.O. Box 41418
Philadelphia PA 19101-1418
215/209-1764

AMOUNT: $200–1500

DEADLINE(S): April 1

FIELD(S): All areas of study

Open to high school seniors who are children of ConRail, Penn Central, or predecessor railroad company employees. Must demonstrate need & take SAT, TSWE, & two achievement tests. For undergraduate study.

12 to 15 scholarships based on financial need and competitive exams. Renewable up to 4 years. Write for complete information.

860

D. D. HACHAR CHARITABLE TRUST FUND
(Undergraduate Scholarships)
Laredo National Bank; Trustee
P.O. Box 59
Laredo TX 78042
512/723-1151 Ext. 670

AMOUNT: Varies

DEADLINE(S): Last Friday of April; last Friday of October

FIELD(S): All areas of study

Open to residents of Laredo (Webb County) Texas. Scholarships available for undergraduate study. College freshmen and sophomores must maintain minimum 2.0 GPA; juniors and seniors at least 2.5 GPA. Must be enrolled full-time.

Annual family income cannot exceed $44,000. US citizenship required. Write for complete information.

861

DANISH SISTERHOOD OF AMERICA
(Scholarship Program)
3429 Columbus Dr.
Holiday FL 34691
Written inquiry only

AMOUNT: Varies

DEADLINE(S): Varies

FIELD(S): Continuing Education; Danish Studies

Open to Danish Sisterhood of America members in good standing (and their children) who are attending approved schools. One-year or longer membership required. Awards are based on high academic achievement.

Write to National Vice President & Scholarship Chair Elizabeth K. Hunter at above address for complete information.

862

DAUGHTERS OF PENELOPE
(Annual Scholarships)
1909 Q St. NW; Suite 500
Washington DC 20009
202/234-9741

AMOUNT: $500–$1000
DEADLINE(S): June 20
FIELD(S): All fields of study

Undergraduate study. Open to females of Greek descent who are members of Daughters of Penelope or Maids of Athena or the daughter of a member of Daughters of Penelope or Order of AHEPA. Academic performance & need are main considerations.

Renewable. Write for complete information.

863

DAUGHTERS OF THE AMERICAN REVOLUTION
(American Indians Scholarship)
Mrs. Lyle A. Ross
3738 South Mission Dr.
Lake Havasu City AZ 86406-4250
Written inquiry

AMOUNT: $500
DEADLINE(S): August 1; December 1
FIELD(S): All fields of study

Open to American Indians (both youth and adults) striving to get an education. Funds help students of any tribe in any state based on need, academic achievement, and ambition.

Send SASE to above address for complete information.

864

DAUGHTERS OF THE AMERICAN REVOLUTION
(Lillian and Arthur Dunn Scholarship)
Office of the Committee/Scholarships
National Society DAR
1776 'D' St. NW
Washington DC 20006-5392
202/879-3292

AMOUNT: $1000 per year for 4 years
DEADLINE(S): February 15
FIELD(S): All fields of study

Open to graduating high school seniors whose mothers are current DAR members (must be sponsored by mother's DAR chapter). Award is for undergrad study & can be renewed with annual transcript review & approval. US citizenship required.

Write for complete information (include SASE).

865

DAUGHTERS OF THE CINCINNATI
(Scholarship Program)
122 East 58th Street
New York NY 10022
212/319-6915

AMOUNT: Varies
DEADLINE(S): March 15
FIELD(S): All fields of study

Open to high school seniors who are daughters of commissioned officers (active, retired, or deceased) in the US Regular Army, Navy, Air Force, Marine Corps, or Coast Guard. For undergraduate study at any accredited four-year institution.

Awards based on need & merit. Include parent's rank and branch of service when writing for application or further information.

866

DAUGHTERS OF UNION VETERANS OF THE CIVIL WAR
(Grand Army of the Republic Living Memorial Scholarship)
503 South Walnut
Springfield IL 62704
Written inquiry (MUST include SASE)

AMOUNT: $200
DEADLINE(S): April 30
FIELD(S): All fields of study

Open to LINEAL descendants of a union veteran of the Civil War. Must be a junior or senior in college, in good scholastic standing; of good moral character, and have a firm belief in the US form of government.

For complete information send a self-addressed stamped envelope and PROOF of direct lineage to a Civil War union veteran (military record). Three to four awards per year.

867

DAVID WASSERMAN SCHOLARSHIP FUND Inc.
(Award Program)
Adirondack Center
4722 St. Hwy. 30
Amsterdam NY 12010
Written inquiry

AMOUNT: $300 per year
DEADLINE(S): Apr 15
FIELD(S): All fields of study

Open to bona fide residents of Montgomery County NY who are pursuing an undergraduate degree and are USA citizens.

20–25 awards per year. Renewable. Make requests for information and applications in writing.

868

DAVIS-ROBERTS SCHOLARSHIP FUND INC.
(Scholarships to DeMolays & Jobs Daughters)
P.O. Box 1974
Cheyenne WY 82003
307/632-2948

AMOUNT: Varies
DEADLINE(S): June 15
FIELD(S): All areas of study

Open to Wyoming residents who are or have been a DeMolays or Jobs daughter in the state of Wyoming. Scholarships for full-time undergraduate study. Financial need is a consideration. US citizenship required.

12 to 14 awards annually. Renewable. Write for complete information.

869

DEMOLAY FOUNDATION INC.
(Scholarships)
10200 N. Executive Hills Blvd.
Kansas City MO 64153
816/891-8333

AMOUNT: $1500 (grottoes)
DEADLINE(S): April 1
FIELD(S): Dental or medical fields

For undergraduate freshmen or sophomores with a 2.0 GPA or better. DeMolay membership is required. Considerations are leadership, academic achievement, and goals.

Three grants per year. Write for complete information.

870

DEPARTMENT OF VETERANS AFFAIRS
(Survivors and Dependents Educational Assistance Program)
810 Vermont Ave. NW
Washington DC 20420
800/827-1000

AMOUNT: $404 per month for full-time study

DEADLINE(S): Varies

FIELD(S): All fields of study

Educational support for children (aged 18–26) and spouses/widows of veterans who are disabled/deceased due to military service or are classified currently as prisoner of war or missing in action. Training in approved institution.

Spouses are eligible up to 10 years after determination of eligibility. Contact the nearest VA office for complete information.

871

DESCENDANTS OF THE SIGNERS OF THE DECLARATION OF INDEPENDENCE
(Scholarship Grant)
Mrs. P. F. Kennedy; Chairperson
417 E. Meadow Lane
Pembroke NH 03275
Written inquiry

AMOUNT: Average $1500

DEADLINE(S): March 15

FIELD(S): All areas of study

Undergrad & grad awards for students who are DSDI members (proof of direct descent of signer of Declaration of Independence necessary). Must be full-time student accepted or enrolled in a recognized USA 4-year college or university.

Applicants must name their ancestor-signer when requesting application and send a self-addressed stamped envelope ($.64) or they will NOT receive a response. Write for complete information.

872

DISABLED AMERICAN VETERANS AUXILIARY
(DAVA Student Loans)
3725 Alexandria Pike
Cold Spring KY 41076
606/441-7300

AMOUNT: Up to maximum of $1000 for 4 years

DEADLINE(S): April 25

FIELD(S): All fields of study

Open to citizens of US who have been accepted by an institution of higher education & are children whose living mother is a life member of DAV Auxiliary or (if mother is deceased) father is a life member of at least 1 year.

40–42 loans per year. Renewable. Write for complete information.

873

DISTRICT OF COLUMBIA
(State Student Incentive Grant Program)
2100 M. L. King Jr. Ave. SE; Suite 401
Washington DC 20020
202/727-3688

AMOUNT: $400–$1500

DEADLINE(S): Last Friday in June

FIELD(S): All fields of study EXCEPT Law & Medicine

Open to US citizens or legal residents who have lived in DC for at least 15 consecutive months, have at least a 2.0 GPA, can demonstrate financial need, & are enrolled in an eligible US institution.

Renewable scholarships for undergraduate study. Must have high school diploma or equivalent. Write for complete information.

874

DOLPHIN SCHOLARSHIP FOUNDATION
(Scholarships)
405 Dillingham Blvd.
Norfolk Naval Station
Norfolk VA 23511
804/451-3660; FAX 804/489-8578

AMOUNT: $1750

DEADLINE(S): April 15

FIELD(S): All fields of study

Children of members or former members of the submarine force who qualified in submarines and served in the submarine force for at least 5 years, or for at least 6 years in direct support of the submarine force, or who died on active duty.

For students seeking BA or BS degree. Financial need is a consideration. Send self-addressed stamped envelope (Business size) for complete information.

875

DOYLE SCHOLARSHIP PROGRAM
(Scholarships)
1501 Mendocino Ave.
Santa Rosa CA 95401
707/527-4740

AMOUNT: Varies
DEADLINE(S): March 1
FIELD(S): All fields of study

Applicants must be enrolled at Santa Rosa Junior College. Applications for the Doyle Scholarship program are made through the SRJC scholarship office. Awards are based on scholastic achievement and financial need. US citizenship required.

Number of awards per year varies. Contact SRJC scholarship office for complete information.

876

EASTER SEAL SOCIETY OF IOWA INC.
(James L. & Lavon Madden Mallory Annual Disability Scholarship Program)
P.O. Box 4002
Des Moines IA 50333
515/289-1933

AMOUNT: $1000
DEADLINE(S): April 15
FIELD(S): All fields of study

Open to Iowa residents with a permanent disability who are graduating high school seniors. Award supports undergraduate study at a recognized college or university.
Write for complete information.

877

EBELL OF LOS ANGELES
SCHOLARSHIP PROGRAM
(Flint Scholarships & Ebell Scholarships)
743 S. Lucerne Blvd.
Los Angeles CA 90005
213/931-1277

AMOUNT: $2000 ($200/month for 10 months)
DEADLINE(S): May 1
FIELD(S): All fields of study

Open to Los Angeles County residents who are undergraduate sophomores, juniors, or seniors enrolled in a Los Angeles County college or university. Must be a USA citizen. GPA of 3.25 must be maintained for renewal.

50–60 awards per year. Financial need is a consideration. Write for complete information.

878

EDUCATION ASSISTANCE
CORPORATION FEDERAL FAMILY
EDUCATION LOAN PROGRAM
115 First Ave. SW
Aberdeen SD 57401
605/225-6423

AMOUNT: Varies
DEADLINE(S): None
FIELD(S): All areas of study

South Dakota resident enrolled in an eligible school on at least a half-time basis. US citizen or legal resident.
Loans are renewable. Write for complete information.

879

EDUCATIONAL COMMUNICATIONS
SCHOLARSHIP FOUNDATION
721 N. McKinley Rd.
Lake Forest IL 60045
708/295-6650

AMOUNT: $1000

DEADLINE(S): June 1 (request applications by March 15)

FIELD(S): All fields of study

Open to current high school students who are US citizens and have taken the SAT or ACT examination. Awards based on GPA, achievement test scores, leadership, work experience, essay, financial need.

150 scholarships per year. Write for complete information. Include name, home address, current year in high school, and approximate grade point average.

880

EDWARD ARTHUR MELLINGER EDUCATIONAL FOUNDATION INC.
(Scholarships & Loans)
P.O. Box 278
1025 East Broadway
Monmouth IL 61462
309/734-2419

AMOUNT: $750 maximum

DEADLINE(S): May 1

FIELD(S): All fields of study

Scholarships are available to students who reside in western Illinois and eastern Iowa and are enrolled in undergraduate programs. Loans are available for graduate study.

250 awards per year. Renewable. Write for complete information.

881

EDWARD RUTLEDGE CHARITY
(College Scholarships)
Box 758
Chippewa Falls WI 54729
715/723-6618

AMOUNT: $1700

DEADLINE(S): July 1

FIELD(S): All fields of study

Scholarships open to residents of Chippewa county Wisconsin ONLY. Awards are for full-time undergrad study at recognized colleges & universities. Grades and financial need are considerations. USA citizens only.

35 awards per year. Renewable. Contact address above for complete information.

882

EDWARDS SCHOLARSHIP FUND
(Undergraduate and Graduate Scholarships)
10 Post Office Square So.; Suite 1230
Boston MA 02109
617/426-4434

AMOUNT: $250 to $2500

DEADLINE(S): March 1

FIELD(S): All fields of study

Open ONLY to Boston residents under age 25 who can demonstrate financial need, scholastic ability, and good character. For undergraduate or graduate study but undergrads receive preference. Family home must be within Boston city limits.

Applicants must have lived in Boston from at least the beginning of their junior year in high school. Metropolitan Boston is NOT included.

883

EISENHOWER MEMORIAL SCHOLARSHIP FOUNDATION
(Undergraduate Scholarships)
223 S. Pete Ellis Dr.; Suite 27
Bloomington IN 47408
812/332-2257

AMOUNT: $2500–$10,000

DEADLINE(S): First Tuesday following Thanksgiving Holiday

FIELD(S): All areas of study

Open to Indiana high school seniors in good standing who have never attended college, have faith in a divine being, and a firm belief in the free enterprise system and the American way of life. Financial need is not a consideration.

The awards are limited to certain Indiana colleges. Write for complete information.

884

ELKS NATIONAL FOUNDATION
(Undergraduate Scholarships)
Check local telephone directory

AMOUNT: $1000 to $5000

DEADLINE(S): Mid-January (can vary with local lodge)

FIELD(S): All fields of study

Scholarships are offered to graduating high school seniors who are USA citizens and reside within the jurisdiction of a local lodge of the BPO Elks of the USA. Elks membership is not required.

Criteria for selection are financial need, leadership, and scholarship. Obtain application forms from local Elks Lodge after November 1.

885

EMANUEL STERNBERGER
EDUCATIONAL FUND
(Loan Program)
P.O. Box 1735
Greensboro NC 27402
910/275-6316

AMOUNT: $1000 (1st year) & $2000 (subsequent years); maximum $5000

DEADLINE(S): April 30

FIELD(S): All fields of study

Open to North Carolina residents who are entering their junior or senior year of college or are graduate students. Considerations include grades, economic situation, references, & credit rating.

Personal interview is required. Can be used at any college or university. Write for complete information.

886

ENGLISH-SPEAKING UNION
(Lucy Dalbiac Luard Scholarship)
16 E. 69th St.
New York NY 10021
212/879-6800

AMOUNT: Full tuition and expenses

DEADLINE(S): November

FIELD(S): All fields of study

Open to students attending a United Negro College or Howard or Hampton University. Full scholarship to spend undergraduate junior year at a university in England. US citizen.

Application must be made through student's college or university. Information and applications are sent each fall to the Academic Dean/VP for Academic Affairs at participating schools.

887

ETHEL N. BOWEN FOUNDATION
(Scholarships)
P.O. Box 1559
Bluefield WV 24701
304/325-8181

AMOUNT: Varies

DEADLINE(S): April 30

FIELD(S): All fields of study

Undergraduate and occasional graduate scholarships open to residents of south West Virginia.

20–25 awards per year. Write for complete information.

888

FALCON FOUNDATION
(Scholarships)
3116 Academy Dr.; Suite 200
USAF Academy CO 80840
719/472-4096

AMOUNT: $3000

DEADLINE(S): April 30

FIELD(S): All areas of study

Scholarships to attend private preparatory schools for students who plan to seek admission to the US Air Force Academy. Open to single students age 17–21, in excellent health, & highly motivated to attend academy. USA citizen.

100 awards per year. Send a self-addressed stamped envelope for application.

889

FEDERAL EMPLOYEE EDUCATION & ASSISTANCE FUND
(FEEA Scholarship Program)
8441 W. Bowles Ave.; Suite 200
Littleton CO 80123
303/933-7580; 800/323-4140;
FAX 303/933-7587

AMOUNT: $300–$1500
DEADLINE(S): First Friday in June (applications available January through May)
FIELD(S): All fields of study

Open to current civilian federal & postal employees (w/ at least 3 yrs. service) & dependent family members enrolled or planning to enroll in a 2-year, 4-year ,or graduate degree program. GPA of 3.0 or better.

Awards are merit based. Involvement in extra-curricular/community activities a factor. Send SASE (business size) for complete information. Student loans available directly through sponsor Signet Bank (1-800-955-0005).

890

FEILD CO-OPERATIVE ASSOCIATION
(Mississippi Resident Loans)
P.O. Box 5054
Jackson MS 39296-5054
601/939-9295

AMOUNT: $2000 per calendar year (12 months)
DEADLINE(S): May apply at any time
FIELD(S): All fields of study

Open ONLY to Mississippi residents who are undergraduate juniors & graduate students with satisfactory academic standing. Demonstrate evidence of need & promise of financial responsibility. US citizenship or legal residency required.

These are loans—NOT scholarships. Loans are renewable. Write for complete information.

891

FIFTH MARINE DIVISION
ASSOCIATION
(Scholarships)
c/o W. A. Armond
260 S. Norwinden Dr.
Springfield PA 19064
215/543-4660

AMOUNT: $500 per semester maximum
DEADLINE(S): June 1
FIELD(S): All fields of study

Open to children of Association members for undergraduate study. Show evidence of financial need and an ability level appropriate to proposed program of study. Limited to residents of the US who are high school graduates or equivalent.

Renewable for not more than eight semesters of undergraduate study. Write for complete information.

892

FIRST CAVALRY DIVISION
ASSOCIATION
(Scholarships)
302 N. Main
Copperas Cove TX 76522
Written inquiry

AMOUNT: $600 per year up to 4 years max
DEADLINE(S): None specified
FIELD(S): All fields of study

Awards to children of soldiers who died or were declared 100% disabled from injuries while serving with the 1st Calvary division during & since the Vietnam War or during Desert Storm.

If death occurred after 3/1/80 deceased parent must have been an Association member and serving with the division at the time of death. Send self-addressed stamped envelope for complete information.

893

FIRST COMMERCIAL BANK
(National Advisory Board Scholarship
Program)
P.O. Box 1471
Little Rock AR 72203
501/371-7012

AMOUNT: Varies
DEADLINE(S): February 1
FIELD(S): All fields of study

Open to Arkansas residents who are high
school seniors and plan to attend an accredited Arkansas college or university that
offers a bachelor's degree. Minimum ACT
score of 28 to apply.
Renewable for up to 4 years. Write for complete information.

894

FIRST MARINE DIVISION ASSN.
(Scholarship Program)
14325 Willard Road; Suite 107
Chantilly VA 22021
703/803-3195

AMOUNT: Varies
DEADLINE(S): Not specified
FIELD(S): All fields of study

For dependent of person who served in the
First Marine Division or in a unit attached
to or in support of the Division and is
deceased from any cause or 100% disabled.
For undergraduate study. Write for complete
information.

895

FLEET RESERVE ASSOCIATION
(Scholarships and Awards)
FRA Scholarship Administrator
125 N. West St.
Alexandria VA 22314
708/683-1400 800/424-1120

AMOUNT: Approximately $500
DEADLINE(S): April 15

FIELD(S): All areas of study

Open to children/spouses of Fleet Reserve
Association members. Dependents of
retired or deceased members also may
apply. For undergraduate study. Awards
based on financial need, scholastic standing,
character, & leadership qualities.
"Dependent child" is defined as unmarried,
under 21, or under 23 if currently enrolled
in college. Write for complete information.

896

FLORENCE EVANS BUSHEE
FOUNDATION
(Scholarships)
One Beacon Street
Boston MA 02108
617/573-0462

AMOUNT: Varies
DEADLINE(S): May 1
FIELD(S): All fields of study

Open ONLY to undergraduate college students who reside in the Massachusetts
towns of Byfield, Georgetown, Newbury,
Newburyport, Rowley, Salisbury, or West
Newbury.
Approx 120 grants per year. Write for complete information.

897

FLORIDA DEPT. OF EDUCATION
(Florida Student Assistant Grants)
Office of Student Financial Assistance
1344 Florida Education Center
Tallahassee FL 32399-0400
904/487-0049

AMOUNT: $200–$1500
DEADLINE(S): Varies with program
FIELD(S): All fields of study

Three separate programs available to full-time
degree-seeking undergrads who are
enrolled at an eligible Florida institution.
US citizenship and Florida residency
requirements apply. Priority to students
with the lowest family resources.

Write for complete eligibility requirements and information.

898

FOUNDATION FOR AMATEUR RADIO
(Scholarships)
6903 Rhode Island Ave.
College Park MD 20740
Written inquiry

AMOUNT: Varies each year
DEADLINE(S): June 1
FIELD(S): All fields of study

Program open to active licensed radio amateurs ONLY. Since this specialized program changes so much each year the Foundation annually places announcements with complete eligibility requirements in the amateur radio magazines.

To determine your eligibility look for announcements in magazines such as QST, CQ, 73, Worldradio, etc. Write for complete information.

899

FOUNDATION FOR EXCEPTIONAL CHILDREN
(Scholarship Awards)
1920 Association Dr.
Reston VA 22091
703/620-1054

AMOUNT: $500 & $1000
DEADLINE(S): February 1
FIELD(S): All fields of study

Undergraduate awards in 4 categories:
1. Students with disabilities. 2. Ethnic minority students with disabilities.
3. Gifted/talented students with disabilities.
4. Ethnic minority gifted/talented with disabilities.

Apply in one category only. Must be entering freshman. Write for complete information.

900

FRANCIS OUIMET CADDIE SCHOLARSHIP FUND
190 Park Rd.
Weston MA 02193
617/891-6400

AMOUNT: $500–$5000
DEADLINE(S): December 1
FIELD(S): All fields of study

Open to Massachusetts residents who are college students and have caddied or serviced golf in some capacity for three or more years at a Massachusetts golf club. Must demonstrate financial need.

200–250 awards per year. Renewable. Write for complete information.

901

FRED A. BRYAN COLLEGIATE STUDENTS FUND
(Trust Fund Scholarships)
Norwest Bank Indiana NA
112 W. Jefferson Blvd.
South Bend IN 46601
219/237-3314

AMOUNT: $1400–$1600
DEADLINE(S): March 1
FIELD(S): All fields of study

Open to male graduates of South Bend, Indiana, high schools with preference to those who are or have been Boy Scouts. For undergraduate study at a recognized college or university. Financial need must be demonstrated. US citizenship required

Renewable for up to 4 years. Write for complete information.

902

FRED B. & RUTH B. ZIGLER FOUNDATION
(Scholarships)
P.O. Box 986
324 Broadway
Jennings LA 70546
318/824-2413

AMOUNT: $1250 per semester
DEADLINE(S): March 10
FIELD(S): All areas of study

Scholarships open to graduating seniors at Jefferson Davis Parish (LA) high schools. Awards are tenable at recognized colleges & universities.

10–18 scholarships per year. Renewable for up to 4 years. Write for complete information.

903

FULLER E. CALLAWAY FOUNDATION
(Hatton Lovejoy Scholarship)
209 Broome Street
La Grange GA 30240
706/884-7348

AMOUNT: $3300 per school year
DEADLINE(S): February 15
FIELD(S): All fields of study

Open to high school graduates who have lived in Troup County GA for at least two years and rank in the upper 25 percent of their class.

10 scholarships per year. Write for complete information.

904

GABRIEL J. BROWN TRUST
(Low Interest Loan Fund)
112 Avenue 'E' West
Bismarck ND 58501
701/223-5916

AMOUNT: Varies
DEADLINE(S): June 15
FIELD(S): All fields of study

Special low-interest loans (6%) open to residents of North Dakota who have completed at least 2 years of undergraduate study at a recognized college or university and have a 2.5 or better GPA. USA citizen.

Approximately 75 loans per year. Renewable. Write for complete information.

905

GEORGE ABRAHAMIAN FOUNDATION
(Scholarships for Local Armenians)
945 Admiral Street
Providence RI 02904
401/831-2887

AMOUNT: Varies
DEADLINE(S): September 1
FIELD(S): All areas of study

Open to undergraduate and graduate students who are US citizens of Armenian ancestry and live in Providence RI, are of good character, have the ability to learn, and can demonstrate financial need.

Renewable. Write for complete information.

906

GEORGE E. ANDREWS TRUST
Blackhawk State Bank
P.O. Box 719
Beloit WI 53512
608/364-8917

AMOUNT: $2000
DEADLINE(S): February 1
FIELD(S): All fields of study

Open to seniors at Beloit Memorial or Beloit Catholic High Schools. Scholarship awarded alternately between these two schools. Awards based on scholastic standing, financial need, moral character, industriousness, and other factors.

Write for complete information.

907

GEORGE GROTEFEND SCHOLARSHIP FUND
(Grotefend Scholarship)
1644 Magnolia Ave.
Redding CA 96001
916/225-0227

AMOUNT: $150–$400
DEADLINE(S): April 20
FIELD(S): All fields of study

Scholarships open to applicants who completed all 4 years of high school in Shasta County California. Awards support all levels of study at recognized colleges & universities.

300 awards per year. Write for complete information.

908

GEORGE T. WELCH
(Scholarships)
Baker Boyer Bank Trust Dept.; PO Box 1796
Walla Walla WA 99362
509/525-2000

AMOUNT: Up to $2500; amount varies
DEADLINE(S): March 1
FIELD(S): All fields of study

Open ONLY to US citizens who reside in Walla Walla County Washington and have graduated from a Walla Walla high school.

Approximately 45 awards per year. Contact Holly T. Howard, address above, for complete information.

909

GLASS, MOLDERS, POTTERY, PLASTICS, & ALLIED WORKERS INTERNATIONAL UNION
(Scholarship Program)
P.O. Box 607
Media PA 19063
215/565-5051

AMOUNT: $2500 per year for 4 years
DEADLINE(S): November 1
FIELD(S): All fields of study

Open to dependent children of union members. Applicants must rank in the top 1/4 of high school senior class. Children of international union officers are NOT eligible. Awards tenable at accredited undergraduate colleges & universities.

Write for complete information.

910

GRAHAM-FANCHER SCHOLARSHIP TRUST
149 Josephine St. Suite; A
Santa Cruz CA 95060
408/423-3640

AMOUNT: Varies
DEADLINE(S): May 1
FIELD(S): All fields of study

Open to graduating seniors from high schools in Northern Santa Cruz County (Calif). School and community activities and financial need are considerations.

20 awards per academic year. Write for complete information.

911

GRAND LODGE OF ILLINOIS
(Illinois Odd Fellow-Rebekah Scholarship Award)
P.O. Box 248
305 North Kickapoo St.
Lincoln IL 62656
217/735-2561

AMOUNT: Up to $1000
DEADLINE(S): December 1 (application request); March 1 (completed application)
FIELD(S): All fields of study

Illinois residents. Scholarships for undergraduate study. Applicants must use the official Odd Fellow-Rebekah scholarship form, submit official transcript of latest grades, & demonstrate need. US citizenship required.

Write to address above for complete information & application forms.

912

GRAPHIC COMMUNICATIONS INTERNATIONAL UNION (GCIU-Aj de Andrade Scholarship Awards Program)
1900 L Street NW
Washington DC 20036
202/462-1400

AMOUNT: $2000 (payable $500 per year)
DEADLINE(S): February 15
FIELD(S): All areas

Open to citizens of USA or Canada who are graduating high school seniors and are dependents of Graphic Communications International Union members.
10 awards per year. Write for complete information.

913

GUIDEPOSTS MAGAZINE (Youth Writing Contest)
16 E. 34th St.
New York NY 10016
212/251-8100

AMOUNT: $1000–$6000
DEADLINE(S): November 28
FIELD(S): All fields of study

Open to any high school junior or senior (USA or foreign citizen) who writes an original 1200-word personal experience story (in English) in which the writer's faith in God played a role. Stories should be true & written in the first person.
The top 30 stories will receive these prizes—1st/$6000, 2nd/$5000, 3rd/$4000, 4th/$3000, 5th/$2000, 6th/10th/$1000 and 1st–30th/portable electronic typewriters. Stories should be submitted between September 1 & the Monday after Thanksgiving.

914

H. T. EWALD FOUNDATION (Scholarship Awards)
15175 E. Jefferson Ave.
Grosse Pointe MI 48230
313/821-2000

AMOUNT: $400 to $2500
DEADLINE(S): April 1
FIELD(S): All fields of study

Open to residents of the metropolitan Detroit (MI) area who will be entering college as freshmen. Awards are available for up to 4 years of undergraduate work. Based on financial need, academic achievement, and extracurricular activities.
10 to 18 awards per year. Write for complete information.

915

HARNESS HORSEMEN INTERNATIONAL FOUNDATION (J. L. Hauck Memorial Scholarship Fund)
14 Main St.
Robbinsville NJ 08691
609/259-3717

AMOUNT: $4000
DEADLINE(S): June 1
FIELD(S): All fields of study

Open to sons & daughters of Harness Horseman International Assn. members. Scholarship supports undergraduate study at any recognized college or university.
Renewable. Write for complete information.

916

HARNESS TRACKS OF AMERICA (HTA-ARAMARK/Harry M. Stevens Scholarship)
4640 East Sunrise; Suite 200
Tucson AZ 85718
520/529-2525; FAX 520/529-3235

AMOUNT: $3000
DEADLINE(S): May 15

FIELD(S): All fields of study

Applicants MUST be children of licensed harness racing drivers, trainers, breeders, or caretakers (including retired or deceased) or young people actively engaged in harness racing. For study beyond the high school level.

Five scholarships per year for 1 year each awarded on the basis of merit & financial need. No student may be awarded more than 2 separate yearly scholarships. Write for complete information.

917

HARRY E. & FLORENCE W. SNAYBERGER MEMORIAL FOUNDATION
(Grant Award)
c/o Pennsylvania National Bank & Trust Company; Trust Dept.
Center & Norwegian
Pottsville PA 17901
717/622-4200

AMOUNT: Varies

DEADLINE(S): Last working day in February

FIELD(S): All areas of study

Applicants must be residents of Schuylkill County PA. Scholarships given based on college expense need.

Contact trust clerk Carolyn Bernatonis for complete information.

918

HARVARD/RADCLIFFE OFFICE OF ADMISSIONS AND FINANCIAL AID
(Scholarships; Grants; Loans & Work Study Programs)
3rd floor—Byerly Hall
8 Garden St.
Cambridge MA 02138
617/495-1581

AMOUNT: Varies

DEADLINE(S): None

FIELD(S): All fields of study

Need-based funds available to all who are admitted and can show proof of need.

Applicants must be accepted for admission to Harvard before they will be considered for funding. Many factors other than family income are considered. Write for complete information.

919

HATTIE M. STRONG FOUNDATION
(No-interest Loans)
1620 Eye St. NW; Room 700
Washington DC 20006
202/331-1619

AMOUNT: Up to $2500

DEADLINE(S): Apply between January 1 & March 31

FIELD(S): All fields of study

Open to USA undergraduate & graduate students in their last year of study in the USA or abroad. Loans are made solely on the basis of individual merit. There is no interest & no collateral requirement. USA citizen.

Financial need is a consideration. Approximately 240 awards per year. For complete information send SASE and include personal history, school attended, subject studied, date expected to complete studies, & amount of funds needed.

920

HAUSS-HELMS FOUNDATION INC.
(Grant Program/Scholarships)
P.O. Box 25
Wapakoneta OH 45895
419/738-4911

AMOUNT: Up to $4500

DEADLINE(S): April 15

FIELD(S): All fields of study

Undergraduate scholarships open to residents of Auglaize or Allen County (Ohio) who are recommended by their high school principal, a responsible faculty member, or their guidance counselor. US citizen.

195 scholarships per year. Renewable with reapplication. Write for complete information.

921

HAWAII EDUCATIONAL LOAN PROGRAM
(PLUS/SLS)
1314 S. King St. #861
Honolulu HI 96814
808/536-3731

AMOUNT: Varies
DEADLINE(S): None
FIELD(S): All fields of study

This is a loan for parents of dependent students. The loan must be repaid. Variable interest rate changes annually.
Write for complete information.

922

HERBERT LEHMAN EDUCATION FUND
(Scholarships)
99 Hudson Street #1600
New York NY 10013
Written inquiry

AMOUNT: $1200
DEADLINE(S): April 15
FIELD(S): All fields of study

Open to needy African American high school students planning to begin undergraduate study at recently desegregated and publicly supported deep South institutions having a below average enrollment of African Americans.

US citizenship required. 50–100 awards per year. Renewable. Requests for application forms must be in writing and requested by the applicant.

923

HERSCHEL C. PRICE EDUCATIONAL FOUNDATION
(Grants Program)
P.O. Box 412
Huntington WV 25708
304/529-3852

AMOUNT: $250 to $2500 per semester
DEADLINE(S): October 1; April 1
FIELD(S): All fields of study

Scholarships are given primarily to students who are residents of West Virginia in attendance at W.V. institutions at the undergraduate level. Some graduate awards are available. US citizen.
Write for complete information.

924

HORACE SMITH FUND
(Walter S. Barr Scholarship Fellowship & Loan Fund)
P.O. Box 3034
1441 Main St.
Springfield MA 01101
413/739-4222

AMOUNT: Varies
DEADLINE(S): December 31 (scholarships); February 1 (fellowships); July 1 (loans)
FIELD(S): All areas of study

Open to graduates of Hampden County MA secondary schools for undergraduate or graduate study. Financial need is of primary importance. Scholarship/fellowship applications available after Sept. 1; loan applications after April 1.

Scholarships are for seniors from Agawam, Chicopee, E. Longmeadow, Longmeadow, Ludlow, Springfield, W. Springfield, & Wilbraham High Schools. Renewable. Write for complete information.

925

HOWARD AND MAMIE NICHOLS SCHOLARSHIP TRUST
(Scholarships)
Wells Fargo Bank Trust Dept.; 5262 N. Blackstone
Fresno CA 93710
Written inquiries only

AMOUNT: Varies
DEADLINE(S): February 28
FIELD(S): All fields of study

Open to graduates of Kern County CA high schools for full-time undergraduate or graduate study at a post-secondary institution. Must demonstrate financial need and have a 2.0 or better GPA.

Approximately 100 awards per year. Renewable with reapplication. Write for complete information.

926

HUALAPAI TRIBAL COUNCIL
(Scholarship Program)
P.O. Box 179
Peach Springs AZ 86434
520/769-2216

AMOUNT: $2500/semester (undergraduate); $6500/semester (graduate)
DEADLINE(S): 4 weeks before each semester
FIELD(S): All areas of study

Scholarships are offered to American Indians only, with priority given to members of the Hualapai Tribe. Must be enrolled as a student full-time and maintain passing grades. US citizenship required.

Write to Sheri K. Yellowhawk at above address for complete information.

927

IDAHO STATE BOARD OF EDUCATION
(Scholarship Programs)
LBJ Building; Room 307
P.O. Box 83720
Boise ID 83720-0037
208/334-2270

AMOUNT: $1500 to $5000
DEADLINE(S): Varies
FIELD(S): All areas of study

Various scholarship programs open to Idaho residents who are graduates of Idaho high schools and who are US citizens. For undergraduate study at recognized colleges & universities. ACT scores (academic & vocational) must be submitted.

Write for complete information.

928

ILLINOIS DEPARTMENT OF THE AMERICAN LEGION
(Scholarships)
P.O. Box 2910
Bloomington IL 61702
309/663-0361

AMOUNT: $500
DEADLINE(S): March 15
FIELD(S): All fields of study

Scholarships are open to dependent children of Illinois American Legion members. Awards are tenable at recognized undergraduate colleges & universities. USA citizen.

20 scholarships per year. Write for complete information.

929

ILLINOIS DEPARTMENT OF THE AMERICAN LEGION
(Scouting Scholarship)
P.O. Box 2910
Bloomington IL 61701
309/663-0361

AMOUNT: $500 & $100

DEADLINE(S): April 30

FIELD(S): All areas of study

Open to scouts or explorer scouts who are residents of Illinois. Essay of 500 words on the Legion's Americanism and scouting program is required.

One $500 and four $100 scholarships per year. Write for complete information.

930

ILLINOIS STUDENT ASSISTANCE COMMISSION

(State & Federal Scholarships; Grants; Loans)

1755 Lake Cook Rd.
Deerfield IL 60015-5209
708/948-8550

AMOUNT: Varies with program

DEADLINE(S): Varies

FIELD(S): All fields of study

Commission administers a number of state and federal scholarship, grant, and loan programs for Illinois residents.

Write for complete information.

931

INDEPENDENCE FEDERAL SAVINGS BANK

(Family Federal Education Loan Program)

1900 L St. NW; Suite 300
Washington DC 20036
202/626-0473 or 800/733-0473

AMOUNT: $2625–$5500 undergrads; up to $10,000 graduates

DEADLINE(S): None

FIELD(S): All fields of study

Loans open to USA citizens accepted for enrollment or enrolled in a school approved by the US Dept. of Education and having a satisfactory academic record.

Write for complete information.

932

INDIANA STATE STUDENT ASSISTANCE COMMISSION

(Higher Education & Freedom of Choice Grants)

150 W. Market St.; Suite 500
Indianapolis IN 46204
317/232-2350

AMOUNT: $200–$4000

DEADLINE(S): March 1

FIELD(S): All fields of study

Open to Indiana residents who are accepted to or enrolled in eligible Indiana institutions as full-time undergraduate students. US citizen or legal resident.

Approx 56,000 grants per year. Financial need is a consideration based on choice of college. Write for complete information.

933

INTERNATIONAL ALLIANCE OF THEATRICAL STAGE EMPLOYEES AND MOVING PICTURE MACHINE OPERATORS

(Richard F. Walsh Foundation)

1515 Broadway; Suite 601
New York NY 10036
212/730-1770

AMOUNT: $750

DEADLINE(S): December 31

FIELD(S): All fields of study

Scholarship is offered to high school seniors who are children of members in good standing. Awards are based on transcripts, SAT scores, and letter(s) of recommendation from clergy or teacher.

Award renewable for 4 years. Write for complete information.

934

INTERNATIONAL ASSN. OF BRIDGE STRUCTURAL & ORNAMENTAL IRON WORKERS
(John H. Lyons Scholarship Program)
1750 New York Ave. NW; Suite 400
Washington DC 20006
202/383-4800

AMOUNT: $2500 per year maximum

DEADLINE(S): January 15 (application request); March 31 (completed application)

FIELD(S): All areas of study

Open ONLY to children of members or deceased members in good standing at the time of death. Applicants must be high school seniors ranking in the upper half of their graduating class. For undergraduate study in the US or Canada.

US or Canadian citizenship required. Scholarships will be awarded for 1 year & may be renewed for 3 academic years. Write for complete information.

935

INTERNATIONAL ASSOCIATION OF MACHINISTS AND AEROSPACE WORKERS
(IAM Scholarship Competition)
9000 Machinists Place
Upper Marlboro MD 20772-2687
301/967-4708 ·

AMOUNT: $2000 (members); $1000 (children of members)

DEADLINE(S): December 1

FIELD(S): All fields of study

Open to members or children of members of IAM having 2 years of continuous membership. Must plan to enroll or be enrolled in an accredited 4-year college or university to attain bachelor's degree. May attend a 2-year college & transfer.

Renewable up to 4 years. Write for complete information; enclose self-addressed label with each application & specify whether you are a member or child of a member.

936

INTERNATIONAL BROTHERHOOD OF TEAMSTERS
(Scholarship Fund)
25 Louisiana Ave. NW
Washington DC 20001
202/624-8735

AMOUNT: $1000–$1500 per year

DEADLINE(S): November 30 (to local union)

FIELD(S): All fields of study

Open to high school seniors who are dependent children of Teamster members. For students in top 15% of their class with excellent SAT/ACT scores. US or Canadian citizen. Must demonstrate financial need.

25 scholarships per year. Top 10 are for $1500 & renewable up to 4 years. Remaining 15 are for $1000 and for 1 year only. Write for complete information.

937

INTERNATIONAL LADIES GARMENT WORKERS UNION
(National College Award Program)
1710 Broadway
New York NY 10019
212/265-7000

AMOUNT: $350 annually; renewable for up to four years

DEADLINE(S): January 31

FIELD(S): All fields of study

Open to sons or daughters of union members who have been members in good standing for at least 2 years. Applications accepted only from high school seniors.

10 scholarships per year. Write for complete information.

938

INTERNATIONAL LADIES GARMENT WORKERS UNION
(Philadelphia-South Jersey District Council Scholarship Awards)
Education Director; 35 S. 4th St.
Philadelphia PA 19106
215/351-0750

AMOUNT: $1000 per year
DEADLINE(S): April 15 (to apply)
FIELD(S): All fields of study

Open ONLY to high school students who are children of Philadelphia-South Jersey District Council ILGWU members (for at least 2 years) or to children of members who have died (within the last 2 years).
Students currently enrolled in college are NOT eligible to apply.

939

INTERNATIONAL ONEXIOCA
(Founders Memorial Award)
911 Bartlett Place
Windsor CA 95492
Written inquiry only

AMOUNT: $250
DEADLINE(S): January 7
FIELD(S): All fields of study

Annual award in memory of Hernesto K. Onexioca/founder. Anyone with the legal surname of Onexioca who is not a relative of Onexioca by blood or marriage and was born on Jan. 1 is eligible to apply.
All inquiries MUST include proof of name and birth date. Those without such proof will NOT be acknowledged.

940

INTERNATIONAL SOCIETY FOR CLINICAL LABORATORY TECHNOLOGY
(David Birenbaum Scholarship Fund)
818 Olive St. #918
St. Louis MO 63101
314/241-1445

AMOUNT: Varies
DEADLINE(S): July 15
FIELD(S): All fields of study

Open to ISCLT members and their dependent children. Requires graduation from an accredited high school or equivalent.
Write for complete information.

941

INTERNATIONAL UNION OF BRICKLAYERS AND ALLIED CRAFTSMEN
(Harry C. Bates Merit Scholarship Program)
815 Fifteenth Street NW
Washington DC 20005
202/783-3788

AMOUNT: $500 to $2000 per year up to 4 years
DEADLINE(S): October PSAT tests
FIELD(S): All areas of study

Open to natural or legally adopted children of current, retired, or deceased BAC members. Competition is administered by National Merit Scholarship Corp., which conducts PSAT/NMSQT during October of student's junior year of high school.
Applicants must be national merit semifinalists. Award tenable at any accredited university or community college the student attends full-time. Write for complete information.

942

INTERNATIONAL UNION OF ELECTRONIC, ELECTRICAL, SALARIES, MACHINE, & FURNITURE WORKERS
(J. B. Carey; D. J. Fitzmaurice; & W. H. Bywater Scholarships)
1126 16th St. NW; Dept. of Social Action
Washington DC 20036
202/296-1200

AMOUNT: $1000—JBC (9 awards); $2000—DJF (1); $3000—WHB (1)
DEADLINE(S): April 15

FIELD(S): All fields of study

Programs open to dependents of union members. JBC scholarships support undergraduate study for 1 year in all fields of study. DJF scholarships support undergraduate study for 1 year in engineering only.

WHB Scholarship available only to children of elected local union officials. Contact local union representative for complete information.

943

IOWA COLLEGE STUDENT AID COMMISSION
(Federal Stafford Loan Program; Federal PLUS Loans)
200 Tenth St.; 4th Floor
Des Moines IA 50309-3609
515/281-3501

AMOUNT: $2625–$4000 undergraduate; $7500 graduate
DEADLINE(S): None
FIELD(S): All fields of study

Loans open to Iowa residents enrolled in or attending approved institutions. Must be USA citizens or legal residents and demonstrate need.

Write for complete information.

944

IOWA COLLEGE STUDENT AID COMMISSION
(Iowa Tuition Grant Program)
200 Tenth St.; 4th Fl.
Des Moines IA 50309-3609
515/281-3501

AMOUNT: $2900
DEADLINE(S): April 20
FIELD(S): All fields of study

Open to Iowa residents enrolled or planning to enroll as undergraduates at eligible privately supported colleges or universities, business schools, or hospital nursing programs in Iowa. Must demonstrate need.

USA citizen or legal resident. 10,140 grants per year. Renewable. Write for complete information.

945

IOWA COLLEGE STUDENT AID COMMISSION
(State of Iowa Scholarships)
200 Tenth St.; 4th Fl.
Des Moines IA 50309-3609
515/281-3501

AMOUNT: $610
DEADLINE(S): November 1
FIELD(S): All fields of study

Open to Iowa high school seniors who are in the top 15% of their class and plan to attend an eligible Iowa college or university. Considerations include ACT or SAT composite test scores, GPA, & class rank. US citizenship required.

3000 scholarships per year. Contact your counselor or write to address above for complete information.

946

IOWA COMMISSION OF VETERANS AFFAIRS
(War Orphans Educational Scholarship Aid)
7700 NW Beaver Dr.
Camp Dodge
Johnston IA 50131
515/242-5331

AMOUNT: $300–$600 per calender year
DEADLINE(S): None specified
FIELD(S): All fields of study

Resident of Iowa for at least 2 years prior to application. Child of parent who died in or as a result of military service. High school graduate or equivalent. Attend a post-secondary institution in Iowa.

Renewable. Write for complete information.

947

IOWA FEDERATION OF LABOR AFL-CIO
(Annual Scholarship Program)
2000 Walker St.
Des Moines IA 50317
515/262-9571

AMOUNT: $1500
DEADLINE(S): March 16
FIELD(S): All areas of study
Competition based on essay. Open only to Iowa high school seniors.
Write for complete information.

948

ITALIAN CATHOLIC FEDERATION INC.
(College Scholarships to High School Seniors)
P.O. Box 640449
1801 Van Ness Ave. #330
San Francisco CA 94164
415/673-8240

AMOUNT: $350
DEADLINE(S): March 21
FIELD(S): All fields of study
Open to graduating high school seniors of Italian ancestry and Catholic faith. Winners may attend any accredited institution. Limited to students who live in states where the federation is located (California, Nevada, and Illinois).
Minimum GPA of 3.0 (4.0 scale). 200 scholarships per year. Send stamped self-addressed envelope to address above for further information.

949

J. H. BAKER SCHOLARSHIP FUND
(Scholarships)
c/o Tom Dechant CPA
P.O. Box 280
La Crosse KS 67548
913/222-2537

AMOUNT: $1600 per year
DEADLINE(S): July 31
FIELD(S): All undergrad fields of study
Open to graduates of high schools in the Kansas counties of Rush, Barton, Ellis, Ness, and Pawnee. Must be under 25 years of age. Selection is based on academic performance, character, ability, and need.
Contact address above for complete information.

950

J. WOOD PLATT CADDIE SCHOLARSHIP TRUST
(Scholarships)
Drawer 808
Southeastern PA 19399
215/687-2340

AMOUNT: Up to $6000
DEADLINE(S): April 1
FIELD(S): All fields of study
Open to high school seniors & undergraduate students who have served as a caddie at a Golf Association of Philadelphia member club, have financial need, & have capability to successfully complete their undergraduate degree.
Renewable. Write for complete information.

951

JACK IN THE BOX RESTAURANTS
(Essay and Photo Scholarship Competition)
c/o Anderson Communications Co.
3 Corporate Plaza; Suite 200
Newport Beach CA 92660
714/644-4414

AMOUNT: $1000
DEADLINE(S): March 1
FIELD(S): All fields of study
Open to high school seniors in Arizona, California, Hawaii, Missouri, Texas, and Washington. Essay and photo contest to encourage students to pursue a college education and reward creativity without emphasizing scholastic achievement.
17 awards in 1994. Theme changes annually. Write for complete information.

952

JACKSONVILLE UNIVERSITY
(Scholarships & Grants Programs)
Director of Student Financial Assistance
Jacksonville FL 32211
904/745-7060

AMOUNT: Varies

DEADLINE(S): January 1 to March 15

FIELD(S): All areas of study

Jacksonville University offers numerous scholarships, grants-in-aid, service awards, and campus employment. Financial need is not necessarily a consideration. Early applications are advised.

Candidates must apply for admission and for financial aid. 100 awards per year for study at Jacksonville University. Write for complete information.

953

JAMES G. K. MCCLURE EDUCATIONAL
AND DEVELOPMENT FUND
(Western North Carolina Scholarships)
11 Sugar Hollow Rd.
Fairview NC 28730
704/628-1044

AMOUNT: $300 to $1500

DEADLINE(S): May 15

FIELD(S): All fields of study

Open to students residing in western North Carolina who are entering the freshman class of a North Carolina college or university. Financial need is a consideration.

Write for complete information.

954

JAMES M. HOFFMAN SCHOLARSHIP
(Undergraduate Scholarship)
Southtrust Bank of Calhoun County
P.O. Box 1000
Anniston AL 36202
205/238-1000 Ext. 338

AMOUNT: Varies

DEADLINE(S): March 1

FIELD(S): All fields of study

Open to high school seniors attending schools within Calhoun County Alabama. For undergraduate study at accredited colleges and universities. Must submit copies of parents' W-2 forms.

Write to attention of William K. Priddy for complete information.

955

JAMES W. COLGAN FUND
(Undergraduate Loans)
P.O. Box 15769
1500 Main St.
Springfield MA 01115
413/787-8700; 413/787-8570

AMOUNT: $1000–$2000

DEADLINE(S): April 15

FIELD(S): All fields of study

Educational loans available to Massachusetts residents under age 30 who are enrolled as undergraduate college students in or outside of Massachusetts. Financial need and grades are considerations.

Must have been a Massachusetts resident for 5 years before applying. Loans are not renewable. Write for complete information.

956

JAMES Z. NAURISON SCHOLARSHIP
FUND
P.O. Box 15769
1500 Main St.
Springfield MA 01115
413/787-8570

AMOUNT: $400–$2000

DEADLINE(S): April 15

FIELD(S): All fields of study

Open to undergraduate and graduate students who are residents of the Massachusetts Counties of Berkshire, Franklin, Hampden, or Hampshire, or of the Cities of Suffield or Enfield CT. Awards based on financial need and academic record.

Approximately 300 awards per year. Self-addressed stamped envelope must accompany request for application.

957

JAPANESE AMERICAN CITIZENS LEAGUE
(Abe & Ester Hagiwara Student Aid Award)
1765 Sutter St.
San Francisco CA 94115
415/921-5225

AMOUNT: Varies
DEADLINE(S): March 1
FIELD(S): All fields of study

Open to JACL members or their children or any American of Japanese ancestry. Scholarship may be used for any level of study. USA citizen or legal resident. Must submit FAF form as proof of financial need.

Send stamped self-addressed envelope for complete information.

958

JAPANESE AMERICAN CITIZENS LEAGUE
(Freshman Scholarships)
1765 Sutter St.
San Francisco CA 94115
415/921-5225

AMOUNT: Varies
DEADLINE(S): February 1
FIELD(S): All fields of study

Open to JACL members or their children or any American of Japanese Ancestry. For high school seniors who are planning to attend a trade school, business school, college, or university. US citizen or legal resident.

14 scholarships per year. Send stamped self-addressed envelope for complete information.

959

JAPANESE AMERICAN CITIZENS LEAGUE
(Undergraduate Scholarships)
1765 Sutter St.
San Francisco CA 94115
415/921-5225

AMOUNT: Varies
DEADLINE(S): March 1
FIELD(S): All fields of study

Open to JACL members or their children or any American of Japanese Ancestry. For undergraduate students currently enrolled in or planning to re-enter a trade school, business school, college, or university. USA citizen or legal resident.

11 scholarships per year. Send stamped self-addressed envelope for complete information.

960

JEANNETTE RANKIN FOUNDATION
(Competitive Awards)
P.O. Box 6653
Athens GA 30604
Written inquiry

AMOUNT: $1000
DEADLINE(S): January 15 (application request); March 1 (application)
FIELD(S): All fields of study (undergraduate & vo-tech)

Open to women aged 35 or older accepted or enrolled in a certified program of vo-tech training or an undergrad program (NOT for grad study or 2nd undergrad degree). US citizenship is required. Financial need is major factor in selection.

Write for complete information. Request application between September 1 & January 15; include business-size SASE labeled "JRF 1996" in the lower left-hand corner & state sex, age, & level of study or training.

961

**JEWISH FAMILY AND CHILDREN'S
SERVICES
(Anna and Charles Stockwitz Children and
Youth Fund)**
    1600 Scott St.
    San Francisco CA 94115
    415/561-1226

AMOUNT: $5000 per year (student loans)
DEADLINE(S): None
FIELD(S): All fields of study

Loans & grants open to undergrads who are
    US citizens of the Jewish faith age 25 or
    less. Must reside in San Francisco, San
    Mateo, Santa Clara, Marin, or Sonoma
    County. Loan repayment is flexible; interest
    is approx. 80% of current prime.
Grant applicants must demonstrate financial
    need. Loan applicants must show ability to
    repay. Contact local JFCS office for com-
    plete information.

962

**JEWISH FAMILY AND CHILDREN'S
SERVICES
(College Loan Fund)**
    1600 Scott St.
    San Francisco CA 94115
    415/561-1226

AMOUNT: $5000 maximum (student loan)
DEADLINE(S): None
FIELD(S): All fields of study

Open to worthy college students of the Jewish
    faith with limited resources but with a
    demonstrated ability to repay. Must be US
    citizen residing in San Francisco, San
    Mateo, Santa Clara, Marin, or Sonoma
    County.
Guarantors or co-makers are required but not
    collateral. Repayment terms flexible; inter-
    est usually set at 80% of current prime rate.
    Contact local JFCS office for forms and
    complete information.

963

**JEWISH FAMILY AND CHILDREN'S
SERVICES
(Fogel Loan Fund)**
    1600 Scott St.
    San Francisco CA 94115
    415/561-1226

AMOUNT: Varies
DEADLINE(S): None
FIELD(S): All fields of study

Loans to help individuals of all ages for col-
    lege or vocational studies and for personal,
    business, or professional purposes.
    Applicant must be a US citizen of Jewish
    faith and have a sound plan for repayment.
Should be resident of San Francisco, San
    Mateo, Santa Clara, Marin, or Sonoma
    County. Guarantor or co-makers required
    but no collateral is needed. Contact JFCS
    office for complete information.

964

**JEWISH FAMILY AND CHILDREN'S
SERVICES
(Jacob Rassen Memorial Scholarship Fund)**
    1600 Scott St.
    San Francisco CA 94115
    415/561-1226

AMOUNT: Up to $2000
DEADLINE(S): None
FIELD(S): Study trip to Israel

Open to Jewish students under age 22 who
    demonstrate academic achievement &
    financial need; desire to enhance Jewish
    identity and increase knowledge of & con-
    nection to Israel. Must be USA citizen.
Must reside in San Francisco; San Mateo;
    Santa Clara; Marin or Sonoma County CA.
    Contact local JFCS office for forms and
    complete information.

965

JEWISH FAMILY AND CHILDREN'S SERVICES
(Stanley Olson Youth Scholarship Fund)
1600 Scott St.
San Francisco CA 94115
415/561-1226

AMOUNT: Up to $2500
DEADLINE(S): None
FIELD(S): All fields of study (preference to liberal arts majors)

Open to undergrad or grad students of Jewish faith who are 25 or younger, have demonstrated academic achievement and financial need, and have been accepted for enrollment in a college or university. Must be USA citizen.
Must reside in San Francisco, San Mateo, Santa Clara, Marin, or Sonoma County CA. Contact local JFCS office for applications and complete information.

966

JEWISH FAMILY AND CHILDREN'S SERVICES
(Vivienne Camp College Scholarship Fund)
1600 Scott St.
San Francisco CA 94115
415/561-1226

AMOUNT: $5000 per year
DEADLINE(S): None
FIELD(S): All fields of study

Open to students of Jewish faith for undergrad or vocational study. Must be US citizen & have demonstrated academic achievement, financial need, broad-based extra-curricular activities, and community involvement.
Must have been accepted to a California college or vocational school and reside in San Francisco, San Mateo, Santa Clara, Marin, or Sonoma County. Contact local JFCS office for forms and complete information.

967

JEWISH SOCIAL SERVICE AGENCY OF METROPOLITAN WASHINGTON
(Loan Fund)
6123 Montrose Road
Rockville MD 20852
301/881-3700

AMOUNT: Up to $2000
DEADLINE(S): June 1
FIELD(S): All fields of study

Open to Jewish applicants 18 or older who are within two years of completing an undergraduate or graduate degree or a vocational training program and are residents of the Washington metropolitan area. No interest loan; one time award.
US citzen or permanent resident who will seek citizenship. Write for complete information.

968

JEWISH SOCIAL SERVICE AGENCY OF METROPOLITAN WASHINGTON
(Undergraduate Scholarship Fund)
6123 Montrose Road
Rockville MD 20852
301/881-3700

AMOUNT: Up to $3500/year
DEADLINE(S): June 1
FIELD(S): All fields of study

Open to Jewish undergraduates no older than 30 who are enrolled in an accredited undergraduate four-year degree program and are from the Washington metropolitan area. Special consideration is given to refugees.
Renewable. Awards based on financial need. Write for complete information.

969

JEWISH SOCIAL SERVICE AGENCY OF METROPOLITAN WASHINGTON
(Irene Stambler Vocational Opportunities Grant Program)
6123 Montrose Road
Rockville MD 20852
301/881-3700

AMOUNT: Up to $2500
DEADLINE(S): None
FIELD(S): All fields of study

Open to Jewish women who are residents of the Washington metropolitan area and need to improve their earning power because of divorce, separation, or death of their spouses.

Grants may be used to complete an educational or vocational program or start or expand a small business. Write for complete information.

970

JOHNSON AND WALES UNIVERSITY
(Gaebe Eagle Scout Scholarships)
8 Abbot Place
Providence RI 02903
401/456-1000

AMOUNT: $300
DEADLINE(S): April 30
FIELD(S): All fields of study

Open to undergraduate freshmen who have been accepted at Johnson and Wales University. Must be Eagle Scout who has received the religious award of his faith.

All eligible freshmen receive award of $300. Write for complete information.

971

JOHNSON CONTROLS FOUNDATION
(Scholarship Program)
5757 N. Green Bay Ave.
Box 591
Milwaukee WI 53201
414/228-2296

AMOUNT: $1750 per year ($7000 over 4 yrs.)
DEADLINE(S): February 1
FIELD(S): All areas of study

Eligibility for scholarships limited to children of employees of Johnson Controls Inc. Must be in upper 30% of high school graduating class and must maintain standards in college for renewal. Scholarships for full-time study only.

US citizenship required. Write for complete information.

972

JUNIATA COLLEGE
(Frederick & Mary F. Beckley Scholarship Fund for Needy "Left-handed" Freshmen)
Financial Aid Office
Huntingdon PA 16652
814/643-4310

AMOUNT: $700 to $1000
DEADLINE(S): None
FIELD(S): All fields of study

Awards are open to needy left-handed students who have junior or senior standing at Juniata College.

Write for complete information.

973

JUNIOR LEAGUE OF NORTHERN VIRGINIA
(Scholarships)
7921 Jones Branch Dr. #320
McLean VA 22102
703/893-0258

AMOUNT: $500 to $2000
DEADLINE(S): December 1
FIELD(S): All fields of study

Open to women who are 23 years old or more & accepted to or enrolled in an accredited college or university as an undergraduate or graduate student. Must be resident of Northern Virginia, US citizen, and demonstrate financial need.

8–10 awards per year. Write for complete information.

974

KANSAS AMERICAN LEGION
(Scholarships)
1314 SW Topeka Blvd.
Topeka KS 66612
Written inquiry

AMOUNT: $150–$1000
DEADLINE(S): February 15; July 15
FIELD(S): All fields of study

Variety of scholarships and awards for Kansas residents to attend Kansas colleges, universities, or trade schools. Some are limited to Legion members and/or designated fields of study.
Write for complete information.

975

KANSAS BOARD OF REGENTS
(Kansas Tuition Grant)
700 SW Harrison; Suite 1410
Topeka KS 66603
913/296-3517

AMOUNT: Up to $900
DEADLINE(S): March 15
FIELD(S): All fields of study

Grants open ONLY to Kansas residents who are full-time undergraduate students at eligible Kansas independent colleges & universities. US citizenship required. Financial need is a consideration.
3600 grants per year. Renewable. Write for complete information.

976

KANSAS COMMISSION ON VETERANS' AFFAIRS
(Scholarships)
700 SW Jackson St. #701
Topeka KS 66603
913/296-3976

AMOUNT: Free tuition and fees in state-supported institutions
DEADLINE(S): Prior to enrollment
FIELD(S): All areas of study

Open to dependent child of person who entered USA military service as a resident of Kansas & was prisoner of war, missing or killed in action, or died as a result of service-connected disabilities incurred during service in Vietnam.
Renewable to maximum of 12 semesters. Write for complete information.

977

KENTUCKY CENTER FOR VETERANS AFFAIRS
(Benefits for Veterans & Their Dependents)
545 S. 3rd St.; Room 123
Louisville KY 40202
501/595-4447

AMOUNT: Varies
DEADLINE(S): None
FIELD(S): All fields of study

Kentucky residents. Open to dependent children, spouses, & non-remarried widows of permanently & totally disabled war veterans who served during periods of federally recognized hostilities or who were MIA or a POW.
Veteran must be a resident of KY or—if deceased—a resident at time of death.

978

KENTUCKY HIGHER EDUCATION ASSISTANCE AUTHORITY
(College Access Program [CAP] Grant)
1050 US-127 South
Frankfort KY 40601
502/564-7990

AMOUNT: $246 to $490 per semester
DEADLINE(S): March 15 priority date
FIELD(S): All fields of study

Open to Kentucky residents who are US citizens or legal residents enrolled or planning to enroll at least half-time in a 2- or 4-year undergrad (or vo-tech) program at an eligible Kentucky institution.

Renewable with reapplication. Write for complete information.

979

KENTUCKY HIGHER EDUCATION ASSISTANCE AUTHORITY
(Student Loan Program)
1050 US-127 South; Suite 102
Frankfort KY 40601-4323
502/564-7990 or 800/928-8926

AMOUNT: $2625 to $18,500 (amount varies according to academic standing and whether student is dependent or independent)

DEADLINE(S): Varies

FIELD(S): All fields of study

Open to US citizens or legal residents enrolled or accepted for enrollment (on at least a half-time basis) at an eligible post-secondary educational institution.

Write for complete information.

980

KNIGHTS OF COLUMBUS
(Educational Trust Fund)
P.O. Drawer 1670
New Haven CT 06507
203/772-2130 ext. 332

AMOUNT: Varies

DEADLINE(S): None specified

FIELD(S): All fields of study

Open to children of KC members who died in military service or became totally and permanently disabled from causes directly connected with a period of conflict or from duties as a policeman or fireman.

Must attend a Catholic college. Unspecified number of awards per year. Write for complete information.

981

KNIGHTS OF COLUMBUS
(Pro Deo & Pro Patria Scholarships)
P.O. Drawer 1670
New Haven CT 06507
203/772-2130 ext. 332

AMOUNT: $1500

DEADLINE(S): March 1

FIELD(S): All fields of study

Open to students enrolling in a Catholic college who can show evidence of satisfactory academic performance. Must be a member or dependent of a Knights of Columbus member in good standing or of a deceased member.

62 scholarships per year; 50 at any Catholic college and 12 at the Catholic University of America in Washington DC. Renewable up to 4 years.

982

KNIGHTS OF COLUMBUS
(Squires Scholarship Program)
P.O. Drawer 1670
New Haven CT 06507
203/772-2130

AMOUNT: $1500

DEADLINE(S): March 1

FIELD(S): All areas of study

Open to students entering their freshman year at a Catholic college who are members in good standing of the Columbian squires and have demonstrated academic excellence.

Renewable up to four years. Write for complete information.

983

KNIGHTS TEMPLAR EDUCATIONAL FOUNDATION
(Special Low-Interest Loans)
5097 N. Elston; Suite 101
Chicago IL 60630
312/777-3300

AMOUNT: $6000 maximum per student

DEADLINE(S): Varies

FIELD(S): All fields of study

Special low-interest loans (5% fixed rate). No payments while in school. Repayments start after graduation or when you leave school. Open to vo-tech students or junior/senior undergraduate students or graduate students.

US citizen or legal resident. Request information from Charles R. Neumann (Grand Recorder-Secretary). Call or write to your local state chapter for proper application.

984

LEAGUE OF UNITED LATIN AMERICAN CITIZENS
(LULAC National Scholarship Fund)
2100 M Street NW; #602
Washington DC 20037
Written inquiry

AMOUNT: $200 and up

DEADLINE(S): None specified

FIELD(S): All fields of study

Open to high school graduates of Hispanic origin who are enrolled in an undergraduate college or university. Open to students residing in states in which LULAC councils exist.

See high school counselor or send self-addressed stamped envelope for complete information.

985

LEONARD H. BULKELEY SCHOLARSHIP FUND
(Scholarship Grants)
c/o R. N. Woodworth; Treasurer
17 Crocker St.
New London CT 06320
203/442-6291

AMOUNT: $1000 (approximately)

DEADLINE(S): April 1

FIELD(S): All fields of study

Open ONLY to residents of New London CT for undergraduate study in an accredited college or university. Must demonstrate financial need.

Write for complete information.

986

LEOPOLD SCHEPP FOUNDATION
(Undergraduate Awards)
551 Fifth Ave.
New York NY 10106
212/986-3078

AMOUNT: Varies

DEADLINE(S): June 1–December 31

FIELD(S): All fields of study

Undergraduates should write detailing their education to date, year in school, length of course of study, vocational goal, financial need, age, citizenship, college choice, and availability for interview in New York City.

Approximately 75 new awards per year with another 75 renewals. Applicants should already be in college and not older than 30. High school seniors may NOT apply. Print or type name and address. Send SASE for info.

987

LLOYD D. SWEET SCHOLARSHIP FOUNDATION
(Scholarships)
Box 217 (c/o Mrs. Betty Sprinkle)
Chinook MT 59523
406/357-3374

AMOUNT: Varies

DEADLINE(S): March 2

FIELD(S): All fields of study

Scholarships open to graduates of Chinook (MT) High School. Awards are for full-time undergraduate or graduate study at accredited colleges and universities in the USA.

Approximately 100 awards per year. Write for complete information.

988

**LOUISIANA DEPT. OF VETERANS
AFFAIRS**
(Awards Program)
P.O. Box 94095; Capitol Station
Baton Rouge LA 70804
504/922-0500; FAX 504/922-0511

AMOUNT: Varies
DEADLINE(S): Varies
FIELD(S): All fields of study

Louisiana resident. Open to children (aged
16–25) & widows/spouses of deceased/dis-
abled (100%) war veterans who were
Louisiana residents for at least 1 year prior
to service. For undergraduate study at state-
supported schools in Louisiana.

Approximately 200 awards per year.
Renewable up to 4 years. Write for complete information.

989

**LOUISIANA OFFICE OF STUDENT
FINANCIAL ASSISTANCE**
(Scholarship, Grant, & Loan Programs)
P.O. Box 91202
Baton Rouge LA 70821-9202
504/922-1011; FAX 504/922-1089

AMOUNT: Varies
DEADLINE(S): April 1
FIELD(S): All fields of study

Various programs for undergraduate or graduate study administered by the LSFA open
to Louisiana residents. Some programs
based on financial need; others on academic
standing and/or specific programs of study.

Check with high school counselor or write for
complete information.

990

LUTHERAN BROTHERHOOD
(Scholarships)
625 Fourth Ave. South
Minneapolis MN 55415
800/328-7168

AMOUNT: $800–$1500
DEADLINE(S): February 12
FIELD(S): All fields of study

Undergraduate scholarships open to Lutheran
Brotherhood members. Recipients are chosen by an independent panel of judges on
basis of scholastic achievement (minimum
high school GPA of 3.5), school & community involvement, & future plans.

$500 award for public school; $1000 award for
private non-Lutheran school; $2000 award
for Lutheran school. Renewable. Write for
complete information.

991

LUTHERAN BROTHERHOOD
(Stafford Student Loans)
625 Fourth Ave. South
Minneapolis MN 55415
800/328-7168

AMOUNT: $2650–$7500
DEADLINE(S): None
FIELD(S): All fields of study

Loans open to Lutheran students on a first-
come first-served basis who have been
accepted for admission by an eligible higher
education institution and are making satisfactory progress. Must meet federal requirements.

Contact address above for complete information.

992

**MAINE BUREAU OF VETERAN
SERVICES**
(Grants for Dependents)
State House; Station 117
Augusta ME 04333
207/626-4464

AMOUNT: Free tuition at state-supported
Maine schools
DEADLINE(S): None
FIELD(S): All fields of study

Maine residents. Undergraduate grants for children aged 17–21 and spouses or widows of military veterans who are totally disabled due to service or who died in service. US citizen or legal resident.

Veteran must have lived in Maine at time of entering service or for 5 years prior to application. Students in private schools can receive up to $300 per year. Renewable for 8 semesters. Write for complete information.

993

MAINE EDUCATION ASSISTANCE DIVISION—FINANCE AUTHORITY OF MAINE
(Scholarships)
State House Station #119
Augusta ME 04333
207/289-2183

AMOUNT: $500 (public institutions); $1000 (private)
DEADLINE(S): May 1
FIELD(S): All fields of study

Open to Maine residents attending regionally accredited colleges in AK, CT, DC, DE, MA, MD, NH, PA, RI, or VT. Awards are for full-time undergraduate study.

8000 awards per year. Application is the Maine Financial Aid form available in college financial aid office.

994

MAKARIOS SCHOLARSHIP FUND INC.
(Scholarships)
13 East 40th Street
New York NY 10016
212/696-4590

AMOUNT: $1000 flexible
DEADLINE(S): May 31
FIELD(S): All areas of study

Open to students of Cypriot heritage. Awards support full-time undergraduate or graduate study at accredited colleges or universities in the US. Must demonstrate financial need. Must be resident of Cyprus with a student visa & study full-time.

Number of awards flexible; write for complete information.

995

MARIN EDUCATIONAL FUND
(Undergraduate Scholarship Program)
1010 'B' St.; Suite 300
San Rafael CA 94901
415/459-4240

AMOUNT: $500–$2000
DEADLINE(S): March 2
FIELD(S): All fields of study

Open to Marin County (CA) residents for undergraduate study in 2- or 4-year colleges; and fifth year teaching credentials. Must be enrolled at least half time and demonstrate financial need.
Write for complete information.

996

MARION BURK KNOTT SCHOLARSHIP FUND
(Scholarships)
c/o St. Mary's Seminary & University
540 Roland Ave.
Baltimore MD 21210
410/323-4300

AMOUNT: Full tuition
DEADLINE(S): None specified
FIELD(S): All fields of study

Open to Catholic students to attend parish elementary or Catholic secondary school in Baltimore (city) or the counties of Baltimore, Carroll, Frederick, Harford, or Howard; or one of the 3 Catholic colleges in Maryland.

Student involvement in church, school, and community taken into account. Send business sized self-addressed stamped envelope for information.

997

MARQUETTE UNIVERSITY
(South African Scholarship Program)
Alumni Memorial Union 425
Milwaukee WI 53233
414/288-7289

AMOUNT: Tuition + lab fees & special course fees
DEADLINE(S): March 15
FIELD(S): All areas of undergraduate study

One award to non-white South African citizen who can meet the admission requirements for academic, personal, & English language abilities. Must have financial sponsor for living expenses.

The maximum duration of any scholarship is normally four calendar years with the duration reduced proportionately for students who receive transfer credit.

998

MARTIN LUTHER KING JR.
SCHOLARSHIP FOUNDATION
(Scholarships)
P.O. Box 751
Portland OR 97207
503/229-3000

AMOUNT: Full tuition
DEADLINE(S): July 31 (Fall); December 2 (Winter); March 3 (Spring)
FIELD(S): All areas of study

Open to students at all levels of study who reside in Oregon and plan to attend or already attend an Oregon school. A GPA of 3.0 or better and proof of admission to a post-secondary institution required.
Write for complete information.

999

MARY M. AARON MEMORIAL TRUST
1190 Civic Center Blvd.
Yuba City CA 95997
Written inquiry

AMOUNT: Approximately $375 to $750
DEADLINE(S): March 15
FIELD(S): All areas of study

Open to any needy student from Sutter County CA attending an accredited 2-year (approx. $375) or 4-year (approx. $750) California college or university. Grants based on financial need. Grades & activities are not considered.
Write for complete information.

1000

MARYLAND HIGHER EDUCATION
COMMISSION
(Distinguished Scholar Awards)
State Scholarship Administration
16 Francis St.
Annapolis MD 21401
410/974-5370

AMOUNT: $3000
DEADLINE(S): Apply in spring of junior year in high school
FIELD(S): All fields of study

Open to Maryland high school students who are National Merit or achievement finalists. Additional awards given to academically gifted or talented students. For undergraduate study in Maryland.

Renewable up to 4 years. Distinguished scholar winners who wish to be teachers are also eligible for $3000 teacher education scholarships. Contact high school counselor or address above for details.

1001

MARYLAND HIGHER EDUCATION
COMMISSION
(Educational Assistance Grant)
State Scholarship Administration
16 Francis St.
Annapolis MD 21401-1781
410/974-5370

AMOUNT: $200–$3000
DEADLINE(S): March 1
FIELD(S): All areas of study

Open to Maryland residents for full-time undergraduate study at a Maryland degree-granting institution or hospital school of nursing. Financial need must be demonstrated.

Renewable with reapplication for up to 3 years. Write for complete information.

1002

MARYLAND HIGHER EDUCATION COMMISSION

(Edward T. Conroy Memorial Scholarships)
State Scholarship Administration
16 Francis St.
Annapolis MD 21401
410/974-5370

AMOUNT: Up to $3480 for tuition & mandatory fees
DEADLINE(S): July 15
FIELD(S): All fields of study

Open to dependent children of persons 100% disabled or killed in the line of military duty who were Maryland residents at the time of disability or death, and to dependent children of MIAs or POWs of the Vietnam conflict. US citizen.

For undergraduate or graduate study; full or part time. Write for complete information.

1003

MARYLAND HIGHER EDUCATION COMMISSION

(House of Delegate Scholarships)
State Scholarship Administration
16 Francis St.
Annapolis MD 21401-1781
410/974-5370

AMOUNT: Varies—$200 minimum
DEADLINE(S): Established by individual delegates
FIELD(S): All fields of study

Open to Maryland residents who are undergraduate or graduate students in Maryland (or out-of-state with a unique major). Must be US citizen or legal resident and live in district of member of House of Delegates.

Duration is up to 4 years; 2–4 scholarships per district. Also for full- or part-time study at certain private career schools and diploma schools of nursing. Write to your delegate for complete information.

1004

MARYLAND HIGHER EDUCATION COMMISSION

(Senatorial Scholarship Program)
State Scholarship Administration
16 Francis St.
Annapolis MD 21401
410/974-5370

AMOUNT: $400–$2000
DEADLINE(S): March 1
FIELD(S): All fields of study

Open to Maryland residents for undergrad study at MD degree-granting institutions, certain private career schools, & nursing diploma schools in Maryland. For full- or part-time study. SAT or ACT required.

Students with unique majors or with impaired hearing may attend out of state. Duration is 1–4 years with automatic renewal until degree is granted. Write for complete information.

1005

MASSACHUSETTS COMPANY
(The M. Geneva Gray Scholarship Fund)
Trust Dept.
125 High St.
Boston MA 02110
617/556-2335

AMOUNT: Up to $1000
DEADLINE(S): April 15
FIELD(S): All fields of study

Open to undergraduate students who are MA residents and are unable to qualify for scholarships due to parental or individual income limitations or are unable to complete their education because of lack of finances.

Candidates from middle-income families ($25,000–$50,000) with several children to be educated are favored. There are no academic requirements other than enrollment and good standing. Write for complete information.

1006

MASSACHUSETTS HIGHER EDUCATION COORDINATING COUNCIL
(Public Service Grant)
Office of Student Financial Assistance
330 Stuart St.; 3rd Floor
Boston MA 02116
617/727-9420

AMOUNT: Varies with school (covers tuition; not fees)
DEADLINE(S): May 1
FIELD(S): All fields of study

Open to permanent Massachusetts residents aged 17–23 whose parent or spouse died (POW/MIA included) during military service or during service as a police officer, firefighter, or correctional officer (while a resident of Massachusetts).
Write for complete information.

1007

MASSACHUSETTS HIGHER EDUCATION COORDINATING COUNCIL
(General Scholarship Program)
330 Stuart Street; 3rd Floor
Boston MA 02116
617/727-9420

AMOUNT: $250–$2500
DEADLINE(S): May 1
FIELD(S): All fields of study

Open to permanent residents of Massachusetts. Awards are for undergraduate study at accredited colleges and universities in Massachusetts.
40,000-50,000 awards per year. Write for complete information.

1008

MASSACHUSETTS OFFICE OF STUDENT FINANCIAL ASSISTANCE
(National Guard Educational Assistance Scholarship Program)
330 Stuart Street; 3rd Floor
Boston MA 02116
617/727-9420

AMOUNT: Tuition waiver
DEADLINE(S): None
FIELD(S): All areas of study

Program open to undergraduate students who are enrolled at a Massachusetts public college or university & are active members of the Massachusetts National Guard or the Massachusetts Air National Guard.
Contact the veterans office at your college or address above for complete information.

1009

MASSACHUSETTS SCHOLARSHIP OFFICE
(Veterans Tuition Exemption Program)
330 Stuart Street; 3rd Floor
Boston MA 02116
617/727-9420

AMOUNT: Tuition exemption
DEADLINE(S): None
FIELD(S): All areas of study

Open to military veterans who are permanent residents of Massachusetts. Awards are tenable at Massachusetts post-secondary institutions.
Contact veterans agent at college or address above for complete information.

1010

MCCURDY MEMORIAL SCHOLARSHIP FOUNDATION
(Emily Scofield Scholarship Fund)
134 West Van Buren Street
Battle Creek MI 49017
616/962-9591

AMOUNT: $100–$1000

DEADLINE(S): March 31

FIELD(S): All areas of study

Scholarships for residents of Calhoun County, Michigan. Must be undergraduate.

4–5 scholarships per year. Renewable with reapplication and satisfactory grades. Write for complete information.

1011

MCCURDY MEMORIAL SCHOLARSHIP FOUNDATION
(McCurdy Scholarship)
134 West Van Buren Street
Battle Creek MI 49017
616/962-9591

AMOUNT: $1000

DEADLINE(S): March 31

FIELD(S): All fields of study

Must be a resident of Calhoun County, Michigan. Program is for undergraduate students.

7 scholarships per year. Renewable with reapplication and satisfactory grades. Write for complete information.

1012

MERCANTILE BANK OF TOPEKA
(Claude & Ina Brey Memorial Endowment Fund)
c/o Trust Dept.
P.O. Box 192
Topeka KS 66601
913/291-1118

AMOUNT: $500

DEADLINE(S): April 15

FIELD(S): All fields of study

Scholarships open to fourth degree Kansas grange members. Awards tenable at recognized undergraduate colleges & universities. US citizen.

8 awards per year. Renewable. For complete information write to Marlene Bush; P.O. Box 186; Melvern KS 66510.

1013

MEXICAN AMERICAN BUSINESS AND PROFESSIONAL SCHOLARSHIP ASSOCIATION
(Scholarship Program)
P.O. Box 22292
Los Angeles CA 90022
Written inquiry only

AMOUNT: $100–$1000

DEADLINE(S): May 1 (postmark)

FIELD(S): All fields of study

Open to Los Angeles County residents who are of Mexican-American descent and are enrolled full-time in an undergraduate program. Awards are based on financial need and past academic performance.

Write for complete information.

1014

MICHIGAN COMMISSION ON INDIAN AFFAIRS; MICHIGAN DEPT. OF CIVIL RIGHTS
(Tuition Waiver Program)
P.O. Box 30026
Lansing MI 48909
517/373-0654

AMOUNT: Tuition (only) waiver

DEADLINE(S): 8 weeks prior to class registration

FIELD(S): All areas

Open to any Michigan resident who is at least 1/4 North American Indian (certified by their tribal nation) & willing to attend any public Michigan community college, college, or university.

Award is for all levels of study and is renewable. Must be Michigan resident for at least 12 months before class registration. Write for complete information.

1015

MICHIGAN DEPT. OF EDUCATION
(Michigan Competitive Scholarships)

Student Financial Assistance Services
P.O. Box 30008
Lansing MI 48909
517/373-3394

AMOUNT: $100–$1200

DEADLINE(S): February 15 for freshmen

FIELD(S): All fields of study/Michigan residents

Open to USA citizens who have lived in Michigan at least a year and are enrolled at least half time in an eligible Michigan college. Must demonstrate financial need and submit ACT scores.

Scholarships renewable. Fact sheets are available from high school counselors. Write for complete information.

1016

MICHIGAN DEPT. OF EDUCATION
(Michigan Tuition Grants)

Student Financial Assistance Services
P.O. Box 30008
Lansing MI 48909
517/373-3394

AMOUNT: $100–$1900

DEADLINE(S): Varies

FIELD(S): All fields of study (except BRE degree)

Open to Michigan residents enrolled at least half time at independent non-profit Michigan institutions (List available from above address). Both undergraduate and graduate students who can demonstrate financial need are eligible.

Grants renewable. Write for complete information.

1017

MICHIGAN GUARANTY AGENCY
(Stafford; SLS; PLUS Loans)

P.O. Box 30047
Lansing MI 48909
517/373-0760

AMOUNT: Up to $8500

DEADLINE(S): None specified

FIELD(S): All fields of study

Guaranteed student loans available to students or parents of students who are enrolled in an eligible institution.
Write for complete information.

1018

MICHIGAN VETERANS TRUST FUND
(Tuition Grants Program)

611 West Ottawa; 3rd Floor
Lansing MI 48913
517/335-1629

AMOUNT: Tuition

DEADLINE(S): None

FIELD(S): All areas of study

Open to Michigan residents of at least 12 months preceding enrollment who are aged 16–22 and are the child of a Michigan veteran killed in action or who later died or was totally disabled due to a service-connected cause.

Grants are for undergraduate study at Michigan tax-supported schools. Write for complete information.

1019

MILITARY ORDER OF THE PURPLE HEART
(Sons, Daughters, & Grandchildren Scholarship Program)

National Headquarters
5413-B Backlick Rd.
Springfield VA 22151
703/642-5360

AMOUNT: $1000 per year (4 years maximum)

DEADLINE(S): June 15

FIELD(S): All fields of study

Open to children & grandchildren of Military Order of Purple Heart Members or Purple Heart Recipients. For full-time study at any level by US citizen or legal resident. Must demonstrate academic achievement and financial need.

Renewable for up to 4 years provided a 2.5 GPA is maintained. Write for complete information.

1020

MINNESOTA CHIPPEWA TRIBE
(Scholarship Fund)
P.O. Box 217
Cass Lake MN 56633
218/335-8584

AMOUNT: Up to $3000

DEADLINE(S): June 1

FIELD(S): All fields of study

Open to enrolled members of the Minnesota Chippewa Tribe and those eligible for enrollment. Awards are tenable at recognized undergraduate and graduate institutions. US citizenship required.

Approximately 850 awards per year. Write for complete information.

1021

MINNESOTA HIGHER EDUCATION COORDINATING BOARD
(Grants)
Capitol Square Bldg.; Suite 400
550 Cedar St.
St. Paul MN 55101
612/296-3974

AMOUNT: $100–$5889

DEADLINE(S): May 31

FIELD(S): All fields of study

Open to Minnesota residents to attend eligible MN colleges & universities. Candidates may not hold 4-year degree or have attended college for 4 years, may not be in default on

a student loan, or delinquent in child support payments.

65,000 awards per year. Write for complete information.

1022

MINNESOTA STATE DEPARTMENT OF VETERANS AFFAIRS
(Deceased Veterans' Dependents Scholarships)
Veterans Service Bldg.; Benefits Div.
St. Paul MN 55155-2079
612/296-2562

AMOUNT: Tuition + $350

DEADLINE(S): None

FIELD(S): All areas of study

Open to 2-year (or more) residents of MN who are sons/daughters of veterans killed or who died as a result of a service-caused condition. Parent must have been a resident of MN at time of entry into service. US citizens or legal residents.

Awards tenable at MN undergraduate colleges & universities. Scholarships are renewable up to a bachelor's degree. Write for complete information.

1023

MINNESOTA STATE DEPARTMENT OF VETERANS AFFAIRS
(Veterans Grants)
Veterans Service Bldg.; Benefits Div.
St. Paul MN 55155-2079
612/296-2562

AMOUNT: $350

DEADLINE(S): None

FIELD(S): All areas of study

Open to veterans who were residents of MN at the time of their entry into the armed forces of the US & were honorably discharged after having served on active duty for at least 181 consecutive days. Must be US citizen or legal resident.

Must attend accredited institution in Minnesota & have time remaining on federal education period. Must have exhausted through use any federal educational entitlement. Financial need must be demonstrated. Write for complete information.

1024

MINNIE PEARL SCHOLARSHIP PROGRAM
2000 Church St.; Box 111
Nashville TN 37236
800/545-HEAR (Voice/TDD)

AMOUNT: $2000 (or amount of tuition; whichever is less)
DEADLINE(S): February 15
FIELD(S): All fields of study

Open to mainstream high school seniors with a significant bi-lateral hearing loss, a 3.0 or better GPA, & who are enrolled in or have been accepted by an accredited college, university, or tech school. For full-time study. US citizens only.

Number of awards varies each year. Renewable throughout college career. Write for complete information.

1025

MISSISSIPPI BOARD OF TRUSTEES OF STATE INSTITUTIONS OF HIGHER LEARNING
(Law Enforcement Officers and Firemen Scholarship Program)
3825 Ridgewood Rd.
Jackson MS 39211
601/982-6570

AMOUNT: Tuition; room; required fees
DEADLINE(S): None specified
FIELD(S): All areas of study

Open to children, step-children, or spouse of Mississippi law enforcement officers or full-time firemen who were fatally injured or were totally disabled while on duty. Children must be under age 23.

Tuition-free scholarships for 8 semesters at any state-supported college or university in Mississippi. Write for complete information.

1026

MISSISSIPPI BOARD OF TRUSTEES OF STATE INSTITUTIONS OF HIGHER LEARNING
(Southeast Asia POW/MIA Scholarship Program)
3825 Ridgewood Rd.
Jackson MS 39211
601/982-6570

AMOUNT: Tuition; room; required fees
DEADLINE(S): None specified
FIELD(S): All areas of study

Open to dependent children of military veterans formerly or currently listed as missing in action in Southeast Asia or as prisoners of war as a result of military action against the US Naval Vessel Pueblo.

Tuition-free scholarships for 8 semesters at any state-supported Mississippi college or university. Write for complete information.

1027

MISSOURI COORDINATING BOARD FOR HIGHER EDUCATION
(Missouri Student Grant Program)
3515 Amazonas Dr.
P.O. Box 6730
Jefferson City MO 65102
314/751-3940

AMOUNT: $100 to $1500
DEADLINE(S): January 1 to April 30
FIELD(S): All fields of study

Undergraduate grants open to Missouri residents who are US citizens attending a Missouri school. Missouri FFS or FAF required.

8300 grants per year. Write for complete information.

1028

MISSOURI COORDINATING BOARD FOR HIGHER EDUCATION
(Missouri Guaranteed Student Loan Program)
P.O. Box 6730
Jefferson City MO 65102
314/751-3940

AMOUNT: Up to $23,000 (total) for undergraduate study; $8500 per year for graduate students to a maximum of $65,000 (both undergrad & grad)

DEADLINE(S): By end of academic period

FIELD(S): All fields of study

Open to Missouri residents or students attending school in Missouri. US citizenship or legal residency required.

Write for complete information.

1029

MISSOURI COORDINATING BOARD FOR HIGHER EDUCATION
(Higher Education Academic Scholarship Program)
3515 Amazonas Dr.
P.O. Box 6730
Jefferson City MO 65102
314/751-3940

AMOUNT: $2000

DEADLINE(S): June 1

FIELD(S): All fields of study

Undergraduate scholarships for Missouri residents who are US citizens. Must be high school graduate accepted or enrolled full-time as an undergraduate & have a composite ACT or SAT score in top 3% for Missouri schools.

Renewable yearly as an undergraduate. Write for complete information.

1030

MOBIL CORPORATION
(Desert Storm Scholarship Program)
3225 Gallows Road
Fairfax VA 22037-0001
Written inquiry only

AMOUNT: Varies

DEADLINE(S): Varies with institution

FIELD(S): All fields of study

Open to veterans of Operation Desert Shield/Desert Storm, their spouses, & children. The spouses & children of those who died in the operations receive highest priority. For full-time undergraduate study leading to a bachelor's degree.

Scholarships are renewable and available at 20 US colleges and universities. Financial need is a consideration. Write for list of participating schools and complete information.

1031

MODERN WOODMEN OF AMERICA
(Fraternal College Scholarship Program)
1701 First Avenue
Rock Island IL 61201
Written inquiry only

AMOUNT: $500–$2000

DEADLINE(S): January 1

FIELD(S): All fields of study

Open to high school seniors who have been beneficial members of Modern Woodmen for at least two years and are in the upper half of their graduating class. For use at any accredited four-year college in the USA.

36 awards per year, renewable for four years. Write for complete information.

1032

MONTANA UNIVERSITY SYSTEM
(Indian Fees Waiver Program)
2500 Broadway
P.O. Box 203101
Helena MT 59620
406/444-6594

AMOUNT: Waiver of registration and incidental fees

DEADLINE(S): None

FIELD(S): All fields of study

One-fourth or more Indian blood & Montana residency for at least 1 year before enrolling in Montana University System required. Financial need must be demonstrated.

Each unit of the Montana University System makes its own rules governing selection. 500 waivers per year. Write for complete information.

1033

MONTANA UNIVERSITY SYSTEM
(Montana Guaranteed Student Loan Program)
2500 Broadway
P.O. Box 203101
Helena MT 59620-3101
406/444-6594

AMOUNT: $2625–$4000 per year undergrads; $7500 per year grads
DEADLINE(S): None
FIELD(S): All fields of study

The MGSLP is not a lender; it does not make loans to students. Rather it guarantees their loans which are made by regular lending institutions such as banks, or Savings and Loan Assns. Must demonstrate financial need.

Must be a resident of Montana attending an eligible Montana school. Write for complete information.

1034

MONTANA UNIVERSITY SYSTEM
(Montana State Student Incentive Grants)
2500 Broadway
P.O. Box 203101
Helena MT 59620
406/444-6594

AMOUNT: UP to $600
DEADLINE(S): None
FIELD(S): All fields of study

Open to Montana residents who are full-time undergraduate students attending accredited schools in Montana. Must demonstrate need.

1150 awards per year. Contact financial aid office of the school you plan to attend as these grants are decentralized.

1035

MOTHER JOSEPH ROGAN
MARYMOUNT FOUNDATION
(Grant Program & Loan Program)
c/o Joseph E. Lynch
2217 Clayville Ct.
Chesterfield MO 63017
314/391-6248

AMOUNT: $400 to $750
DEADLINE(S): May 1
FIELD(S): All areas of study

Grants and loans for students who are US citizens, live in the metropolitan St. Louis area, and are entering or enrolled in a high school; vocational/technical school, college, or university.
Write for complete information.

1036

NAACP NATIONAL OFFICE
(Agnes Jones Jackson Scholarship)
4805 Mt. Hope Dr.
Baltimore MD 21215
401/358-8900

AMOUNT: $1500–$2500
DEADLINE(S): April 30
FIELD(S): All areas of study

Undergraduate ($1500) & graduate ($2500) scholarships open to applicants who have been NAACP members for at least 1 year & will be under the age of 25 on April 30. Minimum GPA of 2.5 high school, 2.0 undergraduate, & 3.0 graduate student.

Send legal size self-addressed stamped envelope to address above for application and complete information.

1037

NATIONAL 4-H COUNCIL
(National 4-H Award Programs)
7100 Connecticut Ave.
Chevy Chase MD 20815
301/961-2904

AMOUNT: $750 to $1500

DEADLINE(S): None specified

FIELD(S): All fields of study

DO NOT USE ADDRESS OR TELE-PHONE ABOVE!!! Contact your LOCAL 4-H agent or state leader for information and applications. Present or former 4-H members are eligible for a multitude of scholarship & award programs for post-secondary education.

The 4-H Digest (a summary of scholarship programs) & national 4-H college scholarship programs checklist should be available from your local or state agent. If not, send self-addressed stamped envelope to address above for details.

1038

NATIONAL AMPUTATION FOUNDATION
(Scholarships)
73 Church St.
Malverne NY 11565
516/887-3600

AMOUNT: $125–$250 per year

DEADLINE(S): None

FIELD(S): All fields of study

Open to any high school senior who is handicapped or an amputee. Awards support undergraduate study at any recognized college or university.

24 awards per year. Write for complete information.

1039

NATIONAL ART MATERIALS TRADE ASSN.
(NAMTA Scholarships)
178 Lakeview Ave.
Clifton NJ 07011
201/546-6400

AMOUNT: Varies

DEADLINE(S): March 15

FIELD(S): Visual arts

Open to NAMTA employees, members, and their relatives, or to individuals in an organization related to Art or the Art materials industry. For undergraduate or graduate study.

Selection based on financial need, grades, activities, interests, and career choice. Write for complete information.

1040

NATIONAL ASSOCIATION OF SECONDARY SCHOOL PRINCIPALS
(National Honor Society Scholarships)
1904 Association Dr.
Reston VA 22091
Inquire of H.S. principal or counselor

AMOUNT: $1000

DEADLINE(S): February 1

FIELD(S): All fields of study

Open to National Honor Society Members. Each chapter nominates two seniors to compete for scholarships at the national level.

250 scholarships per year. Contact your NHS chapter, high school principal, or guidance counselor for complete information.

1041

NATIONAL COUNCIL OF JEWISH WOMEN—GREATER BOSTON SECTION
(Amelia Greenbaum/Rabbi Marshall Lifson Scholarship Program)
831 Beacon St. #138
Newton Centre MA 02159
617/783-9660

AMOUNT: $400 maximum

DEADLINE(S): April 30

FIELD(S): All fields of study

Open to Jewish women who are residents of Boston (or vicinity) & attend a Massachusetts college or university as an undergraduate. Must demonstrate financial need.

Write for complete information.

1042

NATIONAL FEDERATION OF THE BLIND
(Ezra Davis—American Brotherhood for the Blind Scholarship)
814 4th Ave.; Suite #200
Grinnell IA 50112
515/236-3366

AMOUNT: $6000
DEADLINE(S): March 31
FIELD(S): All fields of study

Open to legally blind students pursuing or planning to pursue a full-time post-secondary course of study. Awards are based on academic excellence, community service, and financial need.

Write for complete information.

1043

NATIONAL FEDERATION OF THE BLIND
(Frank Walton Horn Memorial Scholarship)
814 4th Ave,; Suite #200
Grinnell IA 50112
515/236-3366

AMOUNT: $2500
DEADLINE(S): March 31
FIELD(S): All fields of study

Scholarship for legally blind students studying (or planning to study) at any post-secondary level. For all fields of study but preference will be given to architecture and engineering majors.

Awards based on academic excellence, service to the community, and financial need. Write for complete information.

1044

NATIONAL FEDERATION OF THE BLIND
(Hermione Grant Calhoun Scholarships)
814 4th Ave.; Suite #200
Grinnell IA 50112
515/236-3366

AMOUNT: $2000
DEADLINE(S): Mar 31
FIELD(S): All fields of study

Scholarship open to legally blind female undergraduate and graduate students. Awards based on academic excellence, service to the community, and financial need.

Write for complete information.

1045

NATIONAL FEDERATION OF THE BLIND
(Melva T. Owen Memorial Scholarship)
814 4th Ave.; Suite #200
Grinnell IA 50112
515/236-3366

AMOUNT: $2500
DEADLINE(S): March 31
FIELD(S): All fields of study

Open to legally blind students for all post-secondary areas of study directed towards attaining financial independence. Excludes religion and those seeking only to further their general and cultural education.

Awards based on academic excellence, service to the community, and financial need. Write for complete information.

1046

NATIONAL FEDERATION OF THE BLIND
(Scholarships)
814 4th Ave.; Suite #200
Grinnell IA 50112
515/236-3366

AMOUNT: $2000–$4000
DEADLINE(S): March 31
FIELD(S): All fields of study

14 scholarships (2 for $4000 ea; 4 for $2500 ea; 8 for $2000 ea) will be given. Applicants must be legally blind and studying (or planning to study) full time at the post-secondary level.

Awards are on the basis of academic excellence, community service, and financial need. Write for complete information.

1047

NATIONAL FEDERATION OF THE BLIND OF CONNECTICUT
(Scholarships & Awards)
580 Burnside Ave.
East Hartford CT 06108
203/289-1971

AMOUNT: $1250 to $3000
DEADLINE(S): September 15
FIELD(S): All fields of study

For legally blind applicants who are Connecticut residents or non-residents studying in Connecticut. Programs for undergraduate study, vocational-technical training, and personal advancement. Legal US resident.

Write or phone for complete information.

1048

NATIONAL HISPANIC SCHOLARSHIP FUND
(Scholarships)
P.O. Box 728
Novato CA 94948
Written inquiry

AMOUNT: Varies
DEADLINE(S): August 15 October 1
FIELD(S): All fields of study

Open to US citizens or permanent residents of Hispanic parentage enrolled full time as undergraduate or graduate student in USA college or university. Applicants must have completed at least 15 units/credits prior to fall registration.

Community college units must be transferable to a 4-year instutution. Financial need is a consideration. Send business size self-addressed stamped envelope for complete information.

1049

NATIONAL MERIT SCHOLARSHIP CORPORATION
1560 Sherman Ave.; Suite 200
Evanston IL 60201
708/866-5100

AMOUNT: Non-renewable $2000; renewable $250–$2000 (or more)
DEADLINE(S): See PSAT/NMSQT student bulletin
FIELD(S): All areas of study

Open to students who enter the competition for scholarships by taking the PSAT/NMSQT in October of their junior year in high school. US citizenship required.

Scholarship winners are chosen on the basis of abilities, skills, and accomplishments without regard to gender, race, ethnic origin, or religion.

1050

NATIONAL SCIENCE TEACHERS ASSN. SCHOLARSHIP COMPETITION
(Duracell/NSTA Scholarship Competition)
1840 Wison Blvd.
Arlington; VA 22201-3000
703/312-9258

AMOUNT: $100 to $20,000
DEADLINE(S): Jan 15
FIELD(S): All fields of study

Design competition open to all USA high school students who create & build an original working device powered by one or more Duracell batteries. 100 awards given; must be a US citizen or legal resident.

Official entry forms are available from science teachers or by writing to NSTA at the address above. Write for complete information.

1051

NATIONAL SOCIETY OF THE SONS OF THE AMERICAN REVOLUTION
(Eagle Scout Scholarship)
1000 S. Fourth St.
Louisville KY 40203
502/589-1776

AMOUNT: $5000 (1st); $1000 (2nd)
DEADLINE(S): December 31
FIELD(S): All fields of study

Open to the current class of Eagle Scouts who passed their board of review between July 1 & the following June 30 of each year. College plans DO NOT have to be complete in order to receive the cash scholarships.

Contact your local SAR Eagle Scout Chairman for complete information.

1052

NATIONAL TWENTY AND FOUR
(Memorial Scholarships)
c/o Ethel M. Matuschka
6000 Lucerne Ct. #2
Mequon WI 53092
Written Inquiry

AMOUNT: Maximum of $500
DEADLINE(S): May 1
FIELD(S): All areas of study

Open to members & dependents of members between the ages of 16 and 25. Selection is based on financial need, scholastic standing, & school activities.

Write for complete information ONLY if above qualifications are met.

1053

NATIVE SONS OF THE GOLDEN WEST
(Annual High School Public Speaking Contest)
414 Mason St.; Suite 300
San Francisco CA 94102
415/392-1223

AMOUNT: $600–$1600
DEADLINE(S): March 1
FIELD(S): All fields of study

Public speaking competition open to California high school students under age 20. Speeches should be 7–9 minutes in length and may be on any subject related to California's past or present.

District eliminations take place in March and April; finals are in May. Write for complete information.

1054

NAVY SUPPLY CORPS FOUNDATION
(Scholarships)
1425 Prince Ave.
Athens GA 30606-2205
404/354-4111

AMOUNT: $2000
DEADLINE(S): February 15
FIELD(S): All fields of study

Open to children of Navy supply corps officers (including warrant) & supply corps associated enlisted ratings on active duty, in reserve status, retired with pay, or deceased. For undergraduate study at accredited 2-yr/4-yr colleges.

Approx. 50 awards per year. Write for complete information.

1055

NAVY/MARINE CORPS RELIEF SOCIETY
(NMCRS Education Grants)
801 N. Randolph St.; Suite 1228
Arlington VA 22203
202/696-4960

AMOUNT: $2000
DEADLINE(S): None specified
FIELD(S): All fields of study

Undergraduate grants open to unmarried dependent children (under age 23) of US Navy & US Marine Corps personnel who died while on active duty or during retirement after 20+ years of service. US citizen or legal resident.

Renewable. Write for complete information.

1056

NAVY/MARINE CORPS ROTC
(College Scholarships)
801 N. Randolph St.
Arlington VA 22203-1991
Written inquiry

AMOUNT: Tuition; books; fees; $150 per month

DEADLINE(S): December 1

FIELD(S): All fields of study (US Marine Corps Officer)

Open to US citizens between the ages of 17 and 21 who are physically qualified and will have high school diploma by end of August. Must have no qualms about bearing arms and defending the US constitution.

For four years of undergraduate study leading to commission as a reserve officer in the US Navy or Marine Corps. See USN/USMC recruiter or write for complete information.

1057

NEGRO EDUCATIONAL EMERGENCY DRIVE
(NEED Scholarship Program)
643 Liberty Ave.; 17th Floor
Pittsburgh PA 15222
412/566-2760

AMOUNT: $100 to $1000

DEADLINE(S): April 30

FIELD(S): All areas of study

Pennsylvania residency & US citizenship required. Open to Black students with a high school diploma or GED who reside in Allegheny, Armstrong, Beaver, Butler, Washington, or Westmoreland Counties.

400 scholarships per year. Renewable. Write for complete information.

1058

NELLIE MAE
(SHARE; GradSHARE; EXCEL & GradEXCEL Loans)
50 Braintree Hill Park; Suite 300
Braintree MA 02184-1763
617/849-1325 or 800/634-9308

AMOUNT: $2000 to $20,000

DEADLINE(S): None specified

FIELD(S): All fields of study

Variety of loans available for undergraduate and graduate study at accredited degree-granting colleges or universities. Varied repayment and interest rate options. Cumulative maximum loan of $80,000 per student.

Write for complete information.

1059

NEVADA DEPT. OF EDUCATION
(Student Incentive Grant Program)
Capital Complex
400 W. King St.
Carson City NV 89701
702/687-5915

AMOUNT: Up to $5000

DEADLINE(S): None specified

FIELD(S): All fields of study

Student incentive grants available to Nevada residents enrolled in eligible Nevada institutions.

Application must be made through the financial aid office of eligible participating institutions.

1060

NEW BEDFORD PORT SOCIETY— LADIES BRANCH
(Limited Scholarship Grant)
15 Johnny Cake Hill
New Bedford MA 02740
Written inquiry only

AMOUNT: $300–$400

DEADLINE(S): May 1

FIELD(S): All areas of study

Open to residents of greater New Bedford who are descended from seafarers such as whaling masters and other fishermen. For undergrad and marine biology studies. Renewable. Write for complete information.

1061

NEW BRITAIN LABOR COUNCIL AFL-CIO
(Beyer-Ropiak Scholarship)
1 Grove St. #315B
New Britain CT 06051
Written inquiry

AMOUNT: $500

DEADLINE(S): June 1

FIELD(S): All areas of study

Son/daughter/ward of AFL-CIO member whose local is affiliated with New Britain Central Labor Council eligible to apply. For full-time undergraduate study only.
Write for complete information.

1062

NEW ENGLAND BOARD OF HIGHER EDUCATION
(New England Regional Student Program)
45 Temple Pl.
Boston MA 02111
617/357-9620

AMOUNT: Tuition reduction (varies)

DEADLINE(S): Varies

FIELD(S): All fields of study

Under this program New England residents may attend public colleges and universities in other New England states at a reduced tuition rate for certain majors which are not available in their own state's public institutions.

6750 awards given in the '93/'94 academic year. Write for complete information.

1063

NEW HAMPSHIRE AMERICAN LEGION
(Scholarships)
Department Adjutant; State House Annex
Concord NH 03301
Written inquiry only

AMOUNT: $1000

DEADLINE(S): May 1

FIELD(S): All fields of study

Various scholarships and awards open to New Hampshire residents for college or vocational/technical school studies. Some are limited to children of Legion members.
Write for complete information.

1064

NEW HAMPSHIRE CHARITABLE FOUNDATION
(Student Aid Scholarship Funds)
37 Pleasant St.
Concord NH 03301
603/225-6641

AMOUNT: $100–$2500

DEADLINE(S): April 22

FIELD(S): All fields of study

More than 90 separate scholarship and loan programs for New Hampshire residents are administered by the NHCF. Student must be enrolled in an accredited 2-year or 4-year college or university. Must be legal resident of New Hampshire.
Write for complete information.

1065

NEW HAMPSHIRE HIGHER EDUCATION ASSISTANCE FOUNDATION
(Federal Family Education Loan Program)
P.O. Box 877
Concord NH 03302-0877
603/225-6612 or 800/525-2577

AMOUNT: Varies with program

DEADLINE(S): None

FIELD(S): All fields of study

Open to New Hampshire residents pursuing a college education in or out of state and to non-residents who attend a New Hampshire college or university. The foundation administers a variety of student and parent loan programs.

US citizen. Write for complete information.

1066

NEW JERSEY DEPT. OF HIGHER EDUCATION
(Educational Opportunity Fund Grants)
Office of Student Assistance; CN 540
Trenton NJ 08625
609/588-3230; 800/792-8670 IN NJ

AMOUNT: $200–$1950 undergrad; $200-$4000 graduate student

DEADLINE(S): October 1; March 1

FIELD(S): All areas of study

New Jersey resident for at least 12 months prior to application. Grants for economically and educationally disadvantaged students. For undergraduate or graduate study in New Jersey. Must demonstrate need. US citizen or legal resident.

Grants renewable. Write for complete information.

1067

NEW JERSEY DEPT. OF HIGHER EDUCATION
(Public Tuition Benefit Program)
Office of Student Assistance; CN 540
Trenton NJ 08625
609/588-3230; 800/792-8670 in NJ

AMOUNT: Partial to full tuition

DEADLINE(S): October 1; March 1

FIELD(S): All areas of study

Open to New Jersey residents who are dependents of emergency service personnel & law officers killed in the line of duty in NJ. For undergraduate study in NJ. US citizenship or legal residency required.

Renewable. Write for complete information.

1068

NEW JERSEY DEPT. OF MILITARY & VETERANS AFFAIRS
(Veterans Tuition Credit Program)
Eggert Crossing Rd.; CN 340
Attn: DVL6S
Trenton NJ 08625
609/530-6961; 800/624-0508 in NJ

AMOUNT: $400 (full-time); $200 (half-time)

DEADLINE(S): October 1; March 1

FIELD(S): All fields of study

Open to US military veterans who served between Dec. 31, 1960, & May 7, 1975, and were residents of New Jersey for one year prior to application, or were NJ residents at time of induction or discharge. Proof of residency is required.

Applies to all levels of study. Write for complete information.

1069

NEW JERSEY DEPT. OF MILITARY & VETERANS AFFAIRS
(POW/MIA Dependents Grants)
Eggert Crossing Rd.; CN 340
Attn: DVS
Trenton NJ 08625-0340
609/530-6961; 800/624-0508 in NJ

AMOUNT: Full tuition

DEADLINE(S): October 1; March 1

FIELD(S): All fields of study

New Jersey residents. Open to dependent children of USA military personnel who were officially declared POW or MIA after January 1, 1960. Grants will pay undergraduate tuition at any accredited public or independent college/university in NJ.

Write for complete information.

1070

NEW JERSEY STATE GOLF ASSOC.
(Scholarships)
Raintree; 14 Woodmere Ct.
Freehold NJ 07728
201/780-3562 After 6 PM

AMOUNT: $800–$2500

DEADLINE(S): May 1

FIELD(S): All fields of study

Open to students who have served as a caddie at a New Jersey golf club which is a member of the NJ state golf association. For full-time undergraduate study at an accredited college or university.

Awards are based on scholastic achievement, financial need, SAT scores, character, & length of service as a caddie. 30+ new awards per year. Renewable for 3 additional years. Write for complete information.

1071

NEW MEXICO EDUCATIONAL ASSISTANCE FOUNDATION (Student Incentive Grant)
P.O. Box 27020
Albuquerque NM 87125
505/345-3371

AMOUNT: Up to $2000

DEADLINE(S): None

FIELD(S): All areas/New Mexico residents

Open to New Mexico residents who are enrolled at least half time in a public or private undergraduate institution in New Mexico. NMEAF is fiscal administrative agent; individual schools make awards based on financial need.

Approximately 2700 grants per year. Contact college financial aid officer for complete information.

1072

NEW MEXICO VETERANS' SERVICE COMMISSION (Scholarship Program)
P.O. Box 2324
Santa Fe NM 87503
505/827-6300

AMOUNT: Full Tuition + $300

DEADLINE(S): None

FIELD(S): All fields of study

Open to New Mexico residents (aged 17–25) who are son or daughter of person who was killed in action or died as a result of military service in the US Armed Forces during a period of armed conflict.

Veteran must have been NM resident at time of entry into service and must have served during a period of armed conflict. Approx. 13 full-tuition scholarships for undergrads per year. Write for complete information.

1073

NEW YORK STATE EDUCATION DEPARTMENT (Awards, Scholarships, & Fellowships)
State & Federal Scholarship & Fellowship Unit
Cultural Education Center
Albany NY 12230
Written inquiry

AMOUNT: Varies

DEADLINE(S): Varies

FIELD(S): All fields of study

Various state and federal programs administered by the NY State Education Department open to residents of New York state. One year's NY residency immediately preceding effective date of award is required.

Write for complete information.

1074

NEW YORK STATE HIGHER EDUCATION SERVICES CORPORATION (State & Federal Scholarships, Awards, Grants, and Loans)
Student information
99 Washington Ave.
Albany NY 12255
518/474-4898

AMOUNT: Varies with program

DEADLINE(S): Varies

FIELD(S): All fields of study

The corporation administers a variety of federal and state scholarships, awards, grants, and loans. Open to New York state residents attending school in New York state. Some programs carry a service obligation for each year of support.

US citizenship is also required. Write for complete information.

1075

NEW YORK STATE SENATE
(Session Assistants Program)
State Capitol Room 500A
Albany NY 12247
518/455-2611

AMOUNT: $2500 stipend
DEADLINE(S): October 21
FIELD(S): All fields of study

Open to talented undergraduates who want first-hand experience in New York state government on site at the legislature (this is not a scholarship program). All academic majors may apply. Good academic record & US citizenship required.

Write to Dr. Russell J. Williams at above address for complete information.

1076

NEWTON PUBLIC SCHOOLS
(Chaffin Educational Fund Scholarship & Loan Programs)
100 Walnut Street
Newtonville MA 02160
617/552-7652

AMOUNT: $500 per semester; $4000 maximum
DEADLINE(S): None
FIELD(S): All fields of study

Open to graduates of Newton North and Newton South High Schools ONLY. Preference to students enrolling in 4-year accredited undergraduate programs.

Approximately 27 awards per year. Renewable to a maximum of $4000. Write for complete information.

1077

NON-COMMISSIONED OFFICERS ASSOCIATION
(Scholarships)
P.O. Box 33610
San Antonio TX 78265
512/653-6161

AMOUNT: $750–$1000
DEADLINE(S): March 31
FIELD(S): All fields of study

Undergraduate & vocational scholarships open to children and spouses of members. Children of members must be under age 25 to receive initial grants.

35 awards per year. Full-time students who maintain at least a 3.0 GPA may reapply each year for scholarship renewal. Write for complete information.

1078

NORTH AMERICAN PHILIPS CORPORATION
(Scholarship Program)
100 East 42nd Street
New York NY 10017
212/850-5000

AMOUNT: $2500; $500–$1500
DEADLINE(S): March 1 (apply in January)
FIELD(S): All areas of study

Open to dependent children of North American Philips employees. Applicants must be high school seniors who expect to graduate during the current year. Considerations include academic record, SAT, or ACT scores & biographical questionnaire.

52 awards per year. Financial need is considered except for two $2500 awards which are merit-based only. Participation in extracurricular activities and sports are considered. Write for complete information.

1079

**NORTH CAROLINA DIVISION OF
SERVICES FOR THE BLIND
(Rehabilitation Assistance for Visually
Handicapped)**
309 Ashe Ave.
Raleigh NC 27606
919/733-9700

AMOUNT: Tuition + fees; books & supplies
DEADLINE(S): None
FIELD(S): All areas of study

Open to North Carolina residents who are
legally blind or have a progressive eye condition which may result in blindness (there-
by creating an employment handicap for
the individual) and who are undergrad or
grad students at a NC school.
Write for complete information.

1080

**NORTH CAROLINA DIVISION OF
VETERANS AFFAIRS
(Dependents Scholarship Program)**
325 N. Salisbury St.; Suite 1065
Raleigh NC 27603
919/733-3851

AMOUNT: $1200 to $3000 (private college);
tuition & fees + room & board (public
college)
DEADLINE(S): May 31
FIELD(S): All fields of study

Undergraduate scholarships open to children
of veterans who died as a result of wartime
service or were disabled, POW, MIA, or
received pension from the VA, Veteran
entered Service as NC resident or applicant
NC resident since birth.
Awards tenable at private & public colleges in
North Carolina. 350–400 awards per year.
Renewable up to 4 years. Write for complete information.

1081

**NORTH CAROLINA STATE EDUCATION
ASSISTANCE AUTHORITY
(Student Financial Aid for North Carolinians)**
P.O. Box 2688
Chapel Hill NC 27515
919/549-8614

AMOUNT: Varies
DEADLINE(S): Varies
FIELD(S): All fields of study

The state of NC, private NC organizations, &
the federal government fund numerous
scholarship, grant,; work-study, & loan programs for North Carolina residents at all
levels of study.
The NC state education assistance authority
annually publishes a financial aid booklet
describing in detail various programs for
North Carolina residents. A copy is available free to undergrads who plan to attend
a school in NC.

1082

**NORTH CAROLINA STATE
UNIVERSITY
(John Gatling Scholarship Program)**
2119 Pullen Hall
Box 7342
Raleigh NC 27695
919/515-3671

AMOUNT: $6000 per year
DEADLINE(S): Apply for admission to NC
state by February 1
FIELD(S): All fields of study

If you were born with surname of Gatlin or
Gatling, this program will provide $6000
toward the cost of attending NC state university as an undergraduate, provided you
meet NC state university entrance and
transfer requirements. US citizen.
Award is renewable each year if you study full
time (24 or more credits per year) & maintain at least 2.0 GPA. Contact the NCSU
merit awards program coordinator at
address above for complete information.

1083

NORTH DAKOTA INDIAN
SCHOLARSHIP PROGRAM
(Scholarships)
State Capitol Building; 10th Floor
Bismarck ND 58505
701/328-2960

AMOUNT: Up to $2000
DEADLINE(S): July 15
FIELD(S): All fields of study

Open to North Dakota residents who have at least 1/4 Indian blood or are enrolled members of a North Dakota tribe. Awards are tenable at recognized undergraduate colleges & universities in North Dakota. US citizenship required.

100–150 scholarships per year. Renewable. Write for complete information.

1084

NORTH DAKOTA STUDENT FINANCIAL
ASSISTANCE AGENCY
(Grants)
State Capitol; 10th Floor
600 East Blvd.
Bismarck ND 58505
701/328-4114

AMOUNT: Up to $600
DEADLINE(S): April 15
FIELD(S): All fields of study

Open to residents of North Dakota for undergraduate study at colleges & universities in North Dakota. Must be citizen or legal resident of USA.

2400 awards per year. Renewable. Write for complete information.

1085

OHIO NATIONAL GUARD TUITION
GRANT PROGRAM
Adj. Gen. Dept.; Attn: AGOH-TG
2825 W. Granville Rd.
Columbus OH 43235
614/889-7032

AMOUNT: For state schools 60% of tuition; for private schools 60% of avg. state school fees
DEADLINE(S): July 1; November 1; February 1; April 1
FIELD(S): All fields of study

Open to residents of Ohio with an enlisted obligation of six years in the Ohio National Guard. Provides 12 quarter or 8 semester hours.

Write to the tuition grant office at above address for complete information.

1086

OHIO STUDENT AID COMMISSION
(Ohio Academic Scholarship Program)
State Grants & Scholarships Dept.
309 S. Fourth St.
P.O. Box 182452
Columbus; Ohio 43218-2452
614/466-1190

AMOUNT: $1000
DEADLINE(S): February 23
FIELD(S): All fields of study

Open to seniors at eligible Ohio high schools who are Ohio residents and enrolled or intend to be enrolled as full-time undergraduate students in eligible Ohio institutions of higher education. US citizen.

1000 awards per year. Scholarships are automatically renewable for up to four years of undergraduate study provided satisfactory progress is made. Write for complete information.

1087

OHIO STUDENT AID COMMISSION
(Ohio Instructional Grants)
State Grants/Scholarship Dept.
309 S. 4th St.
PO Box 182452
Columbus OH 43218
614/466-7420

AMOUNT: $216 to $1326 (public institution); $540 to $3306 (private institution); $372 to $2268 (proprietary institution)

DEADLINE(S): Last Friday in September

FIELD(S): All fields of study

Open to Ohio residents who are US citizens enrolled full time in an eligible Ohio institution of higher education. Must be in good academic standing and demonstrate financial need.

90,000 renewable grants per year. Write for complete information.

1088

OHIO STUDENT AID COMMISSION
(Ohio Student Choice Grant)
State Grants & Scholarships Dept.
309 S. Fourth St.
P.O. Box 182452
Columbus OH 43218-2452
614/466-1190

AMOUNT: Varies

DEADLINE(S): Determined by institution

FIELD(S): All fields of study except Theology or Religion

Open to Ohio residents who are USA citizens and are enrolled as full-time undergraduate students at an eligible private non-profit Ohio college or university. Not for studies leading to degrees in Religion or Theology.

23,000 awards per year renewable for a maximum of 5 years. Write for complete information.

1089

OHIO UNIVERSITY (Charles Kilburger
Scholarship)
Asst. Dir. Student Services
1570 Granville Pike
Lancaster OH 43130
614/654-6711

AMOUNT: Tuition

DEADLINE(S): February 1

FIELD(S): All fields of study

Scholarship open to seniors graduating from a Fairfield County (Ohio) high school who will enroll at Ohio University Lancaster for

at least two years. For undergraduate study only. US citizenship required.

Applications available ONLY from high school counselors. Must demonstrate financial need.

1090

OHIO WAR ORPHANS SCHOLARSHIP
BOARD
(Scholarships)
Ohio Student Aid Commission
State Grants & Scholarships Dept.
309 S. Fourth St.
P.O. Box 182452
Columbus OH 43218-2452
614/466-1190

AMOUNT: Full tuition at public schools; equivalent amount at private schools.

DEADLINE(S): July 1

FIELD(S): All areas of study

Ohio resident & dependent of veteran who served for at least 90 days during war & as a result is now 60% or more disabled, or 100% disabled for any other reason, and must be receiving VA benefits for the disability.

350 awards per year. Write for complete information.

1091

OMEGA PSI PHI FRATERNITY
(Founders Memorial Scholarships)
2714 Georgia Ave. NW
Washington DC 20001
202/667-7158

AMOUNT: $500

DEADLINE(S): May 15

FIELD(S): All areas of study

Open ONLY to members of Omega Psi Phi fraternity who will be college sophomores or juniors and who have a 3.0 or better grade point average.

Write to the Omega Psi Phi Fraternity District Scholarship Chairman for complete information.

1092

**OPERATING ENGINEERS LOCAL
UNION NO. 3
(IUOE Scholarship Program)**
1620 South Loop Rd.
Alameda CA 94502
510/748-7400

AMOUNT: Up to $3000
DEADLINE(S): March 1
FIELD(S): All areas of study

Open to dependent children of members of
IUOE Local No. 3 who are high school
seniors with at least a 3.0 GPA. Awards tenable at recognized undergraduate colleges
& universities. US citizenship required.
Write for complete information.

1093

**ORDER OF THE EASTERN STAR
(Grand Chapter of California Scholarships)**
870 Market St.; Suite 722
San Francisco CA 94102
Written Inquiry

AMOUNT: $250–$500 (2-year college);
$500–$1000 (4-year college)
DEADLINE(S): May 15
FIELD(S): All fields of study

Open to California residents who are accepted
to or enrolled in a California college or university or trade school and have at least a
3.5 GPA (4.0 scale). Must demonstrate
financial need and be US citizen.
Write to Mrs. Diane Silva, Grand Secretary,
(address above) for complete information.

1094

**OREGON DEPARTMENT OF
VETERANS' AFFAIRS
(Educational Scholarship Aid for Oregon
Veterans)**
700 Summer St. NE; Suite 150
Salem OR 97310
800/692-9666

AMOUNT: $35 to $50 per month
DEADLINE(S): None
FIELD(S): All fields of study

Must be resident of Oregon & US citizen with
a qualifying military service record at time
of application. For study in an accredited
Oregon school.
Applicants must have armed forces expedi-
tionary medal or the Vietnam service medal
or be a veteran of the Korean conflict
(active duty). Write for complete information.

1095

**OREGON STATE SCHOLARSHIP
COMMISSION
(Oregon Cash Awards; Oregon Need Grants)**
1500 Valley River Dr. #100
Eugene OR 97401
503/687-7400

AMOUNT: $3180
DEADLINE(S): April 1
FIELD(S): All areas of study

Open to Oregon residents enrolled full time in
any 2- or 4-year non-profit college or university in Oregon. Must be US citizen or
legal resident and demonstrate financial
need.
It is not necessary to take SAT/ACT for need
grants. 22,000 awards and grants per year.
Renewable. Write for complete information.

1096

**OREGON STATE SCHOLARSHIP
COMMISSION
(Oregon Guaranteed Student Loans)**
1500 Vally River Dr. #100
Eugene OR 97401
800/452-8807

AMOUNT: $2625–$4000 undergrad; $7500
graduate (annual maximum)
DEADLINE(S): None specified
FIELD(S): All fields of study

Open to US citizens or permanent residents who are attending an eligible Oregon institution and to Oregon residents attending any eligible institution outside of Oregon at least half time.

Write for complete information.

1097

OREGON STATE SCHOLARSHIP COMMISSION
(Private Scholarship Programs Administered by the Commission)
1500 Vally River Dr. #100
Eugene OR 97401
503/687-7395

AMOUNT: $250–$3000
DEADLINE(S): March 1
FIELD(S): All fields of study

100 different private scholarship programs are administered by the commission and are open to Oregon residents only. Some are tied to a specific field and/or level of study but in general they are available to all levels and fields of study.

Dependent students must have parents residing in Oregon. Independent students must live in Oregon for 12 months prior to September 1.

1098

ORPHAN FOUNDATION OF AMERICA
(Scholarship Program)
1500 Massachusetts Ave.; Suite 448
Washington DC 20005
Written inquiries only

AMOUNT: $250–$1000
DEADLINE(S): May 15
FIELD(S): All areas of study

Program open to "orphans" (as defined by The Orphan Foundation of America) who have "not been adopted." Awards tenable at any recognized undergraduate or vocational school in the US. Must be US citizen or legal resident.

50+ Scholarships per year. Renewable with reapplication. Write for complete information.

1099

PARENTS WITHOUT PARTNERS
(International Scholarship)
401 N. Michigan Ave.
Chicago IL 60611-4267
312/644-6610

AMOUNT: Varies
DEADLINE(S): March 15
FIELD(S): All fields of study

Open to dependent children (up to 25 years of age) of Parents Without Partners members. Can be a graduating high school senior or college student. For undergraduate study at trade or vocational school, college, or university.

Write for complete information (send postage-paid envelope).

1100

PAUL AND MARY HAAS FOUNDATION
(Scholarship Grants)
P.O. Box 2928
Corpus Christi TX 78403
512/887-6955

AMOUNT: $1000 per semester
DEADLINE(S): Initially fall of high school senior year
FIELD(S): All fields of study

Program open to high school seniors who are Corpus Christi TX residents. Awards support full-time pursuit of first undergraduate degree.

Approximately 50 awards per year. Must prove financial need. Write for complete information.

1101

PENNSYLVANIA DEPARTMENT OF MILITARY AFFAIRS—BUREAU OF VETERANS AFFAIRS
(Scholarships)
Fort Indiantown Gap
Annville PA 17003-5002
717/861-8904 or 717/861-8910

AMOUNT: Up to $500/term ($4000 for 4 years)

DEADLINE(S): None

FIELD(S): All areas of study

Open to children of military veterans who died or were totally disabled as a result of war, armed conflict, or terrorist attack. Must have lived in Pennsylvania for 5 years prior to application, be age 16–23, & demonstrate financial need.

70 awards per year. Renewable. For study at Pennsylvania schools. Must be US citizen. Write for complete information.

1102

PENNSYLVANIA HIGHER EDUCATION ASSISTANCE AGENCY
(Robert C. Byrd Scholarship Program)
P.O. Box 8114
Harrisburg PA 17105
717/257-5220

AMOUNT: $1500 per year

DEADLINE(S): May 1

FIELD(S): All fields of study

Open to Pennsylvania high school seniors in the top 5 percent of their graduating class with a 3.5 or better GPA & an SAT score of 1100 or higher. Must be US citizen & have been accepted for enrollment in an institution of higher education.

Renewable to a maximum of four years. Write for complete information.

1103

PERRY & STELLA TRACY SCHOLARSHIP FUND
(Scholarships)
Wells Fargo Private Banking Group
P.O. Box 2511
Sacramento CA 95812
916/440-4449

AMOUNT: $350–$750

DEADLINE(S): None

FIELD(S): All areas of study

Open to applicants who are graduates of El Dorado County high schools or have resided in El Dorado County CA for at least 2 years. Awards are tenable at recognized undergraduate colleges & universities.

Approximately 125 awards per year. Renewable. Contact high school counselor for complete information. DO NOT contact Wells Fargo.

1104

PHI KAPPA THETA NATIONAL FOUNDATION
(Scholarship Program)
c/o Scott Bova
3901 W. 86th St.; Suite 425
Indianapolis IN 46265
317/872-9934

AMOUNT: Varies

DEADLINE(S): April 30

FIELD(S): All fields of study

Undergraduate scholarships are limited to members of Phi Kappa Theta Fraternity. Applications are sent to all chapters and extras are available at national office. Not available to high school or graduate students.

Five scholarships annually. Financial need is a consideration but is relative to the other applicants. Write for complete information.

1105

**PHILADELPHIA COLLEGE OF
TEXTILES AND SCIENCE
(Scholarship Program)**
Schoolhouse Lane & Henry Avenue
Philadelphia PA 19144
215/951-2800

AMOUNT: $2000–$10,000
DEADLINE(S): May 1
FIELD(S): All areas of study

Open to high school seniors in the top 1/5 of
their class. For study at Philadelphia
College of Textiles & Science. Must submit
SAT or ACT score and be US citizen.
Scholarship renewable if GPA of 3.0 or bet-
ter is maintained.
Write for complete information.

1106

**PICKETT & HATCHER EDUCATIONAL
FUND INC.
(Loans)**
P.O. Box 8169
Columbus GA 31908-8169
706/327-6586

AMOUNT: $16000 max
DEADLINE(S): Varies
FIELD(S): All fields of study EXCEPT Law,
Medicine, & Ministry

Open to US citizens who are legal residents of
& attend colleges located in the southeastern portion of the US. Must enroll in 4-year
program of study in 4-year college. Loans
are not made for graduate or vo-tech studies.
Write for applications & complete information
in January preceding academic year in
which loan is needed. May not have other
educational loans.

1107

**PORTUGUESE CONTINENTAL UNION
(Scholarships)**
899 Boylston Street
Boston MA 02115
617/536-2916

AMOUNT: Varies
DEADLINE(S): February 15
FIELD(S): All areas of study

Open to members of the Portuguese
Continental Union of the USA with at least
one year membership in good standing and
who plan to enroll or are enrolled in any
accredited college or university.
Financial need is a consideration. Write for
complete information.

1108

**PRESBYTERIAN CHURCH—USA
(Native American Education Grants)**
Financial Aid for Studies
100 Witherspoon St.
Louisville KY 40202-1396
502/569-5760

AMOUNT: $200 to $1500
DEADLINE(S): June 1
FIELD(S): All fields of study

Open to Native Americans & Alaska Natives
who are Presbyterian & who have completed at least one semester of work at an
accredited institution of higher education.
Preference to students at the undergraduate
level.
US citizenship or permanent residency
required. Renewal is based on continued
financial need & satisfactory academic
progress. Write for complete information.

1109

**PRESBYTERIAN CHURCH—USA
(National Presbyterian College Scholarships)**
100 Witherspoon St.
Louisville KY 40202-1396
502/569-5745

AMOUNT: $500 to $1400

DEADLINE(S): December 1

FIELD(S): All fields of study

Scholarships for incoming freshmen at one of the participating colleges related to the church. Applicants must be superior high school seniors & confirmed members of the Presbyterian Church—USA. Must be US citizen or legal resident.

Application and brochure available after September 1. Financial need is a consideration. Write for complete information.

1110

PRESBYTERIAN CHURCH—USA
(Samuel Robinson Scholarships)
100 Witherspoon St.
Louisville KY 40202
502/569-5745

AMOUNT: $1000

DEADLINE(S): April 1

FIELD(S): All fields of study

Open to undergraduate students enrolled in one of the 69 colleges related to the Presbyterian Church. Applicants must successfully recite the answers to the Westminster shorter catechism and write a 2000-word essay.

20–30 awards per year. Write for complete information.

1111

PRESBYTERIAN CHURCH—USA
(Student Loan Fund)
National Ministry Division
100 Witherspoon St.
Louisville KY 40202-1396
502/569-5735

AMOUNT: Up to $1000 per year

DEADLINE(S): None specified

FIELD(S): All fields of study

Loans open to communicant members of the Presbyterian Church (USA) who are US citizens or permanent residents. For full-

time undergraduate or graduate study. No interest while in school; repayable at 6.5% APR thereafter.

GPA of 2.0 or better required. Those preparing for professional church occupations can borrow up to $2000 per academic year. Write for complete information.

1112

PRESBYTERIAN CHURCH—USA
(Student Opportunity Minority Scholarships)
100 Witherspoon St.
Louisville KY 40202-1396
502/569-5760

AMOUNT: $100 to $1400

DEADLINE(S): April 1

FIELD(S): All fields of study

Open to minority (Black, Hispanic, Asian, Native American) high school seniors who are members of the Presbyterian Church & entering college as full-time freshmen. Must be US citizen or legal resident.

110–130 awards per year. Renewal of awards is dependent on continued financial need and satisfactory academic progress. Write for complete information.

1113

PRESIDENT'S COMMITTEE ON
EMPLOYMENT OF PEOPLE WITH
DISABILITIES
(National Poster Scholarship Program)
1331 F St. NW
Washington DC 20004
202/376-6200; FAX 202/376-6219;
TDD 202/376-6205

AMOUNT: $500

DEADLINE(S): January 31 (postmark)

FIELD(S): All fields of study

Open to high school students (grades 9–12) & undergrads at schools in the US; Puerto Rico; the Virgin Islands, or the District of Columbia. Applicant must have proof of disability, letter of recommendation, and write an essay.

Write for complete information.

1114

PRINCE GEORGE'S CHAMBER OF COMMERCE FOUNDATION
(Scholarship)

4601 Presidents Drive; Suite 230
Lanham MD 20706
301/731-5000

AMOUNT: Full tuition at Maryland schools; partial tuition at out-of-state schools

DEADLINE(S): May 15

FIELD(S): All fields of study

Open to residents of Prince George's County MD for undergraduate study. Must be US citizen. Financial need is a consideration.

Write for complete information.

1115

PROFESSIONAL BOWLERS ASSOCIATION
(Billy Welu Memorial Scholarship)

1720 Merriman Rd.
P.O. Box 5118
Akron OH 44334
216/836-5568

AMOUNT: $500

DEADLINE(S): May 31

FIELD(S): All fields of study

The scholarship is designed to assist undergraduate students who are enrolled in college and are currently representing their schools in bowling as a team member, coach, or trainer.

The aim of the PBA is to support and promote the sport of bowling. Write for complete information.

1116

PROFESSIONAL HORSEMEN'S ASSOCIATION OF AMERICA INC.
(Financial Assistance)

c/o Mrs. Ann Grenci
284 Old Sleepy Hollow Drive
Pleasantville NJ 10570
201/538-3797

AMOUNT: $500

DEADLINE(S): May 1

FIELD(S): All areas of study

Members or dependents of members of the Professional Horsemen's Association receive first consideration for financial assistance. Awards can be used for college or trade school.

Write to Mrs. Ann Grenci at above address for complete information.

1117

PUBLIC EMPLOYEES ROUNDTABLE
(Public Service Scholarships)

P.O. Box 14270
Washington DC 20044
202/927-5000; FAX 202/927-5001

AMOUNT: $500–$1000

DEADLINE(S): May 15

FIELD(S): All fields of study

Open to graduate students & undergraduate sophomores, juniors, and seniors who are planning a career in government. Minimum of 3.5 cumulative GPA. Preference to applicants with some public service work experience (paid or unpaid).

10 to 15 awards per year. Applications available as of February 1. Send self-addressed STAMPED envelope for application.

1118

RECORDING FOR THE BLIND
(Mary P. Oenslager Scholastic Achievement Awards)
20 Roszel Rd.
Princeton NJ 08540
609/452-0606

AMOUNT: $750; $1500; $5000
DEADLINE(S): February 1
FIELD(S): All fields of study

Open to legally or totally blind college students registered with the RFB who have received or will receive a bachelor's degree from a 4-year college or university and who have a 3.0 GPA or better.

Bachelor's degree must be received between July 1 of year preceding application deadline date and June 30 of year of application deadline date. Write for complete information.

1119

RHODE ISLAND HIGHER EDUCATION ASSISTANCE AUTHORITY
(Loan Program; Plus Loans)
560 Jefferson Blvd.
Warwick RI 02886
401/736-1160

AMOUNT: Up to $5500 for undergrads & up to $8500 for graduates (subsidized); up to $5000 for undergrads & up to $10,000 for graduates (unsubsidized)
DEADLINE(S): None specified
FIELD(S): All fields of study

Open to Rhode Island residents or non-residents attending an eligible school. Must be US citizen or legal resident and be enrolled at least half-time. Rhode Island residents may attend schools outside the state.

Must demonstrate financial need. Write for current interest rates and complete information.

1120

RHODE ISLAND HIGHER EDUCATION ASSISTANCE AUTHORITY
(Undergraduate Grant and Scholarship Program)
560 Jefferson Blvd.
Warwick RI 02886
407/736-1100

AMOUNT: $900
DEADLINE(S): March 1
FIELD(S): All fields of study

Open to Rhode Island residents who are enrolled or planning to enroll at least 1/2 time at an eligible post-secondary institution. US citizen or legal resident.

Must demonstrate financial need. Write for complete information.

1121

RIPON COLLEGE
(Distinguished Honor Scholarship; Pickard Scholarship)
P.O. Box 248; 300 Seward St.
Admissions Office
Ripon WI 54971
414/748-8102 or 800/94RIPON

AMOUNT: Up to $3500 (DHS); $7600 & $15,200 (Pickard)
DEADLINE(S): March 1
FIELD(S): All areas of study

For entering first-year students. Scholarships and distinguished honor scholarships will be awarded on basis of total high school record, recommendations, and interview.

There are nine $7600 Pickard scholarships & one for $15,200. Must apply & be accepted for admission at Ripon College. Write for more information.

1122

RIPON COLLEGE
(ROTC Honor Scholarship)
P.O. Box 248; 300 Seward St.
Admissions Office
Ripon WI 54971
414/748-8102 or 800/94RIPON

AMOUNT: $1700
DEADLINE(S): March 1
FIELD(S): All areas of study

Entering first-year or transfer students. ROTC
scholarships will be awarded on basis of
total high school record, recommendations,
interview, and participation in ROTC at
Ripon.

Must apply and be accepted for admission at
Ripon college. Write for complete information.

1123

ROTARY FOUNDATION OF ROTARY
INTERNATIONAL
(Ambassadorial Scholarships)
1 Rotary Center
1560 Sherman Ave.
Evanston IL 60201
708/866-3000

AMOUNT: Full tuition & living expenses up
to US $21,500
DEADLINE(S): Check with local Rotary
Club
FIELD(S): All fields of study

Applicants pursuing university studies must
have completed 2 years of course work
when scholarship begins. Those pursuing
practical training/vocational study must
have worked in their vocation at least 2
years & have high school diploma.

For study in another country where Rotary
Clubs are located. Applications must be
submitted through local Rotary Clubs.
Deadlines can be as early as March & as
late as July 15.

1124

ROUCH FOUNDATION
(A. P. Rouch & Louise Rouch Scholarship
Grant)
c/o Trust Dept.
Twin Falls Bank & Trust Co.
Twin Falls ID 83303
208/733-1722 Ext. 221

AMOUNT: Varies
DEADLINE(S): May 1
FIELD(S): All areas of study

Open to orphaned, poor, or underprivileged
boys and girls who live in Twin Falls, Idaho,
and the immediate vicinity. Awards can be
used at Idaho schools. Must demonstrate
financial need.

Number of awards per year varies. Renewable.
Contact Assistant Trust Officer Janice
Stover at above address for complete infor-
mation.

1125

ROYAL A. & MILDRED D. EDDY
STUDENT LOAN TRUST FUND; LOUISE
I. LATSHAW STUDENT LOAN TRUST
FUND
(Student Loans)
NBD Bank Trust Dept.
8585 Broadway; Suite 396
Merrillville IN 46410
Written inquiry

AMOUNT: $2000 maximum
DEADLINE(S): First-applied basis
FIELD(S): All fields of study

Loan fund available to undergraduate juniors
& seniors who are US citizens. Loan principal & interest is to be repaid in full & 2
credit-worthy co-signers are required.
Interest rate is 10%. For study in the USA
only.

Repayment in monthly installments is to start
not later than 5 months after graduation.
Write for complete information.

1126

ROYAL NEIGHBORS OF AMERICA
(Fraternal Scholarships)
230 16th Street
Rock Island IL 61201
309/788-4561

AMOUNT: $500 to $2000
DEADLINE(S): December 1
FIELD(S): All areas of study

Open to high school seniors who are RNA members of at least 2 years & in the upper quarter of their class or are recommended by their high school principal. Awards tenable by US citizens at recognized undergrad colleges & universities.

22 non-renewable $500 scholarships for freshman year only and 10 national scholarships that are renewable for 4 years. Write for complete information.

1127

SACHS FOUNDATION
(Scholarship Program)
90 S. Cascade Ave.; Suite 1410
Colorado Springs CO 80903
719/633-2353

AMOUNT: $3000 (undergrad); $4000 (graduate)
DEADLINE(S): March 1
FIELD(S): All fields of study

Open to Black residents of Colorado who are high school graduates, US citizens, have a 3.4 or better GPA, & can demonstrate financial need. For undergrad study at any accredited college or university. Very few graduate grants are awarded.

Approximately 50 scholarships per year. Renewable if 2.5 or better GPA is maintained. Grants are for up to 4 years in duration. Write for complete information.

1128

SACRAMENTO SCOTTISH RITE OF FREEMASONRY
(Charles M. Goethe Memorial Scholarship)
P.O. Box 19497
Sacramento CA 95819
916/452-5881

AMOUNT: Varies
DEADLINE(S): June 10
FIELD(S): All fields of study

For any field of study but preference to students majoring in eugenics or biological sciences. Grants are limited to students who are members or senior members of the Order of Demolay.

Also open to children of members or deceased members of a California Masonic Lodge. Write for complete information.

1129

SAINT ANDREW'S SOCIETY OF THE STATE OF NEW YORK
(Graduate Scholarship Program)
71 W. 23rd St.; 5th Floor
New York NY 10010
212/807-1730

AMOUNT: $13,000 (maximum award)
DEADLINE(S): December 15
FIELD(S): All fields of study

Open to undergraduate seniors at accredited USA institutions who are of Scottish ancestry. Scholarships are for a year of graduate study at a school in Scotland.

Preference to applicants who have not studied in Great Britain. Financial need is a consideration. Write for complete information.

1130

SAMUEL LEMBERG SCHOLARSHIP LOAN FUND INC.
(Scholarships; Loans)
60 East 42nd St.; Suite 1814
New York NY 10165
Written inquiry

AMOUNT: Up to $5000 per academic year

DEADLINE(S): April 1

FIELD(S): All fields of study

Special no-interest scholarship-loans open to Jewish men & women pursuing any undergraduate, graduate, or professional degree. Recipients assume an obligation to repay their loans within 10 years after the completion of their studies.

Write for complete information.

1131

SAN FRANCISCO STATE UNIVERSITY
(Over-60 Program)
Admissions Office
1600 Holloway Ave.
San Francisco CA 94132
415/338-2037

AMOUNT: Admissions & registration fees waiver

DEADLINE(S): None

FIELD(S): All fields of study

Open to California residents over 60 years of age who have lived in the state for at least one year by September 20th. Must meet the university's regular admissions standards. Total cost is $3 per semester.

Write Admissions Office for complete information.

1132

SAN JOSE STATE UNIVERSITY
(Scholarships)
Financial Aid Office SJSU
One Washington Square
San Jose CA 95192-0036
408/924-6063

AMOUNT: $50 to $1000

DEADLINE(S): January 1–March 1

FIELD(S): All fields of study

Scholarships are awarded competitively to students enrolled at San Jose State on the basis of grade point average. Most require a demonstration of financial need.

Students interested in graduate fellowships and assistantships should apply directly to their department Dean's office. 450 scholarships per year. Write for complete information.

1133

SAN RAFAEL INDOOR SPORTS CLUB INC.
(Scholarships for Disabled Students)
c/o College of Marin
Financial Aid Office
Kentfield CA 94904
415/924-3549

AMOUNT: $300 per year

DEADLINE(S): May 1

FIELD(S): All areas of study

Open to students enrolled in or planning to enroll in the disabled students program at the College of Marin. Must have a course load of six units or more and maintain a 3.0 or better GPA.

Write for complete information.

1134

SANTA BARBARA FOUNDATION
(Student Loan Program)
15 E. Carrillo St.
Santa Barbara CA 93101
805/963-1873

AMOUNT: Varies

DEADLINE(S): January 31

FIELD(S): All fields of study

Open to graduates of Santa Barbara County high schools who have attended schools in the county since 7th grade. For 3 years of undergraduate study. Applicants must be US citizens or permanent residents. Financial need is a consideration.

Up to 550 awards per year. Applications available October 1 to January 15. Write for complete information.

1135

SCHOLARSHIP FOUNDATION OF ST. LOUIS
(Interest-free Undergraduate Loan Program)
8215 Clayton Road
St. Louis MO 63117
314/725-7990

AMOUNT: $3000

DEADLINE(S): April 15

FIELD(S): All areas

Residents of the _____ who are high
school gr_____ _an demonstrate
finar_____ _e interest-free. Six
_____ _wing graduation.
_____ _ble up to a maximum of
_____ _r person provided student is in
_____ academic standing and continues to
_____ _ow need. Write for complete information.

CANCELLED

1136

SCREEN ACTORS GUILD FOUNDATION
(John L. Dales Scholarship Fund)
5757 Wilshire Blvd.
Los Angeles CA 90036
213/549-6709

AMOUNT: $2000

DEADLINE(S): April 30

FIELD(S): All areas of study

Scholarships open to SAG members with at
least 5 years membership or dependent children of members with at least 8 years membership. Awards are for any level of undergraduate, graduate, or post-graduate study.
Financial need is a consideration. Renewable
yearly with reapplication. Write for complete information.

1137

SEAFARERS' WELFARE PLAN
(Charlie Logan Scholarship Program for Seamen)
5201 Auth Way
Camp Springs MD 20746
301/899-0675

AMOUNT: $6000–$15,000

DEADLINE(S): April 15

FIELD(S): All areas of study

Open to seaman who has no less than 2 years
of actual employment on vessels of companies signatory to the seafarers' welfare plan.
Must have had 125 days employment in
previous calendar year.

Renewable up to 2 years. Write for complete
information.

1138

SEAFARERS' WELFARE PLAN
(Charlie Logan Scholarship Program for Dependents)
5201 Auth Way
Camp Springs MD 20746
301/899-0675

AMOUNT: $15,000

DEADLINE(S): April 15

FIELD(S): All areas of study

Open to dependent children of seaman who
have been employed for at least 3 years by
a contributor to seafarer's welfare plan.
Student must be H.S. (or equivalent) grad
in upper 1/3 of class; unmarried & under 19
years of age.

Write for complete information and restric-
tions.

1139

SECOND MARINE DIVISION ASSOCIATION
(Scholarship Fund)
P.O. Box 8180
Camp Lejeune NC 28542
Written inquiry

AMOUNT: $700

DEADLINE(S): April 1

FIELD(S): All fields of study

Open to unmarried dependents of individuals
who are now serving or have served in the
USMC 2nd Marine Division. Awards for

undergraduate study only. US citizenship required.

Requests for application should be in student's own handwriting. Include self-addressed stamped envelope.

1140

SELBY FOUNDATION
(Scholarship Program)
  1800 Second St.; Suite 905
  Sarasota FL 34236
  813/957-0442

AMOUNT: $500–$2000

DEADLINE(S): April 30

FIELD(S): All fields of study

For undergraduate study by residents of Sarasota or Manatee County FL who are attending an accredited college and have a GPA of 3.0 or better. Must demonstrate financial need and be US citizen.

Write for complete information.

1141

SEMINOLE TRIBE OF FLORIDA
(Higher Education Awards)
  6073 Stirling Road
  Hollywood FL 33024
  305/584-0400 Ext. 154

AMOUNT: None specified

DEADLINE(S): April 15; July 15; November 15

FIELD(S): All areas of study

Open to enrolled members of the Seminole Tribe of Florida or to those eligible to become a member. For undergraduate or graduate study at an accredited college or university.

Awards renewable. Write for complete information.

1142

SENECA NATION HIGHER EDUCATION
(Education Grants)
  Box 231
  Salamanca NY 14779
  716/945-1790

AMOUNT: Up to $5000

DEADLINE(S): July 15; December 31; May 20

FIELD(S): All fields of study

Open to enrolled members of the Seneca Nation of Indians who are in need of funding for post-secondary education and are accepted in an accredited program of study. May be used toward associate's, bachelor's, master's, or doctor's degree.

Award is based on financial need. Write for complete information.

1143

SERVICE EMPLOYEES INTERNATIONAL UNION
(Scholarship Program)
  1313 'L' St. NW
  Washington DC 20005
  800/448-7348

AMOUNT: $1000

DEADLINE(S): March 12

FIELD(S): All fields of study

Scholarships open to Service Employees International Union members (in good standing) and their dependent children. Awards can be used at a community college or trade/tech school or to continue education at a 4-year college or university.

There are 20 awards per year; 9 are non-renewable. Write for complete information.

1144

SICO FOUNDATION
(Scholarships)
  Scholarships Coordinator
  Mount Joy PA 17552
  717/653-1411

AMOUNT: $1000 per year

DEADLINE(S): February 15

FIELD(S): All fields of study

Open to high school seniors residing in the state of Delaware or the Pennsylvania counties of Adams, Berks, Chester, Cumberland, Dauphin, Delaware, Lancaster, Lebanon, or York.

Also available to residents of New Jersey counties of Atlantic, Cape May, Cumberland, Gloucester, and Salem, and to residents of Cecil County, Maryland. Write for complete information.

1145

SOCIETY OF DAUGHTERS OF HOLLAND DAMES
(Scholarships)
'Thorland'
Valley Road
Locust Valley NY 11560
515/671-8833

AMOUNT: $500

DEADLINE(S): May 1

FIELD(S): All fields of study

Open to applicants of Dutch descent who will be undergraduate juniors or seniors at an accredited US college or university & demonstrate high scholastic standing & good moral character. US citizenship required.

Financial need is a consideration. Renewable for senior year upon reapplication and reevaluation. Write for complete information and include proof of Dutch ancestry.

1146

SOCIETY OF DAUGHTERS OF THE U.S. ARMY
(Scholarships)
7717 Rock Ledge Ct.
Springfield VA 22152
Written inquiry

AMOUNT: $1000

DEADLINE(S): March 1 (to receive application); March 31 (completed application)

FIELD(S): All fields of study

Open to daughters, step- and granddaughters of commissioned officers of the US Army who are on active duty, are retired, or who died on active duty or after eligible retirement. Must demonstrate financial need and merit.

Approximately 8 scholarships per year. Renewable. Include qualifying parent's name, rank, social security number, & dates of service. Send self-addressed stamped envelope between November 1 & March 1.

1147

SONS OF ITALY FOUNDATION
(National Leadership Grants)
219 'E' Street NE
Washington DC 20002
202/547-2900

AMOUNT: $2000 to $5000

DEADLINE(S): March 15

FIELD(S): All fields of study

National leadership grant competition is open to any full-time student of Italian heritage studying at an accredited college or university. For undergraduate or graduate study.

Write for complete information. Also contact local and state lodges for information regarding scholarships offered to members and their children.

1148

SONS OF NORWAY FOUNDATION
(Astrid G. Gates Scholarship Fund)
1455 West Lake St.
Minneapolis MN 55408
Written inquiry

AMOUNT: $250 to $750

DEADLINE(S): March 1

FIELD(S): All fields of study

Applicants must be between the ages of 17 & 22 and be CURRENT members of Sons of

Norwary or children or grandchildren of current Sons of Norway members. Must demonstrate financial need.
Write for complete information.

1149

SOROPTIMIST FOUNDATIONS
(Soroptimist International of the Americas—Training Awards Program)
  Two Penn Center Plaza; Suite 1000
  1500 JFK Blvd.
  Philadelphia PA 19102-1883
  215/557-9300

AMOUNT: $3000 (54 awards); $10,000 (1 award)
DEADLINE(S): December 15
FIELD(S): All fields of study

Open to mature women heads of households furthering their skills/training to upgrade employment status. Preference to vo-tech training or undergrad degree completion. Not available for grad work.

54 regional USA awards; 17 in other countries/territories. Contact local club or send SASE to SIA (Attn: TAP) at above address for complete information.

1150

SOUTH CAROLINA GOVERNOR'S OFFICE; DIVISION OF VETERANS AFFAIRS
(Tuition Scholarships for Children of Veterans)
  1205 Pendleton Street
  Columbia SC 29201
  803/734-0200

AMOUNT: Tuition waiver
DEADLINE(S): None
FIELD(S): All fields of study

For children of veterans who were legal residents of South Carolina at time of entry into military service & who (during service) were MIA, POW, killed in action, totally disabled, or died of disease. Must have received medal of honor.

South Carolina residency & US citizenship required. For undergraduate study at South Carolina state-supported schools. Write for complete information.

1151

SOUTH CAROLINA STUDENT LOAN CORPORATION
  P.O. Box 21487
  Columbia SC 29221
  803/798-0916

AMOUNT: Varies
DEADLINE(S): 30 days before end of loan period
FIELD(S): All areas of study

Open to US citizens or eligible non-citizens. Must be enrolled or accepted for enrollment at an eligible post-secondary school. Amount of loan determined by cost of school and financial need.

Interest begins at 8% and increases to 10% at fifth year of repayment. Loan must be renewed annually. Write for complete information.

1152

SOUTH CAROLINA TUITION GRANTS COMMITTEE
(Higher Education Tuition Grants Program)
  P.O. Box 12159; 1st Floor Keenan Bldg.
  Columbia SC 29211-2159
  803/734-1200

AMOUNT: Up to $3260
DEADLINE(S): None specified
FIELD(S): All fields Of study

Open to residents of South Carolina who are accepted to or enrolled in eligible private post-secondary institutions in South Carolina. Must demonstrate financial need & academic merit. US citizenship or legal residency required.

Approximately 8000 grants per year. Renewable. Contact financial aid office or write to address above for complete information.

1153

**SOUTH DAKOTA DEPT. OF
EDUCATION & CULTURAL AFFAIRS
(State Student Incentive Grant)**
    700 Governors Drive
    Pierre SD 57501-2291
    605/773-3134

AMOUNT: $100 to $600

DEADLINE(S): Established by colleges

FIELD(S): All fields of study

Open to residents of South Dakota who are
    enrolled at an approved undergraduate col-
    lege, university, proprietary, or vocational
    school within the state on at least a half-
    time basis. Must be US citizen or legal resi-
    dent.

Financial need is considered & applicant must
    apply for federal aid. 900 awards per year.
    Renewable until attainment of bachelor's
    degree. Write for complete information.

1154

**SOUTH DAKOTA DEPT. OF
EDUCATION & CULTURAL AFFAIRS
(Tuition Equalization Grant "TEG" Program)**
    700 Governors Drive
    Pierre SD 57501-2291
    605/773-3134

AMOUNT: $100 to $300

DEADLINE(S): Established by college

FIELD(S): All fields of study

Open to residents of South Dakota attending
    an approved undergraduate private college
    or university within the state on a full-time
    basis. Must be US citizen or legal resident.

Financial need is considered and applicant
    must apply for federal aid. Approximately
    700 awards per year. Write for complete
    information.

1155

**SOUTH DAKOTA DIVISION OF
VETERANS AFFAIRS
(Aid to Dependents of Deceased Veterans)**
    500 E. Capitol Ave.
    Pierre SD 57501-5070
    605/773-3269; FAX 605/773-5380

AMOUNT: Free tuition in state-supported
    schools

DEADLINE(S): None specified

FIELD(S): All fields of study

Open to residents of SD under 25 years of age
    who are children of veterans who were resi-
    dents of SD at least 6 months immediately
    prior to entry into active service & who
    died from any cause while in the service of
    the US armed forces.

Must attend a state-supported college or uni-
    versity in SD. Write for complete informa-
    tion.

1156

**STATE COLLEGE AND UNIVERSITY
SYSTEMS OF WEST VIRGINIA—
CENTRAL OFFICE
(WV Higher Education Grant Program)**
    P.O. Box 4007
    Charleston WV 25364-4007
    304/347-1211

AMOUNT: $350 to $1944

DEADLINE(S): January 1; March 1

FIELD(S): All areas of study

Open to high school grads who have lived in
    WV for 1 year prior to application & are
    enrolled full-time as an undergrad in an
    approved WV or PA educational institution.
    Must be US citizen & demonstrate financial
    need.

Approximately 5000 grants per year.
    Renewable up to 8 semesters. Write for
    complete information.

1157

STATE OF NEW JERSEY OFFICE OF STUDENT ASSISTANCE
(Edward J. Bloustein Distinguished Scholars Program)
CN 540
Trenton NJ 08625
609/588-3230; 800/792-8670 in NJ

AMOUNT: $1000 per year for 4 years
DEADLINE(S): October 1
FIELD(S): All areas of study

Open to New Jersey residents who are academically outstanding high school students planning to attend a NJ college or university. US citizenship or legal residency required.

Students may not apply directly to the program. Applications must be made through the high school. Contact guidance counselor or address above for complete information.

1158

STATE OF NEW JERSEY OFFICE OF STUDENT ASSISTANCE
(Tuition Aid Grants)
CN 540
Trenton NJ 08625
609/588-3230; 800/792-8670 in NJ

AMOUNT: $600–$5210
DEADLINE(S): Varies
FIELD(S): All areas of study

New Jersey resident for at least 12 months. For students who are or intend to be enrolled as full-time undergraduates in any college, university, or degree-granting post-secondary institution in NJ. US citizen or legal resident.

Grants renewable. Write for complete information.

1159

STATE OF NEW JERSEY OFFICE OF STUDENT ASSISTANCE
(Garden State Scholarships)
CN 540
Trenton NJ 08625
609/588-3230; 800/792-8670 in NJ

AMOUNT: $500 per year for 4 years
DEADLINE(S): October 1
FIELD(S): All areas of study

Resident of New Jersey for at least 12 months prior to receiving award. For undergraduate study in NJ. Demonstrate scholastic achievement & need. US citizen or legal resident.

Renewable. Write for complete information.

1160

STATE OF NEW JERSEY OFFICE OF STUDENT ASSISTANCE
(Higher Education Loan Program)
CN 540
Trenton NJ 08625
609/588-3200; 800/35-NJ-LOAN

AMOUNT: $2625 undergrad; $8500 graduate student
DEADLINE(S): 2 months prior to date of need
FIELD(S): All areas of study

Open to US citizens or legal residents who have been NJ residents for 6 months prior to filing application or out-of-state students attending school in NJ. Applies to all levels of study.

Write for complete information.

1161

STEVEN KNEZEVICH TRUST
(Grants)
100 E. Wisconsin Ave.; Suite 1020
Milwaukee WI 53202
414/271-6364

AMOUNT: $100 to $800
DEADLINE(S): November 1

FIELD(S): All areas of study

Undergraduate & graduate grants for students of Serbian descent. Must establish evidence of ancestral heritage. It is common practice for students to be interviewed in Milwaukee prior to granting the award.

Address inquiries to Stanley Hack. Include self-addressed stamped envelope.

1162

STUDENT AID FOUNDATION
(Loans)
2520 E. Piedmont Rd.; Suite F180
Marietta GA 30062
404/973-0256

AMOUNT: Undergraduates $2500 per year; graduate students $3000 per year

DEADLINE(S): April 15

FIELD(S): All areas of study

Loans available only to women who are residents of Georgia or are attending schools in Georgia. Grades, financial need, personal integrity, and sense of responsibility are considerations.

35 loans per year. Renewable with reapplication.

1163

STUDENT LOAN GUARANTEE FOUNDATION OF ARKANSAS
(Loan Dept.)
219 South Victory
Little Rock AR 72201
501/372-1491

AMOUNT: $2625 (1st year); $3500 (2nd); $5500 (3rd & 4th); $8500 (graduate)

DEADLINE(S): Varies

FIELD(S): All fields of study leading to a degree or certificate

Loans open to Arkansas resident or non-resident enrolled at eligible Arkansas post-secondary educational institution. Demonstrate financial need. US citizen or legal resident.

Write for complete information.

1164

SUNKIST GROWERS INC.
(A. W. Bodine—Sunkist Memorial Scholarship)
P.O. Box 7888
Van Nuys CA 91409
818/379-7510

AMOUNT: $1000

DEADLINE(S): March 1

FIELD(S): All fields of study

Open to California and Arizona undergraduates who come from an agricultural background and are in need of financial assistance. Confidential application includes personal and financial information.

Write for complete information.

1165

SWEDISH INSTITUTE
(Scholarships for study or research in Sweden)
P.O. Box 7434
S-103 91 Stockholm; Sweden
Written inquiry

AMOUNT: SEK 6700 per month

DEADLINE(S): Applications available only between September 1 and December 1

FIELD(S): All fields of study

Open to students & researchers who are NOT Swedish citizens. For study or research in Sweden when it cannot be done equally well in another country. Duration is normally one academic year. Knowledge of Swedish or English required.

Awards tenable at any Swedish university, educational institution, or for independent research. Write for complete information.

1166

SWISS BENEVOLENT SOCIETY OF CHICAGO
(Scholarship Fund)
6440 N. Bosworth Ave.
Chicago IL 60626
Written inquiry

AMOUNT: $750 to $2500

DEADLINE(S): February 1 (inquiry); March 1 (application)

FIELD(S): All areas of study

Undergraduate scholarships open to Swiss nationals or those of proven Swiss descent who are permanent residents of Illinois or Southern Wisconsin & accepted to or enrolled in accredited colleges or universities. Minimum 3.5 GPA required.

Swiss students studying in the USA on a student or visitors visa are NOT eligible. Write for complete information.

1167

SWISS BENEVOLENT SOCIETY OF SAN FRANCISCO
(Swiss Undergraduate Scholarship Fund)
c/o Swiss Consulate General
456 Montgomery St.; Suite 1500
San Francisco CA 94104
415/788-2272

AMOUNT: Varies

DEADLINE(S): May 15

FIELD(S): All fields of study

Undergrad scholarships at USA colleges open to Swiss nationals who have lived within a 150-mile radius of the San Francisco City Hall for 3 years prior to application date.

15–25 awards per year. Limited to schools in California. Write for complete information.

1168

TEXAS A & M UNIVERSITY
(Academic Excellence Awards)
Student Financial Aid Office
College Station TX 77843
409/845-3236

AMOUNT: $500–$1500

DEADLINE(S): March 1

FIELD(S): All fields of study

Open to full-time undergraduate & graduate students at Texas A&M University. Awards are intended to recognize & assist students who are making excellent scholastic progress.

Approximately 500 awards per year. Awards granted for one year. Applications are available at the student financial aid office during January & February.

1169

TEXAS A & M UNIVERSITY
(Opportunity Awards; Academic Achievement Scholarships)
Student Financial Aid Office
College Station TX 77843
409/845-3236

AMOUNT: $500–$2000

DEADLINE(S): January 15

FIELD(S): All fields of study

These programs are designed to provide scholarships to Texas A&M University for college freshmen & outstanding high school grads. Selection based on leadership ability, SAT scores, & high school record. US citizen or permanent resident.

Approximately 500 awards per year. Awards are granted for 1–4 years. Contact financial aid office for complete information.

1170

TEXAS A & M UNIVERSITY
(President's Achievement Awards for Minority Students)
Office of Honors Programs & Academic Scholarships
College Station TX 77843
409/845-1957

AMOUNT: $2500 per year for 4 years

DEADLINE(S): January 15

FIELD(S): All fields of study

This competitive academic scholarship program provides 4-year scholarships for African-American and Hispanic high school seniors who will be attending Texas A&M University. US citizenship or permanent residency required.

Approximatvely 300 awards per year. Write for complete information.

1171

TEXAS A & M UNIVERSITY
(President's Endowed Scholarships; Lechner Fellowships; McFadden Scholarships)
Office of Honours Programs & Academic Scholarships
College Station TX 77843
409/845-1957

AMOUNT: $2000–$3000 per year over 4 years
DEADLINE(S): January 15
FIELD(S): All fields of study

Open to high school seniors who will be attending Texas A&M, scored 1250 or higher on their SAT (or equivalent of 30 on ACT), and rank in the top 15% of high school graduating class or are National Merit Scholarship semi-finalists.

US citizenship or legal residency required. Approximately 350 awards per year. Write for complete information.

1172

TEXAS HIGHER EDUCATION COORDINATING BOARD
(Scholarships, Grants, & Loans)
P.O. Box 12788
Capitol Station
Austin TX 78711-2788
512/483-6340

AMOUNT: Varies
DEADLINE(S): Varies with program
FIELD(S): All fields of study

Open to students attending Texas institutions. Numerous State-administered student financial aid programs (including scholarships, grants, & loans) are offered.

Contact your school's financial aid office or write to the address above for the booklet "Financial Aid for Texas Students" which describes all programs in detail.

1173

THE BUSINESS PRODUCTS INDUSTRY ASSOCIATION
301 North Fairfax St.
Alexandria VA 22314
703/549-9040

AMOUNT: $2000
DEADLINE(S): March 15
FIELD(S): All fields of study

Open to applicants who are employed by (or related to an employee of) a member company of The Business Products Industry Association. Membership status will be verified.

80 scholarships per year. Write for complete information.

1174

THETA DELTA CHI EDUCATIONAL FOUNDATION
(Scholarship)
135 Bay State Road
Boston MA 02215
Written inquiry

AMOUNT: $1000
DEADLINE(S): April 30
FIELD(S): All fields of study

Scholarships open to active members of Theta Delta Chi. Considerations include past service to the fraternity, scholastic achievement and promise, and financial need. Preference to undergrads but graduate students will be considered.

Write for complete information.

1175

THIRD MARINE DIVISION ASSOCIATION
(Scholarships)
P.O. Box 634
Inverness FL 34451
Written inquiry

AMOUNT: $500–$2400

DEADLINE(S): April 15

FIELD(S): All fields of study

Undergrad scholarships for dependent children of USMC & USN personnel who died as a result of service in Vietnam or the Southeast Asia Operations "Desert Shield" and "Desert Storm" as a result of service with the 3rd Marine Division.

Also open to children of Association members (living or dead) who held membership 2 years or more. Must demonstrate financial need. Awards renewable. Write for complete information.

1176

THOMAS J. WATSON FOUNDATION
(Fellowship Program)
217 Angell St.
Providence RI 02906-2120
401/274-1952

AMOUNT: $16,000 single; $22,500 with accompanying financial & legal dependent

DEADLINE(S): November 1

FIELD(S): All fields of study

Open to graduating seniors at the 48 USA colleges on the foundation's roster. Fellowship provides for one year of independent study and travel abroad immediately following graduation.

Candidates must be nominated by their college. Up to 60 awards per year. Write for list of participating institutions and complete information.

1177

TOWSON STATE UNIVERSITY
(Scholarship & Award Programs)
Scholarship Office
Towson MD 21204
301/321-3702

AMOUNT: Varies

DEADLINE(S): Varies

FIELD(S): All fields of study

Numerous scholarship and award programs available to entering freshmen and to graduate and transfer students.

Write for scholarships and awards booklet which describes each program in detail.

1178

TRANSPORT WORKERS UNION OF AMERICA
(Michael J. Quill Scholarship Fund)
80 West End Ave.
New York NY 10023
212/873-6000

AMOUNT: $1200

DEADLINE(S): May 1

FIELD(S): All fields of study

Open to high school seniors (under 21) who are dependents of TWU members in good standing or of a deceased member who was in good standing at time of death. Dependent brothers or sisters of members in good standing also may apply.

15 scholarships per year. Renewable up to 4 years. Write for complete information.

1179

TULANE UNIVERSITY
(Scholarships & Fellowships)
Admissions Office
New Orleans LA 70118
504/865-5731

AMOUNT: Varies

DEADLINE(S): Varies

FIELD(S): All areas of study

Numerous need-based scholarship & fellowship programs for undergraduate and graduate study at Tulane University. There is also an honors program for outstanding students accepted for enrollment at Tulane.

Write for complete information.

1180

TUPPERWARE HOME PARTIES
(Scholarships)
P.O. Box 2353
Orlando FL 32802
407/826-5050

AMOUNT: Varies
DEADLINE(S): January 15
FIELD(S): All areas of study

Undergraduate scholarships open to independent Tupperware dealers, managers, & their dependent children and to children of franchised distributors. Awards tenable at any recognized college or university. USA citizen or legal resident.
Write for complete information.

1181

TWO/TEN INTERNATIONAL
FOOTWEAR FOUNDATION
(Scholarship Program)
56 Main Street
Watertown MA 02172
617/923-4500 or 800/346-3210

AMOUNT: $200 to $2000
DEADLINE(S): January 15
FIELD(S): All fields of study

Open to children of footwear, leather, & allied industry workers (employed a minimum of 1 year) or to students employed a minimum of 500 hours in one of the above industries. Must be high school senior or within 4 years of graduation.
For full-time undergrad study at 2- or 4-year college, vo-tech, or nursing school. Financial need & superlative academic achievement must be demonstrated. Renewable if criteria continue to be met. Write for complete information.

1182

TY COBB EDUCATIONAL
FOUNDATION
(Undergraduate Scholarship Program)
P.O. Box 725
Forest Park GA 30051
Written Inquiry

AMOUNT: $2000
DEADLINE(S): Juen 15
FIELD(S): All fields of study

Open to Georgia residents who have completed at least one academic year in an accredited college with a "B" grade average. Must demonstrate financial need.
Renewable with reapplication and completion of 45 quarter or 30 semester credit hours. Write for complete information.

1183

UNION OF NEEDLETRADER,
INDUSTRIAL, & TEXTILE
EMPLOYEES—UPPER SOUTH
DEPARTMENT
(UNITE ILGWU Scholarships)
One North Howard Street
Baltimore MD 21201
301/685-0884

AMOUNT: $2500
DEADLINE(S): April 1
FIELD(S): All fields of study

Open to children of current members of Upper South Dept. ILGWU with 3 years of good standing in the union. Awards are tenable at accredited undergraduate colleges & universities.
Write for complete information.

1184

UNITE!
(Duchessi-Sallee Scholarship)
1710 Broadway
New York NY 10019
212/265-7000

AMOUNT: $1000

DEADLINE(S): March 15

FIELD(S): All fields of study

Three winners are selected each year for scholarships to any 2-year or 4-year degree-granting college. Awards are made ONLY to incoming freshmen who are the daughters or sons of union members in good standing for 2 years or more.

Scholarship is renewable for one additional year. Write for complete information.

1185

UNITED DAUGHTERS OF THE CONFEDERACY
(Scholarships)
Business Office; Memorial Bldg.
328 North Blvd.
Richmond VA 23220-4057
804/355-1636

AMOUNT: $400 to $1500

DEADLINE(S): February 15

FIELD(S): All fields of study

Open to descendants of worthy Confederate veterans. Applicants who are collateral descendants must be active members of the United Daughters of the Confederacy or of the Children of the Confederacy & MUST be sponsored by a UDC chapter.

Most awards for undergraduate study. For complete information send self-addressed stamped #10 envelope to address above or contact the education director in the division where you reside.

1186

UNITED FEDERATION OF TEACHERS
(College Scholarship Fund)
260 Park Ave. South
New York NY 10010
212/529-2110

AMOUNT: $4000 ($1000 per year)

DEADLINE(S): December 6

FIELD(S): All fields of study

Open to New York City residents who attend New York City public high schools. Scholarships support undergraduate study at recognized colleges & universities. Financial need and academic standing are considerations.

Approximately 250 awards per year. Renewable. Write for complete information.

1187

UNITED FOOD & COMMERCIAL WORKERS INTERNATIONAL UNION
(UFCW Scholarship Program)
1775 'K' Street NW
Washington DC 20006
201/223-3111

AMOUNT: $1000 per year for 4 years

DEADLINE(S): December 31

FIELD(S): All fields of study

Open to UFCW members or high school seniors who are children of members. Applicants must meet certain eligibility requirements. Awards for full-time study only.

14 awards per year. Contact Douglas H. Dority, President (address above), for complete information.

1188

UNITED FOOD & COMMERCIAL WORKERS UNION—LOCAL 555
(Scholarship Program)
P.O. Box 23555
Tigard OR 97223
503/684-2822

AMOUNT: $900 to $1200

DEADLINE(S): April 22

FIELD(S): All fields of study

Program open ONLY to Local 555 members (in good standing for at least 1 year), their children, & spouses. Scholarships may be used at any accredited university, college, technical-vocational school, junior college, or community college.

Write for complete information ONLY if you are a UFCW Local 555 member or relative of a member.

1189

UNITED NEGRO COLLEGE FUND
(Scholarships)
Educational Services Department
500 E. 62nd St.
New York NY 10021
212/326-1100

AMOUNT: $500 to $7500 per year
DEADLINE(S): Varies
FIELD(S): All areas of study

Scholarships available to students who enroll in one of the 41 United Negro College Fund member institutions. Financial need must be established through the financial aid office at a UNCF college.

For information and a list of the UNCF campuses write to the address above.

1190

UNITED PAPERWORKERS INTERNATIONAL UNION
(Scholarship Program)
P.O. Box 1475
Nashville TN 37202
615/834-8590

AMOUNT: $1000
DEADLINE(S): March 15
FIELD(S): All fields of study

Scholarships open to high school seniors who are sons or daughters of paid-up union members of at least one year. Awards tenable at accredited undergraduate colleges & universities. Must be US or Canadian citizen.

22 awards per year. Recipients are asked to take at least 1 labor course during their college career. Financial need is a consideration. Write for complete information.

1191

UNITED STATES JAYCEES
(War Memorial Fund Scholarship Program)
P.O. Box 7
Tulsa OK 74102
Written inquiry

AMOUNT: $1000
DEADLINE(S): March 1
FIELD(S): All fields of study

Open to US citizens who are enrolled in or accepted for admission to a college or university. Must possess academic potential and leadership traits. Financial need must be demonstrated.

Applications available ONLY between July 1 and February 1. Send self-addressed stamped business size envelope & $5 application fee to JWMF Dept. 94922; Tulsa; OK 74194-0001.

1192

UNITED STEELWORKERS OF AMERICA—DISTRICT 7
(Hugh Carcella Scholarship Program)
1017 W. 9th Ave. A & B
King of Prussia PA 19406
215/265-7577

AMOUNT: $750 to $3000
DEADLINE(S): March 15
FIELD(S): All areas of study

Must be a member in good standing or son or daughter or legal ward of member of United Steelworkers of America—District 7 Local Union, participating in the scholarship program. Must be entering freshman pursuing a BS degree.

8 scholarships per year. Renewable. Write for complete information.

1193

UNITED STUDENT AID FUNDS INC.
(Guaranteed Student Loan Program; Plus
Loans)
1912 Capital Ave. #320
Cheyenne WY 82001
307/635-3259

AMOUNT: $2625 to $5500 (undergrads);
$8500 (grads)
DEADLINE(S): None
FIELD(S): All field of study

Low-interest loans are available to Wyoming residents who are citizens or permanent residents of the USA & enrolled at least 1/2-time in school. Must demonstrate financial need.

Write for complete information.

1194

UNITED TRANSPORTATION UNION
(Scholarship Program)
14600 Detroit Avenue
Cleveland OH 44107
216/228-9400

AMOUNT: $500
DEADLINE(S): March 31
FIELD(S): All areas of study

Open to US or Canadian citizens who are high school graduates under age 25 and are either UTU members or the children or grandchildren of UTU members. Must maintain satisfactory academic record.

50 scholarships per year. Renewable up to 4 years. Awarded on lottery system. Write for complete information.

1195

UNIVERSITY OF NEBRASKA AT
LINCOLN (Regents, David, Davis, National
Merit, & Departmental Scholarships)
16 Administration Bldg.
Lincoln NE 68588-0411
401/472-2030

AMOUNT: Varies
DEADLINE(S): December 15 preceding Fall semester
FIELD(S): All areas of study

Open to Nebraska high school graduates who have taken the ACT or SAT and sent scores to UNL. Variety of scholarships available—some for minorities; some based on financial need; and various other requirements.

By submitting application for freshman scholarship, student is competing for approximately 1500 other individual scholarship programs at UNL. Write for complete information.

1196

UNIVERSITY OF NEW MEXICO
(Scholarships)
Mesa Hall North
Albuquerque NM 87131-2081
505/277-6090

AMOUNT: Varying amounts to $2000
DEADLINE(S): February 1
FIELD(S): All fields of study

The University of New Mexico awards to eligible first-time freshmen more than 1000 scholarships from six major scholarship programs. Considerations include extra-curricular activities and personal statement. Must be US citizen.

Contact Department of Student Financial Aid and Scholarships (address above) for complete information.

1197

UNIVERSITY OF OXFORD—
SOMERVILLE COLLEGE
(Janet Watson Bursary)
College Secretary
Somerville College
Oxford OX2 6HD England
1865-270600

AMOUNT: 3500 pounds sterling
DEADLINE(S): March 1
FIELD(S): All fields of study

Bursary is offered for USA men or women graduates wishing to read for a further degree at Oxford as a member of the college. US citizenship required. Renewable for a second year.

Write for complete information.

1198

UNIVERSITY OF WINDSOR
(Undergraduate Scholarships)
Student Awards Office
Windsor Ontario N9B 3P4 Canada
519/253-4232

AMOUNT: Approximately $600
DEADLINE(S): May 31; December 31
FIELD(S): All fields of study

Open to students who are graduates of a US high school, have superior grades, and wish to study at Windsor University. In-course awards are available to those who are already enrolled. Students must complete all admissions requirements.

Renewable for three years if qualifying average is maintained. Write for complete information and a catalog of available undergraduate scholarships.

1199

URANN FOUNDATION
(Scholarship Program)
Robert C. LeBoeuf; Administrator
P.O. Box 1788
Brockton MA 02403
617/588-7744

AMOUNT: Varies
DEADLINE(S): April 15
FIELD(S): All fields of study

Scholarship program open to children of cranberry growers & their employees (in the state of Massachusetts ONLY). Awards are tenable at eligible 2-year & 4-year undergraduate colleges & universities.

Write for complete information.

1200

US AIR FORCE ACADEMY
(Academy Appointment)
2304 Cadet Dr.; Suite 300
USAF Academy CO 80840
719/472-2520

AMOUNT: Full tuition & all costs + salary
DEADLINE(S): January 31
FIELD(S): All fields of study

Appointment is for a 4-year undergraduate degree followed by a commission as a second lieutenant in the USAF. Recipients are obligated to six years of active duty. Must be US citizen between the ages of 17 & 22. SAT/ACT scores required.

Nomination is required for appointment. Write for information on obtaining nomination and for detailed admission requirements.

1201

US ARMY EMERGENCY RELIEF
(Undergraduate Scholarship Program)
200 Stovall St.
Alexandria VA 22332
Written inquiry

AMOUNT: Up to $1000 per year
DEADLINE(S): March 1
FIELD(S): All fields of study

Open to unmarried dependent children of active, retired, or deceased members of the US Army. Applicants may not have reached their 22nd birthday before June 1 of the school year that begins the following September. For undergraduate study.

Must submit financial aid form and official high school transcript. Write for complete information.

1202

US COAST GUARD MUTUAL ASSISTANCE
(Adm. Roland Student Loan Program)
Coast Guard Headquarters (GZMA)
Washington DC 20593
202/267-1683

AMOUNT: Up to $2700 per year
(undergrads); $7500 (grads)
DEADLINE(S): None specified
FIELD(S): All areas of study

For members & dependents of Coast Guard
Mutual Assistance members who are
enrolled at least half-time in an approved
post-secondary school.

Loans renewable for up to four years. Must
reapply annually. Write for complete information.

1203

US DEPT OF INTERIOR; BUREAU OF INDIAN AFFAIRS
(Higher Education Grant Program)
1849 C St. NW
Washington DC 20240
202/208-4871

AMOUNT: Varies depending on need
DEADLINE(S): Varies
FIELD(S): All areas of study

Open to enrolled members of Indian Tribes or
Alaska native descendants eligible to
receive services from the Secretary of the
Interior. For study leading to associate's,
bachelor's, or graduate degree.

Must demonstrate financial need. Contact
home agency, tribe, or BIA office or financial aid office at chosen college.

1204

US DEPT. OF EDUCATION
(Robert C. Byrd Honors Scholarship Program)
600 Independence Ave. SW
Portals Bldg. Rm. C-80
Washington DC 20202-5329
202/260-3394

AMOUNT: $1500/year
DEADLINE(S): Varies by state
FIELD(S): All fields of study

Open to outstanding high school seniors who
graduate in the same academic year the
award is being made & who have been
accepted for enrollment at an institution of
higher education. Must be US citizen or
permanent resident.

Available for up to 4 years of study. State educational agencies receive funding from the
US Dept. of Education. Apply through
state educational agency or contact school
counselor for complete information.

1205

US MARINE CORPS SCHOLARSHIP FOUNDATION INC.
(Scholarships)
P.O. Box 3008
Princeton NJ 08543
609/921-3534

AMOUNT: $500–$2500
DEADLINE(S): February 1 (applications
available September 1)
FIELD(S): All fields of study

Open to children of US Marine Corps members or the dependent children of former
Marines for undergraduate or vocational
study. Applicant's gross family income
should not exceed $35000.

Renewable with written reapplication each
year. Write for complete information.

1206

US SUBMARINE VETERANS OF WWII
(Scholarship Program)
405 Dillingham Blvd.
Norfolk Naval Station
Norfolk VA 23511
804/451-3660; FAX 804/489-8578

AMOUNT: $1750/year

DEADLINE(S): April 15

FIELD(S): All fields of study

For children of paid-up regular members of
US Submarine Veterans of WWII.
Applicant must be an unmarried high
school senior or have graduated from high
school no more than 4 years prior to applying and be under the age of 24.

List those submarines in which your sponsor
served during WWII and include sponsor's
membership card number when requesting
application.

1207

UTILITY WORKERS UNION OF
AMERICA
(Scholarship Program)
815 16th Street NW
Washington DC 20006
Written inquiry

AMOUNT: $500–$2000 per year

DEADLINE(S): January 1 of junior year in
high school

FIELD(S): All fields of study

Scholarships are for sons and daughters of
utility workers union members in good
standing. Winners are selected from the
group of high school juniors who take the
national merit scholarship exams.

Two 4-year scholarships awarded annually.
Write for complete information.

1208

VERMONT STUDENT ASSISTANCE
CORPORATION
(Incentive Grants)
Champlain Mill; P.O. Box 2000
Winooski VT 05404
802/655-9602

AMOUNT: $400 to $5200

DEADLINE(S): March 1

FIELD(S): All fields of study

Open to Vermont residents enrolled as full-
time undergraduate students in approved
degree programs. Must demonstrate financial need and be US citizen or legal resident.

Write for complete information.

1209

VIKKI CARR SCHOLARSHIP
FOUNDATION
(Scholarships)
P.O. Box 5126
Beverly Hills CA 90210
Written inquiry

AMOUNT: Up to $3000

DEADLINE(S): April 1

FIELD(S): All fields of study

Open to Mexican-American California residents between the ages of 17 and 22.
Awards are for undergrad study at accredited colleges and universities. No U.S. citizenship requirement.

5–10 awards per year. Applications available
Jan 1. Send SASE for complete information.

1210

VIRGIN ISLANDS BOARD OF
EDUCATION
(Exceptional Children Scholarship)
P.O. Box 11900
St. Thomas VI 00801
809/774-4546

AMOUNT: $2000

DEADLINE(S): March 31

FIELD(S): All fields of study

Open to bona fide residents of the Virgin Islands who suffer from physical, mental, or emotional impairment & have demonstrated exceptional abilities & the need of educational training not available in Virgin Islands schools.

NOT for study at the college level. Write for complete information.

1211

VIRGIN ISLANDS BOARD OF EDUCATION
(Territorial Scholarship Grants)
P.O. Box 11900
St. Thomas VI 00801
809/774-4546

AMOUNT: $1000–$3000

DEADLINE(S): March 31

FIELD(S): All fields of study

Grants open to bona fide residents of the Virgin Islands who have a cumulative average of at least 'C' & are enrolled in an accredited institution of higher learning.

300–400 loans & grants per year. Renewable provided recipient maintains an average of 'C' or better. Loans are also available. Write for complete information.

1212

VIRGINIA STATE COUNCIL OF HIGHER EDUCATION
(Tuition Assistance Grant Program)
101 N. 14th St.
James Monroe Bldg.
Richmond VA 23219
804/225-2141

AMOUNT: Up to $1500

DEADLINE(S): July 31; September 14; December 1

FIELD(S): All fields of study EXCEPT Religious Training or Theological Education

Open to Virginia residents who are full-time undergraduate, graduate, or professional students at eligible private colleges and universities in Virginia.

Contact the financial aid office at the college or university you wish to attend for complete information.

1213

VIRGINIA STATE COUNCIL OF HIGHER EDUCATION
(College Scholarship Assistance Program)
101 N. 14th St.
James Monroe Bldg.
Richmond VA 23219
804/225-2141

AMOUNT: $400 to $2000

DEADLINE(S): Varies

FIELD(S): All fields of study except religion

Open to Virginia residents who are undergraduate students with at least 6 credit hours at eligible Virginia colleges and universities. Applicants may NOT be enrolled in a program of religious training or theological education.

Funding reduced for 1995-96 & program may be eliminated for 1996-97. Write for complete information or contact your institution's financial aid office.

1214

VIRGINIA STATE COUNCIL OF HIGHER EDUCATION
(Undergraduate Financial Assistance "Last Dollar" Program)
James Monroe Bldg.
101 N. 14th St.
Richmond VA 23219
804/225-2141

AMOUNT: Minimum $200 per term

DEADLINE(S): Varies (college or university deadline)

FIELD(S): All areas of study

"Last dollar" is a need-based program designed to assist minority Virginia students in attending state-supported colleges on at least a half-time basis. Must be a Virginia resident and enrolled in a public Virginia institution.

Contact the financial aid office at your college or university.

1215

VIRGINIA STATE COUNCIL OF HIGHER EDUCATION
(Virginia Scholars Program)
101 N. 14th St.
James Monroe Bldg.
Richmond VA 23219
804/786-1690

AMOUNT: $3000

DEADLINE(S): December 15 (high school senior); May 15 (college transfer)

FIELD(S): All fields of study

Open to Virginia residents who are outstanding high school seniors or grads of public 2-year colleges planning to enroll as full-time undergrads at a 4-year VA college or university—must be nominated by high school or 2-year college.

Grants are merit based. Renewable up to 3 additional years. Write for complete information.

1216

VIRGINIA STUDENT ASSISTANCE AUTHORITIES
(Guaranteed Student Loan Programs)
411 E. Franklin St.; Suite 300
Richmond VA 23219-2243
804/755-4000 or 800/792-LOAN

AMOUNT: Varies

DEADLINE(S): None

FIELD(S): All fields of study

Various loan programs open to students enrolled in approved institutions. Eligibility governed by SEAA & federal regulations.

Contact college financial aid office or write to address above for complete information.

1217

VON TROTHA EDUCATIONAL TRUST
(Von Trotha Scholarship)
Trust Dept.
P.O. Box 1057
1000 10th St.
Greeley CO 80631
303/356-1000

AMOUNT: $300 to $500

DEADLINE(S): March 31

FIELD(S): All areas of study

Scholarships are open to graduates of Weld County Colorado high schools who are in the upper 25% of their class. To be used only at accredited colleges and universities.

Write for complete information.

1218

WAL*MART FOUNDATION
(Scholarship, Associate Scholarship, & Community Scholarship)
702 SW 8th St.
Bentonville AR 72716-8071
501/273-6878

AMOUNT: $1000 to $6000

DEADLINE(S): March 1 ("Scholarship" & "Associate")—deadline for "Community" established by local store

FIELD(S): All fields of study

Open to high school seniors planning to attend an accredited college or university. Selection is based on academic achievement, ACT/SAT results, extra-curricular activities, leadership qualities, and financial need.

If you or your parents are Wal*Mart associates, contact a member of management in your Wal*Mart facility; if you or your parents are NOT Wal*Mart associates contact your high school counselor for more information.

1219

WASHINGTON HIGHER EDUCATION COORDINATING BOARD
(Washington State Need Grant Program)
P.O. Box 43430
917 Lakeridge Way
Olympia WA 98504
360/753-7850

AMOUNT: Varies
DEADLINE(S): Varies by school
FIELD(S): All fields of study except theology

Open to residents of Washington State for at least 1 year prior to enrollment. Awards tenable at eligible Washington State colleges & universities. For undergraduate study. Must attend at least half-time & be US citizen or legal resident.

35,000+ grants per year. Renewable. DO NOT APPLY DIRECTLY—apply as part of regular financial aid application process at any Washington State college, university, or technical or proprietary school.

1220

WASHINGTON POST
(Thomas Ewing Memorial Educational Grants for Newspaper Carriers)
1150 15th St. NW
Washington DC 20079
202/334-5799

AMOUNT: $1000–$2000
DEADLINE(S): Last Friday in January
FIELD(S): All areas

Open to current post carriers who have been on-route the past 18 months. Award is intended to assist & encourage pursuit of higher education at any level.

25–35 awards per year. Write for complete information.

1221

WASHINGTON STATE PTA
(Financial Grant Foundation Program)
2003 65th Ave. West
Tacoma WA 98466-6215
206/565-2153

AMOUNT: $500 to $1000
DEADLINE(S): March 1
FIELD(S): All fields of study

Open to Washington state residents. Grant program is designed to assist Washington state high school seniors & graduates who will be entering freshmen at an accredited college or university. Financial need is primary consideration.

Write for complete information.

1222

WASIE FOUNDATION
(Scholarship Program)
909 Foshay Tower
Minneapolis MN 55402
612/332-3883

AMOUNT: $1000–$7500
DEADLINE(S): April 15
FIELD(S): All fields of study

Undergraduate and graduate scholarships open to qualified students of Polish descent who are of the Christian faith. Awards tenable only in Minnesota at 10 specified institutions of higher education. 30 awards per year.

Applicants must be full-time students and may not be a member of the Communist party. Applications are sent out in January and must be returned by April 15.

1223

WELLESLEY COLLEGE
(Alice Freeman Palmer Fellowships)
Career Center
Secretary Graduate Fellowships
Wellesley MA 02181-8200
617/283-3525

AMOUNT: Up to $4000 stipend

DEADLINE(S): Mid-December

FIELD(S): All fields of study

Open to unmarried women under 27 years of age who are Wellesley College graduates. Fellowships are for graduate study or research at institutions in the USA or abroad. Should remain unmarried throughout tenure.

Write for complete information.

1224

WELLESLEY COLLEGE
(Fellowships for Wellesley Graduates)
Career Center
Secretary Graduate Fellowships
Wellesley MA 02181-8200
617/283-3525

AMOUNT: $1000 to $14,000 stipend

DEADLINE(S): Mid-December

FIELD(S): All fields of study

Numerous fellowship programs open to Wellesley College graduating seniors and Wellesley College graduates. For graduate study or research at institutions in the USA or abroad.

Applications available starting September 1. Write for complete information.

1225

WELSH GUILD/PHILADELPHIA
(Scholarships)
450 S. Broadway
Camden NJ 08103
Written inquiry only

AMOUNT: $500 to $1500

DEADLINE(S): March 1

FIELD(S): All fields of study

Open to undergrads of Welsh descent who live within 150 miles of Philadelphia or plan to enroll in a college within that area. Must prove Welsh descent & be active in a Welsh organization or church or participate in Welsh activities.

Must be US citizen or legal resident. 5 to 6 awards per year. Renewable. Send SASE to Daniel E. Williams; Ysgrifennydd Cymdeithas Gymreig/Philadelphia (at the above address) for application & complete information.

1226

WEST VIRGINIA DIVISION OF
VETERANS' AFFAIRS
(War Orphans Education Program)
1321 Plaza East; Suite 101
Charleston WV 25301
304/558-3661

AMOUNT: $400 to $500/year

DEADLINE(S): July 15; December 1

FIELD(S): All areas of study

Open to surviving children (aged 16–23) of USA military personnel whose active duty service in US armed forces involved hostile action. Death of parent must have been the result of a disability incurred during such wartime service.

Student must have lived in WV for 1 year prior to initial application. Awards tenable at any state-supported high school, college, or university. Write for complete information.

1227

WESTERN GOLF ASSOCIATION/EVANS
SCHOLARS FOUNDATION
(Caddie Scholarships)
Scholarship Committee
Golf IL 60029
708/724-4600

AMOUNT: Full tuition & housing

DEADLINE(S): November 1

FIELD(S): All fields of study

Open to US high school seniors in the top 25% of their class who have served as a caddie at a WGA member club for at least 2 years. Outstanding personal character & financial need are considerations.

Applications are accepted after completion of junior year in high school (between July 1 and November 1). 200 awards per year; renewable for 4 years. Contact your local country club or write to address above for complete information.

1228

WHITNEY BENEFITS INC.
(Student Loans)
  P.O. Box 691
  403 N. Jefferson
  Sheridan WY 82801
  307/674-7303

AMOUNT: $2000 to $4000
DEADLINE(S): None
FIELD(S): All fields of study

Open to graduates of Sheridan County, Wyoming, high schools who are under 25 years of age & maintain at least a 2.0 GPA. Loans may be used for undergraduate study only. A personal interview is required.
Financial need is considered. Family income should be under $40,000 per year. Approximately 70 awards per year. Write for complete information.

1229

WILLIAM BRADLEY SCHOLARSHIP FOUNDATION INC.
(William Bradley Scholarship)
  125 Ozark Dr.
  Crystal City MO 63019
  314/937-2570

AMOUNT: $400
DEADLINE(S): April 1
FIELD(S): All fields of study

Open to graduating seniors of Crystal City High School, Festus High School, or St. Pius X High School in Jefferson County, Missouri. Must rank in the top 10 percent of class.
Write for complete information.

1230

WILLIAM H. CHAPMAN FOUNDATION
(Scholarships)
  P.O. Box 1321
  New London CT 06320
  203/443-8010

AMOUNT: $200–$850
DEADLINE(S): April 1
FIELD(S): All fields of study

Open ONLY to residents of New London County, CT. Awards support full-time undergraduate study at accredited colleges & universities. US citizenship or legal residency required. Must demonstrate financial need.
Approximately 100 awards per year. Renewable with re-application. Write for complete information.

1231

WINDHAM FOUNDATION INC.
(Scholarships)
  P.O. Box 70
  Grafton VT 05146
  802/843-2211

AMOUNT: Varies
DEADLINE(S): April 1
FIELD(S): All fields of study

Program is open ONLY to students who are RESIDENTS OF WINDHAM COUNTY, VERMONT. Scholarships are tenable at recognized undergraduate colleges & universities.
Approximately 400 awards per year. Renewable up to 4 years. Write for complete information.

1232

WISCONSIN DEPARTMENT OF VETERANS AFFAIRS
(Deceased Veterans' Survivors Economic Assistance Loan/Education Grants)
  P.O. Box 7843
  Madison WI 53707
  608/266-1311

AMOUNT: $4500 maximum

DEADLINE(S): None specified

FIELD(S): All areas of study

Open to surviving spouses (who have not remarried) of deceased eligible veterans and to the minor dependent children of the deceased veterans. Must be residents of Wisconsin at the time of application.

Approximately 5700 grants & loans per year. Contact a Wisconsin veterans' service officer in your county of residence for complete information.

1233

WISCONSIN DEPARTMENT OF VETERANS AFFAIRS
(Veterans Economic Assistance Loan/Education Grants)
P.O. Box 7843
Madison WI 53707
608/266-1311

AMOUNT: $4500 maximum

DEADLINE(S): None specified

FIELD(S): All areas of study

Open to veterans (as defined in Wisconsin Statute 45.35-5) who are living in Wisconsin at the time of application. There are limitations on income.

Approximately 5700 grants and loans per year. Write for complete information.

1234

WISCONSIN HIGHER EDUCATION AIDS BOARD
(Student Financial Aid Program)
P.O. Box 7885
Madison WI 53707
608/267-2206; FAX 608/267-2808

AMOUNT: Varies

DEADLINE(S): None specified

FIELD(S): All fields of study

Board administers a variety of state and federal programs that are available to Wisconsin residents who are enrolled at least half time and maintain satisfactory academic record. Most require demonstration of financial need.

Write for complete information.

1235

WOMEN OF THE EVANGELICAL LUTHERAN CHURCH IN AMERICA
(Scholarship Program)
8765 W. Higgins Rd.
Chicago IL 60631-4189
312/380-2700

AMOUNT: $500 to $2000

DEADLINE(S): March 1

FIELD(S): All fields of study except ministry or church-certified professions

Open to ELCA laywomen age 21 or older who have experienced an interruption in schooling of at least 2 years since high school. Must provide academic record of course work beyond high school.

Must demonstrate scholastic ability, financial need; clear educational goals, & Christian commitment. Write for complete information.

1236

WOMEN'S SPORTS FOUNDATION
(Travel & Training Grants)
Eisenhower Park
East Meadow; NY 11554
516/542-4700

AMOUNT: Up to $1500 (individual); up to $3000 (team)

DEADLINE(S): March 15; July 15; November 15

FIELD(S): All fields of study

This fund was established to provide assistance to aspiring female athletes & female teams to achieve higher performance levels & ranking within their sport. USA citizen.

Grants are available for training, coaching, equipment, & travel to scheduled competitive events. Write for complete information.

1237

YAKIMA INDIAN NATION
(Scholarship Program)
P.O. Box 151
Toppenish WA 98948
509/865-5121

AMOUNT: $1000 per year
DEADLINE(S): July 1
FIELD(S): All areas of study

Program open to enrolled members of the Yakima Indian Nation. Awards tenable at recognized undergraduate & graduate institutions. US citizenship required.

Approximately 200 awards per year. Write for complete information.

1238

YOUTH FOR UNDERSTANDING
INTERNATIONAL EXCHANGE
(Corporate Sponsored Scholarships)
3501 Newark St. NW
Washington DC 20016
800/673-2728

AMOUNT: Program tuition
DEADLINE(S): November and December
FIELD(S): All fields of study

Merit-based scholarships open to high school students who wish to go overseas for a summer or for a school year. Most corporate-sponsored scholarships are available only to children of employees of sponsoring corporations.

Parents of interested students should check with their personnel office at work to see if their firm is a participant.

Helpful Publications

1239

10 STEPS IN WRITING THE RESEARCH PAPER
Roberta Markman, Peter Markman, and
  Marie Waddell
  Barron's Educational Series Inc.
  250 Wireless Blvd.
  Hauppauge NY 11788
  COST—$7.95

Arranged to lead the student step by step
  through the writing of a research paper;
  from finding a suitable subject to checking
  the final copy. Easy enough for the beginner; complete enough for the graduate student. 160 pages.

1240

200 WAYS TO PUT YOUR TALENT TO WORK IN THE HEALTH FIELD
NHC
  National Health Council Inc.
  350 Fifth Ave. Suite; 1118
  New York NY 10018
  COST—25 cents each plus $3.00 per order shipping/handling

Highly recommended. Includes straight
  answers to your questions about health
  careers plus a listing of organizations where
  more information is available about specific
  fields; financial aid and training schools.

1241

ABCs OF FINANCIAL AID (MONTANA FINANCIAL AID HANDBOOK)
Montana Guaranteed Student Loan Program
  Montana Career Information System
  2500 Broadway; P.O. Box 203101
  Helena MT 59620
  COST—Free

Describes educational costs and financial aid
  available in Montana for Montana residents
  or those attending school in Montana only.
  It covers application and award procedures
  and financial aid programs.

1242

ACADEMIC YEAR ABROAD
Sara J. Steen, Editor
  Institute of International Education
  IIE Books; 809 United Nations Plaza
  New York NY 10017
  COST—$42.95 + $4 handling

Provides information on more than 2350 post-
  secondary study programs outside the USA.

1243

AFL-CIO GUIDE TO UNION-SPONSORED SCHOLARSHIPS
AFL-CIO Department of Education
  AFL-CIO
  815 16th St. NW
  Washington DC 20006
  COST—Free to union members; $3.00 non-union

Comprehensive guide for union members and
  their dependent children. Describes local,
  national, and international union-sponsored scholarship programs. Includes a
  bibliography of other financial aid sources.

1244

ANNUAL REGISTER OF GRANT SUPPORT
Reed Reference Publishing
  Reed Reference Publishing Company
  121 Chanlon Rd.
  New Providence NJ 07974
  COST—$165.00 + $11.55 shipping/handling

Annual reference book found in most major libraries. Details thousands of grants for research that are available to individuals and organizations.

1245

ART CALENDAR
Carolyn Blakeslee, Editor in Chief

Art Calendar
P.O. Box 199
Upper Fairmount MD 21867
COST—$32.00/one year

Monthly publication contains articles of interest to artists including listings of grants; fellowships; exhibits; etc. Annual edition lists opportunities without deadlines. Sample copy of monthly is available for $5.

1246

AMERICAN INSTITUTE OF ARCHITECTS INFORMATION POSTER AND BOOKLET
AIA

AMERICAN INSTITUTE OF ARCHITECTS POSTER BROCHURE
1735 New York Ave. NW
Washington DC 20006
COST—Free

Provides list of accredited professional programs and scholarship information.

1247

BARRON'S GUIDE TO LAW SCHOOLS (10TH EDITION)
Barron's College Division;
ISBN 0-8120-1754-4

Barron's Educational Series Inc.
250 Wireless Blvd.
Hauppauge NY 11788
COST—$14.95

Comprehensive guide covering more than 200 ABA-approved American law schools. Advice on attending law school.

1248

BASIC FACTS ON STUDY ABROAD
IIE

Institute of International Education
IIE Books; 809 United Nations Plaza
New York NY 10017
COST—Free

Brochure offering essential information on planning for undergraduate and graduate study outside the USA.

1249

CAREER GUIDE FOR SINGERS
Mary McDonald, Editor

Opera America
777 14th St. NW; Suite 520
Washington DC 20005
COST—$30.00 non-members; $20.00 members

Directory containing information on auditions, grants, and competitions for young singers contemplating a career in opera.

1250

CFKR CAREER MATERIALS CATALOG
CFKR

CFKR Career Materials Inc.
11860 Kemper Rd.; Unit 7
Auburn CA 95603
COST—Free

A catalog of printed materials, software, and videotapes covering career planning, college financing, and college test preparation. Includes materials applicable to all ages—from the primary grades through graduate school.

1251

CHRONICLE CAREER INDEX
CGP; ISBN #1-55631-243-1

Chronicle Guidance Publications
66 Aurora St.
P.O. Box 1190
Moravia NY 13118

COST—$14.25 + $1.43 shipping/handling (Order No. 502CI)

Listings of career and vocational materials for students and counselors. Describes over 500 sources of publications and audio-visual materials. 90 pages. Revised annually.

1252

CHRONICLE FINANCIAL AID GUIDE
CGP; ISBN #1-55631-242-3

Chronicle Guidance Publications
66 Aurora St.
P.O. Box 1190
Moravia NY 13118
COST—$22.47 + $2.25 shipping
Order #502A

Annual guide containing information on financial aid programs offered nationally and regionally by public and private organizations. Programs support study for high school seniors, college undergraduates, and adult learners. 312 pages.

1253

CHRONICLE FOUR-YEAR COLLEGE DATABOOK
CGP; ISBN #1-55631-240-7

Chronicle Guidance Publications
66 Aurora St.
P.O. Box 1190
Moravia NY 13118
COST—$22.49 + $2.25 shipping/handling (Order No. 502CM4)

Reference book in two sections. "Majors" section lists 2133 institutions offering 780 4-year graduate and professional majors. "Charts" section contains information and statistics on each of the schools. 545 pages.

1254

CHRONICLE TWO-YEAR COLLEGE DATABOOK
CGP; ISBN #1-55631-241-5

Chronicle Guidance Publications
66 Aurora St.;

P.O. Box 1190
Moravia NY 13118
COST—$22.46 plus $2.25 shipping/handling (Order No. 502CM2)

Reference book in two sections. "Majors" section lists 2422 institutions offering 728 certificate/diploma, associate, and transfer programs. "Charts" section contains comprehensive information and statistics on each institution.

1255

COLLEGE DEGREES BY MAIL
John Bear Ph.D.; ISBN 0-89815-379-4

Ten Speed Press; Box 7123
Berkeley CA 94707
COST—$12.95 + $2.50 shipping/handling

Listing of 100 colleges that offer bachelors, masters, doctoral, and law degrees through home study. Book is the successor to Bear's Guide to Earning Non-Traditional College Degrees. 214 pages.

1256

COLLEGE FINANCIAL AID EMERGENCY KIT
Joyce Lain Kennedy and Dr. Herm Davis

Sun Features Inc.
Box 368-K
Cardiff CA 92007
COST—$5.95 (includes postage and handling)

40-page booklet filled with tips on how to meet tuition & room and board costs. It tells what is available, whom to ask, and how to ask.

1257

COLLEGE HANDBOOK (THE)
CBP; ISBN #0-87447-479-5

College Board Publications
P.O. Box 886
New York NY 10101

COST—$20.00 + $3.95 shipping/handling. CA and PA residents add sales tax.

Describes in detail over 3200 two- and four-year undergraduate institutions in the USA. Includes information on admission requirements; costs; financial aid; majors; activities; enrollment; campus life and more. 1600 pages.

1258

COLLEGE SMARTS—THE OFFICIAL FRESHMAN HANDBOOK

Joyce Slayton Mitchell; ISBN 0-912048-92-1.

Garrett Park Press
P.O. Box 190
Garrett Park MD 20896
COST—$10.95

Cogent advice for the college freshman. Covers such practical subjects as what things to take, coping with dorm life and your roommate, registration, fraternity/sorority rush, even your laundry. Advice is practical and to the point.

1259

COOPERATIVE EDUCATION UNDERGRADUATE PROGRAM DIRECTORY

NCCE

National Commission for Cooperative Education
360 Huntington Ave.
Boston MA 02115
COST—Free

Explains what co-op education is; details its advantages and lists colleges and universities that offer co-op education programs.

1260

DIRECTORY OF ACCREDITED INSTITUTIONS

ACICS

Accrediting Council for Independent Colleges and Schools
750 1st St. NE; Suite 980
Washington DC 20002
COST—No charge (one copy limit)

Annual directory containing information on more than 650 institutions offering business or business-related career programs and accredited by ACICS.

1261

DIRECTORY OF ATHLETIC SCHOLARSHIPS

Alan Green; ISBN #0-8169-2892-3

Facts on File Inc.
460 Park Ave South
New York NY 10016
COST—$24.95

Discusses the ins and outs of the recruiting process, school by school index; sport by sport index, and state by state index.

1262

DIRECTORY OF FINANCIAL AID FOR MINORITIES (1995–1997)

Gail A. Schlachter & R. David Weber

Reference Service Press
1100 Industrial Rd.; Suite 9
San Carlos CA 94070
COST—$47.50 + $4.00 shipping

Describes over 2000 scholarships, fellowships, grants, loans, awards, and internships set aside for American minorities and minority organizations. Covers all levels of study. 666 pages. Cloth. ISBN 0-918276-28-4.

1263

DIRECTORY OF FINANCIAL AID FOR STUDENTS OF ARMENIAN DESCENT

Armenian Assembly of America

Armenian Assembly of America
122 'C' Street NW; Suite 350
Washington DC 20001
COST—Free

The Armenian Assembly prepares this annual booklet that describes numerous scholarship, loan, & grant programs available from sources in the Armenian community.

1264

DIRECTORY OF FINANCIAL AIDS FOR WOMEN (1995–1997)

Gail A. Schlachter

Reference Service Press
1100 Industrial Rd.; Suite 9
San Carlos CA 94070
COST—$45.00 + $4.00 shipping

Contains over 1500 descriptions of scholarships, fellowships, grants, loans, awards, and internships set aside for women and women's organizations. Covers all levels of study. 498 pages. Cloth. ISBN 0-918276-27-6.

1265

DIRECTORY OF NATIONAL INFORMATION SOURCES ON DISABILITIES (6TH EDITION 1994-95)

National Institute of Disability & Rehabilitation Research

US Department of Education
8455 Colesville Rd.; Suite 935
Silver Spring MD 20910
COST—$15.00

Two-volume directory inventories public/federal/private resources at the national level that offer information &/or direct services to people with disabilities & people involved in educating, training, or helping people with disabilities.

1266

DIRECTORY OF POSTSECONDARY EDUCATIONAL RESOURCES IN ALASKA

ACPE

Alaska Commission on Postsecondary Education
3030 Vintage Blvd.
Juneau AK 99801
COST—Free

Comprehensive directory of postsecondary institutions and programs in Alaska plus information on state and federal grants, loans, and scholarships for Alaska residents (those who have lived in Alaska for two years).

1267

DIRECTORY OF RESEARCH GRANTS

Oryx

Oryx Press
4041 N. Central Ave.; #700
Phoenix AZ 85012
COST—$135.00

Annual reference book found in most major libraries. Excellent tool for any person or organization looking for research funding. Organized by grant title and contains extensive indexes.

1268

DIRECTORY OF SPECIAL PROGRAMS FOR MINORITY GROUP MEMBERS

ISBN 0-912048-39-5

Garrett Park Press
P.O. Box 190F
Garrett Park MD 20896
COST—$30.00

Lists over 4000 scholarships, fellowships, career assistant programs, job training sources, and other resources to help Afro-American, Asian, Hispanic, and Native American students with their education and careers. 348 pages.

1269

DIRECTORY OF UNDERGRADUATE POLITICAL SCIENCE FACULTY
Patricia Spellman

American Political Science Association
1527 New Hampshire Ave. NW
Washington DC 20036
*COST—$35.00 (non-members); $20.00
(APSA members) + $4.00 postage*

Directory listing nearly 600 separate political science departments. It includes department names, addresses, telephone numbers, names, & specializations of faculty members.

1270

EEO BIMONTHLY
Timothy M. Clancy, executive editor

CASS Recruitment Publications Inc.
1800 Sherman Place; Suite 300
Evanston IL 60201
COST—$42.00/Year

Bimonthly publication containing detailed career opportunity profiles on American companies, geographic employer listings, and occupational index.

1271

ENCYCLOPEDIA OF ASSOCIATIONS— VOL. 1
ISBN #0-8103-7945-7

Gale Research Inc.
835 Penobscot Bldg.
Detroit MI 48226
COST—$415.00

An outstanding research tool. 3-part set of reference books found in most major libraries. Contains detailed information on over 22,000 associations, organizations, unions, etc. Includes name and key word index.

1272

EXPLORING CAREERS IN MUSIC
Paul Bjorneberg; ISBN 0-940796-86-4

Music Educators National Conference
1806 Robert Fulton Dr.
Reston VA 22091
COST—$10.00/ $8.00 MENC members

Informative booklet discussing careers in the performing arts, music education, the music business, recording industry, and allied fields.

1273

FACTFILE 2—CAREERS IN FILM AND TELEVISION
Deborah A. Davidson

American Film Institute
P.O. Box 27999
Los Angeles CA 90027
*COST—$9.95 + $2 shipping/handling.
California residents add sales tax.*

Lists unions; guilds and professional organizations and gives information on intern and apprenticeship programs in directing; distribution; film and television production and writing. 46 pages.

1274

FEDERAL BENEFITS FOR VETERANS & DEPENDENTS (S/N 051-000-00202-4)
Veterans Administration

Superintendent of Documents
U.S. Government Printing Office
Washington DC 20402
COST—$2.50

94-page booklet containing details of all Federal benefit programs available to veterans and their dependents.

1275

FELLOWSHIP GUIDE TO WESTERN EUROPE

Gina Bria Vescori, editor

Council for European Studies
c/o Columbia University; 808-809
International Affairs Bldg.
New York NY 10027
COST—$8.00 (prepaid—check to Columbia Univ.)

This booklet is intended to assist USA students in finding funds for European travel and study in the social sciences and humanities.

1276

FINANCIAL AID FOR MINORITIES IN BUSINESS AND LAW

ISBN 0-912048-88-3

Garrett Park Press
P.O. Box 190F
Garrett Park MD 20896
COST—$4.95

This booklet lists sources of financial aid and clarifies application procedures. Includes a bibliography of other sources of funding information.

1277

FINANCIAL AID FOR MINORITIES IN EDUCATION

ISBN 0-912048-99-9

Garrett Park Pres
P.O. Box 190F
Garrett Park MD 20896
COST—$4.95

This booklet lists financial aid opportunities for minorities interested in elementary, secondary, and administrative programs in such fields as counseling, special education, and speech pathology.

1278

FINANCIAL AID FOR MINORITIES IN ENGINEERING AND SCIENCE

ISBN 0-912048-98-0

Garrett Park Press
P.O. Box 190F
Garrett Park MD 20896
COST—$4.95

Individual awards and general programs offered for graduate and professional study by private organizations, foundations, federal and state governments, colleges, and universities.

1279

FINANCIAL AID FOR MINORITIES IN HEALTH FIELDS

ISBN 0-912048-96-4

Garrett Park Press
P.O. Box 190F
Garrett Park MD 20896
COST—$4.95

Includes individual awards and general programs offered for graduate or professional study by private organizations, foundations, federal and state governments, colleges, and universities.

1280

FINANCIAL AID FOR MINORITIES IN JOURNALISM AND MASS COMMUNICATIONS

ISBN 0-912048-84-0

Garrett Park Press
P.O. Box 190F
Garrett Park MD 20896
COST—$4.95

This booklet lists specific sources of financial aid for minority students and tells how to apply for it.

1281

FINANCIAL AID FOR MINORITIES—AWARDS OPEN TO STUDENTS WITH ANY MAJOR
ISBN 0-912048-93-1

Garrett Park Press
P.O. Box 190F
Garrett Park MD 20896
COST—$4.95

This booklet lists sources of financial aid and clarifies application procedures. Includes a bibliography of other sources of funding information.

1282

FINANCIAL AID FOR THE DISABLED AND THEIR FAMILIES
Gail Ann Schlachter and R. David Weber

Reference Service Press
1100 Industrial Rd.; Suite 9
San Carlos CA 94070
COST—$38.50 + $4.00 shipping

Contains descriptions of 900 scholarships, fellowships, grants, loans, awards, and internships set aside for the disabled and their families. Covers all levels of study. 310 pages.

1283

FINANCIAL AID FOR VETERANS, MILITARY PERSONNEL, & THEIR FAMILIES
Gail Ann Schlachter and R. David Weber

Reference Service Press
1100 Industrial Rd.; Suite 9
San Carlos CA 94070
COST—$38.50 + $4 shipping

Contains over 950 descriptions of scholarships, fellowships, grants, loans, awards, and internships set aside for veterans; military personnel, and their families. Covers all levels of study. 300 pages.

1284

FINANCIAL ASSISTANCE FOR LIBRARY & INFORMATION STUDIES
ALA

American Library Association
Office for Library Personnel Resources
50 E. Huron St.
Chicago IL 60611
COST—$1.00 for postage/handling

An excellent summary of fellowships, scholarships, grants-in-aid, loan funds, and other financial assistance for library education. Published each fall for the following year.

1285

FINDING MONEY FOR COLLEGE
John Bear; Ph.D.

Ten Speed Press
P.O. Box 7123
Berkeley CA 94707
COST—$7.95 + $3.50 shipping and handling

In this book Dr. Bear builds on the extensive research he has done in education, searching out unconventional, overlooked, ordinary but not well understood sources of assistance and tells how to pursue them. 168 pages.

1286

FISKE GUIDE TO COLLEGES—1995 EDITION
New York Times Books; ISBN 812-92534-1

Times Books
400 Hahn Rd.
Westminster MD 21157
COST—$18.00

Describes the top-rated 265 out of 2000 possible 4-year schools in the USA. They are rated for academics, social life, and quality of life.

1287

FLORIDA STUDENT FINANCIAL AID—FACT SHEETS
Department of Education

Florida Dept. of Education
1344 Florida Education Center
Tallahassee FL 32399
COST—Free

Booklet containing information on Florida grants, scholarships, and teacher programs.

1288

GED. . . THE KEY TO YOUR FUTURE
American Council on Education

GED Testing Service of the American Council on Education
One Dupont Circle NW
Washington DC 20036
COST—Free

If you or someone you know left high school before graduation, this free brochure will explain what the GED tests are and how they provide the opportunity to earn a high school equivalency diploma.

1289

GET SMART FAST
Sondra Geoffrion

Access Success Associates
P.O. Box 1686
Goleta CA 93116
COST—$6.95 each + $2.50 postage USA; $4.00 foreign. California residents add sales tax.

61-page handbook for academic success which explains how to master the art of studying, writing essays, preparing for and taking tests strategically, etc.

1290

GOVERNMENT ASSISTANCE ALMANAC (9TH EDITION)
J. Robert Dumouchel; ISBN 0-7808-0061-3

OmniGraphics Inc.
2500 Penobscot Bldg.
Detroit MI 48226
COST—$135.00

Comprehensive guide to more than $834 billion worth of federal programs available to the American public. Contains 825 pages and 1370 entries detailing programs of benefit to students, educators, researchers, and consumers.

1291

GUIDE TO SOURCES OF INFORMATION ON PARAPSYCHOLOGY
Eileen J. Garrett Library

Parapsychology Foundation
228 E. 71st St.
New York NY 10021
COST—$3.00

An annual listing of sources of information on major parapsychology organizations, journals, books, and research.

1292

GUIDELINES FOR THE PREPARATION OF SCHOOL ADMINISTRATORS
AASA

American Association of School Administrators
1801 N. Moore St.
Arlington VA 22209
COST—$7.00 prepaid

People who are planning a career in school administration will find this book helpful in explaining the demands and expectations of schools as well as those who play key roles in recommending or establishing certification requirements.

1293

HANDBOOK OF PRIVATE SCHOOLS
ISBN #0-87558-135-8

Porter Sargent Publishers Inc.
11 Beacon St.; Suite 1400
Boston MA 02108
COST—$85.00 + $2.74 postage and handling

Annual reference book found in most major libraries. Describes in detail 1700 American elementary and secondary private schools. 1396 pages.

1294

HAPPIER BY DEGREES
Pam Mendelsohn

Ten Speed Press
P.O. Box 7123
Berkeley CA 94707
COST—$8.95 + $3.50 shipping/handling

Excellent book for women just starting out or returning to college. This is a comprehensive guide to the entire process of entering into a new academic field including financial aid; child care; etc. 266 pages.

1295

HIGH SCHOOL STUDENT'S APPLICATION WORKBOOK
Ken and Pat Voak

Ken & Pat Voak Publications
230 Old Graham Hill Rd.
Santa Cruz CA 95060
COST—$5.00

Complete workbook designed to help students record and evaluate their high school years. Includes standardized forms that give the student an idea of what information will be asked on applications for colleges, jobs, scholarships, etc.

1296

HOW TO FIND OUT ABOUT FINANCIAL AID
Gail Ann Schlachter

Reference Service Press
1100 Industrial Rd.; Suite 9
San Carlos CA 94070
COST—$37.50 + $4.00 shipping

A comprehensive guide to more than 700 print and online directories that identify over $21 billion in financial aid available to undergraduates, graduate students, and researchers.

1297

INDEX OF MAJORS & GRADUATE DEGREES
CBP; ISBN #0-87447-480-9

College Board Publications
P.O. Box 886
New York NY 10101
COST—$17.00 + $3.95 shipping/handling—CA and PA residents add sales tax.

Describes over 580 major programs of study at 2900 undergraduate and graduate schools. Also lists schools that have religious affiliations, special academic programs, and special admissions procedures. 700 pages.

1298

INTERNATIONAL JOBS
Eric Kocher

Addison-Wesley Publishing Co.
1 Jacob Way
Reading MA 01867
COST—$14.38

A handbook listing more than 500 career opportunities around the world.

1299

INTERNSHIPS
Peterson's ISBN 1-56079-286-8

Peterson's Guides
202 Carnegie Center; P.O. Box 2123
Princeton NJ 08543
COST—$29.95 + $6.75 shipping/handling

Lists on-the-job training opportunities in today's job market. Listings are arranged by career field and indexed geographically.

1300

JOB OPPORTUNITIES FOR THE BLIND (JOB)
NFB

National Federation of the Blind
1800 Johnson St.
Baltimore MD 21230
COST—Free

JOB is operated by the NFB in partnership with the US Dept. of Labor. It offers national reference service to blind job seekers on all aspects of looking for work, to employers, and to those assisting blind persons.

1301

JOURNALISM AND MASS COMMUNICATION DIRECTORY
AEJMC

Association for Education in Journalism & Mass Communications
Univ. of SC; 1621 College St.
Columbia SC 29208
COST—$25.00 USA; $35.00 foreign

Annual directory listing over 350 schools and departments of journalism and mass communication, information on national funds, fellowships, and foundations, collegiate and scholastic services. Over 3000 individual members.

1302

JOURNALISM CAREER GUIDE FOR MINORITIES
DJNF

Dow Jones Newspaper Fund Inc
PO Box 300
Princeton NJ 08543-0300
COST—Free

Comprehensive guide listing financial aid available to students studying for print journalism careers. Also includes career information, jobs, salaries, intern programs, and more. To order call 800/DOW FUND.

1303

JOURNALIST'S ROAD TO SUCCESS—A CAREER AND SCHOLARSHIP GUIDE
DJNF

Dow Jones Newspaper Fund Inc.
P.O. Box 300
Princeton NJ 08543
COST—$3.00 per copy

Highly recommended for print or broadcast communications students or journalists. Comprehensive booklet describing what and where to study, how to pay for it; where the jobs are, and how to find them. To order call 800/DOW-FUND.

1304

LEARNING DISABILITY INFORMATION
ODS

Orton Dyslexia Society
Chester Building Suite 382; 8600 LaSalle Rd.
Baltimore MD 21286
COST—Free + $5.00 shipping and handling

National organization formed to help learning disabled children and their parents. There are local chapters throughout the USA. Contact address above for details on membership, services offered, and location of the nearest chapter.

1305

LEARNING DISABILITY INFORMATION

Scholarships offered to local persons who attend summer teacher training.

Orton Dyslexia Society; Northern California Branch
1244 Sierra Ave.
San Jose CA 95126
COST—Free

Orton Dyslexia Society (ODS) is a national organization formed to help learning disabled children and their parents. Send SASE to address above for details on membership and services offered by the Northern California chapter.

1306

MAKING A DIFFERENCE—CAREER OPPORTUNITIES IN DISABILITY-RELATED FIELDS

The Arc

The Arc; National Headquarters
P.O. Box 1047
Arlington TX 76004
COST—$10.00 (includes S/H)

A handbook of over 50 professions that serve people who have disabilities. Includes career overview, employment settings, populations served, salary/educational/certification requirements.

1307

MAKING IT THROUGH COLLEGE

PSC

Professional Staff Congress
25 W. 43rd St.; 5th Floor
New York NY 10036
COST—$1.00

Handy booklet containing information on coping with competition, getting organized, study techniques, solving work overloads, and more. 14 pages.

1308

MEDICAL SCHOOL ADMISSION REQUIREMENTS

Cynthia T. Bennett

Association of American Medical Colleges
2450 N St. NW
Washington DC 20037
COST—$15.00 + shipping

Contains admission requirements of accredited medical schools in the USA and Canada.

1309

MEDICINE—A CHANCE TO MAKE A DIFFERENCE

AMA

American Medical Association
Order Processing
P.O. Box 109050
Chicago IL 60610
COST—$5.00 + $4.95 shipping/handling (pkg. of 10 brochures)

For college students considering a career in medicine. Answers questions about the profession and medical education, including prerequisites, admission requirements, and choosing a medical school.

1310

MITCHELL EXPRESS—THE FAST TRACK TO THE TOP COLLEGES

Joyce Slayton Mitchell; ISBN 1-880774-03-8

Garrett Park Press
P.O. Box 190
Garrett Park MD 20896
COST—$15.00

A college catalog-sized directory of America's most popular colleges. It profiles the colleges and provides information on admissions and financial aid. 269 pages.

1311

MUSIC SCHOLARSHIP GUIDE (3RD EDITION)
Sandra V. Fridy; ISBN 1-56545-050-7

Music Educators National Conference
1806 Robert Fulton Dr.
Reston VA 22091
COST—$27.50 ($22.00 MENC members)

Lists over 1300 undergraduate music scholarships in the United States and Canada, including eligibility requirements, application deadlines, contact information.

1312

NAEA ART SCHOLARSHIP BOOK
NAEA

National Art Education Association
1916 Association Dr.
Reston Va 22091
COST—$12 plus $3.50 shipping/handling

Listing of undergraduate scholarships and other financial aid from America's art schools, colleges, and universities. 60 pages.

1313

NATIONAL DIRECTORY OF CORPORATE GIVING
TFC; ISBN 0-87954-400-7

Foundation Center (The)
79 Fifth Ave./16th Street
New York NY 10003
COST—$199.50 (Including shipping/handling)

Book profiles 2000 programs making contributions to nonprofit organizations. A valuable tool to assist grant seekers in finding potential support.

1314

NEED A LIFT?
American Legion

American Legion Education Program
P.O. Box 1055
Indianapolis IN 46206
COST—$3.00

Outstanding guide to US government-related financial aid. Contains information on the financial aid process (how, when, & where to start), addresses for scholarship, loan & career information. 126 pages.

1315

OCCUPATIONAL OUTLOOK HANDBOOK
US Bureau of Labor Statistics (1994-95); S/N 029-001-03157-2 (cloth bound); S/N 029-001-031-1 (paperback)

Superintendent of Documents
US Government Printing Office
Washington DC 20402
COST—$26.00 (cloth bound); $23.00 (paperback)

Annual publication designed to assist individuals in selecting appropriate careers. Describes over 200 occupations in great detail and includes current and projected job prospects for each. 492 pages.

1316

OFF TO COLLEGE
Guidance Research Group

Order Fulfillment Dept-95-RSCH
P.O. Box 931
Montgomery AL 36101
COST—$5.00

An excellent annual booklet in magazine form that helps incoming freshmen prepare for sucess in college living through personal essays concerning a variety of campus experiences.

1317

OFFICIAL HANDBOOK FOR THE CLEP EXAMINATIONS
CBP; ISBN #0-87447-455-8

College Board Publications
P.O. Box 886
New York NY 10101
COST—$15.00

Official guide to College Level Examination Program (CLEP) tests from the actual sponsors of the tests. Contains sample questions and answers, advice on how to prepare for tests, which colleges grant credit for CLEP, and more. 500 pages.

1318

PETERSON'S COLLEGES WITH PROGRAMS FOR STUDENTS WITH LEARNING DISABILITIES; 4TH ED.
Peterson's Inc.; ISBN 1-56079-400-3

Peterson's Inc.
P.O. Box 2123
Princeton NJ 08543-2123
COST—$24.95

Comprehensive guide to over 1000 two-year and four-year colleges and universities offering special academic programs for students with dyslexia and other learning disabilities.

1319

PETERSON'S GUIDE TO FOUR-YEAR COLLEGES 1995
Peterson's Inc.; ISBN #1-56079-364-3

Peterson's Inc.
P.O. Box 2123
Princeton NJ 08543-2123
COST—$19.95

Detailed profiles of over 1900 accredited 4-year colleges in the USA and Canada. Also includes entrance difficulty directory, majors directory, and college cost directory.

1320

PHARMACY SCHOOL ADMISSION REQUIREMENTS
AACP

American Association of Colleges of Pharmacy
Office of Student Affairs; 1426 Prince St.
Alexandria VA 22314
COST—$25.00 prepaid

114-page booklet containing comparative information charts along with the general history of accredited pharmacy programs and current admission requirements.

1321

PILOT TRAINING GUIDE
FAPA

Future Aviation Professionals of America (FAPA)
4959 Massachusetts Blvd.
Atlanta GA 30337
COST—$38.00

Booklet designed to help beginner and advanced pilots make decisions about their training. Includes list of FAA-approved flight training schools in the USA.

1322

PLANNING FOR A DENTAL EDUCATION
AADS

American Association of Dental Schools
1625 Massachusetts Ave. NW
Washington DC 20036-2212
COST—Free

Brochure discusses dentistry as a career and offers advice on planning for a dental education.

1323

POWER STUDY TO UP YOUR GRADES AND GPA
Sondra Geoffrion

Access Success Associates
P.O. Box 1686
Goleta CA 93116
COST—$4.95 + $2.50 USA Postage ($4.00 foreign postage). California residents add sales tax.

One of 5 excellent booklets explaining techniques to discover what will be tested, cut study time in half, prepare thoroughly, write essays, & take tests. Other titles cover Math, English, Social Studies, & Science.

1324

POWER STUDY TO UP YOUR GRADES IN MATH
Sondra Geoffrion

Access Success Associates
P.O. Box 1686
Goleta CA 93116
COST—$4.95 + $2.50 USA postage ($4.00 foreign postage). California residents add sales tax.

One of 5 excellent booklets explaining correct procedures to solve problems with speed, accuracy, & correctness. Also how to prepare for & take tests.

1325

POWER STUDY TO UP YOUR GRADES IN ENGLISH
Sondra Geoffrion

Access Success Associates
P.O. Box 1686
Goleta CA 93116
COST—$4.95 + $2.50 USA postage ($4.00 foreign postage). California residents add sales tax.

One of 5 excellent booklets explaining techniques to discover what will be tested, cut study time in half; prepare thoroughly, write essays, & take tests. Other titles cover math, social studies, science, & improving grade point average.

1326

POWER STUDY TO UP YOUR GRADES IN SOCIAL STUDIES
Sondra Geoffrion

Access Success Associates
P.O. Box 1686
Goleta CA 93116
COST—$4.95 + $2.50 USA postage ($4.00 foreign postage). California residents add sales tax.

One of 5 excellent booklets explaining techniques to discover what will be tested, cut study time in half, prepare thoroughly, write essays, take tests. Other titles cover Math, English, Science, and improving grade point average.

1327

POWER STUDY TO UP YOUR GRADES IN SCIENCE
Sondra Geoffrion

Access Success Associates
P.O. Box 1686
Goleta CA 93116
COST—$4.95 + $2.50 USA postage ($4.00 foreign postage). California residents add sales tax.

One of 5 excellent booklets explaining how to discover what will be tested, cut study time in half, prepare thoroughly, write essays, & take tests. Other titles cover Math, English, Social Studies, & improving grade point average.

1328

PRINCETON REVIEW—COLLEGE ADMISSIONS—CRACKING THE SYSTEM

Adam Robinson and John Katzman, Editors

Villard Books
201 E. 50th St.
New York NY 10022
COST—$7.95

Offers high school students bold strategies for getting into the college of their choice. 153 pages.

1329

PROCEEDINGS AND ADDRESSES OF THE AMERICAN PHILOSOPHICAL ASSN.

APA

American Philosophical Association (The)
University of Delaware
Newark DE 19716
COST—$10

Annual issue contains lists of grants and fellowships of interest to philosophers.

1330

SAVE A FORTUNE

Phillip Godwin; ISBN # 0-945332-05-X

Agora Books
842 E. Baltimore St.
Baltimore MD 21202
COST—$14.95

A common-sense plan for building wealth through saving rather than earning. Includes information on how to save on taxes, education, housing, travel, health, etc. 209 pages.

1331

SCHOLARSHIPS & LOANS FOR NURSING EDUCATION

NLN; ISBN #0-88737-580-4

National League for Nursing
350 Hudson St.
New York NY 10014
COST—$14.95 + $3.75 postage/handling

Guide to financial aid for nursing and health care professions. Lists scholarships, fellowships, grants, traineeships, loans, and special awards. 113 pages.

1332

STUDENT FINANCIAL AID AND SCHOLARSHIPS AT WYOMING COLLEGES

University of Wyoming

University of Wyoming Office of Student Financial Aid
P.O. Box 3335
Laramie WY 82071-3335
COST—Free

Describes post-secondary student aid and scholarship programs that are available to Wyoming students. Booklets can be obtained at all Wyoming high schools and colleges.

1333

STUDENT GUIDE—FINANCIAL AID FROM THE US DEPARTMENT OF EDUCATION

U.S. Department of Education

Federal Student Aid Information Center
P.O. Box 84
Washington DC 20044
COST—Free

Lists qualifications and sources of information for federal grants, loans, and work-study programs.

1334

STUDY ABROAD (VOLUME 29; 1996–1997)
UNESCO

United Nations Educational, Scientific, and Cultural Organization
UNIPUB; UNESCO Agent; 4611-F Assembly Drive
Lanham MD 20706
COST—$29.95 + postage/handling

Printed in English, French, & Spanish, this volume lists 3700 international study programs in all academic and professional fields in more than 124 countries.

1335

THE FACTS ABOUT ARMY ROTC
U.S. Army

U.S. Army - College Army ROTC
Gold Quest Center
P.O. Box 3279
Warminster PA 18974
COST—Free

Provides information on types of scholarships available, eligibility, deadlines, application procedures, and monetary value.

1336

THE FOUNDATION DIRECTORY
ISBN #0-87954-449-6 (soft cover); 0-87954-484-8 (hard cover)

The Foundation Center
79 Fifth Ave.
New York NY 10003
COST—$160.00 soft cover; $185.00 hard cover; + $4.50 shipping by UPS

Authoritative annual reference book found in most major libraries. Contains detailed information on over 6300 of America's largest foundations. Indexes allow grantseekers, researchers, etc., to quickly locate foundations of interest.

1337

THEIR WORLD
NCLD

National Center for Learning Disabilities
381 Park Ave. South; Suite 1420
New York NY 10016
COST—$10.00

Annual magazine devoted to helping parents of learning disabled children as well as professionals in the learning disabled field, and to increasing public awareness of learning disabilities.

1338

UAA COLLEGIATE AVIATION SCHOLARSHIP LISTING
Gary W. Kiteley; Executive Director

University Aviation Assn.
3410 Skyway Dr.
Auburn AL 36830
COST—$4.95 members; $9.95 non-members + $3 shipping/handling

Listing of financial aid sources, methods of applying for general purpose aid, and a listing of aviation scholarships arranged by broad classification.

1339

UNIVERSITY CURRICULA IN OCEANOGRAPHY AND RELATED FIELDS
Marine Technology Society

Marine Technology Society
1828 L St. NW; Suite 906
Washington DC 20036
COST—$5 shipping/handling

A guide to current marine degree programs and vocational instruction available in the marine field. Consolidates and highlights data needed by high school students as well as college students seeking advanced degrees.

1340

UNLOCKING POTENTIAL

Barbara Scheiber and Jeanne Talpers; ISBN 0-917561-30-9

Adler & Adler Publishers Inc.
Woodbine House
6510 Bells Mill Road
Bethesda MD 20817
COST—$12.95

A step-by-step guide to colleges & other choices for people with learning disabilities. Discusses choosing the right post-secondary schools, the admission process, overcoming academic hurdles, and more. 195 pages.

1341

VACATION STUDY ABROAD

Sara Steen; Editor

Institute of International Education
IIE Books; 809 United Nations Plaza
New York NY 10017
COST—$36.95

Guide to some 1600 summer or short-term study-abroad programs sponsored by USA colleges, universities, private institutions, and foreign institutions. 400 pages.

1342

WHAT COLOR IS YOUR PARACHUTE?

Richard N. Bolles; ISBN #0-89815-492-8

Ten Speed Press
P.O. Box 7123
Berkeley CA 94707
COST—$14.95 + $2 postage

Step-by-step career planning guide. Highly recommended for anyone who is job hunting or changing careers. Valuable tips on assessing your skills, resume writing, handling job interviews. 464 pages.

1343

WINNING SCHOLARSHIPS FOR COLLEGE—AN INSIDER'S GUIDE

Marianne N. Ragins

The Scholarship Workshop
P.O. Box 6845
Macon GA 31208
COST—$13.95 (includes shipping and handling)

As a high school senior the author was offered college scholarships totalling over $400,000. This 158-page book describes the application process, reveals strategies for finding scholarships, & offers advice on presenting credentials.

1344

WORK-STUDY-TRAVEL ABROAD—THE WHOLE WORLD HANDBOOK

Council on International Educational Exchange

Council on International Educational Exchange
205 E. 42nd St.; Publications Dept.
New York NY 10017
COST—$13.95

Excellent book on the basics of traveling, working, and studying abroad. How to find out about study-abroad opportunities, grants, scholarships, exchange programs, and teaching opportunities. Also information on the cheapest ways to travel.

1345

WORLD DIRECTORY OF MEDICAL SCHOOLS

WHO

World Health Organization
(1211 Geneva 27; Switzerland)
WHO Publication Center;
49 Sheridan Ave.
Albany NY 12210
COST—$35 (shipping/handling included)

Comprehensive book that describes the medical education programs and schools in each country. Arranged in order by country or area.

Career Information

1346

AMERICAN SOCIETY OF
AGRONOMY
677 S. Segoe Rd.
Madison WI 53711

1347

(career information)
AMERICAN MANAGEMENT ASSN.
135 W. 50th St.
New York NY 10020

1348

ACCOUNTING
(career information)
INSTITUTE OF MANAGEMENT
ACCOUNTANTS
10 Paragon Dr.
Montvale NJ 07645

1349

ACCOUNTING
(career information)
AMERICAN INSTITUTE OF
CERTIFIED PUBLIC ACCOUNTANTS
1211 Avenue of the Americas
New York NY 10036

1350

ACCOUNTING
(career information)
NATIONAL SOCIETY OF PUBLIC
ACCOUNTANTS
1010 N. Fairfax St.
Alexandria VA 22314

1351

ACTUARIAL SCIENCE
(career information)
SOCIETY OF ACTUARIES
475 N. Martingale Rd.; Suite 800
Schaumburg IL 60173-2226

1352

ADVERTISING
(career information)
AMERICAN ADVERTISING
FEDERATION
Education Services; Suite 500; 1101
Vermont Ave. NW
Washington DC 20005

1353

AERONAUTICS
(career information)
AMERICAN INSTITUTE OF
AERONAUTICS AND ASTRONAUTICS
(Student Programs Department)
370 L'Enfant Promenade SW
Washington DC 20024

1354

AEROSPACE EDUCATION
(career information)
AEROSPACE EDUCATION
FOUNDATION
1501 Lee Highway
Arlington VA 22209

1355

AGRICULTURAL ENGINEERING
(career information)
ASAE SOCIETY FOR ENGINEERING
IN AGRICULTURAL FOOD AND
BIOLOGICAL SYSTEMS
2950 Niles Rd.
St. Joseph MI 49085

1356

AGRICULTURE
(career information)

AMERICAN FARM BUREAU
FEDERATION
225 Touhy Ave.
Park Ridge IL 60068

1357

AGRICULTURE MANAGEMENT & AGRIBUSINESS
(career information)

US DEPT OF AGRICULTURE; RURAL
ECONOMIC & COMMUNITY
DEVELOPMENT
Human Resources; 14th & Independence
Ave. SW
Washington DC 20250-0700

1358

AIR FORCE
(career information)

AIR FORCE OPPORTUNITY CENTER
P.O. Box 3505
Capitol Heights MD 20791

1359

AIR FORCE ACADEMY/AFROTC
(career information)

DIRECTOR OF SELECTIONS
2304 Cadet Dr. Suite 200
USAF Academy CO 80840

1360

AIRLINE
(career information)

AIR TRANSPORT ASSOCIATION OF
AMERICA
1301 Pennsylvania Ave. NW; Suite 1100
Washington DC 20004-1707

1361

ANIMAL SCIENCE
(career information)

NATIONAL ASSN. OF ANIMAL
BREEDERS Inc.
401 Bernadette Dr.; P.O. Box 1033
Columbia MO 65205

1362

ANIMAL SCIENCE
(career information only)

AMERICAN SOCIETY OF ANIMAL
SCIENCE
Business Office; 309 W. Clark St.
Champaign IL 61820

1363

ANTHROPOLOGY
(career information)

AMERICAN ANTHROPOLOGICAL
ASSOCIATION
1703 New Hampshire Ave. NW
Washington DC 20009

1364

APPRAISER—REAL ESTATE; GEMOLOGY; MACHINERY & EQUIPMENT; PERSONAL PROPERTY
(career information)

AMERICAN SOCIETY OF
APPRAISERS
P.O. Box 17265
Washington DC 20041

1365

APPRENTICESHIP
(career information)

US DEPT. OF LABOR; BUREAU OF
APPRENTICESHIP AND TRAINING
200 Constitution Ave. NW; Room N-4649
Washington DC 20210

1366

ARCHAEOLOGY
(career information)
ARCHAEOLOGICAL INSTITUTE OF
AMERICA
656 Beacon St.
Boston MA 02215-2010

1367

ARCHITECTURE
(career information)
AMERICAN INSTITUTE OF
ARCHITECTS
Education Dept.; 1735 New York Ave. NW
Washington DC 20006

1368

ASTRONOMY
(career information)
AMERICAN ASTRONOMICAL
SOCIETY
Education Officer; Astronomy Dept.
University of Texas
Austin TX 78712-1083

1369

AUDIOLOGY; SPEECH PATHOLOGY
(career information)
AMERICAN SPEECH-LANGUAGE-
HEARING ASSOCIATION
10801 Rockville Pike
Rockville MD 20852

1370

AUTHOR/WRITER
(career information)
PEN AMERICAN CENTER
568 Broadway; Suite 401
New York NY 10012

1371

AUTOMOTIVE ENGINEERING
(career information)
SOCIETY OF AUTOMOTIVE
ENGINEERS INC.
400 Commonwealth Dr.
Warrendale PA 15096

1372

BANKING
(career information)
AMERICAN BANKERS ASSOCIATION
Library & Information Systems
1120 Connecticut Ave. NW
Washington DC 20036

1373

BIOLOGIST
(career information)
AMERICAN INSTITUTE OF
BIOLOGICAL SCIENCES
730 11th St. NW
Washington DC 20001

1374

BIOTECHNOLOGY
(career information)
INDUSTRIAL BIOTECHNOLOGY
ASSN.
1625 'K' St. NW; Suite 1100
Washington DC 20006

1375

BLACK FILMMAKERS
(career information)
BLACK AMERICAN CINEMA
SOCIETY
3617 Montclair St.
Los Angeles CA 90018

1376

BROADCAST NEWS
(career information)
> RADIO & TELEVISION NEWS
> DIRECTORS ASSN.
> 1000 Connecticut Ave. NW; Suite 615
> Washington DC 20036

1377

BROADCASTING
(career information)
> AMERICAN WOMEN IN RADIO &
> TELEVISION
> 1650 Tysons Boulevard; Suite 200
> McLean VA 22102

1378

BUSINESS EDUCATION
(career information)
> NATIONAL BUSINESS EDUCATION
> ASSN.
> 1914 Association Dr.
> Reston VA 22091

1379

**CAREERS IN THE MATHEMATICAL
SCIENCES**
(career information)
> MATHEMATICAL ASSOCIATION OF
> AMERICA
> 1529 18th St. NW
> Washington DC 20036

1380

CARTOONING
(career information)
> NEWSPAPER FEATURES COUNCIL
> 37 Arch St.
> Greenwich CT 06830

1381

CHEMICAL ENGINEERING
(career information)
> AMERICAN INSTITUTE OF
> CHEMICAL ENGINEERS
> Communications Dept., 345 E. 47th St.
> New York NY 10017

1382

CHIROPRACTIC
(career and school information)
> INTERNATIONAL CHIROPRACTORS
> ASSOCIATION
> 1110 N. Glebe Rd.; Suite 1000
> Arlington VA 22201

1383

CHIROPRACTIC
(career information)
> AMERICAN CHIROPRACTIC ASSN.
> 1701 Clarendon Blvd.
> Arlington VA 22209

1384

CIVIL ENGINEERING
(career information)
> AMERICAN SOCIETY OF CIVIL
> ENGINEERS
> 345 E. 47th St.
> New York NY 10017-2398

1385

CLINICAL CHEMIST
(career information)
> AMERICAN ASSOCIATION FOR
> CLINICAL CHEMISTRY
> 2101 L St. NW; Suite 202
> Washington DC 20037-1526

1386

COMMUNICATIONS
(career and schools information)

ACCREDITING COUNCIL ON
EDUCATION IN JOURNALISM &
MASS COMMUNICATIONS
Stauffer-Flint Hall; University of Kansas
School of Journalism
Lawrence KS 66045

1387

COMPUTER SCIENCE
(career information)

IEEE—USA
1828 L St. NW; Suite 1202
Washington DC 20036

1388

CONSTRUCTION
(career information)

ASSOCIATED GENERAL
CONTRACTORS OF AMERICA
1957 'E' St. NW
Washington DC 20006

1389

COSMETOLOGY
(career information)

AMERICAN ASSOCIATION OF
COSMETOLOGY SCHOOLS
901 N. Washington St.; Suite 206
Alexandria VA 22314

1390

CRAFTS
(career information)

AMERICAN CRAFT INFORMATION
CENTER
72 Spring St.
New York NY 10012

1391

CREATIVE WRITING
(career information)

NATIONAL WRITERS ASSOCIATION
1450 S. Havana; Suite 424
Aurora CO 80012

1392

DANCE
(career information)

AMERICAN ALLIANCE FOR
HEALTH, PHYSICAL EDUCATION,
RECREATION, & DANCE
1900 Association Dr.
Reston VA 22091

1393

DATA PROCESSING MANAGEMENT
(career information)

DATA PROCESSING MANAGEMENT
ASSN.
505 Busse Highway
Park Ridge IL 60068

1394

DEMOGRAPHY
(career information)

POPULATION ASSOCIATION OF
AMERICA
1722 N St. NW
Washington DC 20036

1395

DENTAL ASSISTANT
(career information)

AMERICAN DENTAL ASSISTANTS
ASSN..
203 N. LaSalle St.; Suite 1320
Chicago IL 60601

1396

DENTAL HYGIENIST
(career information)
> AMERICAN DENTAL HYGIENISTS
> ASSN. INSTITUTE FOR ORAL
> HEALTH
> 444 N. Michigan Ave.; Suite 3400
> Chicago IL 60611

1397

DENTAL LABORATORY TECHNOLOGY
(career information)
> NATIONAL ASSN. OF DENTAL
> LABORATORIES
> 555 E. Braddock Rd.
> Alexandria VA 22314

1398

DENTAL PROFESSION
(career information)
> ADA ENDOWMENT AND
> ASSISTANCE FUND INC.
> 211 E. Chicago Ave.
> Chicago IL 60611

1399

DIETITIAN
(career information)
> AMERICAN DIETETIC ASSN
> Attn: Membership Department; 216 W.
> Jackson Blvd.; Suite 800
> Chicago IL 60606

1400

DISABLED
(career information)
> THE ARC
> P.O. Box 1047
> Arlington TX 76004

1401

DRAMA/ACTING
(career information)
> SCREEN ACTORS GUILD
> 5757 Wilshire Blvd.
> Los Angeles CA 90036-3600

1402

EDUCATION
(career information)
> AMERICAN FEDERATION OF
> TEACHERS
> Public Affairs Department; 555 New Jersey
> Ave. NW
> Washington DC 20001

1403

ELECTRICAL ENGINEERING
(career information)
> INSTITUTE OF ELECTRICAL &
> ELECTRONICS ENGINEERS—United
> States Activities (IEEE—USA)
> 1828 L St. NW; Suite 1202
> Washington DC 20036

1404

ENGINEERING
(programs & career information)
> JUNIOR ENGINEERING TECHNICAL
> SOCIETY INC. (JETS)
> 1420 King St.; Suite 405
> Alexandria VA 22314

1405

ENGINEERING
(career information)
> NATIONAL SOCIETY OF
> PROFESSIONAL ENGINEERS
> 1420 King St.
> Alexandria VA 22314

1406

ENTOMOLOGY
(career information)
ENTOMOLOGICAL SOCIETY OF
AMERICA
9301 Annapolis Rd.
Lanham MD 20706

1407

ENVIRONMENTAL
(studies and career information)
US ENVIRONMENTAL PROTECTION
AGENCY
401 M St. SW; Office of Communications,
Education, and Public Affairs
Environmental Education Division
Washington DC 20460

1408

FAPA
(career information)
FUTURE AVIATION PROFESSIONALS
OF AMERICA (FAPA)
4959 Massachusetts Blvd.
Atlanta GA 30337

1409

FBI
(career information)
FEDERAL BUREAU OF
INVESTIGATION
Department of Justice
Washington DC 20535

1410

FASHION DESIGN
(educational information)
FASHION INSTITUTE OF
TECHNOLOGY
Seventh Ave. @ 27th St.
New York NY 10001-5992

1411

FIRE SERVICE
(career information)
NATIONAL FIRE PROTECTION ASSN.
1 Batterymarch Park; PO Box 9101
Quincy MA 02269

1412

FISHERIES
(career and university information)
AMERICAN FISHERIES SOCIETY
5410 Grovesnor Lane; Suite 110
Bethesda MD 20814

1413

FLORISTRY
(career information)
SOCIETY OF AMERICAN FLORISTS
1601 Duke St.
Alexandria VA 22314

1414

FOOD SERVICE
(career information)
EDUCATIONAL FOUNDATION OF
THE NATIONAL RESTAURANT
ASSOCIATION
250 S. Wacker Dr.; Suite 1400
Chicago IL 60606

1415

FOOD TECHNOLOGY/SCIENCE
(career information)
INSTITUTE OF FOOD
TECHNOLOGISTS
221 N. LaSalle St.
Chicago IL 60601

1416

FOOD AND NUTRITION SERVICE
(career information)

US DEPT. OF AGRICULTURE. FOOD,
AND NUTRITION SERVICE
Personnel Division; Rm. 620; 1301 Park
Center Dr.
Alexandria VA 22302

1417

FOREIGN LANGUAGES
(career information)

MODERN LANGUAGE ASSN. OF
AMERICA
10 Astor Place
New York NY 10003

1418

FOREIGN SERVICE OFFICER
(career information)

US DEPT. OF HEALTH;
RECRUITMENT DIVISION
P..O. Box 9317; Rosslyn Station
Arlington VA 22219

1419

FOREST SERVICE
(career information)

US DEPT. OF AGRICULTURE
14th & Independence Ave.; Room 801 RPE
Washington DC 20250

1420

FORESTRY
(career information)

SOCIETY OF AMERICAN FORESTERS
5400 Grovesnor Lane
Bethesda MD 20814

1421

FUNERAL DIRECTOR
(career information)

NATIONAL FUNERAL DIRECTORS
ASSN.
11121 W. Oklahoma Ave.
Milwaukee WI 53227

1422

GEOGRAPHY
(career information)

ASSOCIATION OF AMERICAN
GEOGRAPHERS
1710 16th St. NW
Washington DC 20009-3198

1423

GEOLOGICAL SCIENCES
(career information)

AMERICAN GEOLOGICAL
INSTITUTE
4220 King St.
Alexandria VA 22302

1424

GEOPHYSICIST
(career information)

SOCIETY OF EXPLORATION
GEOPHYSICISTS (SEG) FOUNDATION
P.O. Box 702740
Tulsa OK 74170

1425

GRAPHIC ARTS
(career information)

EDUCATION COUNCIL OF THE
GRAPHIC ARTS INC.
1899 Preston White Dr.
Reston VA 22091-4367

1426

GRAPHIC ARTS
(career information)

AMERICAN INSTITUTE OF GRAPHIC
ARTS
164 Fifth Ave.
New York NY 10010

1427

GRAPHIC COMMUNICATIONS
(career information)

EDUCATIONAL COUNCIL OF THE
GRAPHIC ARTS INDUSTRY
1899 Preston White Dr.
Reston VA 22091-4367

1428

HEALTH FIELDS
(career information)

NATIONAL HEALTH COUNCIL INC.
1730 M St. NW; Suite 500
Washington DC 20036

1429

HEALTH PROFESSIONAL STUDENT OPPORTUNITIES
(career information)

US DEPT. OF HEALTH & HUMAN
SERVICES—NATIONAL HEALTH
SERVICE CORPS
2070 Chain Bridge Road; Suite 450
Vienna VA 22182

1430

HEATING AND AIR CONDITIONING ENGINEER
(career information)

REFRIGERATION SERVICE
ENGINEERS SOCIETY
1666 Rand Rd.
Des Plaines IL 60016

1431

HOME ECONOMICS
(career information)

AMERICAN ASSOCIATION OF
FAMILY & CONSUMER SCIENCES
1555 King St.
Alexandria VA 22314

1432

HORTICULTURE
(career information)

AMERICAN ASSOCIATION OF
NURSERYMEN
1250 'I' St. NW
Washington DC 20005

1433

HOSPITAL ADMINISTRATION
(career information)

AMERICAN COLLEGE OF HEALTH
CARE EXECUTIVES
One N. Franklin St.; Suite 1700
Chicago IL 60606-3491

1434

HOTEL MANAGEMENT
(career information)

AMERICAN HOTEL FOUNDATION
1201 New York Ave. NW; Suite 600
Washington DC 20005

1435

ILLUMINATING ENGINEERING
(career information)

ILLUMINATING ENGINEERING
SOCIETY OF NORTH AMERICA
120 Wall St.; 17th Floor
New York NY 10005

1436

INSURANCE
(career information)
  INSURANCE INFORMATION
  INSTITUTE
  110 William St.
  New York NY 10038

1437

INSURANCE
(career information)
  ALLIANCE OF AMERICAN INSURERS
  1501 Woodfield Rd.; Suite 400W
  Schaumburg IL 60173

1438

JOURNALISM
(career information)
  AMERICAN SOCIETY OF
  NEWSPAPER EDITORS
  P.O. Box 4090
  Reston VA 22090-1700

1439

LANDSCAPE ARCHITECTURE
(career information)
  AMERICAN SOCIETY OF
  LANDSCAPE ARCHITECTS
  4401 Connecticut Ave. NW; 5th Floor
  Washington DC 20008

1440

LAW
(career information booklet)
  AMERICAN BAR ASSOCIATION
  750 N. Lake Shore Dr.
  Chicago IL 60611

1441

LAW LIBRARY
(career information)
  AMERICAN ASSOCIATION OF LAW
  LIBRARIES
  53 W. Jackson Blvd.; Suite 940
  Chicago IL 60604

1442

LEARNING DISABLED
(education and career information)
  LEARNING DISABILITIES ASSN. OF
  AMERICA
  4156 Library Rd.
  Pittsburgh PA 15234

1443

LIBRARY SCIENCE
(career information)
  AMERICAN LIBRARY ASSN.
  Office for Library Personnel Resources;
  50 E. Huron St.
  Chicago IL 60611

1444

MACHINE TECHNOLOGY
(career information)
  AMT—THE ASSOCIATION FOR
  MANUFACTURING TECHNOLOGY
  7901 Westpark Dr.
  McLean VA 22102

1445

MACHINE TECHNOLOGY
(career information)
  NATIONAL TOOLING AND
  MACHINING ASSN.
  9300 Livingston Rd.
  Ft. Washington MD 20744

1446

MANAGEMENT
(career information)
CLUB FOUNDATION (THE)
1733 King St.
Alexandria VA 22314

1447

MATHEMATICS TEACHER
(career information)
NATIONAL COUNCIL OF TEACHERS
OF MATHEMATICS
1906 Association Dr.
Reston VA 22091-1593

1448

MECHANICAL ENGINEERING
(career information)
AMERICAN SOCIETY OF
MECHANICAL ENGINEERS
United Engineering Center; 345 E. 47th St.
New York NY 10017

1449

**MEDICAL LABORATORY
TECHNOLOGY**
(career information)
AMERICAN SOCIETY OF CLINICAL
PATHOLOGISTS
Careers; 2100 W. Harrison
Chicago IL 60612

1450

MEDICAL RECORDS
(career information)
AMERICAN HEALTH INFORMATION
MANAGEMENT ASSOCIATION
919 N. Michigan Ave.; Suite 1400
Chicago IL 60611

1451

MEDICAL TECHNOLOGY
(career information)
AMERICAN MEDICAL
TECHNOLOGISTS
710 Higgins Rd.
Park Ridge IL 60068

1452

MEDICINE
(career information)
AMERICAN MEDICAL ASSOCIATION
515 N. State St.
Chicago IL 60610

1453

**METALLURGY AND MATERIALS
SCIENCE**
(career information)
ASM INTERNATIONAL
Student Outreach Program
Materials Park OH 44073

1454

MICROBIOLOGY
(career information)
AMERICAN SOCIETY FOR
MICROBIOLOGY
Office of Education & Training
1325 Massachusetts Ave. NW
Washington DC 20005

1455

MOTION PICTURE
(career information)
SOCIETY OF MOTION PICTURE AND
TELEVISION ENGINEERS
595 W. Hartsdale Ave.
White Plains NY 10607

1456

MUSIC
(career information)
MUSIC EDUCATORS NATIONAL
CONFERENCE
1806 Robert Fulton Drive
Reston VA 22091

1457

MUSIC THERAPY
(career information)
NATIONAL ASSN. FOR MUSIC
THERAPY
8455 Colesville Rd.; Suite 930
Silver Spring MD 20910

1458

NAVAL ARCHITECTURE
(career information)
SOCIETY OF NAVAL ARCHITECTS &
MARINE ENGINEERS
601 Pavonia Ave.
Jersey City NJ 07306

1459

NAVAL/MARINE ENGINEERING
(career information)
SOCIETY OF NAVAL ARCHITECTS &
MARINE ENGINEERS
601 Pavonia Ave.
Jersey City NJ 07306

1460

NEWSPAPER INDUSTRY
(career information)
NEWSPAPER ASSN. OF AMERICA
The Newspaper Center; 11600 Sunrise
Valley Dr.
Reston VA 22091

1461

NURSE ANESTHETIST
(career information)
AMERICAN ASSOCIATION OF NURSE
ANESTHETISTS
222 S. Prospect Ave.
Park Ridge IL 60068-4001

1462

NURSING
(career information)
NATIONAL LEAGUE FOR NURSING
Inc.
350 Hudson St.
New York NY 10014

1463

NURSING
(graduate research grants)
AMERICAN NURSES FOUNDATION
600 Maryland Ave. SW; Suite 100 West
Washington DC 20024

1464

**OCEANOGRAPHY AND MARINE
SCIENCE**
(career information)
MARINE TECHNOLOGY SOCIETY
1828 L St. NW; Suite 906
Washington DC 20036

1465

OPTOMETRIC ASSISTANT/TECHNICIAN
(career information)
AMERICAN OPTOMETRIC ASSN.
Paraoptometric Section
243 N. Lindbergh Blvd.
St. Louis MO 63141

1466

OPTOMETRY
(career information)
NATIONAL OPTOMETRIC ASSN.
2838 S. Indiana Ave.
Chicago IL 60616

1467

OPTOMETRY
(career information)
AMERICAN OPTOMETRIC ASSN.
243 N. Lindbergh Blvd.
St. Louis MO 63141-7881

1468

ORNITHOLOGIST
(career information)
AMERICAN ORNITHOLOGISTS'
UNION
Smithsonian Institution; Division of Birds;
MRC-116
Washington DC 20560

1469

OSTEOPATHIC MEDICINE
(career information)
AMERICAN OSTEOPATHIC
ASSOCIATION
Dept. of Predoctoral Education; 142 East
Ontario
Chicago IL 60611

1470

PALEONTOLOGY
(career information)
PALEONTOLOGICAL SOCIETY
Dr. Donald L. Wolberg, Secretary; P.O. Box
1937
Socorro NM 87801

1471

**PATHOLOGY AS A CAREER IN
MEDICINE**
(career information brochure)
INTERSOCIETY COMMITTEE ON
PATHOLOGY INFORMATION
4733 Bethesda Ave.; Suite 700
Bethesda MD 20814

1472

PEDIATRICS
(career information)
AMERICAN ACADEMY OF
PEDIATRICS
141 NW Point Blvd.; P.O. Box 927
Elk Grove Village IL 60009

1473

PETROLEUM ENGINEERING
(career information)
SOCIETY OF PETROLEUM
ENGINEERS
P.O. Box 833836
Richardson TX 75083

1474

PHARMACOLOGY
(career information)
AMERICAN SOCIETY FOR
PHARMACOLOGY &
EXPERIMENTAL THERAPEUTICS
INC.
9650 Rockville Pike
Bethesda MD 20814-3995

1475

PHARMACY
(career information)
AMERICAN ASSOCIATION OF
COLLEGES OF PHARMACY
Office of Student Affairs; 1426 Prince St.
Alexandria VA 22314

1476

PHARMACY
(career information)
> AMERICAN FOUNDATION FOR
> PHARMACEUTICAL EDUCATION
> P.O. Box 7126; 618 Somerset St.
> North Plainfield NJ 07060

1477

PHARMACY
(school information booklet)
> AMERICAN COUNCIL ON
> PHARMACEUTICAL EDUCATION
> 311 W. Superior #512
> Chicago IL 60610

1478

PHOTOJOURNALISM
(career information for university-level photo-journalism students)
> NATIONAL PRESS PHOTOGRAPHERS
> ASSN.
> 3200 Croasdaile Dr. #306
> Durham NC 27705

1479

PHYSICAL THERAPY
(career information)
> AMERICAN PHYSICAL THERAPY
> ASSN.
> 1111 N. Fairfax St.
> Alexandria VA 22314

1480

PHYSICS
(career information)
> AMERICAN INSTITUTE OF PHYSICS
> One Physics Ellipse
> College Park MD 20740

1481

PILOT
(career information)
> INTERNATIONAL WOMEN PILOTS
> (99s)
> Will Rogers World Airport
> Oklahoma City OK 73159

1482

PODIATRY
(career information)
> AMERICAN PODIATRIC MEDICAL
> ASSN..
> 9312 Old Georgetown Rd.
> Bethesda MD 20814

1483

POLITICAL SCIENCE
(career information)
> AMERICAN POLITICAL SCIENCE
> ASSN.
> 1527 New Hampshire Ave. NW
> Washington DC 20036

1484

PSYCHIATRY
(career information)
> AMERICAN PSYCHIATRIC ASSN.
> DIVISION OF PUBLIC AFFAIRS
> 1400 'K' St. NW
> Washington DC 20005

1485

PSYCHOLOGY
(career information)
> AMERICAN PSYCHOLOGICAL ASSN.
> 750 1st St. NE
> Washington DC 20002

1486

PUBLIC RELATIONS
(career information)
PUBLIC RELATIONS SOCIETY OF
AMERICA
33 Irving Place
New York NY 10003

1487

RADIOLOGIC TECHNOLOGY
(career information)
AMERICAN SOCIETY OF
RADIOLOGIC TECHNOLOGISTS
15000 Central Ave. SE
Albuquerque NM 87123

1488

RANGE MANAGEMENT
(career information)
SOCIETY FOR RANGE
MANAGEMENT
1839 York St.
Denver CO 80206

1489

REAL ESTATE
(career information)
NATIONAL ASSN. OF REALTORS
777 14th St. NW
Washington DC 20005

1490

REHABILITATION COUNSELING
(career information)
NATIONAL REHABILITATION
COUNSELING ASSN.
8807 Sudley Road #102
Manassas VA 22110-4719

1491

RESPIRATORY THERAPY
(career information)
AMERICAN RESPIRATORY CARE
FOUNDATION
11030 Ables Ln.
Dallas TX 75229

1492

RURAL ELECTRIFICATION
(career information)
US DEPT. OF AGRICULTURE; RURAL
ELECTRIFICATION
ADMINISTRATION
14th and Independence Ave. SW; Room
4032
Washington DC 20250

1493

SAFETY ENGINEER
(career information)
AMERICAN SOCIETY OF SAFETY
ENGINEERS
1800 E. Oakton St.
Des Plaines IL 60018

1494

SCHOOL ADMINISTRATION
(career information)
AMERICAN ASSOCIATION OF
SCHOOL ADMINISTRATORS
1801 N. Moore St.
Arlington VA 22209

1495

SCIENCE TEACHER
(career information)
NATIONAL SCIENCE TEACHERS
ASSN.
Attn Office of Public Information
1840 Wilson Blvd.
Arlington VA 22201

1496

SECRETARY
(career information)
> PROFESSIONAL SECRETARIES
> INTERNATIONAL
> P.O. Box 20404
> Kansas City MO 64195-0404

1497

SOCIAL WORK
(career information)
> NATIONAL ASSN. OF SOCIAL
> WORKERS
> 750 First St. NE; Suite 700
> Washington DC 20002

1498

SOCIOLOGY
(career information)
> AMERICAN SOCIOLOGICAL ASSN.
> 1722 'N' St. NW
> Washington DC 20036

1499

SOIL CONSERVATION
(career information)
> SOIL & WATER CONSERVATION
> SOCIETY
> 7515 NE Ankeny Rd.
> Ankeny IA 50021

1500

SPECIAL EDUCATION TEACHER
(career information)
> NATIONAL CLEARINGHOUSE FOR
> PROFESSIONS IN SPECIAL
> EDUCATION
> 1920 Association Dr.
> Reston VA 22091

1501

SPEECH & HEARING THERAPY
(career information—please send self-addressed 8-1/2 x 11 envelope + $1.25 postage/handling)
> ALEXANDER GRAHAM BELL
> ASSOCIATION FOR THE DEAF
> 3417 Volta Place NW
> Washington DC 20007-2778

1502

US NAVY OFFICER
(career information)
> US NAVAL ACADEMY
> Candidate Guidance Office
> Annapolis MD 21402

1503

UNITED STATES ARMY
(career information)
> US MILITARY ACADEMY
> Director of Admissions; 606 Thayer Rd.
> West Point NY 10996

1504

UNITED STATES COAST GUARD
(career information)
> US COAST GUARD ACADEMY
> Director of Admissions; 15 Mohegan Ave.
> New London CT 06320

1505

UNITED STATES MARINE CORPS OFFICER
(Marine Corps Reserve Officers Training Corps and US Naval Academy career opportunities)
> MARINE CORPS COMMANDANT
> Headquarters; US Marine Corps
> 2 Navy Annex
> Washington DC 20380

1506

URBAN PLANNER
(career information)

AMERICAN PLANNING ASSN.
1776 Massachusetts Ave. NW
Washington DC 20036

1507

VETERINARIAN
(career information)

AMERICAN VETERINARY MEDICAL
ASSN.
1931 N. Meacham Rd.; Suite 100
Schaumburg IL 60173

1508

WATER POLLUTION CONTROL
(career information)

WATER POLLUTION CONTROL
FEDERATION
Education Dept.; 601 Wythe St.
Alexandria VA 22314

1509

WELDING TECHNOLOGY
(career information)

HOBART INSTITUTE OF WELDING
TECHONOLOGY
Trade Square East
Troy OH 45373

1510

WOMEN AIRLINE PILOTS
(career information)

INTERNATIONAL SOCIETY OF
WOMEN AIRLINE PILOTS
ISA+21; P.O. Box 66268
Chicago IL 60666

1511

WOMEN PILOTS
(career information)

NINETY-NINES (International
Organization of Women Pilots)
P.O. Box 59965
Oklahoma City OK 73159

1512

YOUTH LEADERSHIP
(career information)

BOYS & GIRLS CLUBS OF AMERICA
1230 W. Peachtree Street NW
Atlanta GA 30309

1513

YOUTH LEADERSHIP
(career information)

BOY SCOUTS OF AMERICA
National Eagle Scout Association; S220;
1325 W. Walnut Hill Lane; P.O. Box 152079
Irving TX 75015

Alphabetical Index